ETHNIC IDENTITY AND EQUALITY

Varieties of Experience in a Canadian City

According to conventional wisdom, the United States deals with its diverse cultures by encouraging assimilation in the melting pot, but Canadian society is a cultural mosaic in which diverse cultures are encouraged to maintain their distinctiveness. It has been argued, most notably by John Porter in *The Vertical Mosaic*, that the maintenance of ethnic cultures is a sustaining factor in the Canadian class system.

In recent years Porter's thesis has been challenged by those who maintain that ethnicity in Canada is not a significant factor in determining status. This study addresses the debate with evidence from a major interview survey of eight ethnic groups in Toronto.

The authors focus on the relationship between two aspects of ethnicity: the persistence of individual ethnic cultures and the degree of equality with which ethnic groups participate in the social, economic, and political life of the wider society. They provide in-depth analysis of ethnic-identity retention, residential segregation, occupational and labour-market concentrations, and political organization.

They conclude that the relation between ethnic persistence and inter-ethnic equality is highly variable. Sometimes, and in some respects, ethnic persistence is an obstacle and a liability; sometimes, and in other respects, it is an asset and actually enhances economic and political participation. And sometimes ethnicity does not seem to matter at all.

At a time when racial tensions are rising across Canada, this study offers a new and more comprehensive understanding of the place of ethnic and racial groups and the complex forces that shape them.

RAYMOND BRETON is Professor of Sociology at the University of Toronto.

WSEVOLOD W. ISAJIW is Professor of Sociology, Scarborough Campus, University of Toronto.

WARREN E. KALBACH is Professor of Sociology, Erindale Campus, University of Toronto.

JEFFREY G. REITZ is Professor of Sociology and Research Associate, Centre for Industrial Relations, at the University of Toronto.

Ethnic Identity and Equality: Varieties of Experience in a Canadian City

Raymond Breton
Wsevolod W. Isajiw
Warren E. Kalbach
Jeffrey G. Reitz

UNIVERSITY OF TORONTO PRESS
Toronto Buffalo London

BRESCIA COLLEGE
LIBRARY
58485

© University of Toronto Press 1990
Toronto Buffalo London
Printed in Canada

ISBN 0-8020-5860-4 (cloth)
ISBN 0-8020-6776-X (paper)

Printed on acid-free paper

Canadian Cataloguing in Publication Data

Main entry under title:

Ethnic identity and equality

ISBN 0-8020-5860-4 (bound) ISBN 0-8020-6776-X (pbk.)

1. Minorities – Ontario – Toronto. 2. Ethnicity – Ontario – Toronto. 3. Toronto (Ont.) – Ethnic relations. 4. Assimilation (Sociology). I. Breton, Raymond, 1931–

FC3097.9.A1E75 1990 305.8'09713'541
F1059.5.T689A22 1990 C89-090628-9

Contents

Acknowledgments

We wish to express our deepest gratitude to all persons who have accepted participation in our study and who have patiently given their time to be interviewed. Their essential participation, though anonymous, is greatly appreciated. We also wish to thank the professional, interviewing, and administrative staff of the York University Survey Research Centre for its valuable work in connection with the technical design and selection of the sample and with the field-work.

Many persons have assisted us at one point or another in the course of the study: the design and pre-testing of the interview schedule, the administration of the project, the processing of census data, and the analysis of the survey data. In one respect or another, we are indebted to the following persons for their valuable assistance: Linda Bell-Deutschmann, Laurie Bridger, Joe Bryant, Peter Carrington, Maisey Cheng, Joel Clodman, Giuliana Colalillo, Larry Comeau, June Corman, Rosalinda Costa, Deborah Coyne, Cindy Creighton, Ab Currie, Donna Dasko, James Dickinson, Phyllis Jensen, Richard Kalwa, Janet Lum, Clayton Mosher, Tomoko Makabe, Keiko Minai, Liviana Mostacci-Calzavara, Chrystyna Mulkewich, David Neice, Momo Podolsky, Madeline Richard, Susan Russell, Daiva Stasiulis, and Tania Wanio.

We are grateful as well for the support of the Social Sciences and Humanities Research Council of Canada, whose successive grants over the years have made this study possible. We owe a special debt to our colleague Professor Ken Dion, who encouraged us to prepare this manuscript for publication in its present form. This book has been published with the help of a grant from the Social Science Federation of

Canada using funds provided by the Social Sciences and Humanities Research Council of Canada.

ETHNIC IDENTITY AND EQUALITY

1

Introduction

This study addresses three major issues – issues that have been central in the work of students of ethnicity.

The first issue concerns the persistence of ethnicity over time and through generations. What is the extent of persistence? How does ethnicity change as a basis of identity and social organization? How is its content transformed? What are the social conditions associated with diverse patterns of evolution within or between ethnic collectivities?

The second issue concerns the incorporation of members of ethnic collectivities in society as a whole. How successfully are they incorporated in social, economic, and political structures? What is the degree and nature of their participation in the institutions of the society? What forms of equality or inequality arise? What social conditions facilitate or hinder their full incorporation in the social fabric?

These two issues have a long history of research and debate. Traditionally, they have been seen, implicitly or explicitly, almost as opposites. They have seemed to be two dimensions of reality varying together, but in opposite directions. As one increased, the other decreased. Thus, successful incorporation into society was taken to be more or less automatically associated with loss of ethnic social and cultural attachments. In recent years, however, this automatic negative association between persistence and incorporation began to be questioned.

Thus, a third issue concerns the dynamic interaction of ethnic persistence and incorporation in society. Is ethnic social organization always a liability with regard to incorporation? Which aspects may be compatible with social incorporation? Under what conditions can ethnicity act as a facilitator rather than as an obstacle? In short, is the loss of ethnicity necessary for full social incorporation, or can ethnicity persist in certain social forms, and even be a positive factor in bringing about full incorporation?

This book attempts to provide answers to these questions for the case of one major multi-ethnic urban centre: Toronto. The book is based on a study of a number of different ethnic and racial minority groups, as well as the dominant or 'majority' group (which, depending upon the precise definition, is no longer actually a numerical majority). Each of the groups has been surveyed to permit an analysis of ethnic social formations, ethnic group incorporation into society, and the relation between the two. Because of the inclusion of a variety of groups, the study permits an examination of ways in which the answers to our questions may vary from one ethnic group to another.

Our results should be of interest to students of ethnicity, and also to policy makers dealing with ethnic minorities. The study is research-oriented, and is addressed primarily to readers concerned with research results, such as professional researchers, graduate students, and senior undergraduates. However, the issues have serious policy implications as well, and the results should be of interest to those who are mainly preoccupied with public policy, whether they are in government or in ethnic or other civic organizations.

In this chapter, the broad issues of concern are specified in somewhat greater detail. As well, information is provided about the history and present ethnic composition of the city of Toronto, and about the data base for the study. Subsequent chapters examine the issues in terms of several specific domains of ethnicity. The concluding chapter brings together the main findings and indicates the conclusions we have reached regarding our basic questions of ethnicity and social incorporation.

Research Issues: Ethnicity and Social Incorporation

Ethnic social formations, and the incorporation of ethnic group members in the larger society, are concepts that must be made more specific for any detailed study. As well, the interrelation between the two has several distinct aspects in the various domains of social life. Some further points are needed to indicate how these ideas will be used as a framework for this study.

ETHNICITY AS A BASIS OF SOCIAL ORGANIZATION

An important line of variation to be considered in the study of ethnicity and ethnic groups is the extent to which ethnic ancestry and culture play a role in the way people think of themselves and in the choices they make concerning such matters as work, residence, socio-cultural activities, and political behaviour. To what extent do people retain their ethnic heritage and use it, individually or collectively, as 'cultural capital' in coping with problems of identity and of social and economic well-being?

There are many areas of life in which ethnicity can be an active force. At a fundamental level, it can shape identities by determining who people are in their own eyes and those of others. Social identities provide social roots and a sense of belonging, of not being lost in the multitude. As Isaacs (1975: 35) put it: 'An individual belongs to his basic group in the deepest and most literal sense that he is not alone, which is what all but a very few human beings most fear to be. He is not only not alone, but here, as long as he chooses to remain in and of it, he cannot be denied or rejected. It is an identity that no one can take away from him.' Ethnicity can be the basis of such a social identity (Dashefsky 1972, 1975; Deshen 1974; Driedger 1975, 1977).

Ethnicity can also be the basis for the construction of neighbourhoods. The psychological sense of belonging, of having a home, can be supported or reinforced by a geographical or social belonging (Driedger and Church 1974; Driedger 1978). Thus ethnicity not only affects the daily lives and social relations or urban dwellers; it also contributes to the structure of the physical and social configuration of the urban environment (Lieberson 1961; Glazer and Moynihan 1963; Fischer 1975; Taylor 1979; Darroch and Marston 1984). At one level, the map of the city is based on an ethnic code.

The market for jobs and the social relations at work can also be structured along ethnic lines. It is as if family, kinship, and neighbourhood ties were transposed into the work domain. Ethnic solidarity is extended beyond the private to the public sphere of economic activity. In other words, economic action is embedded in structures of social relations (Granovetter 1985) and some of these relations are based on ethnicity (Hughes and Hughes 1952; Lieberson 1963; Hannerz 1974; Hechter 1978).

Finally, ethnic solidarity can be mobilized for collective action. Such action can be for the construction or expansion of community institutions; for the performance of community functions; for the shaping of electoral outcomes; and for protection against external expressions of hostility. In short, ethnic solidarity can have a political dimension (Glazer and Moynihan 1963; Cohen 1974a; D. Bell 1975; Dahlie and Fernando 1982). In other words, political action, like economic and cultural activities, is embedded in structures of social relations, some of which are ethnic.

Ethnicity, however, can also become progressively insignificant in these same areas. Sometimes, and in several respects, the identity of individuals is not based on their ethnic origin. Many persons have few, if any, social relations with others of the same origin. They have forgotten the language, history, and traditions of their group and find little meaning in its customs, even if they occasionally practise them. They do not participate in ethnic associations and activities. They are unconcerned with the possibility that their children might marry outside the ethnic collectivity. To the extent that this is true, ethnicity has lost its importance as a factor in individual lives and as a basis of social, economic, and political organization (M. Gordon 1964; Borhek 1970; Greeley 1974; Reitz 1980b). Ethnic solidarity is weak or absent; ethnic cultures are phenomena of the past. People may retain some sense of their ethnic identity, but may be less interested in the cultural and organizational expressions of this identity (Gans 1979).

Clearly, the impact of ethnicity in shaping identities and social organization is a variable. It may vary in degree and in the ways in which it operates. Ethnicity can be critical, totally insignificant, or have a whole range of effects in between. It can affect several, a few, or no areas of individual and collective life. As Yancey et al. have said, it does not make sense to think of ethnicity as merely 'a constant ascribed trait that is inherited from the past ... The assumption of a common heritage as the essential aspect of ethnicity is erroneous. Ethnicity may have relatively little to do with Europe, Asia or Africa, but much more to do with the exigencies of survival and the structure of opportunity in this country' (1976: 400). Ethnicity is also a reflection of the present and the anticipated future. The impact of ethnicity varies depending upon current conditions and the experiences of individuals and groups in relation to the members and institutions of the larger society.

THE INCORPORATION OF ETHNIC GROUP MEMBERS INTO SOCIETY

One important respect in which ethnicity is not simply 'a constant ascribed trait that is inherited from the past' is that ethnic heritages tend to be transformed through the group's interaction with other groups in their environment, especially the dominant group. As Glazer and Moynihan note, 'the ethnic group in American society became not a survival from the age of mass immigration but a new social form. One could not predict from its first arrival what it might become or, indeed, whom it might contain' (1963: 16). The organization and culture of ethnic groups is not simply brought from the society of origin and preserved in the new social environment. Much of it is a new creation in a context that is itself in evolution (Thomas and Znaniecki 1927; Cohen 1974a; Yancey et al. 1976; Isajiw 1977; Reitz 1980b). It is through the process of becoming members and participants in the society that the ethnicity of groups is selectively retained, transformed, reconstructed, or disappears. As a result, the ethnicity of destination, if one exists at all, can be significantly different from the ethnicity of origin.

Thus, another line of variation that needs to be considered in the study of ethnic groups is the extent to which and the ways in which they become incorporated in the structure of the society. Incorporation can occur at several levels. The economic sector is one of the most basic, and a considerable amount of attention has been devoted to it by researchers and policy makers. Identity and culture, residence, and politics are also important domains of incorporation (Richmond 1964, 1967a; Blishen 1970; Darroch 1979; Lieberson 1980; Richmond and Kalbach 1980). Each of these is considered in the subsequent chapters.

Incorporation in the larger society entails involvement in institutions, the construction of social ties, participation in socio-cultural activities, and, most important, equal access to the rewards that the economic and political systems generate and distribute. Incorporation is a matter of degree. It usually occurs over a fairly long period of time and frequently over generations.

ETHNIC SOCIAL FORMATIONS: ASSETS OR LIABILITIES IN SOCIAL INCORPORATION?

Incorporation entails two sets of processes: one on the side of members of ethnic groups; another on the part of individuals and institutions of the larger society. Gordon (1964: 71) has included the two dimensions in his typology of assimilation, the second part of which referred to the 'reception' by the larger society in different areas of activity ('attitude receptional assimilation,' or absence of prejudice, and 'behaviour receptional assimilation,' or absence of discrimination).

In other words, incorporation is the result of factors and processes internal and external to the ethnic group, or internal or external to the larger society. Two sets of ethnic boundaries are involved: those of the established groups in the society and those of the groups seeking full membership and equal participation in it. That is to say, incorporation involves ethnic boundaries both of the dominant and of the minority groups (Isajiw 1974).

Ethnic social formations, and the boundaries they imply, can be obstacles or barriers to incorporation for individual minority-group members (and hence for entire groups). They may prevent or make difficult the development of more encompassing levels of solidarity and integration. They can be the basis of inequality and inequity in the functioning of economic and political institutions. They can be used for the maintenance of inequalities in social status and separateness in social relations and neighbourhoods.

For instance, particular ethnic identities may not be as respected and accepted as others. They may be considered less worthy or inferior; they may be seen as alien, less Canadian than that of the dominant group. Also, just as ethnic identities can find a social and psychological space in a neighbourhood, the assignment of a low status to them may result in the refusal to accept those with the stigmatized identity as neighbours.

The control of job networks and career lines provides advantages to some that may be used to the detriment of others. The solidarity that includes some may exclude others – a line of differentiation that tends to follow the dominant-minority axis. In addition, members of various ethnic groups can bring different skills, values, and attitudes to the job market, the workplace, and other institutions. These may be associated with factors such as cultural background, past advantages or discrimination, and conditions at the time of immigration. But whatever their sources, these differences can reinforce ethnic barriers and generate separateness and inequalities among groups. On the side of the ethnic minority, they can do so by creating and maintaining 'mobility traps' (Wiley 1967). On the side of the dominant groups, they can do so by facilitating the control of positions of advantage and the exclusion of minorities (Porter 1972, 1975).

Ethnic social formations may facilitate, as well as hinder, the process of becoming part of the larger society. They may provide the resources necessary to overcome the obstacles or barriers to participation in the society's institutions. Indeed, social networks and collective action can be oriented to making gains for group members; to combating discrimination; to overcoming the disadvantages generated by the policies and practices of individuals and of organizations, whether public or private. In short, the cultural, social, economic, and political resources of ethnic groups can be used to challenge entrenched systems of privileges, to open up the institutions of the larger society and facilitate full participation in them on the part of minorities.

Thus, there are two related but distinct lines of variations in the situation of ethnic groups: in the extent to which the ethnic heritage constitutes a basis of individual life and social organization, and in the degree of incorporation in the larger society. When we say that they constitute two distinct lines of variation, we are asserting strongly that one cannot be taken as the obverse of the other. Incorporation does not necessarily mean that ethnicity is disappearing as a basis of social organization and individual identity. The existence of a vibrant ethnic community does not imply that incorporation is failing to occur. The variations in the two phenomena may be correlated; but they are not the same.

A central hypothesis is that the two dimensions can be put together to constitute a conceptual space in which ethnic groups can be located depending on their position in each of them. This space can be visualized as in the diagram on page 10. If incorporation necessarily entailed the disappearance of ethnicity as an operative social factor, then all groups would fall along the diagonal from the lower left to the upper right segments of the diagram. If no single necessary relationship is assumed between the two dimensions, groups could be located in other portions of the two-dimensional space (as well as along that diagonal).

OBJECTIVES OF THE STUDY, AND FOUR RESEARCH FOCI

There are, then, four major objectives pursued in the analysis that follows. They are to describe and analyse

1 the variations among several ethnic groups in the degree and pattern of incorporation in the larger society;
2 the variations among groups in the ways in which ethnicity shapes their identity, social relationships, and activities;
3 variations across groups in the impacts (positive and negative) on incorporation in the larger society of ethnicity and of social relations based on ethnicity; and

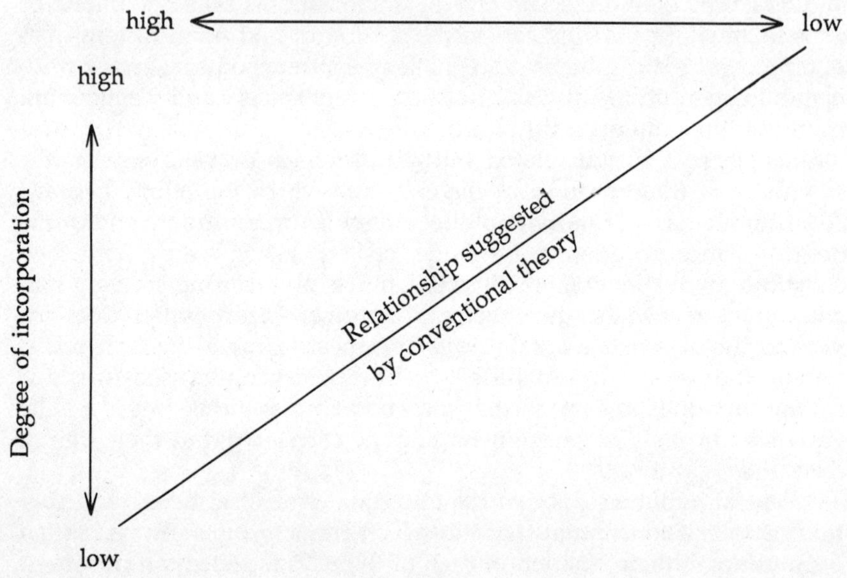

4 variations over time, specifically across generations, in the role of ethnicity for members of different ethnic groups, and in the degree of their incorporation.

The study deals with these issues in four areas: ethnic identity, residential segregation, participation in the socio-economic opportunity structure, and socio-political organization.

Ethnic Identity and Retention

Ethnicity consists of at least one, or a combination, of six components: (a) distinct overt and covert cultural behaviour patterns; (b) personal ties, such as family, community, and friendship networks; (c) organizations such as schools, churches, enterprises, media; (d) associations such as clubs, 'societies,' youth organizations; (e) functions, sponsored by ethnic organizations, such as picnics, concerts, teas, rallies; and (f) identity as a social psychological phenomenon.

Ethnic identity is conceived as a specific phenomenon rather than as an omnibus combination of all the components. Thus, ethnic identity is defined as *one* aspect of the way in which individuals conceive of their location within and their relationship to the social system at large and to others in it. Ethnic identity can have a variety of contents or forms: not all persons who locate themselves in the group of their ancestors do so in the same way. One may perceive oneself as inferior or superior in relation to others. One may identify with an ethnic group by feeling an obligation to attend as many functions sponsored by ethnic organizations as possible, or one may feel no such obligation at all, yet identify with the group in terms of other obligations or on some other basis. One may simply choose to live in an ethnic neighbourhood as an expression of ethnic identity.

Chapter 2 analyses the retention of ethnicity by focusing primarily on retention of ethnic identity and analysing the other components in relation to it. Its objective is to study which aspects of ethnicity in general and which forms and intensities of ethnic identities in particular are retained from generation to generation.

Ethnic Residential Segregation

The growth of urban communities is usually accompanied by increased specialization and differentiation of economic activity, which, in turn, is reflected in the spatial distribution of these activities and of residential neighbourhoods according to the socio-economic and cultural characteristics of their inhabitants. The traditional model of urban growth relates the expansion of the central business district to the expansion of middle- and upper-class residential areas into suburban areas at the expense of deteriorating neighbourhoods in the inner core. Residential mobility becomes a vehicle for social mobility, and the move to better housing and better neighbourhoods commensurate with improved economic status and changing housing needs reflects both upward-mobility aspirations and achievement.

In the classical model of urban growth, the areas of transition, between the expanding business district and the retreating middle- and upper-class residential areas, provide housing opportunities for the relatively unskilled workers, including native-born internal migrants as well as immigrants from abroad. Ethnic and racial enclaves develop and serve as general reception areas to assist the new arrivals in getting established. Subsequent moves from these initial areas of settlement, either by the original migrants or their children, are possible as the individuals manage to acquire the necessary skills and economic means to improve their position in the economic and social system. It has been generally assumed that those who remain in the original reception areas do so because they have not acquired the necessary skills to improve their economic status, because they have experienced racial or ethnic prejudice, or because of their own preferences. In any event, the patterns of residential distribution exhibited or perceived by various ethnic and racial groups would tend to reflect the extent of their adaptation to the social and economic system of the community as a whole.

Chapter 3 addresses some of these issues. Specifically, it seeks (a) to establish the extent and pattern of ethnic residential segregation by generation; (b) to determine the significance of ethnic origin relative to other social and economic characteristics and with respect to existing patterns of segregation; and (c) to analyse the relationship between various indicators of segregation and ethnic identity, participation, and networks.

Ethnicity and Labour Markets

Occupational opportunities and rewards available in labour markets are frequently unequally allocated among individuals of different ethnic origins. The rewards associated with occupation include status or prestige and income. The allocation of job rewards is, in part, affected by the qualifications of incumbents. Job qualifications include years and type of education, years of work experience, and knowledge of English. Ethnic inequalities are partly due to such qualifications, but inequalities can remain after these qualifications have been taken into account.

How do ethnic economic formations, or ethnic concentrations in labour markets, alter the allocation of job rewards? Several theories suggest ways in which ethnic concentrations in occupations or work groups may reinforce existing inequalities. When this happens, then ethnic economic formations represent obstacles to social incorporation. However, such negative effects may apply only in extreme cases. Or, they may depend upon the type of labour-market concentrations. Sometimes ethnic businesses may provide a basis for altering the distribution of occupational rewards, generating resources and reallocating them within the ethnic group.

Three forms of ethnic concentration in labour markets will be considered: concentrations in occupational categories (such as Italians in construction trades, or Chinese in certain service occupations), in minority businesses as entrepreneurs and as employees, and in work groups within organizations.

Chapter 4 describes ethnic inequalities of occupational opportunities and rewards, and examines ways in which ethnic concentrations in labour markets influence those inequalities. The analysis will examine the extent to which the allocation of rewards depends on factors other than qualifications, and the extent to which these are reduced or enhanced by ethnic concentrations for each ethnic group.

Ethnicity and Collective Political Action

Collective action can be organized in order to take advantage of opportunities, to pursue commonly agreed upon goals, or to deal with problems experienced by members of the community. In other words, members of ethnic groups can have interests that they can, if the necessary conditions are met, pursue through collective action.

The organization of such action involves at least three broad categories of processes: the identification of matters as requiring concerted action; the mobilization of commitment and participation, including material support; and the organization of the action itself to deal with the problems or objectives identified. These processes require leadership, a decision-making structure, conflict-resolution mechanisms, and means of communication and co-ordination. The existence of material resources in the ethnic population and a degree of social cohesion are important resources in this regard. So are attitudes favourable to collective action, perceptions of its possible effectiveness, and the perceived legitimacy of the leadership and organizations in the community.

Chapter 5 deals with the latter elements, namely with the perceptions and attitudes of members of ethnic groups with regard to the problems faced by their group, to the type of action that could be effective in dealing with them, and to the existing leadership and decision making in the community. In other words, the analysis examines the public opinion in different ethnic groups with regard to matters of importance for concerted action.

Population Growth and Ethnic Diversity in Toronto

As background for the present study, it is important to review some of the basic facts about the history of Canadian immigration as it affects Toronto, and the growth and formation of the ethnic groups that constitute the population of Toronto today.

ETHNIC BACKGROUND OF TORONTO

Toronto emerged as the capital of Upper Canada in 1793 and since that time has been the dominant urban and cultural centre of English Canada. It was established by the English and its growth was assured by the British Empire Loyalists who came to Canada from the American colonies following the American Revolution. The War of 1812 further strengthened Toronto's resolve to remain British, but it did not stem the flow of immigrants from either the United States or abroad (Mulvany 1884). The British Empire Loyalists included Germans, French, and Hessians in addition to the British; and later immigrants included both well-to-do British families and military types from abroad as well as destitute Scots and Irish refugees from the great potato famine (Mulvany 1884: 18–19; Burnet 1972: 5–29). The various ethnic origins and religious groups of early Toronto were not members of a classless, egalitarian society. The ruling English élite were well established and in a good position to maintain old-world class distinctions and prejudices through judicious government appointments and land grants. The class structure seems to have evolved from the top down as the founding fathers distributed largesse, and the more successful merchants and other entrepreneurs gradually occupied the niche between the élite and the less skilled workers who where dependent on employment as wage earners for their economic survival. From the beginning, Toronto had a distinctive class structure controlled by the élite and linked to the social and economic characteristics of immigrants and the circumstances surrounding their arrival in Upper Canada.

After the early period of relatively free immigration, increasingly restrictive policies and regulations were imposed to restrict entry to those ethnic and cultural groups thought to be most suited for life in Canada, given its British heritage and the rigours of the environment and northern climate (Canada, Department of Manpower and Immigration 1974b: 7–13). While the preference had been for British, northern and western Europeans, and those born in the United States, the ethnic composition of the continuing immigrant stream gradually shifted to central, eastern, and southern Europeans, and more recently to non-Europeans (Kalbach and McVey 1979: 48–51). The consequences of Canada's history of settlement by a variety of ethnic- and cultural-origin groups of varying socio-economic characteristics over the years are reflected in the results of a recent national study of race and ethnic attitudes (Berry, Kalin, and Taylor 1977). What was revealed was the presence of a hierarchy of ethnic preferences within the Canadian population. It is not surprising that these preferences closely parallel the picture of the preferred immigrant set forth in Canada's immigration policies and regulations prior to the 1960s. While all references to ethnic and cultural origins were finally eliminated from the government's selection criteria (Canada, Department of Manpower and Immigration 1974a: 45), preferential ethnic and racial attitudes do not appear to have diminished to any significant degree among Canadians.

For the hundred-year period shown in table 1.1 (parts A and B), Toronto's population grew rapidly and its degree of ethnic diversity increased steadily. When Toronto was first incorporated as a city in 1834, its population stood at 9,254 (Mulvany 1884: 31). By 1851 it had reached 30,775, and by 1881 it was beginning to spill over its political boundaries and was taking on the characteristics of a metropolitan centre with a core city of 86,415 and a total population of over 100,000 including its suburbs (Kralt 1976: 29–33).

The city of Toronto approached a quarter million at the beginning of the twentieth century, and by 1921 had exceeded the half million mark. Between 1941 and 1951, the CMA (Census Metropolitan Area; that is the city of Toronto and its built-up suburbs) passed the one million population mark, and twenty years later reached a population of 2,628,325. During the 1970s, the Toronto CMA became the largest in Canada. In 1981, its population was reported to be 2,975,495, and in 1986, 3,399,680.

Only a cursory glance at the data on population growth by ethnic origin groups, in tables 1.1 and 1.2, is necessary to appreciate the increasing ethnic diversity of Toronto's population during this period of growth. The increasing size of the ethnic minority groups settling in Toronto and its suburbs had reduced the overwhelming position of dominance enjoyed by the population of British origins from 95.6% in 1871 to just slightly over 50% in 1971. Unfortunately, it is not possible to derive comparable data for populations by ethnic origins in 1981.[1]

RECENT CHANGES IN TORONTO'S ETHNIC POPULATIONS

Minority ethnic populations showing spectacular relative gains have been the so-called 'new' immigrants, that is, the Italians, Portuguese, and other southern Europeans, and those of non-European origins. During the 1950s and 1960s, the Germans, Italians, and Dutch dominated the immigrant streams, but during the early 1970s, Portugal

TABLE 1.1
Population of the City of Toronto by Ethnic-Origin Groups, 1871 to 1921, and the Toronto Census Metropolitan Area (CMA), 1941 to 1971[a]

A. City of Toronto, Canada, 1871–1921

Ethnic origin	1871 Number	1871 %	1881 Number	1881 %	1901 Number	1901 %	1921 Number	1921 %
English	21,204	37.8	34,608	40.0	94,021	45.2	260,860	50.0
Irish	24,101	43.0	32,177	37.2	61,435	29.5	97,361	18.7
Scottish	8,212	14.6	13,754	15.9	34,547	16.6	83,620	16.0
Other British	85	0.2	211	0.2	785	0.4	3.389	0.6
French	572	1.0	1,230	1.4	3,015	1.4	8,350	1.6
German	985	1.8	2,049	2.4	5,986	2.9	5,864	1.0
Dutch	62	0.1	163	0.2	737	0.4	3,961	0.8
Scandinavian	.20	–	89	0.1	253	0.1	1,109	0.2
Polish	81	0.1	132	0.2	142	0.1	2,380	0.5
Russian	g		g		g		1,332	0.3
Ukrainian					g		1,149	0.2
Italian	34	0.1	104	0.1	1,054	0.5	8,217	1.6
Jewish	11		124	0.1	3,090	1.5	34,619	6.6
Other European	31	0.1	108	0.1	124	0.1	812	0.2
Swiss	(21)		(83)	(0.1)	(124)	(0.1)	b	
Greek	(1)		b		b		(812)	(0.2)
Portuguese and Spanish	(9)		(25)		b		b	
Yugoslavian			b		b		b	
Chinese			10		219	0.1	2,176	0.4
Japanese			e		e		e	
East Indian							f	
Other Asian							450	0.1
Negro	551	1.0	593	0.7	674	0.3	1,236	0.2
West Indian							b	
Native Indian	5		6		42		183	
Other	10		199	0.2	295	0.1	3,337	0.6
Not stated	27		858	1.0	1,578	0.8	1,488	0.3
Total	56,092	100.0	86,415	100.0	207,998	100.0	521,893	100.0

a Data are for the City of Toronto except for 1971, which are for the Census Metropolitan Area.
b Included in 'Other.'
c Included in 'Other European.'
d Includes Eskimo.
e Included with Chinese.
f Included with Other Asian
g Included with Polish.

B. Toronto Census Metropolitan Area: 1941–1971

Ethnic group	Number 1941	1951	1961	1971	Per cent 1941	1951	1961	1971
British Isles	730,480	812,498	1,107,203	1,495,355	81.1	72.7	60.7	56.9
French	19,423	31,853	61,421	91,935	2.2	2.9	3.4	3.5
German	11,529	19,329	80,300	116,610	1.3	1.7	4.4	4.4
Netherlands	9,606	12,452	33,434	44,500	1.1	1.1	1.8	1.7
Scandinavian	3,926	6,657	16,050	18,310	0.4	0.6	0.9	0.7
Polish	13,094	26,998	58,578	51,210	1.4	2.4	3.2	1.9
Russian	2,367	5,846	14,186	5,200	0.3	0.5	0.8	0.2
Ukrainian	11,823	29,262	46,650	60,705	1.3	2.6	2.6	2.3
Jewish	52,779	59,448	53,123	109,865	5.9	5.3	2.9	4.2
Italian	17,887	27,962	140,378	271,775	2.0	2.5	7.7	10.3
Other Europeans	20,095	41,482	136,610	238,530	2.2	3.7	7.5	9.2
Asian	3,645	9,786	20,534	71,195	0.4	0.9	1.1	2.7
Other	3,873	33,897	56,041	53,135	0.4	3.0	3.0	2.0
Total	900,491	1,117,470	1,824,481	2,628,325	100.0	100.0	100.0	100.0

SOURCE: Statistics Canada, Censuses of Canada

became the third most important source country. The Portuguese, in turn, were replaced by the Hong Kong Chinese. In addition to Hong Kong and Portugal, other countries showing up among the leading source countries of immigration to Canada during the 1970s (in descending order of importance) were Jamaica, India, Philippines, Greece, Italy, and Trinidad (Canada, Department of Manpower and Immigration 1974b: 84). The liberalization of immigration policies during the 1960s and 1970s significantly increased the non-European component of immigration, the bulk of which has been destined for Ontario, and in particular, its largest CMAS (Kalbach and McVey 1971: 192–4).

The net effects of post-war immigration for the ethnic composition of the Toronto area population can be seen in table 1.1, part B. Note that for the major western, northern, and eastern European populations, their greatest increases occurred during the 1951–61 decade. For the Italians other southern Europeans (included in the 'other European' category), their growth was fairly constant throughout the post-war period, while the Asian origin population experienced its greatest intercensal increases after 1961.

The survey data for the present study were collected in 1978 and 1979. The omission of the ethnic-origin question from the 1976 Census

TABLE 1.2
Population by ethnic origin, Toronto CMA, 1971 and 1981

Ethnic origin	Number 1971	Number 1981	Per cent 1971	Per cent 1981
British	1,495,355	1,390,005	56.9	46.7
Italian	271,775	297,205	10.3	10.0
German	116,610	82,930	4.4	2.8
Jewish	109,865	109,240	4.2	3.7
French	91,935	74,800	3.5	2.5
Ukrainian	60,705	50,705	2.3	1.7
Greek	51,470	65,025	2.0	2.2
Polish	51,210	47,690	1.9	1.6
Netherlands	44,500	34,220	1.7	1.2
Portuguese	43,640	88,885	1.7	3.0
West Indian and Black[a]	27,965	78,445	1.1	2.6
Chinese	26,355	89,590	1.0	3.0
Hungarian	23,345	22,685	0.9	0.8
Other Asian[b]	16,145	49,955	0.6	1.7
Other European[c]	77,630	80,135	3.0	2.7
Scandinavian	18,310	12,310	0.7	0.4
Indo-Pakistani	14,545	69,725	0.6	2.3
Czech and Slovak	14,450	11,900	0.5	0.4
Japanese	11,725	12,600	0.4	0.4
Finnish	8,980	8,155	0.3	0.3
Austrian	7,870	6,875	0.3	0.4
Native Indian and Inuit	6,935	11,380	0.3	0.4
Spanish	6,495	20,060	0.2	0.7
Russian	5,200	4,190	0.2	0.1
Belgian and Luxembourg[d]	2,465	1,885	0.1	0.1
Romanian	2,185	2,590	0.1	0.1
British and French		44,425	0.0	1.5
British and Other		109,825	0.0	3.7
French and Other		8,830	0.0	0.3
British, French, and Other		11,175	0.0	0.4
European and Other		31,435	0.0	1.1
Native Peoples and Other		6,020	0.0	0.2
Other Single and/or Mult. Origin[e]	20,660	40,625	0.8	1.4
Total	2,628,325	2,975,495	100.0	100.0

SOURCE: Statistics Canada, 1981 and 1971 Censuses of Canada

a 1981 data for Black and Caribbean.

b In 1971, Other Asian includes Other East Indian. In 1981, Other Asian includes Asian Arab, Indo-Chinese, Pacific Islands, and West Asian.

c In 1981, Other European includes Armenian, Balkans, Baltic, Romanian, and Swiss.

d In 1971, data for Belgian only.

e Includes Unknown, Other, and Syrian-Lebanese.

TABLE 1.3
Population by selected mother tongues*
Toronto CMA: 1971, 1976, and 1981

	Number			Per cent		
Mother-tongue group	1971	1976	1981	1971	1976	1981
Italian	220,430	200,965	221,390	8.4	7.2	7.4
German	67,050	53,130	57,120	2.6	1.9	1.9
French	44,775	39,805	44,265	1.7	1.4	1.5
Greek	43,565	38,180	50,075	1.7	1.4	1.7
Portuguese	39,745	61,005	77,790	1.5	2.2	2.6
Ukrainian	35,085	32,710	34,155	1.3	1.2	1.1
Polish	32,195	25,775	34,200	1.2	0.9	1.1
Croation, Serbian	26,390	31,835	31,060	1.0	1.1	1.0
Chinese and Japanese	25,700	42,605	74,035	1.0	1.5	2.5
Japanese			5,620			
Chinese			68,415			
Estonian, Lithuanian	20,910	16,410	n/a	0.8	0.6	0.0
Hungarian	20,560	17,300	21,225	0.8	0.6	0.7
Netherlands, Flemish	18,580	12,815	16,845	0.7	0.5	0.6
Yiddish	16,940	8,930	12,515	0.6	0.3	0.4
Czech and Slovak	10,430	7,780	9,290	0.4	0.3	0.3
Indo-Pakistani	8,005	18,665	34,205	0.3	0.7	1.1
Spanish	7,310	18,200	25,265	0.3	0.6	0.8
Scandinavian	6,170	4,540	5,510	0.2	0.2	0.2
Russian	3,845	3,590	6,345	0.1	0.1	0.2
Native Indian and Inuit	1,335	1,665	n/a	0.1	0.1	0.0
Other Non-English	40,065	125,340	104,070	1.5	4.4	3.5
Total			859,360	26.2	27.2	28.9

SOURCE: Statistics Canada, 1981 Census of Canada. Volume 2, Catalogue 93-930, table 1, 1-117–1-120; 1976 and 1971 Censuses of Canada.
*Percentage of the total population, excluding English Mother Tongue, which comprised 72.8% in 1976, and 71.1% in 1981.

of Canada prevents analysis of the nature of changes in the ethnic composition of the population closer to that period. However, data on non-English mother tongues were collected during the 1971, 1976, and 1981 censuses. These data provide additional evidence of continuing increases in ethnic and cultural diversity, insofar as the non-English mother-tongue populations are concerned. Note in table 1.3 that the largest relative gains occurred during the first five-year inter-censal period, that is, between 1971 and 1976. The population reporting Spanish as their mother tongue increased from 7,300 to 18,200 or by

149% between 1971 and 1976, compared to only 39% during the 1976–81 period. Indo-Pakistanis recorded a 133% increase (from 8,000 to 18,700) between 1971 and 1976, and another 83% increase during the following five years. The combined Chinese and Japanese mother-tongue group increased from 25,700 to 42,600, or by 65%, followed by another 74% increase. The Portuguese increased by 53%, from 39,700 to 61,000, but only by 28% during the second half of the decade. The residual 'other' category, comprising mostly the newer and smaller immigrant groups with non-English mother tongues, showed a 213% increase between 1971 and 1976, but only a 160% increase over the whole decade.

While immigration itself may have been somewhat slowed by the introduction of annual target levels in 1978, there does not seem to be any evidence to suggest that the diversity of the immigration stream has shown any significant decline in so far as the mother-tongue characteristics of a population can be taken as an approximate indicator of its ethnic diversity. The large number of rapidly growing ethnic minority groups represented in the Toronto population makes it one of the more ethnically diverse urban communities in Canada, and an ideal population in which to study inter-ethnic relations. The number of ethnic minority groups, their size, and the varying degrees of similarity to the dominant cultural population are important factors underlying the nature of inter-ethnic and inter-racial relations.

Survey of Ethnic Groups in Toronto

The results of this study come from a survey of 2,338 respondents in Toronto. The survey was designed for the purpose of examining the theoretical issues of concern to this study. These considerations affected both the selection of ethnic groups for inclusion in the study and the design of the sample within specific groups. Further technical features of the sample design, the respresentativeness of the ethnic-group samples, and the weighting scheme used in the data analysis are presented in appendix A. The interview schedule is included as appendix B.

ETHNIC GROUPS INCLUDED IN THE STUDY

An important feature of the study is that it is comparative in nature. It was designed in such a way as to allow systematic comparisons among several ethnic groups. The minority groups were selected so that the study would include variations along the dimensions required by the objectives of the sub-projects: generational composition, the size and socio-economic standing of groups, their degree of ethnic organization and retention, their residential distribution, and the racial background of their members. Mainly because of considerations of costs, but also of manageability, the number of groups selected for analysis is necessarily limited. Many groups could not be included. At the same time, most *types* of groups in Toronto were represented, and the survey does represent the diversity of ethnicity within the city of Toronto.

Nine groups were selected; the 'Majority Canadian group' and eight minority groups. The Majority Canadian group includes persons of English, Irish, and Scottish origin whose families have been in Canada three or more generations. Four minority groups were included within which there is substantial generational variation: German, Italian, Jewish, and Ukrainian. There are also three groups composed primarily of immigrants: Chinese, Portuguese, and West Indians. An eighth minority group is the 'first- and second-generation English.' This last group was included to permit analysis of generational variations within a group whose members comprise part of the Majority Canadian group.

The terms 'majority' and 'minority' are used in their sociological sense. They are not meant to refer to the numerical size of groups but rather to the power relationship they have with each other. Thus, in this study, the expression 'Majority Canadian group' refers to the segment of the population that has been and continues to be dominant in Toronto. It refers to the historical collectivity that has shaped the political, economic, and socio-cultural institutions of the city, and that, to a significant extent, continues to control them. Elsewhere in Canada, the 'majority group' might be different, depending upon the particular configuration of groups. In Montreal, for example, both French- and British-origin Canadians are powerful groups. Our use of the term 'Majority-Canadian' is intended to apply in Toronto only.

SAMPLE DESIGNS WITHIN GROUPS

The groups included in the study vary by size, by generational distribution, and by geographical distribution across the city. All of these factors affected the sample design. The geographical distributions for several groups in the study, as reflected in indexes of relative concentration, are shown in maps prepared from the 1981 census data, which follow figure 1 (outline of study area).[2] These maps show

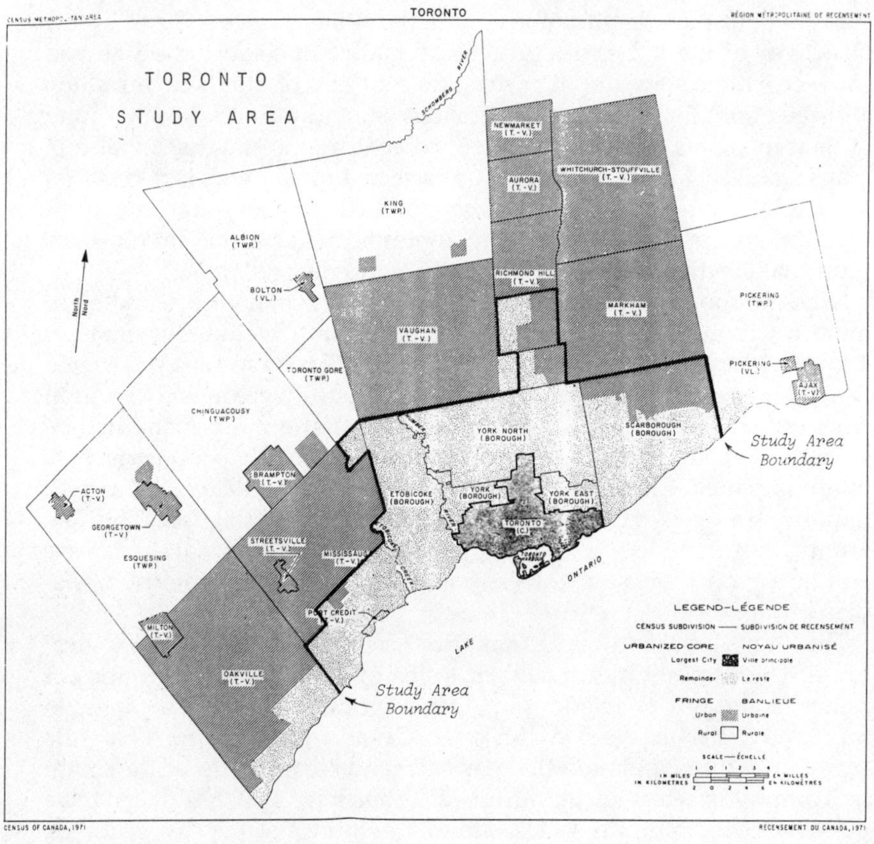

Figure 1
Outline of the study area

Variations in the index of relative concentration of populations of selected ethnic origins in the Toronto Census Metropolitan Area are shown on the following nine pages. The maps, produced by the Population Research Laboratory, Erindale College, University of Toronto, are based on a special tabulation of the 1981 Census data by Statistics Canada. See note 3 on page 314 for an explanation of the index of relative concentration.

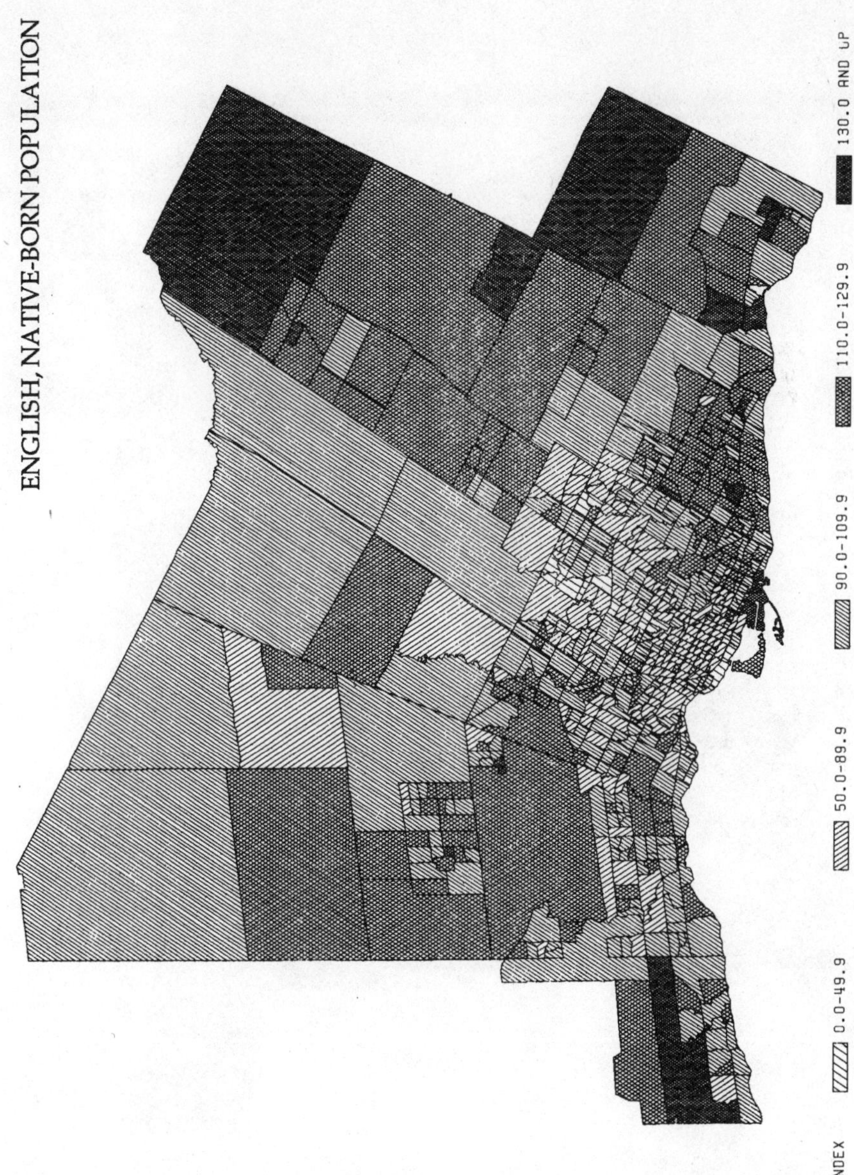
ENGLISH, NATIVE-BORN POPULATION
INDEX
0.0-49.9
50.0-89.9
90.0-109.9
110.0-129.9
130.0 AND UP

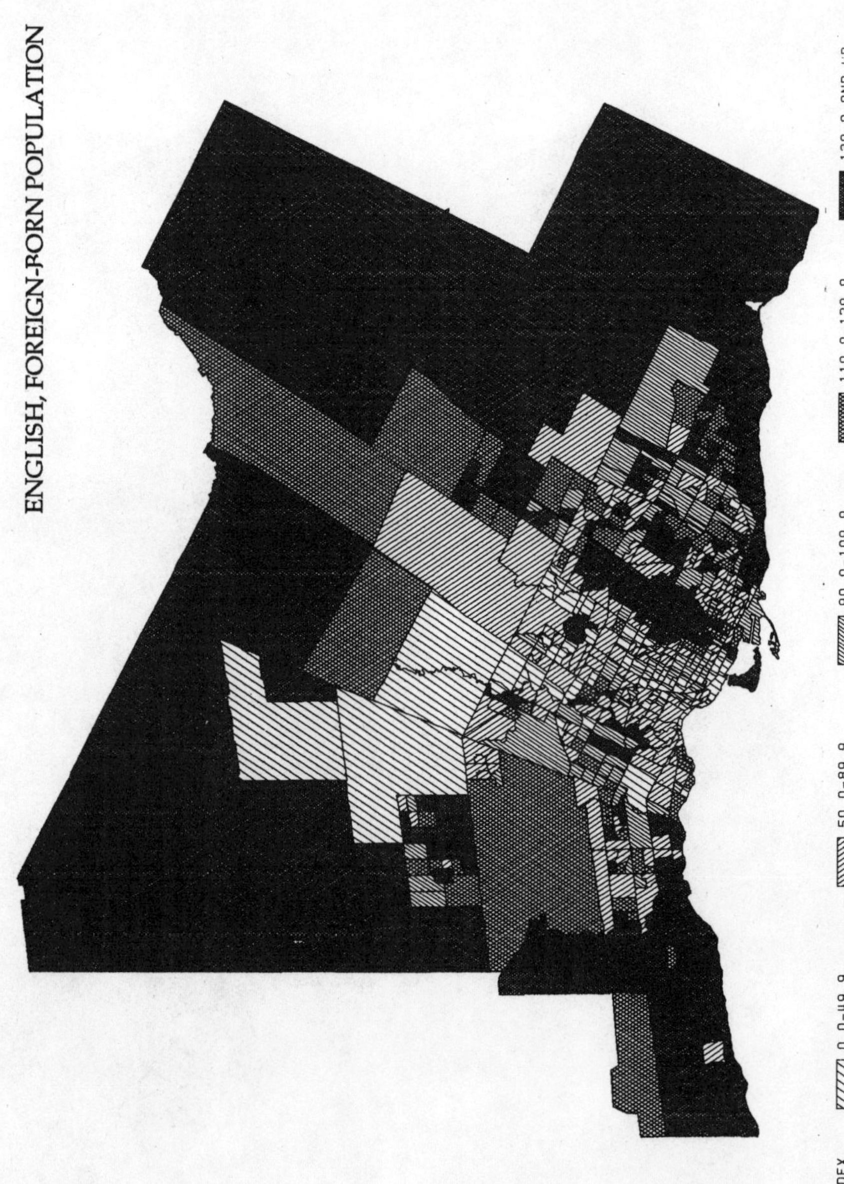
ENGLISH, FOREIGN-BORN POPULATION
INDEX
0.0-49.9
50.0-89.9
90.0-109.9
110.0-129.9
130.0 AND UP

GERMAN, TOTAL POPULATION

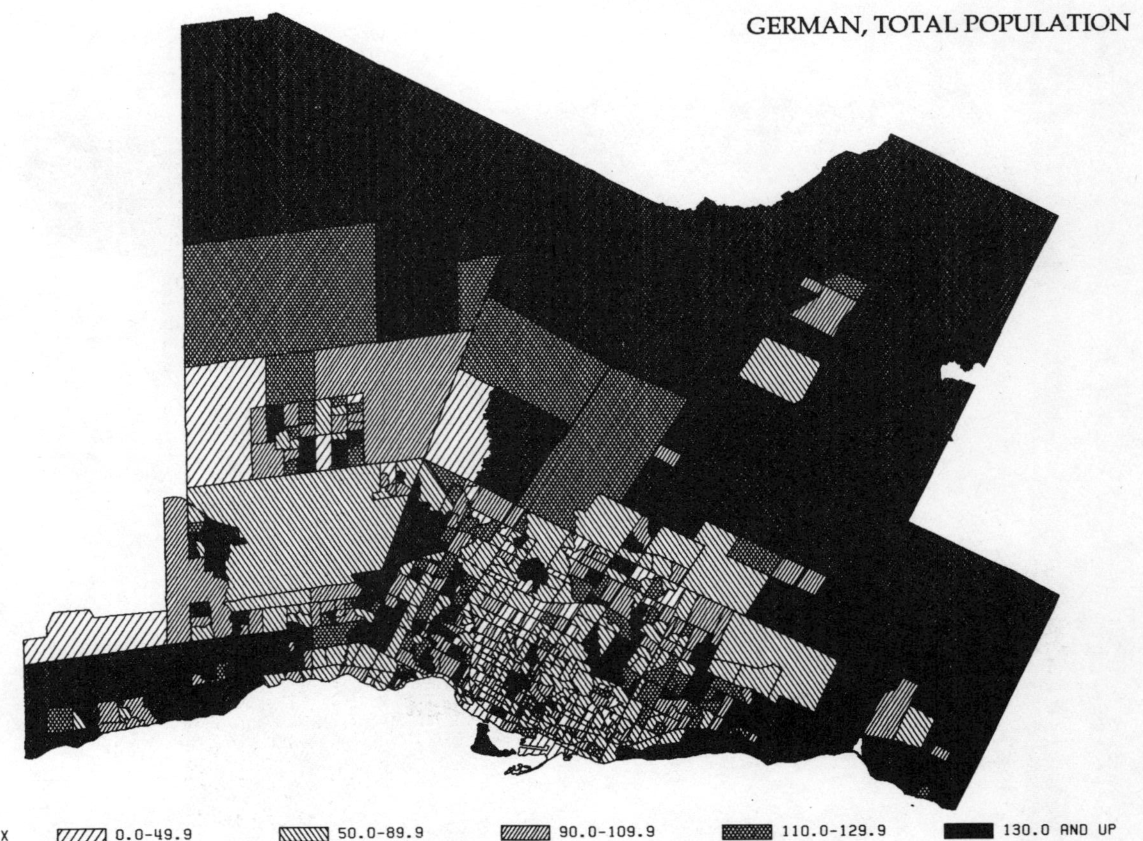

UKRAINIAN, TOTAL POPULATION

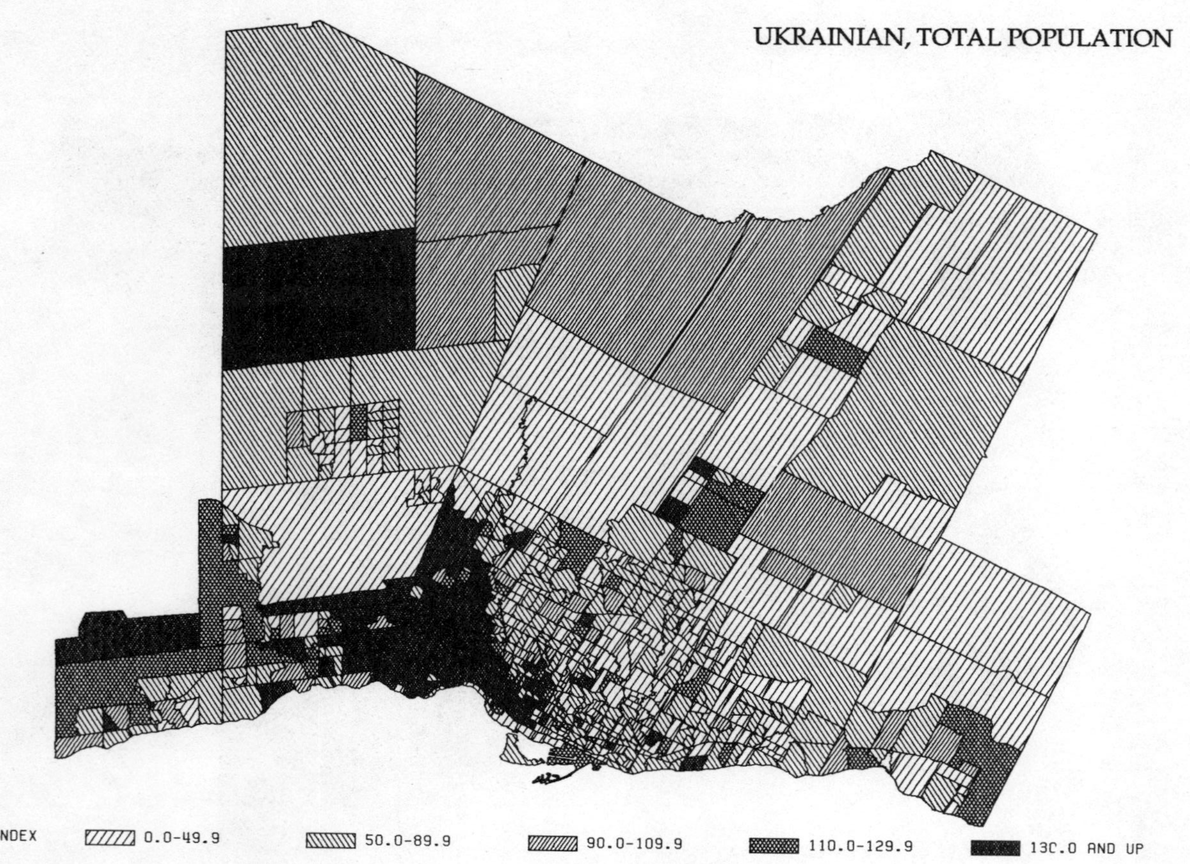

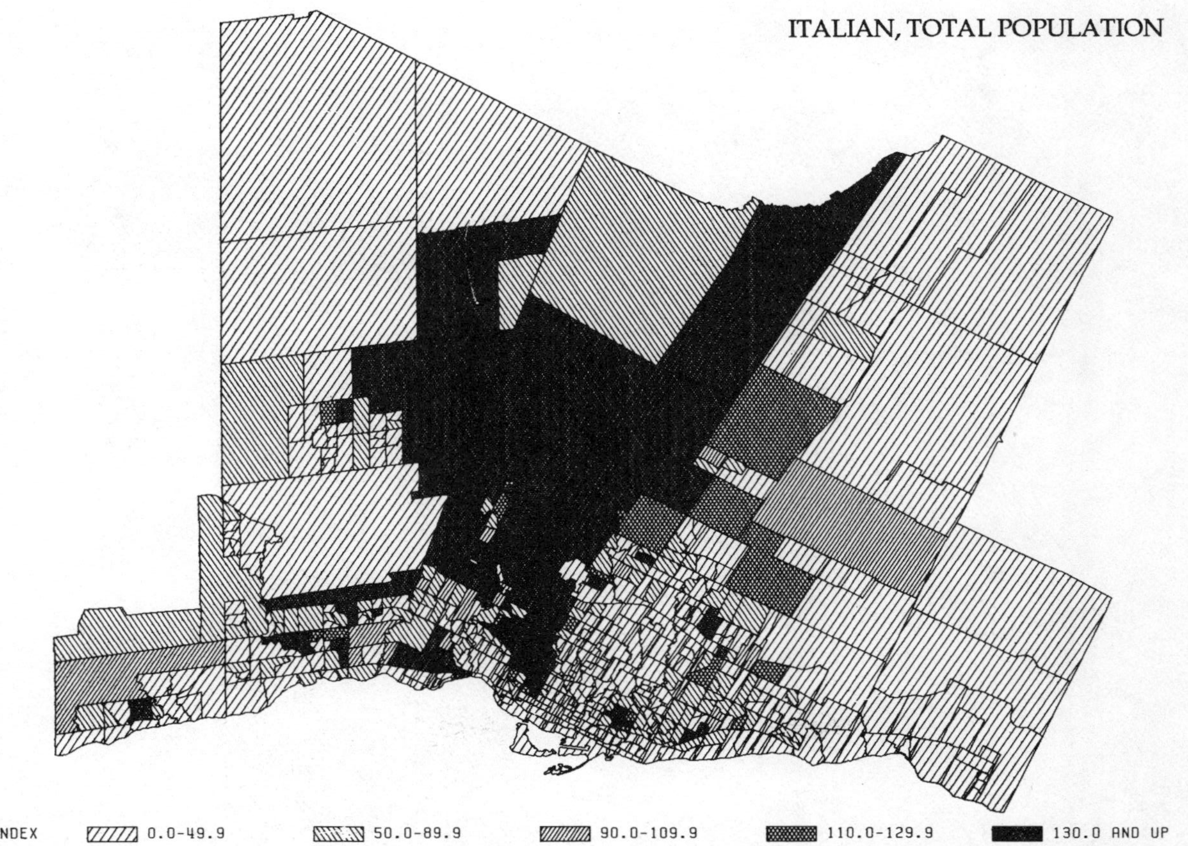
ITALIAN, TOTAL POPULATION
INDEX
0.0-49.9
50.0-89.9
90.0-109.9
110.0-129.9
130.0 AND UP

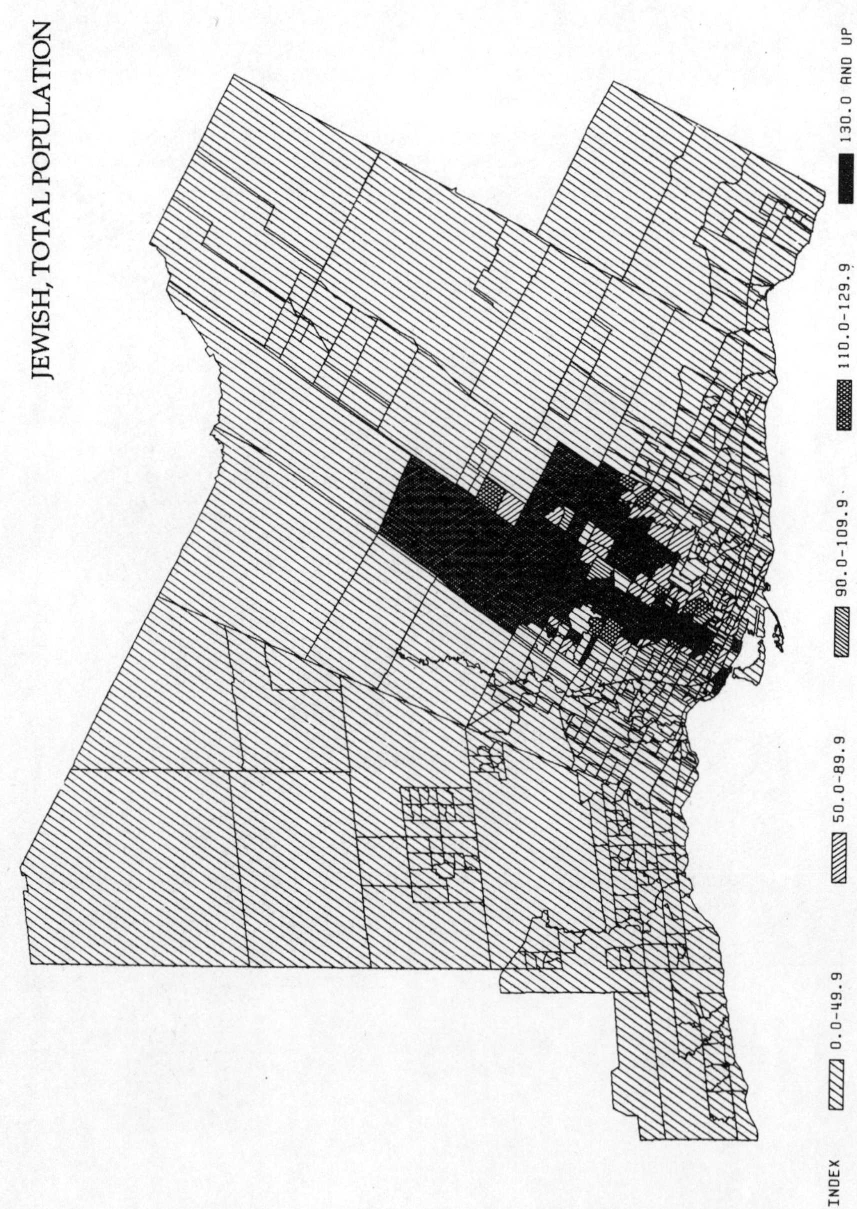
JEWISH, TOTAL POPULATION
INDEX
0.0-49.9
50.0-89.9
90.0-109.9
110.0-129.9
130.0 AND UP

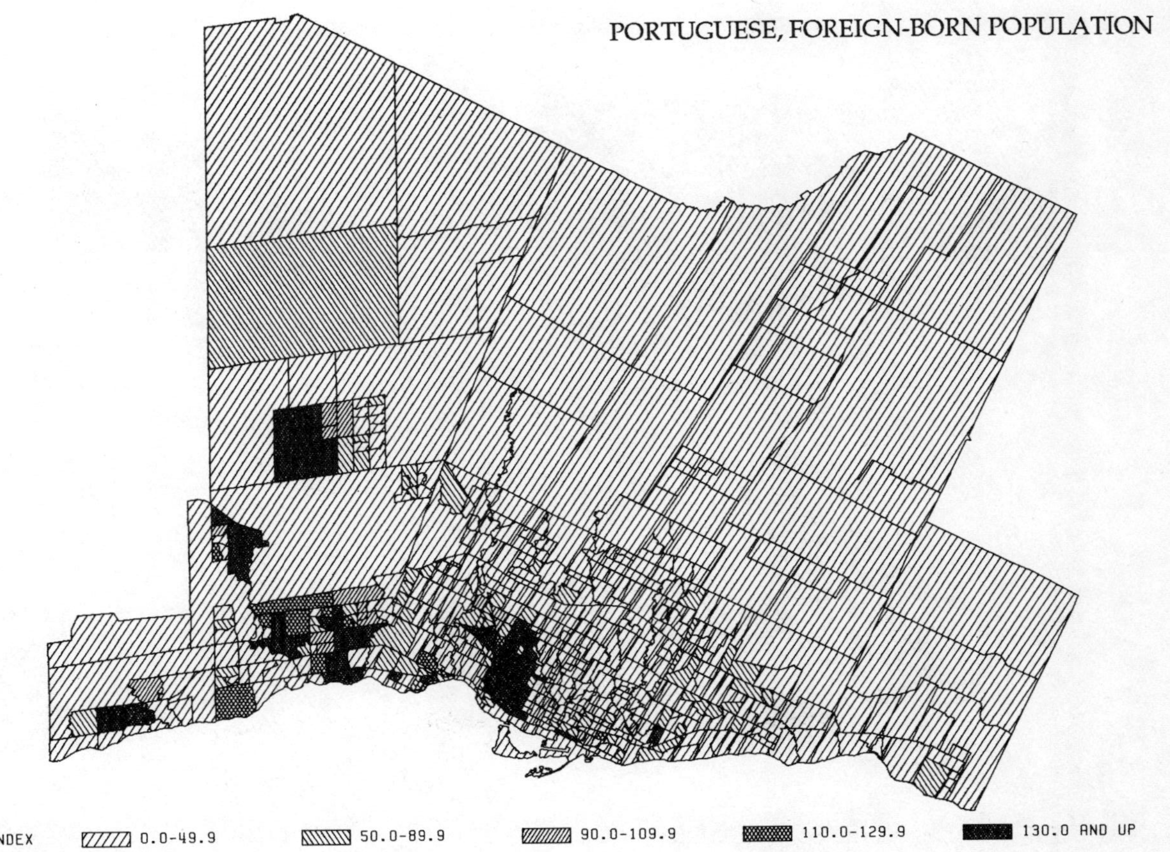
PORTUGUESE, FOREIGN-BORN POPULATION
INDEX
0.0-49.9
50.0-89.9
90.0-109.9
110.0-129.9
130.0 AND UP

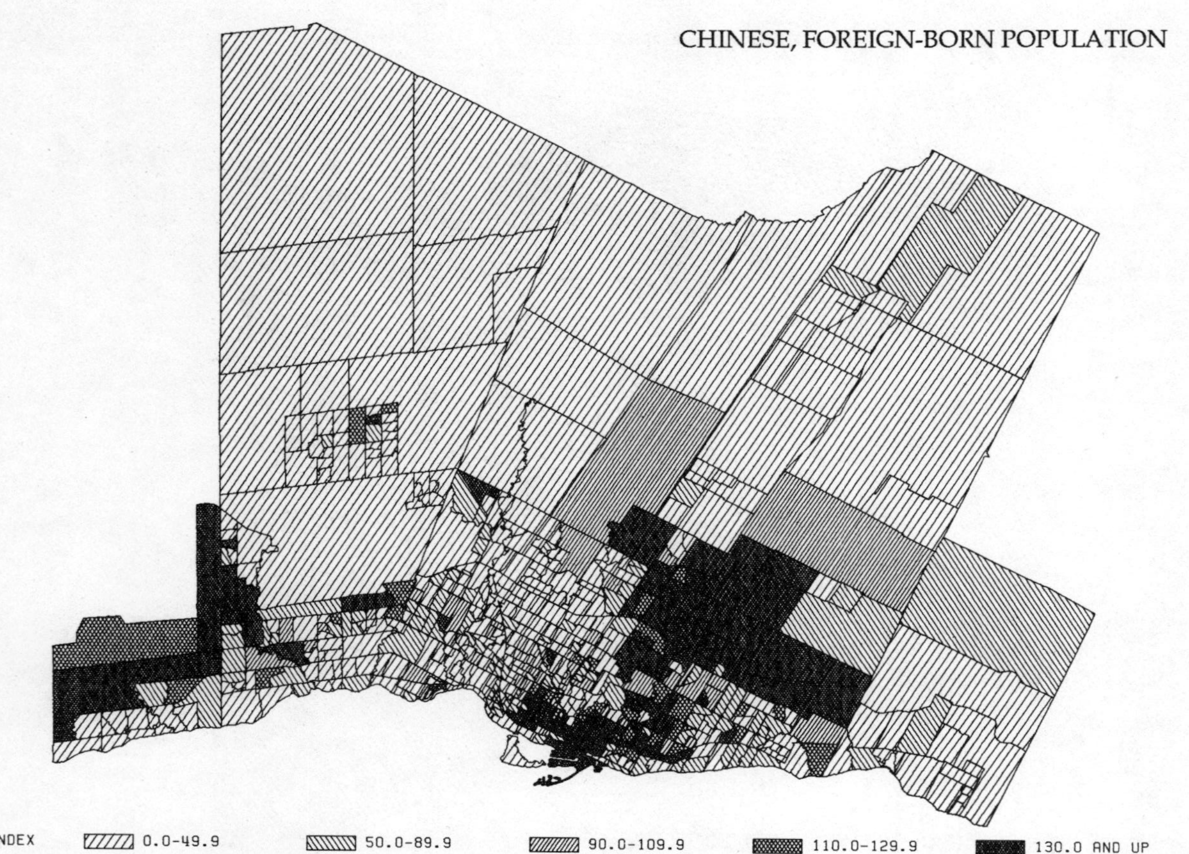
CHINESE, FOREIGN-BORN POPULATION
INDEX
0.0-49.9
50.0-89.9
90.0-109.9
110.0-129.9
130.0 AND UP

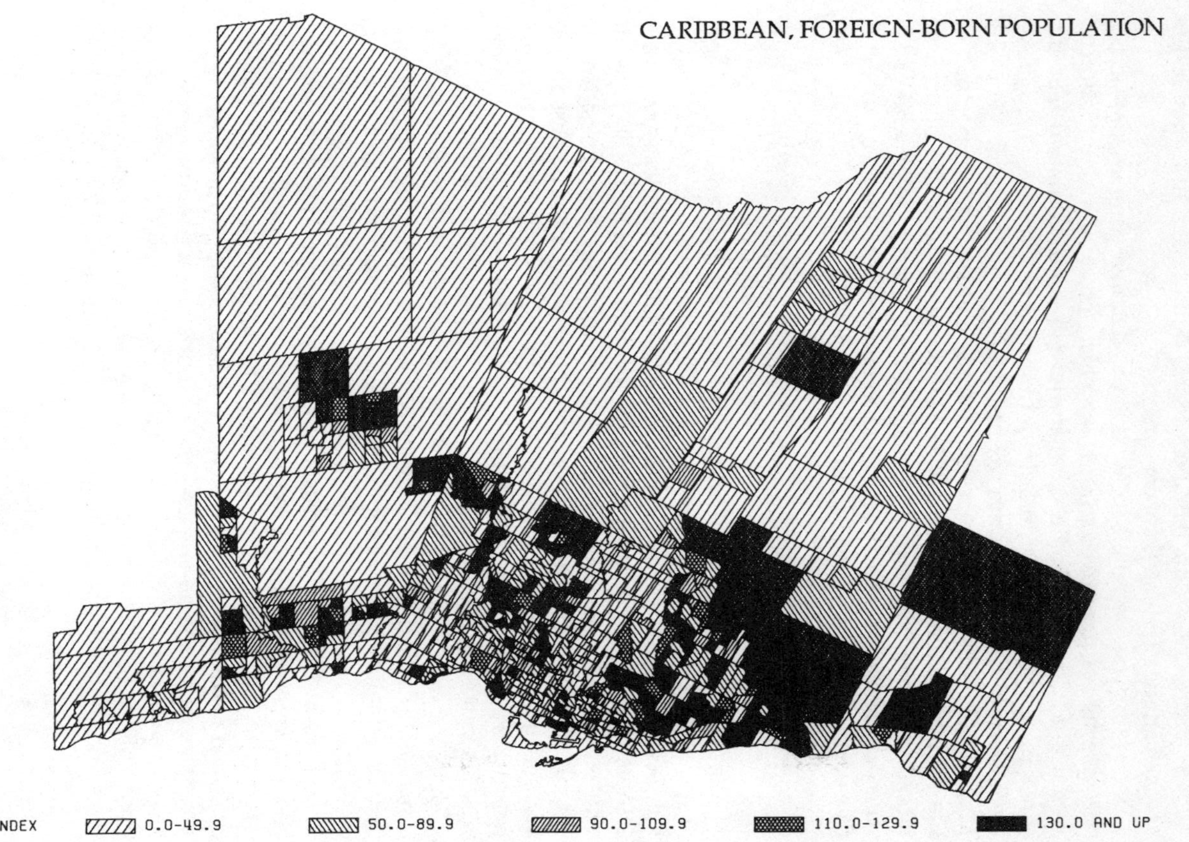
CARIBBEAN, FOREIGN-BORN POPULATION
INDEX
0.0-49.9
50.0-89.9
90.0-109.9
110.0-129.9
130.0 AND UP

extreme variations in the degree and patterns of residential concentration. These patterns (examined in more detail in chapter 3) posed asignificant challenge in the design of a proper sample that would adequately represent group members living both inside and outside the areas of ethnic residential concentration.

The study was designed so as to allow detailed comparisons across generations for the five groups in which generational variation is significant (German, English, Italian, Jewish, and Ukrainian). For the three groups composed primarily of immigrants (Chinese, Portuguese, and West Indians) the sample includes *only* immigrants. (For the Majority Canadians, of course, the sample consists only of persons in the third or higher generation). For all groups it was also desired to include persons who live in areas of ethnic concentration and those who do not. The sample is restricted to persons aged eighteen to sixty-five years who were in the labour force or were students.

WEIGHTING

The problem of sampling such diverse ethnic groups is quite complex. Disproportionate sampling probabilities must be used. The sample is not self-weighted: certain ethnic-generational categories are over-sampled given their relative size in the Toronto population. There were also some disproportionate sampling probabilities across residential neighbourhoods. This means that to achieve representativeness in the analysis it is necessary to weight the data to compensate for the disproportionate sampling probabilities. Respondents may have different weights in the sample.[3]

Thus, the data reported in this study are weighted to best reflect the actual distribution of ethnic-group members in Toronto by group, generation, and residential location. As an example, consider the case of Italians. The Italian group in Toronto is one of the largest ethnic minorities in the city. It consists of a high proportion of immigrants, and the third-generation group, while large numerically, is a small proportion of all Italians in Toronto. The group is residentially concentrated in certain areas of the city. The Italian sample, however, is the same size as for the other established groups, has a fixed proportion of respondents in each generation, and is skewed towards respondents from Italian areas. Thus, respondents are weighted to compensate for these sampling disproportions, so that the weighted sample corresponds to the actual numbers of Italians, their distribution by generation, and residence in Italian neighbourhoods.

In order to avoid confusion in interpreting the results, each table presented in the data analyses throughout chapters 2 through 5 includes both the weighted number of cases and the actual number of interviews that each weighted *N* represents. In each case, the weighted numbers of interviews (*WN*) vary from the actual numbers of interviews on which a given statistic is based (*N*). Both numbers are reported in the tables. Within the parameters of the sample design, the survey data based on weighted results can be considered representative of these various ethnic groups. Technical features of the sample design and the weighting procedures are discussed in appendix A.

THE INTERVIEWS

The persons included in the sample were interviewed with the use of the schedule in appendix B. On the average, interviews lasted one hour and a half. The interviews were carried out in 1978 and 1979, by the York University Survey Research Centre. Wherever possible, the ethnic origin of interviewers was taken into account in making field assignments. Further details on the interviewing procedures are provided in appendix A.

2

Ethnic-Identity Retention

Wsevolod W. Isajiw

One of the three basic ways in which ethnic groups become incorporated into the broader society is by developing a new identity. Nevertheless, quite often ethnic identity is also retained. That is, many members of ethnic groups, while becoming 'Canadian' in their identity in some respects, also remain 'ethnic' in some other respects. They do not necessarily define the latter to be contradictory to the former. Because identity is multi-sided, it is not a zero-sum phenomenon; Canadian identity is not necessarily gained to the extent that ethnic identity is lost and, vice versa, ethnic identity is not necessarily retained to the extent that Canadian identity is not acquired.

This chapter tries to determine to what extent ethnic identity is retained from one generation to another. Retention of ethnic identity refers to the extent to which attributes that can be identified as characteristic of the specific ethnic group are present among second or subsequent generations. These attributes may or may not be the same as those found among the first generation. In fact, evidence shows that subsequent generations do develop ethnic patterns of behaviour or a subjective identity of a type not present in the first generation. By the third generation, members of an ethnic group have become, in some manner, incorporated into the larger society and their ethnic identity has gone through a process of transformation. Ethnic-identity transformation is a shift in identity from a form that is inconsistent with the identity of the total society to one that is consonant with it. Ethnic identity can have a variety of forms, some of which may be less and others more consonant with the general societal identity. Some forms of identity may place a strong emphasis on ethnic friendship or endogamous marriage, but not necessarily ethnic language or customs. Other forms may place strong emphasis on language, but less on marriage. This chapter tries to ascertain what forms of ethnic identity are retained longest and by which ethnic groups, since some ethnic groups may retain one form of identity more than other groups, and will attempt to ascertain variations in this regard. These variations, then, will be seen as different patterns through which different groups incorporate their identity into the larger society.

It should be remembered that this study deals with ethnic-identity retention and, inversely, with ethnic-identity loss. It does not deal with assimilation as such. Ethnic-identity loss should not, by itself, be interpreted as an indicator of assimilation. Assimilation into the culture of a larger society and retention of some forms of ethnic identity can and often do take place concomitantly.

Nature of Ethnic Identity

In general terms, ethnic identity can be conceived as a social-psychological phenomenon that derives from membership in an ethnic group. A definition of an ethnic group has been given elsewhere (Isajiw 1974). What is important here is that an ethnic group is a phenomenon that gives rise to (1) social organization, an objective phenomenon that provides the structure for the ethnic community, and (2) identity, a subjective phenomenon that gives to individuals a sense of belonging and to the community a sense of oneness and historical meaning. Ethnic identity can thus be defined in Lewinian (1948) terms as a manner in which persons, on account of their ethnic origin, locate themselves psychologically in relation to one or more social systems, and in which they perceive others as locating them in relation to those systems. By ethnic origin is meant either that a person has been socialized in an ethnic group or that his or her ancestors, real or symbolic, have been members of the group. The social systems may be one's ethnic community or society at large, or other ethnic communities and other societies, or a combination of all these.

Locating oneself in relation to a community and society is not only a psychological phenomenon, but also a social phenomenon in the sense that the internal psychological states express themselves objectively in external behaviour patterns that come to be shared by others. Thus, individuals locate themselves in one or another community internally by states of mind and feelings, such as self-definitions or feelings of closeness, and externally by behaviour appropriate to these states of mind and feelings. Behaviour according to cultural patterns is thus an expression of identity and can be studied as an indication of its character.

We can thus distinguish external and internal aspects of ethnic identity. External aspects refer to observable behaviour, both cultural and social, such as (1) speaking an ethnic language, practising ethnic traditions, and so on; (2) participation in ethnic personal networks, such as family and friendship; (3) participation in ethnic institutional organizations, such as churches, schools, enterprises, media; (4) participation in ethnic voluntary associations, such as clubs, 'societies,' youth organizations; and (5) participation in functions sponsored by ethnic organizations such as picnics, concerts, public lectures, rallies, dances.

The internal, subjective aspects of ethnic identity refer to images, ideas, attitudes, and feelings. These, of course, are interconnected with the external, or objective, behaviour. But it should not be assumed that, empirically, the two types are always dependent upon each other. Rather, they may vary independently; one may retain a higher degree of internal than of external aspects, and vice versa. We can distinguish at least three types of internal aspects of identity: (1) cognitive, (2) moral, and (3) affective.

The cognitive dimension of identity includes, first, self-images and images of one's group. These may be stereotypes of self or of the group and perceived stereotypes by others of oneself and one's group. It also includes knowledge of one's group's heritage and its historical past. This knowledge may not necessarily be extensive or objective. It may rather focus on selected aspects or events or historical personalities that are highly symbolic of the group's experiences and that thus have become a legacy. Finally, the cognitive dimension includes knowledge of one's group's values, since these are part of the group's heritage.

The moral dimension of identity involves feelings of group obligations. In general, feelings of group obligations have to do with the importance a person attaches to his or her group and the implications the group has for the person's behaviour. Specifically, it would include such feelings of obligation as the importance of teaching the ethnic language to one's children, of marrying within the group, or of helping members of the group with finding a job. Feelings of obligation account for the commitment a person has to his group and for the group solidarity that ensues. They can be said to constitute the central dimension of subjective identity. So far, no theory of ethnic identity has conceptualized group obligations as constituting its core dimension. A number of researchers, such as Geismar, have asked questions of their respondents about such obligations, without, however, conceptualizing them as a central notion of subjective ethnic identity.

The affective, or cathectic, dimension of identity refers to feelings of attachment to the group. Two types of such feelings can be distinguished: (1) feelings of security with and sympathy and associative preference for members of one's group as against members of other groups and (2) feelings of security and comfort with the cultural patterns of one's group as against the cultural patterns of other groups or societies.

The Problem of Ethnic-Identity Retention

It is a basic assumption of this study that the retention of ethnic identity from one generation to another does not necessarily mean retention of both its aspects, or all the components of each aspect in the same degree. Some components may be retained more than others; some may not be retained at all. A member of the third generation may subjectively identify with his ethnic group without having knowledge of the ethnic language or without practising ethnic traditions or participating in ethnic organizations. Or, inversely, he or she may practise some ethnic traditions without having strong feelings of attachment to the group. Furthermore, the same components of external identity may acquire different subjective meaning for different generations, ethnic groups, or other subgroups within the same ethnic group. Therefore, it should not be assumed that the ethnic identity retained by the third generation is of the same type or form of identity as that retained by the first or the second generation.

The differential variation of the components of ethnic identity thus allows us to distinguish various forms of ethnic identity. For example, a high level of retention of the practice of ethnic traditions accompanied by a low level of such subjective components as feelings of group obligation may be one form of ethnic identity: say, a ritualistic ethnic identity. By contrast, a high intensity of feelings of group obligation accompanied by a low level of practice of traditions would be a completely different form of ethnic identity: say, an ideological identity with different implications for the collective aspects of ethnic group behaviour. Negative images of one's own ethnic group, accompanied by a high degree of awareness of one's ethnic ancestry, may be still another form of ethnic identity, a rebelling identity, and positive images of one's ancestral group accompanied by a practice of highly selected traditions, particularly by the third or a consecutive generation, may be still another form of ethnic identity, that of ethnic rediscovery. As part of its conclusions this study will single out a few possible forms of ethnic identity derived from the empirical findings, but no attempt will be made to link various identity components in the manner suggested above.

Much of the literature on the retention of ethnic identity has been related to the Hansen hypothesis. According to this hypothesis, the second generation removes itself or rebels against its ethnic group, and the third returns to it. Until now, however, the research evidence informing this issue has been to a large extent confusing.

Studies done in the United States have shown varying degrees of ethnicity retention. Some American authors would conclude that by the second or third generation little ethnic identity is retained and would imply that the process of assimilation is rapid and effective. Others would show that these generations retain a significant degree of their ethnic identity. The facts have shown both loss and retention of ethnic identity.

Most studies of the three generations have been American. Canadian work on this subject began in a more systematic way in the 1970s, but the number of studies has been small.

The brief, selected review of studies that follows focuses on the ethnic identity of the three generations, particularly the second and third. The studies that deal with ethnic identity but that do not consider generational differences or generational peculiarities are not considered here.

Ludwig Geismar's early study (1954) used a rather sophisticated measure of ethnic identification. He tested sixty-seven campers at a Zionist summer camp and found that no children with low ethnic identification were from homes where much Jewish ritual was present. However, he also found that a number of campers who identified highly with their ethnicity came from families in which Jewish observances were at a minimum.

Herbert Gans (1956) was among the first to observe that if the third generation returns to ethnicity, it is unlikely to return to the traditional ethnic culture as it was known and practised by the grandparents. Yet Herberg, in his study (1955) of the relationship between ethnicity and religion, found that second-generation Jews developed their ties with their religious community fairly easily, and that third-generation members did not sever their religious ties, but on the contrary further reinforced them. For the Polish and Italian groups, however, Herberg found that the third generation became disillusioned with the ethnic group, whereas the second generation identified with it.

The decade of the sixties produced much more data on ethnic generations. The students of ethnicity were also given a challenge by Glazer and Moynihan's issue-raising work (1963) in which the authors pointed to the persistence of ethnic communities in the American cities in spite of the melting-pot ideology. Yet, again, the studies carried out at that time have come down on both sides of the Hansen hypothesis. The data gathered, however, have introduced several important qualifications to the question of generations. Thus, several studies have shown that only a certain percentage of the second generation rebels or removes itself from its parental ethnicity, not the entire generation. It has also been found that the second generation may rebel against ethnicity in some respects, yet may remain ethnic in other respects.

Kramer and Leventman (1961), for example, found that in the entire second generation of the Jewish community they surveyed, only a few rejected their ethnic identity, even though many of them were turning away from traditional religion. Eugene Uyeki (1960), in his study of the Japanese in the United States, found that the Nisei (second generation) did acculturate and assimilate in the host society at a rather rapid rate. The Nisei considered themselves to be American, and made no association with Japan, except as a country from which their parents came. He concluded that the absence of a segregated, organized Japanese community made difficult any reinforcement of Japanese cultural values and practices. However, the study did find that the respondents strongly identified with other Nisei, and that the majority of their friendships were with Nisei.

Lenski's findings (1961) on the Jews in Detroit parallel Uyeki's results. Lenski found that while there had been a weakening of ties to religious associations among the Jews in Detroit, Jewish communal ties have remained strong. Unlike Lenski's findings, but more in accord with those of Will Herberg, Lazarewitz and Rowitz (1964) found that, among the Jewish population studied, increasing church attendance was positively correlated with increasing Americanization.

Gans in his famous study of Italians in Boston (1962) found that in spite of overt conflicts between parents and children, in both the second and the third generation, certain attitudes towards work have remained constant. Thus, first-generation parents did not encourage their children to get emotionally involved in work or to seek satisfaction from it, because the conditions of their own work in America included little satisfaction. Second-generation parents, however, encouraged their children to equip themselves for better jobs, and to get as much education as they could for this purpose. However, Gans noted that the children seemed to internalize the attitudes towards work held by the majority of their ethnic group and thus continued to express the group's lack of interest in thinking about the future. While the parents were often disappointed that their children did not continue their education beyond the legal minimum, Gans reported that this disappointment was not intense. Indeed, in the end a certain continuity in attitudes came to be maintained among the generations.

Simirenko, however, in his study of the first and second generation (1964), pointed out that one should not generalize about each generation as a whole. His interviews showed that there are at least two types of persons among the second generation, those who are more conservative and retain more of their ethnic background, and those who are more radical, who adjust and acculturate to the general society faster and retain less of their ethnic identity.

The Lakeville studies (Sklare and Greenblum 1967; Ringer 1967), predominantly of second- and third-generation Jews in suburban areas, indicate both continuity and conflict between generations. In the study parents were asked: 'Do you think there is more agreement or less agreement between your outlook and interest in Jewish affairs and your children's than there was between yours and your father's (mother's) when you were a child?' One-half of the persons surveyed saw no difference between their own early experiences and their children's; of the rest, three-quarters thought there was more family harmony now than a generation ago, and one-quarter thought there was less.

In the mid-sixties a study appeared that tried to ascertain ethnic-language retention (Fishman et al. 1966: 34–50). Although its main empirical source was the United States census, it was a first attempt to analyse the census data for language retention by the three generations. Some of the analysis, however, had to be based on estimates. The results showed a substantial overall drop from the first to the third generation. Yet, variations among ethnic groups were also substantial. Some groups showed sharp gains from one generation to another, others sharp losses. The work, however, raised many important questions about ethnic generations and suggested some interesting ideas as to the different relationship of each generation to the society at large (Fishman et al. 1966: 343–52).

The seventies and the eighties have witnessed more sophisticated and careful conceptualizations of ethnicity and ethnic identity. The question as to whether the second generation rebels and the third returns is still not clearly answered. A review of studies, however, suggests that perhaps Hansen's question about generational continuity was not phrased in the right way. By now there seems to be a general agreement that culturally the second generation assimilates relatively quickly, and also that the third generation, or at least part of it, retains a degree of ethnic identification. The question of rebellion and return still remains, but it has to be approached in a different context.

Is it that the second generation rebels against its ethnicity, or is it that the rapid process of cultural assimilation has been interpreted as rebellion? Is it that the third generation exhibits a regained interest and identification with ethnicity, or is it that the ethnic identification that has always been there has been interpreted as a return? Or perhaps interest and identification with ethnicity, as Michael Novak (1971) insisted, is a stage in the history of ethnic groups in which they are asserting themselves.

Arnold Dashefsky (1970, 1972) and jointly with H. Shapiro (1974) has produced one of the most interesting studies of this problem. Dashefsky is careful with his concepts of 'generation,' 'ethnic self-conception,' 'ethnic group identification,' and 'participation in ethnic activities.' He also develops a more sophisticated measure of ethnic identification. His study consisted of two samples of males, sons aged 22 to 29, and their fathers, with a total of 302 persons from the Jewish community of St Paul, Minnesota, to whom questionnaires were distributed. His findings show that sons participate in a greater number of ethnic interpersonal contacts and of ethnic situational contexts than do their fathers, yet they have a less, rather than a more, distinctive ethnic identity. Save for specifically Jewish education, higher levels of general education and occupation tended to be associated with less distinctive identity, regardless of ethnic interaction and contact patterns. Dashefsky, like Lenski, concludes that the weakening of religious ties from father to son has been matched by the weakening of a distinctive Jewish self-conception, while the enduring strength of communal bonds can be seen in the continuing strength of interactional factors.

Paralleling Dashefsky's findings, Sharot (1973), in his study of American Jews, found that the second generation did not revolt against their ancestral religion but simply became indifferent to it, and that the third generation did not return to it.

Studies of the Irish, Italian, East European, and Japanese ethnic groups, however, are much more supportive of the Hansen hypothesis. Goering (1971) studied a sample of one hundred Irish and Italian third-generation individuals, and found that while there was little ethnic organizational activity among them, there was a significant questioning of the 'American dream,' accompanied by an opposition to the demands of the blacks, and by a heightened ethnic consciousness. Goering concludes that the declining importance of ethnic constraints serves as a condition for the emergence of ethnic consciousness. The third generation does return to ethnicity but less as a source of cultural or religious refreshment than as the basis for organizing the scepticism associated with discontent and racial confrontation.

Neil Sandberg, in his study of Polish Americans in Los Angeles (1974: 50–5), found that there was a consistent but irregular decrease of ethnic identity levels from the first to the fourth generation. The decrease from the first to the second generation was not very significant, as was also true of the decrease from the third to the fourth generation. The big drop was from the second to the third generation.

Yet, Greeley (1972) and McCready (1974; and jointly 1974) have compared Anglo-Saxons, Irish, and Italians in the United States and have shown that the cultural heritages of the Old World, especially their distinctive values, have persisted among the second and third generations. Frideres and Goldenberg's study (1977), however, seemed to show that students in western Canada have a low level of ethnic identity. Only about 33% of their sample felt that their fate was bound up with their ethnic group at least to some extent. Their sample, however, did not differentiate between any of the generations.

Masuda, Matsumoto, and Meredith (1970) have shown that among the Japanese of Seattle there was a considerable process of acculturation of both the first and the second generation, that is, the Issei and the Nisei. The process was accelerated by social contact with and mobility into the majority society. However, both the Issei and the Nisei had problems in adjusting to the host society, though their problems were of two different types. Those of the Issei arose from their tendency to segregate themselves from the society at large, whereas those of the Nisei arose from their cultural marginality – from having one foot in the Japanese community and the other outside of it. As a result, the Nisei were faced with the type of conflict described by Hansen, while the Issei were free of it. By contrast, the Sansei (third generation) exhibited a high degree of acculturation, but not much structural assimilation. They did show, however, a rather considerable degree of ethnic identity.

Hasakawa (1973) confirmed the findings of Masuda et al. on the Sansei. Her conclusion was that the ethnic identification of the Sansei is based on a combination of both their interaction with the majority members and their interaction with ethnic peers. Ethnic identification is thought to result because the interaction with ethnic members is rewarding, while interaction with non-ethnic members is costly.

In a study of the Japanese in Toronto, Makabe (1976, 1978, 1979) also substantiates the hypothesis that the Sansei maintain a degree of ethnic identity. However, she draws attention to differences in attitudes towards one's ethnic identity. Thus, a high proportion of Nisei saw their ethnicity as having a negative connotation, whereas the Sansei expressed a high degree of pride in their relationship to Japan since it was an internationally respected country.

The idea that the second generation is between two cultures and the third assimilates yet retains some significant ethnic-identity characteristics was clearly illustrated in Connor's major study (1977) of the Japanese Americans in Sacramento, California. His sample consisted of 847 interviewees and 1,200 mailed questionnaires, and was stratified for the three generations. The study involved five different instruments in an attempt to measure a large variety of characteristics that could be identified as Japanese. It also included comparisons with a non-Japanese sample. Like the other studies, Connor's results show both considerable assimilation from one generation to another and relatively high identity retention. On some counts, his data also support Hansen's hypothesis of 'return' inasmuch as a few scores for the Sansei were higher than those for the Nisei. Yet Connor concludes that the Sansei are interested in retaining the symbolic rather than the behavioural aspects of their heritage.

Although most of the studies reviewed so far indicate a loss in ethnic practices from generation to generation, religious practices remain most problematical. In a study of New York City Catholics, Nelsen and Allen (1974) indicate that in focusing on the differences between the generations, one has to take into account cultural differences between ethnic groups as units. Thus, in their sample of 885 white Catholics, the authors included representative numbers of Western, Eastern, and Southern Europeans, and representative numbers of the three generations. Their findings show that there were no meaningful differences in religious attendance among the first-generation Catholics, but among the second-generation respondents the differences were substantial. Western Europeans show an increase in religious attendance from the first to the second generation, while Southern Europeans show a decrease. The findings thus give support to both Herberg's and Hansen's hypotheses. The authors interpret their findings by stating that the pattern of second-generation religious attendance depends on the extent of differences between the ethnic culture and the dominant American culture. The smaller the difference, the higher the retention of the religious practices, and vice versa.

Similar findings, showing large differences in the retention of religious identity between different ethnic groups, were reported by Abramson (1975). His results induced him to distinguish at least three different patterns of loss and retention. Some groups lose religious identity in a straight-line pattern from generation to generation; others increase it from the first to the second generation and then drop off; still others lose their identity from the first to the second generation, but then regain it to a higher degree in the third generation.

This variation appears to be also true of other practices, especially the knowledge and use of the ethnic language. In a study of ethnic-language retention in Canada, O'Bryan, Reitz, and Kuplowska (1975) examined a national sample of 2,433 persons representing ten different ethnic groups. They found that the highest proportion of those in the second and third generation who had at least some knowledge of the ethnic language were among the Eastern and Southern Europeans. However, such groups as the Germans and the Dutch also had relatively high proportions of second- and third-generation members with at least some knowledge of their ethnic language.

The study also showed that, in the total sample, the actual use of ethnic language decreased rather sharply with each generation; yet 39% of the third and 64% of the second generation reported at least some knowledge of their ethnic language. Furthermore, 66% of the second and 59% of the third generation supported either strongly or somewhat the idea of their ethnic group retaining the use of its language, and the majority supported language retention, regardless of whether they themselves knew the language. In terms of self-identification, almost 35% of the second generation and about 30% of the third report themselves as hyphenated Canadians (see also Reitz 1980).

Further research has to a large extent dispelled the notion that ethnic identity retention is exactly the same process for all groups. Driedger (1975, 1977) has studied territorial, institutional, and cultural identity factors among various ethnic groups in Winnipeg. He concluded that some groups score high on some identity factors, whereas other groups do so on other identity factors. Thus, the French and Jewish university students ranked high on attendance in parochial schools, endogamy, and in-group friends. Other groups, such as Ukrainians, ranked high on ethnic language knowledge scores, whereas others, such as the Scandinavians, tended to rank low on all scores.

By the end of the 1970s and the beginning of the 1980s the researchers of ethnicity had come to accept the fact that in spite of assimilation some percentage and some form of ethnic identity often remains in the second, third, and even later generations. Studies appeared that tried to explore more precisely the nature of this type of identity. Yancey et al. (1976) pointed to the 'emergent' rather than 'transmitted' properties of ethnic persistence. Gans (1979) labelled the type of ethnic identity prevalent among the third generation as 'symbolic.'

In Canada, Doucette and Edwards (1987) studied a sample of university students in the Atlantic coast region, an area with the least ethnic diversity in Canada. Of the sample, only 32% considered themselves definitely members of an ethnic group, while 56% felt somewhat differentiated from those of other backgrounds. When asked about the factors responsible for ethnic continuity, 71% of all the respondents referred to a 'sense of groupness' or 'belonging.' They felt that this alone would be sufficient in maintaining the continuity of ethnic identity. Other factors mentioned by them were language and religion. The authors interpret this emphasis on the sense of groupness as indicating the symbolic nature that ethnicity has acquired.

Baar (1983) interviewed a sample of several generations of Mennonite church members in Ontario's Niagara Peninsula. The interviews showed that in the second and subsequent generations the behavioural prescriptions of the communal life became de-emphasized but religious commitment became stronger. Baar claims this change made adjustment to the non-Mennonite environment easier but it required a redefinition of ethnic group boundaries. Most Mennonites, however, did not perceive this redefinition as a threat to the persistence of their group. Baar concludes that her study replaces Gordon's concept of 'assimilation' with a concept of 'selective accentuation,' by which the importance of the patterning or re-patterning of inter-group relations in defining and maintaining identity is emphasized.

Some studies have delved in depth into the nature and meaning of the new awareness of ethnicity. Aversa (1978) has tried to specify different motifs around which the new ethnicity has been constructed among the Italian Americans, such as the 'renaissance-grandeur' motif, 'contadino-pastoralism' motif, or 'immigrant experience' motif. Tricarico (1984) explored the attitudes of three generations of Italians and focused on some of the successful institutions established as a product of the new ethnicity.

An interesting, even if controversial, study of ethnic identity is Nicks's ethnohistorical approach to understanding an individual's identity. The history of an ethnic group provides, as it were, a substitute for generational analysis. It also plays a role in forming the ethnic identity of younger generations. Nicks (1985) describes the identity of her subject, Mary Anne, a Red River Metis, as a positive and strong ethnic identity, associated with the history of the Metis as interpreted today by Metis historians and represented by the new style of exhibiting Metis art and history in museums or galleries. This identity, however, was formed as a product of a conscious rejection of a culture that epitomized only adaptation to the fur trade and that represented the Metis as half-breeds, caught mid-way between a 'primitive' state and assimilation into the white society. The new Metis identity is seen as a product of Canadian history, but is something distinct and positive.

Similarly to that of Nicks, Kienetz's study discusses the impact and consequences of the ethnic resurgence among the young generations of native Indians and Inuits in Canada since the 1970s. Kienetz (1986) reports on school surveys conducted among grade 7 to 10 students in a school of the Status Indian reserve community of Pukatawagan, Manitoba. The results of the study showed that more than five times as many students identified with some native Indian category than with simply being Canadian. In another, non-native environment, however, the results were much different. Kienetz concludes that this difference is a consequence of the new awareness among native Indians, which is the only ethnic identity among the natives of Canada's North that is of practical significance today to mainstream Anglo-Canadians.

Yet, the end of the 1970s and the decade of the 1980s also present studies that more or less re-emphasize the old unilinear pattern of assimilation of the three generations. Alba (1976) used Andrew Greeley's 1963 data to assess intermarriage rates for four generations of eight different ethnic groups. His analysis showed that although the ethnic groups analysed showed some ethnic-identity retention as judged by in-marriage rates, nevertheless, the overall picture across four generations is one of extensive and increasing assimilation, contradicting any assumption of 'universal ethnic vitality.' Farber, Gordon, and Mayer's (1979) data on 564 children of the respondents interviewed corroborated this conclusion. It showed a rather large amount of intermarriage of young Jewish persons with non-Jewish mates.

The same conclusion was reached by Montero (1981), who derived his findings from a sample of 2,304 second-generation and 802 third-generation Japanese Americans. He employed six different indicators of assimilation, including intermarriage. On all of them his data showed a definite increase of assimilation from the Issei to the Nisei to the Sansei. He concludes by stating that these findings do not lend support to Hansen's third-generation ethnic-revival thesis. Rather, they point to a pattern that is more consistent with R.E. Park's unilinear concept of assimilation. He also indicates that education and social mobility hasten the assimilation process (see also Makabe 1979). In his later study of Italians, Alba (1985a, b) went on to emphasize that assimilation is the major process among ethnic groups and that the key forces that have made it so are structural.

The emphasis on the assimilation process has moved some scholars to look more closely at, as it were, the product of assimilation. Lieberson (1985) used the NORC surveys to look at the identity of the different generations and observed that, among those whites who were unable to name any ancestral country and those who gave 'American' as their ancestry, almost all were at least fourth-generation. He estimated that these 'Unhyphenated whites' make up about 20% of all non-black Americans with at least four generations' residence in the country. According to him, these whites constitute an ethnicity of its own type, perhaps the American ethnicity, resulting from the assimilation of at least four generations of many other ethnic groups.

Assuming that intermarriage is still the most important indicator of assimilation, Alba and Chamlin (1983) undertook an analysis of the NORC General Social Survey data on intermarriage for the years 1977, 1978, and 1980. As could have been expected, their analysis showed that the odds of multiple as against single ethnic ancestry among the younger generations were two times higher than those for the older generations. Yet, they were surprised to find that in spite of this fact, for the younger cohorts with mixed ancestry the odds that they ultimately will identify with only one ancestry were markedly higher than those for the older cohorts. That is, in spite of their mixed ancestry there was a rather strong tendency among the younger generations of various ethnic backgrounds to identify with a single ethnicity to which they felt closer. The education factor only increased these odds. The authors conclude that this finding corroborates the claim of ethnic resurgence and that ethnic identification may remain an issue even for the socially assimilated (see also Alba 1985b). Once again the reality proved to be elusive. Willingly or not, the authors' conclusion completely reformulates the issue of assimilation and identity retention. Alba and Chamlin might not have drawn out the implications of this reformulation. Nevertheless, other research in the late 1970s and early 1980s has been showing similar results.

Chrisman (1981), for example, approached the question of ethnic persistence not directly through generational continuity but by means of organizational continuity. Studying the Danish American community in the San Francisco Bay Area, a group that is usually assumed to be one of those groups who assimilate rather quickly, Chrisman showed that a non-localized organizational continuity of the Danish group had existed for about one hundred years. He indicated that the organizational structure of the community has allowed the younger generations to form their own organizational units with different goals from the units made up primarily of older generations. The need for personal networks and the opportunity to establish them offered by the ethnic community organizations have apparently been the dynamic factors responsible for the group's organizational continuity.

Several other studies (Driedger 1980; Hurh 1980; Zenner 1985; Sandberg 1986) have also observed the relationship between ethnic institutional differentiation and change of the subjective meaning of ethnic identity. A study of a sample of 634 Japanese in California by O'Brien and Fugita, reported by McCready (1983), accepted the fact that by the 1970s about 50% of all new marriages involving Japanese were marriages to Caucasians and that many social boundaries between the Japanese and other Americans have been disappearing. Yet, their interviews showed that the Sansei, even significantly more than the Nisei, perceived the differences between Japanese and Caucasian ways of behaving, and by far the majority of both the Nisei and the Sansei placed a positive value on the Japanese culture.

The problem with the question of ethnic identity retention by successive generations is that the answer depends on which components of ethnicity are studied in a given case. Among the studies reviewed, some focus on the retention of ethnic practices and cultural patterns, others on participation in the organized ethnic community or on interaction with members of the ethnic groups, and still others on subjective ethnic identity.

What is indicated, therefore, is a methodology that would compare ethnic-identity retention of the different generations using as many components of ethnicity as possible. Only when such a comparison is done systematically for a variety of ethnic groups will it be possible to determine the general degree of ethnic-identity retention.

In our discussion, only those groups in the sample will be included that, in addition to the first generation, have a significantly large mature second and third generation. The Portuguese, West Indians, and Chinese will not be included in the comparison because their second generation in Toronto is still rather young. The 'Majority Canadians' that include the combined British third and consecutive generations are included. For the English, however, only two generations have been singled out.

Retention of External, Behavioural Aspects of Ethnic Identity

ETHNIC-LANGUAGE RETENTION

Ethnic language has been often considered one of the most socially significant ethnic patterns. Is it equally significant to all ethnic groups, and how well is it retained in Canada by successive generations?

Questions about language retention can be considered from at least four points of view. First is the ethnic language the mother tongue for all those who report themselves as being of a specific ethnic origin? Secondly, do those of any specific ethnic origin for whom English rather than the ethnic language is the mother tongue have any knowledge of their ethnic language? Thirdly, how well is the language known by all those who have any knowledge of it? Finally, how frequently do those who have a knowledge of their ethnic language use it in their everyday life?

Mother Tongue

A mother tongue is defined as the language first learned in childhood and still understood.

Table 2.1 breaks down the data on the mother tongue of all respondents by ethnic origin and generation. The table shows a steady and sharp increase across generations in the number of respondents with English as their mother tongue and a parallel decline in the number of respondents reporting their ethnic language as their mother tongue.

In at least one of the groups, the Jewish, a significant proportion of the first generation, about one-third, report English as their mother tongue. This phenomenon can probably be explained by the fact that many Jews came to Canada from the United States and England.

There are variations in the rate of decline in reporting of the ethnic mother tongue across generations. Italians and Germans exhibit a much more rapid rate of decline than do Jewish and Ukrainian respondents as measured by percentage drops from one generation to another. Ukrainian respondents retain their mother tongue to a higher degree in both second and third generations than do the other three groups. None the less, the majority of the second generation of both Ukrainians and Italians learned the ethnic language as their mother tongue. The majority of the Jewish and German second generation, however, learned English as their mother tongue. In the third generation almost one hundred per cent of all groups, except Ukrainians, report English as their mother tongue. For Ukrainians, the mother tongue seems to have a much greater significance in ethnicity retention than it has for the other groups.

Knowledge of Ethnic Language

Among the groups studied there are significant differences in the knowledge of the ethnic language among those for whom English is the mother tongue. In this instance the data on ethnic-language knowledge are presented only for those whose mother tongue is English; such data were not collected for the rest of the sample. For the first generation, two groups, Jewish and Germans, have proportions of those whose mother tongue is English, but who still have at least some knowledge of their ethnic language (table 2.2). These are most probably individuals who came to Canada from the United States and Britain. In the second generation Germans show the lowest proportion of such knowledge, 41%, while Jewish show the highest, 86%. Italians and Ukrainians are in between, with 55 and 56%. As could be expected, the percentage of the third generation whose mother tongue was English but who know some ethnic language is lower than that for the second generation. The German and Jewish groups show the greatest decline. On the whole, however, the knowledge level remains relatively high: 69, 48, 46, and 12% for Jews, Ukrainians, Italians, and Germans respectively.

When the data on the retention of ethnic language as the mother tongue are compared with knowledge of the ethnic language by those

TABLE 2.1
Mother tongue of respondents, by ethnic origin and generation, in percentages*

Ethnic origin	Mother tongue	Generation 1	2	3
German	English	9	64	99
	Ethnic language	90	34	1
	Other/combination	1	2	0
		(88/150)	(46/77)	(44/94)
Italian	English	1	37	94
	Ethnic language	99	62	3
	Other/combination	0	1	3
		(269/156)	(137/96)	(25/71)
Jewish	English	32	77	100
	Ethnic language	34	23	0
	Other/combination	34	0	0
		(64/144)	(64/116)	(40/88)
Ukrainian	English	2	25	88
	Ethnic language	92	71	12
	Other/combination	6	4	0
		(32/148)	(37/114)	(20/91)

*In all tables, the first number in parentheses represents the weighted number of respondents who answered the question; the second number refers to the actual number of interviews involved in each question.

TABLE 2.2
Percentage of respondents who know at least some ethnic language, among those with English as their mother tongue, by ethnic origin and generation

Ethnic origin	Generation 1	2	3
German	60	41	12
	(8/12)	(29/48)	(43/91)
Italian	–	55	46
	–	(49/31)	(23/65)
Jewish	60	86	69
	(19/36)	(49/89)	(40/87)
Ukrainian	–	56	48
	–	(9/27)	(17/73)

for whom English is the mother tongue, an interesting fact is revealed. More respondents in the third generation know their ethnic language as a second language than as their mother tongue (compare tables 2.1 and 2.2). This fact shows that the mother tongue, although often used as such, by itself, is not a good indicator of ethnic identity loss.

Ethnic-Language Literacy

Two questions have served as indicators of how well the ethnic language is known: how well the respondents feel they can read the language and how well they feel they can write it. For each ethnic group and for each generation larger numbers of respondents can read their ethnic language than can write it (table 2.3). Except for the Ukrainians and Italians, this discrepancy between reading and writing increases from the first to the second generation.

The reading and writing abilities themselves decline sharply from generation to generation. For Italians and Germans the decline from the first to the second generation is the sharpest: 60 percentage points for Italians and around 36 points for Germans for reading; 62 percentage points for Italians and 42 points for Germans for writing.

For the Jewish and Ukrainian groups the decline in the reading and writing ability from the first to the second generation is smaller than for the other two groups: for the Jewish group the percentage points of decline is 16 for reading and 24 for writing; for the Ukrainian group, 25 for reading and 28 for writing. The Jewish first generation, however, has the lowest percentage of respondents of all the four groups with an ability to read and write well either of their two languages. This fact probably reflects the comparatively large percentage of the Jewish first generation whose mother tongue is English rather than Hebrew or Yiddish.

A dramatic decline in reading and writing knowledge is evident in the third generation in all the groups except the Jewish. The Jewish group stands out as highest in the retention of these skills. For them the prevalence of these skills remains the same and even slightly increases from the second to the third generation. Thus, 46% of the Jewish third generation can read, and 25% can write, Hebrew, and some possibly Yiddish, relatively well. This fact may even indicate the process of ethnic rediscovery. Among the other three groups the percentages of the third generation who are able to read their ethnic language well or very well fall to 17 or below, with the Italians and Germans highest, 17, followed by Ukrainians, 10. The writing ability also falls to 17 or below,

TABLE 2.3
Percentage of respondents with ethnic and English mother tongue who read or write ethnic language very or fairly well, by ethnic origin and generation

		Generation		
Language skill	Ethnic origin	1	2	3
Read ethnic language	German	89 (85/145)	54 (28/47)	17 (6/11)
	Italian	92 (267/155)	38 (111/81)	17 (12/20)
	Jewish	58 (53/124)	42 (57/104)	46 (281/61)
	Ukrainian	78 (32/146)	58 (32/102)	10 (10/50)
Write ethnic language	German	85 (85/145)	43 (28/47)	17 (6/11)
	Italian	89 (267/155)	27 (111/81)	8 (12/20)
	Jewish	49 (53/124)	25 (57/104)	25 (28/61)
	Ukrainian	78 (32/14)	50 (32/102)	10 (10/50)

with Germans as the highest, 17, followed by the Ukrainians, 10, and the Italians as the lowest, with a percentage of 8.

Obviously, save for small groups of people, the knowledge of the ethnic language for these three groups is not retained by the third generation – even by those who still have some knowledge of it – as a literary skill. Nor, as the data in the next section will show, is it retained by the third generation in any of the groups as an instrument of regular communication. In the case of the Jewish group, the relatively high retention of the reading and writing skills can possibly be explained by the role that Hebrew plays in religious services. The fact of travel to, and the symbolic value of, Israel may also be a factor.

Frequency of Ethnic-Language Use

The data on language use are available only for those respondents who still can speak their ethnic language (table 2.4). For the first generation there are two basic patterns: in two groups, Italians and Ukrainians,

TABLE 2.4
Frequency of use of ethnic language among those who can speak it, by ethnic origin and generation in percentages

Ethnic origin	Frequency of use	Generation 1	2	3
German	Every day, often	57	29	0
	Occasionally	27	31	25
	Rarely, never	16	39	75
		(84/144)	(26/45)	(5/9)
Italian	Every day, often	94	74	10
	Occasionally	3	10	23
	Rarely, never	3	16	67
		(269/156)	(110/80)	(12/20)
Jewish	Every day, often	43	15	9
	Occasionally	23	24	17
	Rarely, never	34	61	74
		(51/121)	(55/100)	(26/57)
Ukrainian	Every day, often	84	58	9
	Occasionally	10	23	24
	Rarely, never	6	19	67
		(31/145)	(33/103)	(10/51)

over 80% use the language every day or often, and in two groups, Germans and Jews, less than 60% use it every day or often. For the Jewish group the majority of the first generation use it either occasionally or rarely or never.

For the second generation, the frequency of ethnic-language use drops substantially for all the groups, except Italians. Italians still remain very high users, so that the difference between their first and second generation is not as dramatic as in the other groups. Among Ukrainians the shift is towards both occasional use and non-use of the language. Yet still more than half of the second generation use it every day or often. Among the Germans the main shift is very clearly towards occasional use and non-use.

The lowest degree of ethnic-language use among the second generation was in the Jewish group. More than half of the Jewish second generation used the language rarely or never, and only about 15% used it every day or often.

The big break with the use of ethnic language among those who still can speak it comes with the third generation. By far the majority of the third generation used their ethnic language rarely or never. Among those who did use it, most used it only occasionally. If we combine the occasional use with the more frequent use, then the largest percentages of use remain among Ukrainians and Italians, 33% in each case, followed by Jews, 26%, and Germans, 25%.

Summary and Interpretation

The data show a general decline from generation to generation in the retention of the ethnic language as the mother tongue, in ethnic-language knowledge, and in the frequency of use of the ethnic language. The specific patterns of shift from generation to generation differ significantly for each ethnic group.

On the whole, the ethnic language as mother tongue is retained in large proportion in the second generation of some groups (71% for Ukrainians, 62% for Italians, 34% for Germans), but not in the third generation. The only group that retains it in some comparatively significant percentage in the third generation is Ukrainians. Yet of those for whom English is their mother tongue, on an overall average, over 70% of Jews, 50% of Italians and Ukrainians, and about 40% of Germans still have some knowledge of their ethnic language. Although as an overall picture this knowledge decreases across the three generations, rather significant percentages of persons who have such knowledge remain both in the second and in the third generations. The level of knowledge of the ethnic language as judged by the ability to read and write is relatively high for the first and second generations – on the average close to 70% for the first and 40% for the second generation. This level, however, is very low for the third generation of all the groups, around 10% with the exception of the Jewish, for whom it remains not far from 40%.

Whereas some ethnic-language knowledge – albeit without high facility in reading or writing – still remains in significant proportions in the third generations, frequent use of the language does not. Predominantly, the second generation still uses the language at least occasionally, save for one ethnic group. The third generation predominantly uses it rarely, if ever.

How can the discrepancy between ethnic-language knowledge and ethnic-language use be explained? Is the knowledge of the language without any practical use simply a left-over of childhood socialization? The data on ethnic-identity retention suggest a different answer. On the average about 64% of the second and 32% of the third generation reported that it is important to them that their children learn their ethnic language. This comment suggests that for those in the successive generations who retain a knowledge of the language, the language changes its function – rather than being instrumental it becomes symbolic, that is, rather than being a means for practical communication, it becomes a symbol or means of identity reinforcement (Isajiw 1975). This may also be the function of other overt ethnic behaviour patterns.

ETHNIC-GROUP FRIENDSHIPS

It has often been argued that the persistence of ethnicity in North American societies is most evident in the sphere of interpersonal relations. Despite the large extent of assimilation or mobility achieved by the ethnic-group members, individuals still tend to form personal associations with members of their own community. Empirical evidence has been produced in the past indicating that closer or more intimate friends are more likely to be chosen from the respective ethnic community rather than randomly from the society at large. Some of the studies referred to earlier have shown that regardless of the presence of the opportunity to associate freely with persons outside ethnic-group boundaries, a significant proportion of ethnic-group members will tend persistently to maintain a closer friendship circle among their own group members. This pattern of association has been demonstrated with the second, third, or even fourth generation of certain ethnic groups. Do these findings hold true in the metropolitan community studied in the present research?

Apart from the three immigrant groups – Chinese, Portuguese, and West Indian – who are all first-generation and tend to form a more exclusive pattern in their friendships, the variation in the degree of exclusiveness of ethnic-friendship formation among the other groups is substantial.

With regard to the five groups with generational components, it is clear from table 2.5 that the respondents in each group vary greatly with regard to the ethnicity of their three closest friends. The German group is least likely to have close ethnic friendships across the generations, while the Jewish group retains the highest degree of exclusivity in friendship formation. For the Jewish group there is no substantial decrease in ethnic friendships across generations. Only 12% of the first generation have no Jewish close friends at all, and for 52% all three of the closest friends are also Jewish. In the second and third generations only about 7 and 4% have no close Jewish friends, whereas for 51% of the second and 55% of the third generations all three closest friends are of the same ethnic background.

TABLE 2.5
Percentage of respondents with none to three closest friends of own ethnicity, by ethnic origin and generation

Ethnic origin	Number of friends of own ethnicity	Generation 1	2	3
Majority Canadian	0			42
	1–2	–	–	39
	3			19
				(770/225)
English	0	30	22	
	1–2	43	35	–
	3	27	43	
		(230/148)	(179/115)	
German	0	34	71	76
	1–2	51	29	23
	3	15	0	1
		(88/150)	(46/77)	(44/94)
Italian	0	5	21	45
	1–2	30	47	45
	3	65	32	10
		(269/156)	(137/96)	(25/71)
Jewish	0	12	7	4
	1–2	36	42	41
	3	52	51	55
		(64/144)	(64/116)	(40/88)
Ukrainian	0	13	34	62
	1–2	41	46	35
	3	46	20	3
		(32/148)	(36/112)	(20/90)

Italians, too, have highly exclusive friendships in the first generation, with only 5% with no Italian close friends and 65% with all three closest friends of Italian background. The percentages, however, shift substantially for the second and third generations. Thus, 21% of the second generation and 45% of the third generation have no close Italian friends at all, and only about one-third of the second and one-tenth of the third generation have all three close friends of Italian origin.

For the Ukrainians the decline from generation to generation is even sharper. The first generation has a much higher percentage of persons than do the other two groups, 13, with no close friends of the same ethnicity at all, and this percentage increases sharply for the second and the third generations, 34 to 62. Inversely, the percentage with three closest Ukrainian friends declines from 46 to 20 to only 3 from generation to generation.

The Germans are least exclusive in their friendship patterns. Already 34% of the first generation have no close German friends at all and this percentage increases to 71 and 76 in the subsequent generations. At the same time, only 15% of the German first generation has all three closest friends of German background, and in the second and third generations all three closest friends are German for virtually no one.

Yet in both the Ukrainian and the German third generations approximately one-quarter to one-third of all respondents still report that one or two of their closest friends are of the same ethnicity.

The English and the Majority Canadian groups are interesting in this regard. Of the English first generation, 30% have no English close friends at all and 27% have all three of their closest friends who are also English. In the second generation these percentages shift more in what would be an expected direction, with 22% with no English close friends and 43% with all three English close friends. Yet among the Majority Canadians, who are all third or subsequent generations, the percentage of respondents with no English or Scottish or Irish close friends is rather high, 42, and fewer respondents than one may expect, 19%, report all three friends to be also Majority Canadians.

Some respondents do not specify the ethnicity of their out-group friends any further than calling them 'Canadian.' Most others, however, are specific in naming their ethnic-cultural background. Is there any tendency to have British as against non-British persons as out-group friends? Does any particular ethnic group prefer to choose the British more than any other as their close friends outside of their own group? Does generation make any difference as to the ethnicity of out-group friends?

Table 2.6 presents the results of the analysis of the ethnic origin of the first closest friend outside of one's ethnic group by generation and the respondents' own ethnic origin. The data show significant variations in the results. What is most striking is that they show no definite tendency to have more British or 'Canadian' friends from the first to the third generation.

Of the first generation, the groups with the highest percentages of British and Canadian closest out-group friends combined are the Jewish and the Germans: 55 and 50% of the first closest out-group friends respectively. The groups whose first generation has the lowest

TABLE 2.6
Ethnic origin of first closest out-group friend, by ethnic origin and generation, in percentages

Respondent's ethnic origin	Out-group friend's ethnic origin	Generation 1	2	3
Majority Canadian	British*			24
	Canadian	–	–	6
	Other			70
				(609/178)
English	British*	2	0	
	Canadian	18	15	–
	Other	80	85	
		(160/103)	(101/65)	
German	British	36	36	39
	Canadian	14	7	9
	Other	50	57	52
		(70/118)	(44/74)	(41/87)
Italian	British	33	33	31
	Canadian	5	9	7
	Other	62	58	62
		(93/54)	(94/61)	(22/59)
Jewish	British	46	51	47
	Canadian	9	7	9
	Other	45	42	44
		(29/50)	(31/55)	(15/32)
Ukrainian	British	26	44	49
	Canadian	4	4	5
	Other	70	52	46
		(16/62)	(29/80)	(19/86)

*Other than own group

percentages of the British and Canadian first closest friends are the Ukrainians and Italians, 30 and 38% respectively.

In the second generation the picture changes drastically. The two groups whose first generations have the lowest percentages of British and Canadian friends now are among those with the highest percentages. Thus, for the Ukrainians the percentage jumps to 48, for the Italians to 42, and for the Jews it remains about the same as for the first generation, 58.

What is interesting is that for the German second generation, rather than increasing, the percentage decreases slightly from 50 in the first generation to 43 in the second. Yet in the third generation the percentage goes back to 48.

In the third generation, for the Ukrainians the percentage of those with British and Canadian close friends increases from that of the second generation by only about 6 percentage points; for the Jews and Italians it remains more or less the same. For the last two groups the percentages of closest out-group friends of ethnicities other than British or Canadian, rather than decreasing from the second to the third generation, as one would expect, actually increase, albeit very slightly.

For the English themselves the number of the other than British or Canadian friends also increases from the first to the second generation by 5 percentage points, and for the Majority Canadians who are all third-plus generation, the number is rather high, 70%.

How can these data be interpreted? All the implications of these data are not immediately apparent. It is possible that these findings could be explained by demographic factors, such as neighbourhood concentration patterns or the structure of other opportunities for friendship formation. The British, for example, seem to show less exclusive neighbourhood concentration than do other ethnic groups (Kalbach 1980). More research is necessary into these aspects of the issue. One implication, however, is that British ethnicity is not a friendship selection factor any more than are other ethnicities. Hence, in regard to the incorporation of diverse ethnic groups into the structure of the informal, friendship relationships in Canadian society, friendship with the British community members is not a strong positive factor, at least not any stronger than friendship with other groups, and in fact may be weaker. The data indicate a pattern of incorporation into general society that does not depend exclusively on the dominant ethnic groups.

PARTICIPATION IN ETHNIC-GROUP FUNCTIONS

Ethnic-group persistence is sometimes considered to be dependent on the persistence of ethnic organizations and institutions. Although this may not necessarily be so, all groups in our study had some organizations. An important question in this regard is how viable these organizations are. Organizational viability can be determined by either the size and activity of the membership or by participation of the community in the functions sponsored by these organizations. This section will attempt to assess community participation in its various functions. Respondents were asked about their participation in two types of ethnic activities: (1) such activities as picnics, concerts, rallies, dances, parties, and public lectures; and (2) group-sponsored vacation facilities, such as vacation resorts or summer camps. Does participation in these activities persist from generation to generation and what are the differences between ethnic groups? In addition, the respondents were asked about their participation in non-ethnic-group, 'Canadian' functions, such as dances, parties, and informal affairs.

Overall there is a decrease in participation in ethnic-group functions and an increase in participation in general non-group functions from one generation to another, but for some ethnic groups the rate of persistence is rather high.

Table 2.7 records the percentage distribution of participation in the three types of functions by generation and ethnic group. It should be noted that the rate of decrease in participation has to be evaluated in relation to the participation of the first generation. The average rate of participation in the ethnic functions for the first generation for all the five groups studied here is rather low, 49%, but the range is big. The highest percentage is 71, the lowest 22.

The highest participants in the first generation are Italians and Ukrainians, 71% in both cases. Among the Jews, 46% of the first generation participate. Substantially fewer first-generation German and English respondents do so, 33 and 22% respectively.

In the second generation there is a rapid decline in the percentage of those who attend ethnic-group functions in all three groups – Italians, Ukrainians, and Germans. The Jews, however, show persistence and even a slight increase in their participation in their group's functions. By the third generation, however, three types of groups emerge: low, medium, and relatively high participants. Germans, with 6%, are rather low in their third-generation participation, but Jews, Ukrainians, and Italians are relatively high, with 41, 33, and 28% of their third generation still involved in ethnic-group functions.

The Majority Canadians are in between the high and the low participants, with 17% of their third-plus generation attending English, Scottish, or Irish functions. Obviously, if the Majority Canadians do represent a standard for assessing incorporation into Canadian society, medium attendance at ethnic-group functions can be said to be a measure of incorporation.

Table 2.7 also shows that attendance at ethnic vacation resorts or camps is relatively less popular among the ethnic-group respondents.

TABLE 2.7
Participation in ethnic-group social functions, ethnic-group–sponsored vacation facilities, and non-ethnic-group functions, by ethnic origin and generation, in percentages*

Function	Ethnic origin	Generation 1	Generation 2	Generation 3
Ethnic-group functions	Majority Canadian	–	–	17 (787/230)
	English	22 (233/150)	32 (182/117)	–
	German	33 (88/150)	7 (46/77)	6 (44/93)
	Italian	71 (269/156)	46 (137/96)	28 (25/71)
	Jewish	46 (64/144)	50 (64/116)	41 (40/88)
	Ukrainian	71 (32/148)	49 (37/114)	33 (20/91)
Ethnic-group vacation facilities	Majority Canadian	–	–	5 (784/229)
	English	12 (233/150)	13 (182/117)	–
	German	5 (87/149)	2 (46/77)	4 (44/93)
	Italian	17 (267/155)	4 (137/96)	6 (25/71)
	Jewish	19 (64/144)	28 (64/116)	37 (39/87)
	Ukrainian	46 (32/148)	13 (37/114)	2 (20/91)
Non-ethnic-group 'Canadian functions'	Majority Canadian	–	–	80 (787/230)
	English	62 (233/150)	57 (182/117)	–
	German	67 (88/150)	74 (46/77)	79 (44/93)
	Italian	42 (267/155)	80 (137/96)	80 (25/71)
	Jewish	33 (64/144)	55 (64/116)	48 (40/88)
	Ukrainian	52 (32/148)	69 (37/114)	82 (20/91)

*Percentages refer to combined 'frequently,' 'often,' and 'sometimes' answers.

Of the first generation, large numbers of Ukrainians (46%) enjoy such ethnic-group facilities. A smaller percentage of Jewish (19%), Italian (17%), and English (12%) first-generation do so as well.

In the second and third generation there is a gradual increase in the percentage of Jewish respondents who use such ethnic facilities. For all other groups there is a steady decrease, so that by the third generation extremely few respondents go to ethnic vacation resorts or summer camps. Thus, for most groups summer resorts and camps are mainly a first-generation, and, in a smaller degree, a second-generation phenomenon.

With regard to the degree of participation in non-ethnic, 'Canadian' functions, table 2.7 clearly shows that there is an increase across the generations as well as some variation across the ethnic groups.

Over 50% of the German, English, and Ukrainian first-generation respondents participate in non-ethnic, 'Canadian' functions, while around 40% or less of Italian and Jewish first-generation respondents do so. In the second generation there is a dramatic increase in the percentage of Italians attending non-ethnic functions, a significant increase for the Jewish and Ukrainian groups, and a small increase for the Germans. The German group, however, is the highest of all in the first-generation participation in 'Canadian' functions (67%). By the third generation, save for the Jews, about 80% of all respondents attend non-ethnic, 'Canadian' functions. Only 48% of Jews attend non-ethnic functions.

If attendance at 'Canadian' functions is taken to be an indicator of incorporation into the larger society, then in this sense the third generation is more incorporated than the second generation. But it is also evident from the data that a rather substantial percentage of the first- and second-generation members are equally 'incorporated' on this measure. The two types of functions, the ethnic and the 'Canadian,' however, are not necessarily contradictory. In fact they may be complementary. As the data show, many respondents participate in both ethnic and 'Canadian' functions. That is, they both retain their ethnicity and are in some sense incorporated. While this duality of participation diminishes by the third generation, it does not completely disappear.

ETHNIC MEDIA

Ethnic radio and television programs and the ethnic press are important means of ethnic-identity retention because they perform at least three significant functions for the ethnic community. They serve as means of 'being in touch' with the community by informing its members of events and community activities, and thus develop and reinforce the members' knowledge of their community and facilitate physical participation in it. Secondly, they mould the public opinion and attitudes within the community, providing its members with a certain 'ethnic' perspective on the events taking place in society at large. Thirdly, they reinforce ethnic symbolism through artistic presentations that stimulate the ethnic consciousness and identity of those community members who are regularly exposed to them. Hence listening to ethnic radio or watching ethnic TV programs or reading the ethnic press is an indicator of ethnicity retention not only because such activities are ethnic patterns in their own right, but also because they are a means of retaining other ethnic patterns.

Exposure to the ethnic media is not only a function of interest, but also of availability of the media in the ethnic group and of knowledge of the language in which the media present their contents. Some groups have more audio or video programs than others, and some groups have more written periodical materials than others. Yet all the groups studied have at least some audio or video programs available, and all the groups have at least one periodically written medium. Some groups, however, have more English-language ethnic media than others. This fact would reflect itself especially in the extent of exposure to the ethnic media by the third generation.

The extent to which individuals get exposed to ethnic media varies greatly from one ethnic group to another and from one generation to another. As table 2.8 shows, in the first generation the highest percentages of those who listen to ethnic radio or watch ethnic television are among the Italians (84) and the lowest among the Jewish (48). In regard to reading ethnic newspapers, magazines, and periodicals, roughly two-thirds of the first-generation Italians, Ukrainians, and Jews are users – 69, 63, and 59% respectively. Only about half (51%) of the German and one-third (31%) of the English first generation are users.

The decrease from the first to the third generation divides the groups into three categories, the persistent users, the decreasing users, and the third-generation non-users of the ethnic media. The distinction between the three categories depends on the sharpness of drop from the first to the third generation and the extent of use by the third generation. The Ukrainians and the Italians are the decreasing users of the electronic ethnic media. The Germans are third-generation non-users. The Ukrainians show a relatively sharp drop in use from the first

TABLE 2.8
Use of ethnic radio, television, and ethnic newspapers, magazines, or periodicals, by ethnic origin and generation in percentages*

		Generation		
Function	Ethnic origin	1	2	3
Hear/watch ethnic radio/TV programs	Majority Canadian	–	–	30 (787/230)
	English	65 (233/150)	51 (182/117)	–
	German	61 (88/150)	24 (46/77)	1 (44/93)
	Italian	84 (269/156)	30 (137/96)	13 (25/71)
	Jewish	48 (62/142)	30 (64/116)	26 (40/88)
	Ukrainian	61 (32/148)	35 (37/114)	18 (20/91)
Read ethnic newspapers, magazines, or periodicals	Majority Canadian	–	–	15 (787/230)
	English	31 (233/150)	17 (182/117)	–
	German	51 (88/150)	15 (46/77)	2 (44/93)
	Italian	69 (269/156)	17 (137/96)	6 (25/71)
	Jewish	59 (64/144)	57 (64/116)	55 (40/88)
	Ukrainian	63 (32/148)	20 (37/114)	1 (20/91)

*Percentages refer to combined 'frequently,' 'often,' and 'sometimes' answers.

to the second and to the third generation, from 61 to 35 to 18%, but still a significant portion of the third generation uses the electronic media.

For the Italians, the drop in the electronic ethnic-media use from the first to the second generation is extremely sharp, sharper than for any other group in the sample, and it continues from the second to the third generation (from 84 to 30 to 13%). The third generation is quite close to becoming non-users. The Germans drop very sharply from the first to the second generation (from 61 to 24%) and become non-users by the third generation (only 1%).

The persistent users of the ethnic electronic media are the Jews and the British (both the English and the Majority Canadians). For the Jews the percentage drop from the first to the second to the third generation is not very sharp, from 48 to 30 to 26. For the English the drop from the first to the second generation is also not so steep (65 to 51%) and the percentage of users among the Majority Canadian third-plus generation (30%), is also relatively large, larger than for any other second or third generation. The reference here is to other than 'Canadian' electronic media programs, as defined by the respondents themselves.

In regard to the ethnic printed media, the only definitely persistent users across generations are the Jews. The others are sharply decreasing users and by the third generation, non-users. The only exception among these are the Majority Canadians. The Jewish respondents show practically no decrease in the percentage of printed media users from generation to generation and the percentage of users in the second and third generation remains high (59 to 57 to 55).

The Ukrainians, Italians, English, and Germans still have a small but significant meaningful proportion of printed-media users in the second generation (20, 17, and 15%), but these represent a rather sharp drop from the first generation. The sharpest drop from the first generation is presented by the Italians, from 69 to 17. The percentage of their third-generation users, is low, 6, though it is slightly higher than the negligible percentage for the Ukrainians (1) and the Germans (2). Yet the percentage is still meaningful for the Majority Canadian third-plus generations (15).

The persistence of printed-media use among the Jewish three generations and, inversely, the lack of it among the three generations of the other groups can probably be explained by the fact that a high percentage of the Jewish third generation can read Hebrew and at the same time there are many Jewish periodical publications that are written in English. The publications of the other groups rely to a large extent on their ethnic languages, yet, as was pointed out previously, the reading knowledge of the ethnic languages in the third generation of these groups is relatively poor. The data again indicate a higher degree of ethnic-identity retention among the Jewish second and third generation than among the second and third generations of any of the other groups.

ETHNIC TRADITIONS

Ethnic traditions such as foodstuffs, customary celebration of holidays or events in the life cycle, and preference for and retention of certain artistic objects (items of home decoration, costume dress, and so on) are those aspects of ethnic cultures that link with the peasant societies of the past and often have origins going back to prehistory. These patterns are one basic part of a culture that makes it unique.

A person, or a group of persons such as the family, may continue to practise many or few of such patterns or they may not practise them at all, and yet acknowledge that they are traditions of one's group of identity. This section attempts to analyse the differential patterns of retention of selected ethnic traditions. Four types of traditional patterns are considered: eating ethnic foods on ethnic holidays and at other times, practising ethnic religious or non-religious customs, and retaining artistic objects in one's home. The results are summarized in table 2.9.

Overall the custom of eating ethnic food is rather widespread. All ethnic groups studied have very high proportions of people eating ethnic food, both on holiday occasions and at other times.

In the first generation it is highly consumed by all groups, save for the English. Not only on holidays but at other times as well about 9 out of 10 Italian, Ukrainian, and Jewish respondents report that they eat some type of ethnic food often or sometimes. The Germans are as high on ethnic-food consumption at times other than holidays. On holiday consumption their percentage drops to 70. The only exception to this very high percentage of consumption of ethnic food by the first generation is the English. Yet, even their ethnic-food consumption is relatively high, 52% on holiday occasions and 67% at other times. What constituted ethnic food for the English and the Majority Canadians was left up to their own definition, as in the case of the other groups, as long as the food was not considered to be 'Canadian.'

What is interesting is that all groups tend to eat ethnic food just as often, or even more often, outside of holiday occasions or special events.

The tradition of eating ethnic food is retained from generation to generation more than any other ethnic pattern of behaviour. Although there is a decrease in the percentages of those who eat ethnic food from one generation to the next (table 2.9), the percentages of those who eat

TABLE 2.9
Practice of ethnic traditions (consumption of ethnic food at holidays or more often, observance of ethnic customs and possession of ethnic articles), by ethnic origin and generation in percentages*

Ethnic tradition	Ethnic origin	Generation 1	2	3
Consumption of ethnic food associated with holidays	Majority Canadian	–	–	30 (787/230)
	English	52 (233/150)	38 (182/117)	–
	German	70 (88/150)	58 (46/77)	28 (44/93)
	Italian	96 (269/156)	87 (137/96)	74 (25/71)
	Jewish	90 (64/144)	95 (64/116)	91 (40/88)
	Ukrainian	92 (32/148)	89 (37/114)	86 (20/91)
Consumption of ethnic food at times other than holidays	Majority Canadian	–	–	34 (787/230)
	English	67 (233/150)	54 (182/117)	–
	German	94 (88/150)	77 (46/77)	52 (44/93)
	Italian	97 (269/156)	98 (137/96)	92 (25/71)
	Jewish	92 (64/144)	91 (64/116)	87 (40/88)
	Ukrainian	91 (32/148)	92 (37/114)	82 (20/91)
Practice of ethnic customs	Majority Canadian	–	–	25 (787/230)
	English	31 (232/149)	20 (182/117)	–
	German	59 (88/150)	45 (46/77)	15 (44/93)
	Italian	70 (269/156)	59 (137/96)	39 (25/71)
	Jewish	85 (64/144)	90 (64/116)	90 (40/88)
	Ukrainian	92 (32/148)	67 (37/114)	47 (20/91)

TABLE 2.9 (*continued*)

Ethnic tradition	Ethnic origin	Generation 1	2	3
Possession of ethnic articles	Majority Canadian	–	–	34 (787/230)
	English	59 (233/150)	32 (182/117)	–
	German	63 (88/150)	54 (46/77)	23 (44/94)
	Italian	84 (269/156)	74 (137/96)	64 (25/71)
	Jewish	87 (64/144)	85 (64/116)	93 (40/88)
	Ukrainian	96 (32/148)	80 (37/114)	64 (20/91)

*Percentages refer to combined 'everytime,' 'often,' and 'sometimes' answers.

ethnic food often in the second and third generation remain very high for all groups except the Germans, the English, and the Majority Canadians. The Germans are the only group whose third generation does not eat ethnic food as much, although 28% of them do it on holidays and 52% at other times. The second-generation English and the Majority Canadians, though low in comparison to most of the other groups, still have a significant proportion of people eating ethnic food, 38 and 30% at holidays or special events and 54 and 34% at other times. The highest in the overall ethnic-food consumption across generations are the Jewish and Italian groups: 95% of the second and 91% of the third Jewish generation eat ethnic food often or sometimes on holidays and 91% of the second and third generation eat it often or sometimes at other times. Among the Italians the percentages are 87 and 74% for the second and third generation for holiday-food consumption and 98 and 92% for more frequent consumption.

For the Ukrainians, ethnic-food consumption by the second generation for holidays and for more frequent occasions is 89 and 92%. From the second to the third generation the percentage decreases slightly, but remains high, 86 and 82.

With regard to the practice of religious or non-religious ethnic customs, table 2.9 shows that, unlike for the foodstuffs, the practice of group customs decreases more substantially with each generation, except for the Jews. The largest drop occurs between the second and third generation. There are, however, significant variations between the three generations of the five groups. The Jewish group is the highest in retention. Of the first generation, 85% practise ethnic customs. But for the second and the third generations the percentages slightly increase, showing again the rediscovery pattern. Thus 90% of the second and 90% of the third generation still practise ethnic customs. Ukrainians and Italians are somewhat similar in their pattern of decrease from generation to generation, but overall Ukrainians are somewhat higher retainers. For the Ukrainians the pattern from the first to the third generation is 92, 67, and 47%; for the Italians, 70, 59, and 39%. The Germans show a sharp decline in the practice of ethnic customs from the second to the third generations; 45% of the second generation still retain some customs, but 15% of the third generation do so.

Among the English first and second generations, the practice of English, other than Canadian, customs is much lower than among the other groups: 31 and 20%. It is also low among the Majority Canadians: 25%. It is interesting that, unlike the case of the foodstuffs, the practice of ethnic customs among the Chinese and West Indians, who are all first-generation, is relatively low: 59 and 56.

The last question dealing with ethnic traditions concerned itself with whether the respondents possess any artistic articles, religious objects, or traditional clothing characteristic or symbolic of their ethnic group. The pattern of responses produced is similar to the one observed in the practice of group customs, except that the responses that show a difference tend, on the average, to be about 10 to 20 percentage points higher. The Jewish group again is highest in generational retention, followed by Ukrainians, Italians, and Germans. By the third generation, Germans are again the lowest of all groups, 23%, whereas Jews, Ukrainians, Italians, and the Majority Canadians still retain such articles in a significant degree: 93, 64, 64, and 34% respectively.

To sum up, if for all the ethnic groups studied we average out the percentage of retention of the four types of ethnic traditions, that is, eating ethnic foods at holidays or other special occasions, eating ethnic food at other times, practising religious or non-religious ethnic customs, and possessing ethnic artistic articles, then the retention average for the first generation is 79%, for the second, 69%, and for the third, 57%. There are, however, large variations among the ethnic groups. For the first and the second generation the range of variation from the average is about 48 percentage points, for the third, it is around 42 percentage points. This variation indicates relatively large differences in retention patterns among the different groups.

Of the groups with three generations, the Jewish group has the highest degree of retention, followed by the Italians and Ukrainians, and by the Germans with the lowest degree. It is interesting that the Majority Canadians, who are all third-plus-generation in our sample, have a higher degree of retention than do the Germans.

If we compare the two generations of the English with those of the other groups, then for these generations the English are the lowest retainers of traditions of all the groups including the Germans. It is interesting to note here that the first generations of the 'new' groups in Toronto, that is, the Chinese, the West Indians, and the Portuguese, on the average practise their traditions somewhat less than do the first generations of the other groups, other than the English. It is quite possible that the problems of adjustment resulting from the more recent process of immigration make it more difficult for the new groups to practise their traditions. This difficulty is especially indicated in the case of the religious and non-religious ethnic customs.

The data on the retention of traditions raises a question as to why, of all the traditions, eating ethnic food and possessing ethnic articles is retained across generations more than any other external identity pattern. In fact, eating ethnic food is the single pattern retained more than any other item of both the external and internal aspects of ethnic identity. Only a few possible avenues for answering this question can be suggested here.

On theoretical grounds it can be said that the further 'removed' the generation, the more the items from ethnic traditions retained are those that are more relevant to life in the general society, those that complement the cultural patterns of the society, or those that fulfil needs – individual or collective – which the society's general institutional structure is unable to fulfil satisfactorily (Isajiw 1975, 1977). Food and possessions are things that, in general, have a high social value. Furthermore, technological society itself is not distinguished by unique and uniquely prepared foods. It thus creates a need that ethnic foods can easily fill. For this reason, although there are many prejudices against different ethnic groups, there are probably few prejudices against different ethnic foods.

Moreover, ethnic food is retained by the third generation probably less as a skill than as something used by them but prepared by someone else. It is quite probable that the third generation avails itself of ethnic food either from restaurants or from its first- or second-generation relatives. More research is needed to clarify this issue, but it is possible that in regard to ethnic food, subsequent generations behave the way they do regarding ethnic languages, whereby some knowledge of the language is retained, not as a skill but as a symbol. This pattern may be consistent also with a high rate of retention of ethnic artistic articles.

Finally, the power of food as a symbol of identity should not be underestimated. Food can be classified as a primary symbol of identity, primary in at least three meanings of the word. It is a simple symbol inasmuch as it is something very concrete, the use of which is easily recognizable. But it is also something that is very close to the biological process and hence united the organic with the socio-moral order into a unity representing a unique control over the organic (Turner 1969: 52–3). Lastly, the consumption of food is one of the earliest experiences in one's lifetime and thus becomes part of one's basic personality. Again, more research is needed into foods as symbols of identity. Certainly such widespread retention of ethnic foods across generations indicates their deeper significance.

Retention of Internal Aspects of Ethnic Identity

The data in this study were collected to measure the retention of all four internal aspects of ethnic identity. Only some of these data, however, can be discussed in this report. Two approaches are taken: first, a synoptic strategy is followed, by which an attempt is made to ascertain the retention of all internal aspects of ethnic identity, that is, the cognitive, the moral, and the affective, with one measure. To this end an Ethnic Identity Index was devised. It includes three questions. Each question is considered to be an indicator of one of the three aspects.

The second strategy takes the opposite approach. Rather than using one question as the only indicator of each aspect of the phenomenon, it uses many questions as indicators of only one aspect of that phenomenon. Furthermore, rather than collapsing answers to questions into one measure, it considers answers to questions independent of one another and compares them against each other. Since it is necessary to be selective, the aspect of ethnic identity chosen for analysis here is that dealing with commitment and group obligations. As pointed out above, the moral dimension of the internal aspects of ethnic identity can be considered to be central to its study.

The value of the synoptic approach lies in that it guards against the bias by which one aspect of a phenomenon is considered to be more important than others to the study of that phenomenon. The value of the extended approach is that once a theoretical or practical decision is made that one aspect is more important, it allows for a greater precision in the analysis of the phenomenon by drawing attention to details that otherwise would be lost or overlooked. The use of both approaches, therefore, should be complementary.

ETHNIC IDENTITY INDEX

The three questions chosen to make up the Ethnic Identity Index inquire into (1) the respondents' self-definition in terms of the hyphenated or unhyphenated ethnic or Canadian label, (2) the importance the respondents place on their ethnicity, and (3) the respondents' perception of the closeness of their ethnic ties. The three questions were meant to measure the three elements of the internal side of the identity: that is, the first question, the cognitive aspect, or self-definition; the second, the moral aspect, or general feeling of commitment to the group; the third, the affective aspect, or attachment to the group. The three questions are also correlated with each other. In each case the Pearson correlation coefficient was significant at the 0.001 level. Factorial analysis also showed only one factor.

The questions will be analysed as measuring levels of intensity of ethnic identity. The answers to the second and third questions are on a Lickert scale. By offering such choices as 'very important,' 'somewhat important,' and 'not at all important,' the scale is intended to measure intensity of feeling in regard to the issue asked about by the question. The scale thus measures three levels of intensity: high, medium, low. A person whose answers to the respective questions are consistently 'very important,' or 'very close' can be said to have a 'high' level of intensity of identity, as against a person whose answers are consistently 'somewhat important,' or 'moderately close' or 'not at all important,' or 'not close at all.' The latter can be characterized as 'medium' or 'low' levels of identity intensity. The three levels, although they are relative to one another, indicate qualitative differences. The first question, which assesses hyphenated and non-hyphenated identities, is dealt with in a manner analogous to the Lickert scale and hence is included in the index.

When weights were assigned to each answer, the index-score range was from 3 (indicating low intensity of ethnic identity) to 8 (indicating high intensity of ethnic identity).

The mean scores and the percentages for each question vary rather significantly according to the ethnic group. In general, the mean score decreases with each generation (table 2.10). This decrease indicates a loss of intensity of ethnic identity from generation to generation for all groups. However, when the three generations are broken down by ethnicity, the data show again that not all groups lose the intensity of identity in the same degree.

The least intensity of ethnic identity in the third generation is retained among the Germans: a mean score of 3.3, indicating a level of intensity even lower than that for the Majority Canadians, 3.7. Only 14% of the first, 9% of the second, and a negligible 1% of the third German generation have an identity that is 'high' on the Ethnic Identity Index. More than one-third, 39%, of the German first generation can be considered to have a 'medium' level of intensity of ethnic identity. It declines to 24% in the second and 10% in the third generation (table 2.11). This is the lowest index score of all groups for the third generation, even lower than that of the Majority Canadians. While an explanation of this low-intensity-of-identity phenomenon among the Germans is beyond the scope of this paper, it would be interesting to investigate in this connection the impact on the German identity of the Second World War.

The highest degree of ethnic-identity retention across generations in the sample was in the Jewish group. The mean score for both the second and the third generations is the highest of all the groups studied, indicating the highest level of intensity of identity (table 2.10). Of the first generation 51% indicate 'high' identity. Interestingly, this is not the highest percentage of all groups in the sample. Yet, of the second generation, 46% are in the 'high' category and 34% in the 'medium' category. Of the third generation, however, 49% are in the 'high' category and 25% in the 'medium' category. Thus, in the Jewish group, although there is a slight drop in intensity of identity between the first and the second generation, intensity remains high from the second to the third generation and even slightly increases.

The Italian and the Ukrainian groups are in between and rather similar to each other. Both experience a sharp drop in 'high' levels of identity from generation to generation. From 58 and 60% respectively for the first generation to 29 and 27% for the second generation to only 14 and 10% for the third generation. This similarity continues in the 'medium' levels of intensity: 32 and 28% respectively for the first generation to 41 and 38% for the second generation to 33 and 35% for the third generation (table 2.11). Unlike in the Jewish group, in which the predominant feature of the third generation is high intensity of

TABLE 2.10
Mean scores of Ethnic Identity Index, by ethnic origin and generation

Ethnic origin	Generation 1	2	3
Majority Canadian	–	–	3.7
English	5.8	4.4	–
German	4.6	4.1	3.3
Italian	6.4	5.3	4.5
Jewish	5.8	5.9	5.9
Ukrainian	6.1	5.1	4.5

TABLE 2.11
Intensity of ethnic identity as measured by Ethnic Identity Index, by ethnic origin and generation in percentages

Ethnic origin	Intensity of ethnic identity	Generation 1	2	3
Majority Canadian	High	–	–	3
	Medium	–	–	17
	Low	–	–	80
				(787/228)
English	High	29	5	–
	Medium	38	32	–
	Low	33	63	–
		(233/147)	(182/113)	
German	High	14	9	1
	Medium	39	24	10
	Low	47	67	89
		(88/144)	(46/75)	(44/91)
Italian	High	58	29	14
	Medium	34	41	33
	Low	8	30	53
		(269/155)	(137/96)	(25/70)
Jewish	High	51	46	49
	Medium	32	34	25
	Low	17	20	26
		(64/131)	(64/115)	(40/87)
Ukrainian	High	60	27	10
	Medium	28	38	35
	Low	12	35	55
		(32/143)	(37/113)	(20/89)

ethnic identity, for the Italians and Ukrainians the predominant feature of the third generation is low intensity of identity.

The English were much higher than the Germans in the level of identity intensity of their first generation, 29% 'high' as against 14%, but only 5% of the second generation could be classified as 'high.' Still, in the medium levels the percentages were substantial, 38 for the first generation and 32 for the second.

The Majority Canadians show significantly only 17% in the medium level of intensity. Like the Germans, most of them by far, 80%, were in the 'low' category. No group went over 61% in the high level of intensity even in the first generation, including the 'new' groups with only the first generation, the Chinese, Portuguese, and the West Indians.

To sum up, the main value of the index is that it allows us to measure the differences, in both the intensity and extent of ethnic-identity retention, between different ethnic groups. The results show that for all the groups, except the Jewish, the *intensity* of ethnic identity decreases from one generation to the next. For the Jewish group it remains the same, at a high level, from the second to the third generation. The *extent* of ethnic identity, however, that is, the proportion of people who have a meaningful level of intensity of ethnic identity ('medium' and 'high' combined), remains substantial for the second and even for the third generation of most groups. For the second generation the lowest percentage of medium- and high-intensity retainers combined was 33% for the Germans, followed by 37% for the English, 65% for the Ukrainians, 70% for the Italians, and the highest, 80% for the Jewish. For the third generation, the percentage of the combined high- and medium-level retainers was 11 for the Germans, 20 for the Majority Canadians, 45 for the Ukrainians, 47 for the Italians, and 74 for the Jewish.

ETHNIC-GROUP OBLIGATIONS

As was pointed out above, feelings of group obligation can be considered to be an indicator of group commitment. Six questions were asked in the survey regarding feelings of obligation. Three of these referred to the issue of jobs. Only one of these three will be considered, since the response to the other two by any of the three generations was not high. Thus, the four questions referred to (1) how important the respondents felt it was to help people of their own ethnic background to get jobs; (2) the importance attached by the respondents to their actual or potential children marrying into their own ethnic group; (3) the extent to which they felt obliged to support their group's special causes and needs; and (4) the importance they attached to their children, actual or potential, learning their ethnic language.

When the data are analysed for both generation and ethnic origin, variations among the obligations become apparent (table 2.12).

First of all, the by now familiar pattern of groups dividing up between high retainers, medium retainers, and low retainers appears quite clearly. On all four feelings of obligations, the high-retainer group is Jewish. The distinguishing feature for this group is not only the fact that unlike the other groups the subjective identity as measured by the feelings of obligation remains high from generation to generation, in the range between 54 and 86% for any of the generations, but in at least three out of the four obligations it increases either from the first to the second generation or from the first to the second to the third. This increase, again, indicates the rediscovery pattern. It is particularly evident in the case of the feeling of obligation to help their group members find a job. Thus, 57% of the first generation feel this to be an important thing to do; yet 62 and 67% of the second and third do so.

Nevertheless, the highest overall percentage of retention in the Jewish group is displayed in the feeling of obligation to support the group's needs and causes; 82% of the first generation feel this to be important, yet 86% of the second and 80% of the third generation do so. The second-highest retained feeling of obligation in the Jewish group is the obligation to marry within the group; 73% of the first, 78% of the second, and 66% of the third generation feel this obligation to be important.

Behavioural facts seem to correspond to this emphasis on in-marriage. In our sample the in-marriage statistics for the Jewish group were 91% for the first generation, 87% for the second, and 81% for the third generation.

For children to speak the ethnic language was not as important for the members of the Jewish group as were the other obligations. Still, the percentages of those who felt this factor to be important were relatively high across the three generations: 64, 60, and 54 respectively.

The medium retainers, Ukrainians and Italians, showed a pattern different from the Jewish group. First, all percentages, with only one exception, are lower for these groups than they are for the Jewish. Furthermore, unlike for the Jewish, with one exception, all percentages show a downward slide from generation to generation. The basic

TABLE 2.12
Group obligations, by ethnic origin and generation in percentages*

Group obligation	Ethnic origin	Generation 1	2	3
Help group member find job	Majority Canadian	–	–	26 (773/226)
	English	26 (232/149)	25 (182/117)	–
	German	34 (87/149)	32 (46/76)	20 (43/92)
	Italian	56 (265/154)	45 (132/93)	45 (25/70)
	Jewish	57 (63/142)	62 (64/116)	67 (39/86)
	Ukrainian	66 (31/145)	54 (37/113)	53 (20/90)
Marry in group	Majority Canadian	–	–	7 (784/229)
	English	8 (227/146)	14 (177/114)	–
	German	7 (87/148)	2 (45/75)	2 (43/91)
	Italian	39 (263/153)	10 (136/95)	4 (25/71)
	Jewish	73 (63/143)	78 (63/114)	66 (38/84)
	Ukrainian	61 (31/143)	20 (36/112)	5 (20/91)
Support group needs and causes	Majority Canadian	–	–	11 (784/229)
	English	24 (230/148)	27 (179/115)	–
	German	24 (87/149)	7 (45/76)	7 (43/92)
	Italian	65 (259/150)	40 (137/96)	20 (25/70)
	Jewish	82 (63/142)	86 (64/116)	80 (40/88)
	Ukrainian	79 (32/145)	49 (36/112)	36 (20/90)

TABLE 2.12 (*continued*)

Group obligation	Ethnic origin	Generation 1	2	3
Children speak ethnic language	German	65 (86/148)	42 (45/75)	15 (41/88)
	Italian	94 (267/155)	58 (136/95)	31 (25/70)
	Jewish	64 (63/143)	60 (63/115)	54 (39/86)
	Ukrainian	83 (31/145)	66 (37/113)	37 (20/91)

overall pattern of identity retention for the two groups is very similar, but on the whole Ukrainians are somewhat higher retainers than are the Italians.

For both groups, the highest retained feeling of obligation by the third generation is to help group members find a job. But this is not necessarily the predominant feeling of obligation for the first or even second generation of both these groups. For these the predominant feeling is the importance that children speak the ethnic language. Thus, in regard to the job obligation, the percentages for the Ukrainians are 66, 54, and 53 for the three generations respectively, and for the Italians, 56, 45, and 45. In regard to children speaking the language, the percentages for the Ukrainians are 83, 66, and 37, and for the Italians, 94, 58, and 31. The difference in emphasis on cultural vs social factors between these generations is quite interesting. That is, it appears that the third generation places a greater emphasis on the social obligation, helping with a job, than on the cultural obligation of language retention.

Furthermore, the Ukrainian third generation remains somewhat more group-conscious than the Italian third generation. Of them, 36% feel that they should support group needs and causes, as against 20% of the Italian third generation. The percentages for the first and second generation were also slightly higher for Ukrainians: 79 and 49 respectively, and 65 and 40 respectively for the Italians.

A very interesting fact is presented by the answers to the obligation to marry within the group. For Jews, this is one of the most important feelings of obligation, but not so either for Ukrainians or particularly

Italians. Whereas 61% of the Ukrainian and 39% of the Italian first generation consider this obligation to be important, only 20% of Ukrainian and 10% of Italian second generations and a negligible 5 and 4% of their third generations, respectively, still think so. Apparently, both groups, in their second and third generations, do not connect ethnic endogamy with ethnic-identity retention.

Behavioural facts substantiate this attitude. The rate of endogamy for the first generation Ukrainians in our sample was 79%, for the second generation, 41%, and for the third generation, only 13%. For the Italians the endogamy percentages for all three generations were significantly higher, yet they also showed a substantial drop from generation to generation: 91% for the first generation, 64% for the second, and 29% for the third.

The low retainers are the Germans, the English, and the Majority Canadians. In some respects, the Germans are closer to the Italians and Ukrainians, as for example in regard to the importance of children speaking the ethnic language: 65, 42, and 15% of the three generations think that it is important that they should, yet in other respects the English and the Majority Canadians are intermediate between the medium retainers and the lowest retainer, the Germans. Thus, although 34% of the German first and 32% of their second generation and only 26% of the English first and 25% of their second generation feel that they should help their group members to find a job, 26% of the Majority Canadian third-plus and 20% of the German third generation feel so. In regard to support of group needs and causes and endogamous marriages the difference between the two becomes even more pronounced. The first generation of both groups is very similar on both feelings of obligation: about 24% of both groups agree that it is important to them to support their group needs and causes, and around 8% of the first generation of both groups agree that it is important to them that their children marry within the group. The second generations, however, diverge completely. Thus, 27% of the English, as against only 7% of the German second generation, feel that support of group needs and causes is important. Likewise, 14% of the English second generation, as against only 2% of the German second generation, think that marrying within the group is important. Thus, the English second generation, unlike the first generation, in terms of group obligations, is closer to the Italians and Ukrainians than it is to Germans. It can be said that the English in their second generation become more like a typical Canadian ethnic group. The Majority Canadian third-plus generation is much more in between the low German retainers and the medium retainers, with 11% considering it important to support their group needs and causes, and 7% considering in-group marriage as important.

The behavioural reference for this last attitude for the Germans is 60% of the first generation marrying endogamously, 9% of the second generation, and only 4% of the third. For the English, the endogamy rate is 54% for the first generation and 40% for the second. For the Majority Canadian third-plus generation it is 72%.

To sum up, the analysis of a variety of feelings of obligations has made it possible to uncover those feelings that are typical to some groups but not others and those that appear to be shared and retained by consecutive generations in all ethnic groups, particularly the third generation in a relatively large proportion. The latter feelings can be characterized as being of two types, one referring to the structural, the other to the cultural position of a group. The first bears upon the relationship of the ethnic group to the occupational structure of the society at large. This relationship could be interpreted in two ways. A greater involvement of the third ethnic generation in the occupational structure of the society, as for example through their social mobility, may stimulate greater awareness of the group's relationship to society at large. Alternatively, an increasing awareness of one's ethnicity among the third generation of some ethnic groups may focus on those areas of relationship between the group and society at large in which the minority-majority status is most important and through which other aspects of this status may be most readily modified, that is, through the occupational betterment of the group.

The second type of feelings of obligations shared by a substantial percentage of the third generation of all groups is the importance of children knowing the ethnic language. Language appears to carry high value as a symbol of ethnic identity and this value is perceived whenever the question of future generations is raised. Perhaps the respondents perceive the language as being the key to teaching their cultural heritage to younger generations. They may also see the process of learning the language as the simplest practical way of imprinting ethnic identity.

These two types of feelings of obligation may be the more generally accepted ways of incorporation into the larger society on this social-psychological level that allow ethnic-identity retention. The other feelings of obligation show a more substantial variation between the groups.

Conclusion: Summary and Implications

A basic finding of the chapter is that the extent of retention of ethnic identity across generations varies according to different ethnic groups. Some groups are high retainers, other groups are low retainers. The highest overall retainers in the study were the Jewish group, followed by Ukrainians, Italians, British, and Germans. Germans were by far the lowest overall retainers. Table 2.13 presents a summary of the percentages of the ethnic-identity attributes retained by the three generations.

HIGH RETAINER: THE JEWISH

If we average the eight highest retained items in the Jewish group, including both external and internal aspects of identity, then the percentage of retention in the second generation is 84 and in the third generation 82. The Jewish are the only group in our sample whose percentage of retention does not decline substantially from generation to generation in almost all items. As we have seen, in some cases it actually goes up from the second to the third generation, thus showing the pattern of ethnic rediscovery.

Of the Jewish second generation more than 80% retain ethnic food, three closest friends of the same ethnicity, ethnic customs, some knowledge of ethnic language among those whose mother tongue is English, feel the obligation to support ethnic causes, and possess ethnic artistic articles. Between 60 and 80% of the second generation feel the obligation to marry in the group, to help other members with finding a job, and to teach children the ethnic language.

Of the third generation, still more than 80% have their three closest friends of the same ethnicity, and of all the patterns this is the highest retained pattern around the third generation. Further, in this category are included the possession of artistic articles, ethnic food, the observance of ethnic customs, and a feeling of obligation to support ethnic causes. In the 60 to 80% category are knowledge of the language by those whose mother tongue is English, obligation to help group members with a job, and obligation to marry within the group.

MEDIUM RETAINERS: UKRAINIANS AND ITALIANS

On the average, both Ukrainians and Italians are lower than the Jewish group in ethnic-identity retention by about 15 percentage points for the

TABLE 2.13
Summary table: Ethnic-identity retention by ethnic origin and generation in percentages

Table reference	Aspects of ethnic identity retained	Generation	Ethnic origin: Majority Canadian	English	German	Italian	Jewish	Ukrainian
	External Aspects							
1	Ethnic mother tongue	1	–	–	90	99	34	92
		2	–	–	34	62	23	71
		3	–	–	1	3	0	12
2	Knowlege of ethnic language (by those whose mother tongue is English)	1	–	–	60	–	60	–
		2	–	–	41	55	86	56
		3	–	–	12	46	69	48
3	Read ethnic language	1	–	–	89	92	58	78
		2	–	–	54	38	42	53
		3	–	–	17	17	46	10
	Write ethnic language	1	–	–	85	89	49	78
		2	–	–	43	27	25	50
		3	–	–	17	8	25	10
4	Frequent use of ethnic language ('every day' and 'often')	1	–	–	57	94	43	84
		2	–	–	30	74	15	58
		3	–	–	0	10	9	9
	Occasional use of ethnic language	1	–	–	27	3	23	10
		2	–	–	31	10	24	23
		3	–	–	25	23	17	24
5	1–2 closest friends of own ethnicity	1	–	43	51	30	36	41
		2	–	35	29	47	42	46
		3	39	–	23	45	41	35
	3 closest friends of own ethnicity	1	–	27	15	65	52	46
		2	–	43	0	32	51	20
		3	19	–	1	10	55	3

TABLE 2.13 (*continued*)

Table reference	Aspects of ethnic identity retained	Generation	Ethnic origin: Majority Canadian	English	German	Italian	Jewish	Ukrainian
7	Participation in ethnic-group functions	1	–	22	33	71	46	71
		2	–	32	7	46	50	49
		3	17	–	6	28	41	33
	Usage of ethnic-group-sponsored vacation facilities	1	–	12	5	17	19	46
		2	–	13	2	4	28	13
		3	5	–	4	6	37	2
8	Hear/watch ethnic radio/TV	1	–	65	61	84	48	61
		2	–	51	24	30	30	35
		3	30	–	1	13	26	18
	Read ethnic newspapers/magazines, periodicals	1	–	31	51	69	59	63
		2	–	17	15	17	57	20
		3	15	–	2	6	55	1
9	Practice of ethnic traditions:							
	1 Eat ethnic food on holidays and special occasions	1	–	52	70	96	90	92
		2	–	38	58	87	95	89
		3	30	–	28	74	91	86
	2 Eat ethnic food at times other than holidays and special occasions	1	–	67	94	97	92	91
		2	–	54	77	98	91	92
		3	34	–	52	92	87	82
	3 Observe ethnic customs	1	–	31	59	70	85	92
		2	–	20	45	59	90	67
		3	25	–	15	39	90	47
	4 Possess ethnic articles	1	–	59	63	84	87	96
		2	–	32	54	74	85	80
		3	34	–	23	64	93	64

TABLE 2.13 (*continued*)

Table reference	Aspects of ethnic identity retained	Generation	Ethnic origin					
			Majority Canadian	English	German	Italian	Jewish	Ukrainian
	Internal Aspects							
11	Intensity of ethnic identity (Ethnic Identity Index):							
	'High'	1	–	29	14	58	51	60
		2	–	5	9	29	46	27
		3	3	–	1	14	49	10
	'Medium'	1	–	38	39	34	32	28
		2	–	32	24	41	34	38
		3	17	–	10	33	25	35
12	Group obligations:							
	1 Help group members find job	1	–	26	34	56	57	66
		2	–	25	32	45	62	54
		3	26	–	20	45	67	53
	2 Marry in-group	1	–	8	7	39	73	61
		2	–	14	2	10	78	20
		3	7	–	2	4	66	5
	3 Support group needs and causes	1	–	24	24	65	82	79
		2	–	27	7	40	86	49
		3	11	–	7	20	80	36
	4 Teach children ethnic language	1	–	–	65	94	64	83
		2	–	–	42	58	60	66
		3	–	–	15	31	54	37

second generation, and 30 percentage points for the third generation. In the 80% and above category the Ukrainian group retains in the second generation only ethnic-food consumption and possession of ethnic artistic articles, but in the third generation, only ethnic-food consumption. The Italians retain in this category only ethnic-food consumption in both the second and the third generations.

In the second generation, 60 to 80% of Ukrainians know their ethnic language as mother tongue, practise ethnic customs, have three closest friends from the same group, and feel an obligation to teach their ethnic language to their children. Italians in this percentage category, in the second generation, also include three closest friends and a knowledge of their ethnic language as mother tongue. They also include use of the ethnic language and possession of artistic articles. It is interesting that in the second generation significantly more Italians than Ukrainians use their ethnic language. In the third generation, however, the situation changes for both Ukrainians and Italians: only one pattern is retained in the 60–80% category, that is, possession of ethnic artistic articles.

In the 40–60% category, the Ukrainian second generation includes the use of their language, knowledge of the language by those whose mother tongue is English, a feeling of obligation to help their group members find a job, reading and writing their language, and participation in ethnic functions. The Italian second generation includes in this category practising ethnic customs, the obligation to teach children the ethnic language, knowledge of the language by those whose mother tongue is English, and participation in ethnic functions. In the third generation in the 40–60% category, Ukrainians include the obligation to help members with a job, knowledge of the ethnic language by those whose mother tongue is English, and the practice of ethnic customs. The Italians in their third generation are similar. They also include in this category knowledge of the ethnic language by those whose mother tongue is English and an obligation to help members with a job. Unlike Ukrainians, however, on the top of this category Italians include three closest friends of the same ethnicity. For Ukrainians in the third generation this item is in the lower percentile, below 40%.

LOW RETAINERS: ENGLISH, MAJORITY CANADIANS, AND GERMANS

The average percentage of the eight highest retained patterns for the English, the Majority Canadians, and the Germans is much lower than for any of the other groups studied. Thus, for the German second generation it is 47% and for the English second generation 40%. Yet, for the Majority Canadians, third-plus generation, it is 30%, whereas for the German third generation it is 22%. Overall, the Germans are the lowest retainers of all the groups studied.

For both the Majority Canadians and the Germans in the third generation ethnic retention does not reach beyond 40%, with one exception. Among the German third generation, 52% consume ethnic food more often than on holiday or special occasions.

The Majority Canadians have six patterns in the category of 20 to 40%, four of which are in the 30% range. These are having one to two friends of the same ethnicity, the consumption of ethnic food, possession of ethnic articles, and the use of ethnic electronic media. Others in the 20% range are an obligation to help members with a job and the retention of ethnic customs. Among the German third generation, five patterns are in the 20 to 40% category, and all of them are in the 20% range: they are occasional use of ethnic language, having three closest friends of the same ethnicity, eating ethnic food on holidays and special occasions, possession of ethnic artistic articles, and the feeling of obligation to help members with a job. Everything else is retained in the magnitude of less than 20%.

FORMS OF ETHNIC IDENTITY AND SOCIETAL INCORPORATION

The highest percentage of retention of several patterns suggests a distinction of different specific forms of ethnic identity retained by the second and third generations. At least five such forms can be singled out, deriving either from the external or the internal aspects of identity or from a combination of both. They are (1) an identity revolving around concrete objects, as symbols, including food and artistic articles; (2) an identity revolving around having friends of the same ethnicity and marrying within the group; (3) an identity revolving around the practice of customs and community participation; (4) an identity revolving around the language itself; and (5) an identity related to giving support to the group's causes or needs and/or helping group members with a job. Our data show that the most common form is (1), followed by (2).

These can be seen as five different routes to ethnic-identity retention among the second and the third generations consonant with incorporation into the Canadian society. This does not mean that the same persons may not share elements of all five forms of identity, but probably in specific cases or situations one form may gain primacy over the others. Some groups appear to rely on some forms more than on others.

Thus, for example, the feeling of obligation to marry within the group has a special significance to the Jewish group. This feeling of obligation is quite highly retained, in both the second and the third generation of the group, but no other group in the study is even close to this high rate of retention. It also correlates with a rather high rate of exclusive friendship pattern. The latter is also highly retained by the British groups, including the English and the Majority Canadians. The British groups, however, have no especially strong feelings of obligation to marry within the group. Thus, it appears that while for the Jewish group marrying within the group is an important focus of identity retention, for the British groups the focus is exclusivity of close personal relations as such.

For Ukrainians, and possibly for Italians, the language seems to perform this function. Thus, although Ukrainians or Italians are not the highest of all groups in regard to the feelings of obligation to have children learn the ethnic language, nevertheless, in the second generation this feeling of obligation is by far the single highest retained feeling of obligation in both groups. For Ukrainians in particular, the language seems to have a special significance as mother tongue. In the second generation, Ukrainians reported the highest rate of language retention as mother tongue of all the groups. For the Italians, however, in the second generation the use of the language is even more important than its role as mother tongue, although the latter is also quite significant. It is interesting that the obligation to marry within the group is not a highly significant feeling for either the Ukrainian or the Italian second or third generation.

For the German group, the preferred route to identity retention appears to be connected with the third generation's emphasis on food and friends of the same ethnicity.

IMPLICATIONS FOR FURTHER RESEARCH

The data presented here raise a number of further questions that subsequent analysis and more research should pursue. One question is to what extent there is an overlap of the different types of ethnic identity in individual persons. That is, if a person possesses a high degree of one form of ethnic identity, will he or she also tend to have a high degree of other forms of ethnic identity? An analysis of the overlap of the external and internal aspects of ethnic identity should also be made.

The variations in the aspects of ethnic identity retained from generation to generation that have been discovered in this study indicate the importance of researching more complex forms of ethnic identity, such as were suggested earlier in this study. These forms are based on combinations of various ethnic patterns, such as self-images and community participation, or self-images and feelings of group obligation, or feelings of group obligation and community participation. These combinations may involve variables from both the external and the internal aspects of identity or only combinations from one or the other aspect. The significance of studying such combinations derives from the fact that it is easy to misinterpret the empirical results obtained on single ethnic-identity variables when their relation to other variables is not assessed. For example, lack of participation in ethnic community functions, when studied by itself, may be seen as an indicator of the disappearance of ethnic identity. But when it is associated, say, with heightened feelings of obligation to help members of one's group in finding a job, it may indicate the presence of a specific form of ethnic identity rather than a lack of it.

Furthermore, the influence of the intervening variables, such as the socio-economic characteristics, must be assessed. Do better-educated people, or people with higher-status positions, retain ethnic identity less than do less-educated, lower-status people? How does the parental socio-economic level affect the retention of ethnic identity by their children? Do people who come from lower socio-economic family backgrounds retain ethnic identity more than those who come from higher socio-economic family backgrounds? Preliminary analysis suggests that this also is a complex issue. On some aspects of ethnic identity, such as language knowledge, it appears that retention is associated with lower levels of the respondents' education. On other items it appears to be associated with both the lower and higher, but not the middle levels of education. On a number of internal ethnic-identity variables, retention seems to be associated with low levels of the respondents' fathers' education, but with higher levels of the respondents' own education. This correlation raises the question of the role of social mobility as a major factor in ethnic-identity retention or ethnic-identity loss.

Analysis of this survey's data has shown that ethnic socialization is a major factor associated with ethnic-identity retention (Isajiw and Makabe 1982). This relation could be expected. But the analysis shows two further things. First, socialization becomes more salient as an explanatory factor with each consecutive generation and, secondly, besides socialization there are other factors related to identity retention. That is, the later the generation, the more retention of ethnic identity is explainable by ethnic socialization, but in all generations large percentages of ethnic-identity retention cannot be explained by socialization alone. Further research should explain both these facts. We can hypothesize, however, that with each consecutive generation retention of ethnic identity depends more on factors related to the family than to the ethnic community as a whole. The first generation's identity can depend to a large extent on participation in the organizational and general social life of the ethnic community. By the third generation participation in the total ethnic community is uncommon and one's identity may be conditioned to a large extent by the parents' emphasis on the importance of their ethnic background or their opportunities or willingness to enrol their children in ethnic schools or classes, or by their attempts to provide their children with exclusive friendships. Still, further research is needed to refine the concept and measurement of ethnic socialization.

For the third generation, however, factors in ethnic-identity formation other than ethnic socialization may derive also from social structures or processes outside of the family. These, however, may not be the ethnic community at all, but the society at large. It is quite possible that ethnic rediscoveries among the third generation derive from interethnic competition or discrimination encountered, especially in the process of social mobility into higher-middle-class levels. Thus, the very processes leading to societal incorporation may stimulate ethnic-identity retention.

Two mechanisms may work in this regard. First, since higher-middle-class occupations are more prestigious, better-paying, and more scarce, there is a higher degree of competition for them. Competition is a mechanism through which self-awareness is increased, especially awareness of one's ascribed background characteristics (Morse and Gergen 1970; Whiteside 1971). Since ethnic background is one of the most significant ascribed background characteristics, competition of this type will tend to heighten one's awareness of it.

The second mechanism through which social mobility may influence ethnic-identity retention or rediscovery has to do with the role that the ascriptive criteria play in the process of hiring for higher-status occupations. Leon Mayhew (1968) has pointed out that on higher-middle-class occupational levels, the use of ascriptive criteria is often seen by the employers as a more efficient and safer way of personnel selection. The reason is that certain background characteristics are defined by administrators as achievement characteristics, for instance, the type of university or school a person attended. The administrators often consider the prestige of a school, which is an ascriptive characteristic, to be an indicator of achievement or of the quality of prospective performance by the person who has attended the school. In this process of hiring into the higher-middle-class occupations, persons become more conscious of all their ascriptive characteristics, including their ethnicity.

In addition to social mobility, other factors of ethnic-identity retention or rediscovery may derive from the self-awareness created by the conflict between the different ethnic or racial groups, or from the desire to find one's 'roots' created by the anomic structure of industrial society and the impersonal nature of the technological culture (Isajiw 1977). Further research is needed to ascertain the salience of all these factors in relation to both ethnic-identity retention and incorporation into society at large.

3

Ethnic Residential Segregation and Its Significance for the Individual in an Urban Setting

Warren E. Kalbach

The resurgence of interest in cultural pluralism has again brought into question the underlying assumptions of the classical models of urban growth and immigrant assimilation developed during the 1920s. Specifically, the initial residential segregation along ethnic and racial lines that was commonly observed in areas near the urban core was seen as transitory in nature, serving the needs of recently arrived immigrants until they or their children could become more completely incorporated into, or established in, the larger community. Thus, subsequent desegregation, or outward movement of the first and second generations from the primary reception areas for immigrants, was perceived as being synonymous with economic improvement, increasing acculturation, and the weakening or possible severing of ethnic community ties. The Burgess model of urban growth (Burgess 1925) explicitly assumed an original state of ethnic segregation for recently arrived and relatively impoverished immigrant groups from which existing residential patterns evolved. Within this theoretical framework, the level of residential segregation at any time was assumed to be reflective of an ethnic population's degree of acculturation and assimilation into the larger socio-economic structure of the community. This chapter specifically examines the general patterns of ethnic residential segregation in Canada's largest metropolitan area and their relationship to individual ethnic identity and ethnic-related behaviour as part of the process by which immigrant groups become incorporated into Canadian society.

The analysis of residential segregation in the Toronto Census Metropolitan Area is based on special tabulations of the 1971, 1976, and 1981 censuses of Canada provided by Statistics Canada. The data used to assess the significance of these patterns for the individual within the urban context were obtained from the sample survey of 2,338 residents carried out during 1978 and 1979. Information was obtained in the survey on the respondents' perceptions of the ethnic character of their neighbourhoods; on their ethnic cultural origins, socio-economic characteristics, and attitudes towards their own ethnicity; and on the extent of their participation in ethnic-related activities. These data were analysed with respect to the subjectively perceived and objectively determined characteristics of the respondents' residential contexts as well as the ethnic group's propensity for residential segregation by generation. Similar analyses of perceived and objective measures of a neighbourhood's ethnic character have been reported by Reitz (1980b) and Richmond (1972); but the attempt to determine the extent to which individuals actually perceive and are affected by such aggregate-level phenomena as are reflected in patterns of ethnic residential segregation is one of the unique features of the analysis presented in this chapter.

Population Growth and Residential Segregation

Studies of Toronto's early settlement and growth have shown that socio-economic distinctions between ethnic populations were an early part of Toronto's existence, and that existing group preferences and prejudices tended to be reflected in terms of both social and spatial distances (Mulvany 1884: 39–45). Analysis of residential distributions, provided by the census of 1851–2, showed that of the ethnic populations enumerated, the Scottish and Irish were residentially distributed most like the English. Next to the Irish, in degree of segregation, were those who had been born in the United States. By way of contrast, the Jewish population showed the greatest dissimilarity in their residential distribution, vis-à-vis the English, with the French showing almost as much. Germans and those of Netherlands origin were in an intermediate position between those from the United States and the French (Kalbach 1980: 12).

According to the data in table 3.1, the rank order of Toronto's major ethnic groups, in terms of their relative degree of residential segregation in 1851–2, has persisted as the population has grown and become

TABLE 3.1
Indexes of dissimilarity[a] for selected ethnic-origin populations: Toronto, 1871–1971

Ethnic origin	1871	1881	1901	1901[f]	1931	1941	1951	1961	1971
English	b	b	b	b					b
Scottish	7.4	9.5	5.6	11.3	c	c	c	c	7.9
Irish	6.0	5.9	3.2	7.2					7.9
Welsh	–	16.4	8.6						23.9
French	22.6	15.8	14.0	19.8	12.4	14.8	20.0	20.7	17.6
German	16.6	14.8	5.0	8.0	d	d	d	16.6	13.0
Dutch	–	22.4	8.4	10.2	d	d	d	21.6	25.8
Scandinavian	–	16.1	10.6	17.1	d	d	d	15.2	d
Polish	–	–	–	–	54.7	52.9	52.1	46.8	40.4
Russian	20.6	36.8	40.6	47.8	d	d	d	53.0	40.9
Ukrainian	–	–	–	–	38.2	53.2	51.2	42.6	36.4
Italian	31.5	41.4	52.3	56.6	24.8	28.6	34.6	56.0	56.9
Jewish	–	49.2	51.4	55.5	64.4	67.9	63.0	79.5	74.0
Chinese	–	–	23.8	27.2	d	d	d	e	53.2
African/Blacks	37.7	43.8	32.9	35.2	d	d	d	e	50.8
Other	–	55.7	51.3	55.9	d	d	d	e	e
Number of areas used in analysis	7	9	6	16	8	9	9	338	452

SOURCE: Censuses of Canada: 1871 to 1901, 1931 to 1951, 1961, and 1971; and L. Rosenberg, 'Population characteristics of the Jewish community of Toronto,' *Canadian Jewish Population Studies*, Jewish Community Series, no. 3 (Montreal: Canadian Jewish Congress, February 1955), table 1

a The Index of Dissimilarity, a commonly used measure of residential segregation, ranges in value from 0 to 100, and indicates the degree of similarity between the percentage distributions of two populations across all census tracts or other areas. The index represents the percentage of one population that would have to be moved in order for its distribution to become similar to the other (Darroch and Marston 1969; Balakrishnan 1976).

b English origins are used as the reference population for the period 1871 to 1901 and 1971.

c Combined British origins are used as the reference population for 1931, 1941, 1951, and 1961.

d Data for these groups were not made available in the report.

e Index for comparable category was not calculated.

f Based on political wards, 1871 to 1951, and census tracts for 1961 and 1971. For 1901 two combinations of wards are presented for comparative purposes.

more ethnically diverse over the years. Among the newer immigrants, that is, the eastern and southern Europeans, the Russians and Italians exhibited a fairly consistent degree of segregation up to the beginning of the twentieth century almost as high as that which characterized the Jews in Toronto during the same period. The population of Jewish origin has continued to exhibit the highest levels of residential segregation following the 1931 census, while the eastern European-origin groups appear to have declined to more intermediate levels reflected by indexes of dissimilarity between 36 and 41. The increasing numbers of 'visible' minority ethnic groups, such as Chinese and Africans/Blacks, arriving in Canada subsequent to the liberalization of immigration regulations during the 1960s have contributed to the emergence of distinctive residential patterns reflected by indexes of dissimilarity of 53 and 51 respectively. The somewhat higher degree of segregation exhibited by the population of Italian origin in 1971, as well as 1961, would appear to be the consequence of the rapid growth of the Italian community caused by continuing heavy immigration to Canada.

The patterns of segregation that evolved as immigrants continued to arrive seem to have reflected the social and economic status differences of the time, and have remained surprisingly stable with respect to their rank ordering in terms of segregation levels. There are some problems of comparability between the indexes presented in table 3.1, especially with respect to variations in the number of areas used to calculate the indexes. However, the similarity between the two sets of indexes presented for 1901 increases confidence in the comparability of the measures, particularly for the period up to 1951 (see footnote 'e,' table 3.1).

Generally speaking, if there has been any decline in residential segregation, it would appear to have been limited to a few of the northern and western Europeans, for example, the populations of French and German origins. Increases in the populations of other origins seem to have been more area-specific, involving shifts in concentrations rather than a general diffusion outward from the initial reception areas for immigrants. The occurrence of the latter, of course, would have reduced the degree of residential segregation reflected by the indexes of dissimilarity. For most of the post-Second World War period, the picture has not changed very much, even though Toronto has experienced both an economic and a population boom, as well as a significant rise in the degree of ethnic diversity of its population as a result of heavy post-war immigration.[1] Recent research by Balakrishnan has also shown that the rank ordering of Toronto's major ethnic populations, in terms of their residential segregation, has remained much as before. While there is some evidence that levels of segregation declined between 1951 and 1961, they appear to have remained relatively stable or increased slightly between 1961 and 1971.[2]

THE ETHNIC DIMENSION OF RESIDENTIAL SEGREGATION, 1971–81

Like that of many other North American metropolitan centres that have experienced rapid growth and have populations characterized by ethnic and racial diversity, Toronto's present population still shows evidence of residential segregation along ethnic and cultural lines as well as by differences in socio-economic status (Darroch and Marston 1971; Balakrishnan 1976; Guest and Weed 1976). Since Burgess's pioneering work (1925) no one has seriously argued that spatial differentiation on the basis of economic activities or the characteristics of residents does not occur. The continuing debates have centred more around the nature of the residential patterns, and the relative importance of such causal factors as economic status and ethnic origin, than on the determination of the degree of segregation that characterizes the metropolis's constituent ethnic populations, or how such segregation might affect the individual's perception of his or environment and behaviour.

A visual examination of the distributions of several ethnic populations by census tracts, in terms of their relative concentrations, will provide a general view of the nature of Toronto's ethnic mosaic circa 1981.[3] Given the dynamics of urban population growth and distribution, the development of uniformly distributed ethnic populations would be most unlikely. The more recent, and often relatively disadvantaged, immigrant groups would be expected to be more heavily concentrated in areas nearer the central business district, while the older and more established populations would be expected to be more heavily concentrated in the suburban areas (especially the culturally dominant ethnic population and those who have achieved some degree of economic integration and acculturation). The extent to which this expectation is true in a general sense may be seen by examining the distributions for the ten ethnic populations presented in figure 1 (in chapter 1). The population of English origin clearly shows the most widespread dispersion throughout the census metropolitan area, but with relatively greater concentrations in the peripheral suburban and scattered lakeshore areas, a fact consistent with the Burgess model for a culturally and economically dominant group within a large North

American metropolis. This is the established culturally dominant group in Toronto that is generally thought to provide the standard against which other minority ethnic groups measure success in the socio-economic sector. This is also the population that provides the standard for determining the extent of residential segregation exhibited by the other ethnic populations included in this analysis.[4]

The German-origin population has a type of distribution that looks very similar to that of the English reference population, and is indicative of one that has become almost fully incorporated into the English-dominated social and economic systems of Toronto. The Ukrainians appear to be considerably less dispersed and more concentrated than the Germans, but not to as great a degree, it appears, as the Italians. Being a more recent and more visible immigrant population, the Caribbeans (primarily West Indians) might be expected to be more segregated than the Italians. However, their areas of relatively high concentration are a bit more scattered and their overall level of segregation is somewhat less. The Portuguese exhibit yet a different pattern of more widely dispersed clusters within the metropolitan area; and the rather compact cluster of high indexes of relative concentration, with very little scatter, accounts for the Jewish population's position as one of the more highly segregated groups in the Toronto area. Because it is difficult to make visual comparisons between maps of this kind, a more precise, comparative measure of differences between residential distributions should be employed, for instance, the Index of Dissimilarity. While the Index of Dissimilarity is among the more commonly used quantitative measures of relative differences between two population distributions in residential-segregation studies, it provides no clues as to the specific locations of the ethnic groups within the boundaries of the metropolitan area. Distributional maps of the type presented in figure 1 are still required to put the measures of segregation for the various ethnic populations into a fuller geographical perspective.

General impressions of ethnic concentrations gained by areal mapping of measures of relative concentration can be made more precise with the indexes of dissimilarity presented in table 3.2. Indexes have been calculated for a number of the major ethnic populations based on census-tract data from both the 1971 and 1981 censuses of Canada. While the indexes are not strictly comparable for the two census years, they do provide some indication of the extent and nature of the ethnic variations in residential segregation at the beginning and end of the decade during which the ethnic-pluralism survey data were collected in the field.

TABLE 3.2
Indexes of dissimilarity[a] showing degree of residential segregation of selected ethnic populations; Toronto CMA, 1971 and 1981

Ethnic origin	Index of dissimilarity 1971	1981
English 3rd-plus	–	b
English	4.9	18.5
Irish	9.1	16.7
Scottish	10.2	17.7
German	14.2	18.5
French	16.3	19.6
Scandinavian	20.6	–
Netherlands	23.2	31.5
Hungarian	34.2	48.1
Ukrainian	36.5	32.6
Yugolsav	37.5	–
Japanese	39.9	–
Polish	40.5	37.1
Russian	41.3	52.2
West Indian[c]	47.6	–
Blacks	–	49.7
Greek	52.1	44.6
Chinese	52.2	45.3
Italian	56.7	49.8
Portuguese	67.5	62.1
Jewish	73.2	72.6

SOURCE: Indexes based on special tabulations, 1971 and 1981 Censuses of Canada, Statistics Canada.

a Indexes based on the population 15 years of age and over.

b The 1981 indexes of dissimilarity compare the residential distribution of each ethnic group to that of the remaining population. The 1971 IDs use the 3rd-plus generation of English origins as its comparison group.

c Includes blacks.

Taking into account the expected effects of using slightly different populations for the standard of comparison for the 1971 and 1981 indexes, the two sets of segregation indexes are quite similar, with respect to both their general levels of segregation and the rank order of individual ethnic-origin groups. Those of British and other northern and western European origins show the lowest degree of segregation regardless of which particular population serves as the standard for comparison. Central and eastern Europeans are characterized by intermediate levels of segregation, somewhat lower than that exhibited by populations of southern European origins. Asians (for instance, Chinese), West Indians, and blacks show higher levels of segregation comparable to the range for southern Europeans, but lower than the Portuguese, who exhibited the second-highest degree of segregation in both 1971 and 1981. The Jewish population continued to be the most highly residentially segregated of any of the ethnic-minority populations included in the analysis of residential segregation during this period.

These results are quite consistent with the findings of other research, with respect to levels of ethnic segregation in Toronto (Darroch and Marston 1969) and in Canada's other major metropolitan areas (Balakrishnan 1976, 1982; Richmond and Kalbach 1980). The rank order of ethnic populations with respect to their levels of segregation in Toronto was found to be more highly correlated with the rank orders for Winnipeg and Vancouver than it was with Montreal's, while the average level of segregation was similar to that in Winnipeg and intermediate to the higher average levels in Montreal and lower levels in Vancouver (Richmond and Kalbach 1980: 187–90). In general, the findings for the Toronto Census Metropolitan Area would appear to be fairly representative of Canada's largest urban centres, with the possible exception of those centres in Quebec.

As previously mentioned, considerably less is known about the changes that may be occurring with respect to levels of segregation over time, that is, whether or not segregation has been increasing or decreasing, or perhaps remaining stable. Earlier research by Lieberson (1963) in the United States and by Balakrishnan (1976) in Canada has suggested that residential segregation was declining, but a more recent analysis by Balakrishnan (1982) failed to find any evidence of continuing overall declines during the 1960s. Furthermore, Kantrowitz (1969) has made the point that evidence of a possible decline in the segregation of ethnic populations in American cities, reported earlier by

Lieberson, may be misleading. The apparent decline, in fact, may only be the consequence of changes in the native-born comparison group rather than a real change in the residential distribution of second-generation ethnics.

INTRA-ETHNIC-GROUP VARIATIONS

Difficulties in establishing the existence of any trend in residential segregation, based on indexes of segregation, may arise from the fact that indexes based on total ethnic populations may obscure differences in the degree of segregation for each of their separate generational components. Darroch and Marston (1969) showed that levels of segregation tended to be higher for the foreign-born as a whole than for the native-born, and higher for recent immigrants than for those who had been in Canada for longer periods of time. If this is the case, then it would appear that the degree of segregation exhibited by any ethnic population (all generations combined) could be affected by the relative size of its foreign-born population or its other generational groups. All other things being equal, a population whose foreign-born segment is declining in size relative to its native-born component would exhibit declining segregation even though the degree of segregation for its component parts remained unchanged. The indexes are not additive and the segregation index for the combined population is not necessarily the arithmethic mean of the indexes of its separate parts. In short, to understand fully the variations that may be occurring in segregation levels for the various ethnic populations, it is necessary to determine the levels of segregation that characterize their foreign-born, their second generations comprising the native-born children of foreign-born immigrants, and all subsequent generations of native-born from native-born parents. The examination of segregation by generation has been made possible in this analysis through the provision of special cross-tabulations of ethnic-origin data by period of immigration for the foreign-born and birthplace of parents for the native-born, at the census-tract level for the Toronto Census Metropolitan Area from the 1971 Census of Canada.[5]

VARIATIONS IN SEGREGATION BY GENERATIONS

Indexes of dissimilarity between residential distributions for selected ethnic-origin groups and the third-plus generations of English origin, by generation, and by period of immigration for the foreign-born, are

TABLE 3.3
Indexes of dissimilarity for selected ethnic-origin populations, 15 years of age and over, by generation and period of immigration for the foreign-born; Toronto CMA, 1971

	Generation			Period of immigration		
	First	Second	Third+	Pre-1946	1946–60	1961–70
English 3rd-plus (comparison group)	–	–	–	–	–	–
English	12.4	11.0	–	20.8	17.9	26.8
Irish	16.7	13.6	9.3	25.4	22.2	31.1
Scottish	16.9	14.6	11.8	24.3	20.3	32.0
German	19.5	20.2	15.8	33.2	21.7	29.6
French	34.0	23.1	17.9	56.6	49.9	53.4
Scandinavian	27.4	29.7	37.9	48.6	35.7	53.5
Netherlands	29.9	34.2	25.1	60.8	34.6	43.1
Hungarian	36.2	46.1	76.9	55.3	51.4	52.8
Ukrainian	52.6	27.5	28.8	50.1	57.2	–
Yugoslav	39.3	47.7	74.8	56.8	37.8	46.9
Japanese	52.5	42.9	68.5	66.7	–	67.5
Polish	48.6	35.1	36.6	53.4	47.6	61.0
Russian	53.9	60.4	–	81.3	61.8	–
West Indian[a]	48.7	69.9	66.1	–	57.6	51.1
Greek	53.5	57.5	73.2	67.5	49.6	60.8
Chinese	53.9	63.6	82.4	82.1	63.4	53.5
Italian	60.9	32.4	40.1	47.9	59.7	66.3
Portuguese	67.8	–	87.0	–	65.4	–
Jewish	74.1	75.3	68.6	81.0	75.0	68.7

SOURCE: Indexes based on special tabulations, 1971 Census of Canada, Statistics Canada.
a Includes blacks.

given in table 3.3. Interestingly, it is among the least segregated ethnic populations, for example, the English, Irish, Scottish, Germans, and French, that the classical assimilation pattern is found with diminishing segregation observed for successive generations. It may also be observed, albeit less clearly, for the population of Netherlands origin, the Italians, Polish, and Ukrainians. In the latter cases most of the decline in segregation appears to occur between the first and second generations with little further change for subsequent generations. Among the remaining groups, increases in segregation by generation are apparent for the Scandinavians, Hungarians, Russians, Yugoslavs, Greeks, and Portuguese. Also, for such non-European groups as the Chinese and West Indians, and somewhat less consistently for the Japanese, the degree of segregation tends to be higher for subsequent generations vis-à-vis the first generation. The most segregated overall, those of Jewish origin, have the highest indexes of segregation for both first and second generations. They are somewhat less segregated beyond the second generation than are the Portuguese, Chinese, Hungarians, Yugoslavs, and Greeks. However, these differences must be regarded somewhat tentatively because of the relatively small numbers of third-plus generations found in these particular ethnic populations.

VARIATIONS BY PERIOD OF IMMIGRATION

The assimilationist perspective regarding immigrant adaptation also underlies the notion that those immigrants who have been here the longest will also be most like the resident population in terms of the convergence of various social and economic characteristics. The indexes in table 3.3 for ethnic origin by period of immigration, like those for generation, show a variety of patterns. About twelve of the groups shown, including all of the western and northern European origins, show curvilinear relationships between degree of segregation and period of immigration. The Ukrainians and Italians are the only two for whom increased length of residence in Canada appears to be (positively) associated with greater assimilation (that is, an increasing similarity of their residential distributions with that of the third-plus generation of English origin). This pattern also prevails for twelve of the nineteen groups in table 3.3 if the analysis is limited to the post-war period only. For a few groups, for example, the Chinese and Jews, longer periods of residence appear to be associated with high degrees of residential segregation. Other variations from the patterns expected under the simple assimilation model draw attention to the possibility that perhaps attitudes towards some immigrants, as well as socio-economic and other characteristics of arriving immigrants of specific ethnic origins, have varied significantly over the years. Because of changing policies and admission requirements, the most recent immigrants tend to be more highly educated than those who came to Canada during the immediate post-war period; and both groups vary significantly from the pre-war immigrants, many of whom came to Canada as unskilled labourers and agricultural workers with relatively little formal education. Thus, the differences in observed levels of segregation between groups of immigrants who have been in Canada for varying lengths of time reflect differences in their initial skills (entrance status) as well as their achieved levels of socio-economic adaptation and assimilation since immigrating to Canada. There are clearly a variety of patterns by which immigrants are incorporated into Canadian society.

STATUS EFFECTS IN SEGREGATION

Previous research has shown that status differences have been an important factor in accounting for variations in residential segregation between ethnic populations (Murdie 1969; Darroch and Marston 1971; Guest and Weed 1976). The thrust of more recent segregation research has been to show that status differences, while still important, do not explain all the observed variance in segregation between ethnic populations. Therefore, it is important to determine the extent to which the intergenerational patterns of segregation apparent in table 3.3 are a function of differences in the socio-economic-status characteristics of subsequent generations of immigrants of the same ethnic and cultural origins.

Of the several commonly used indexes of socio-economic status, educational attainment is the one employed as a control variable in this analysis. It is a particularly valid and stable index to use for the segregation analysis of populations that include both males and females of varying ages and labour-force status, and who are at differing stages of their individual life cycles. The educational attainment of individuals who have finished their schooling tends to be correlated with income and occupation, while at the same time remaining fixed and generally independent of life-cycle changes during the adult years. In this analysis, indexes of dissimilarity were calculated for each generation within each of three broad educational-attainment levels as a means of determining the extent of intergenerational variation within ethnic groups while controlling for the effects of variations in educational status.

Table 3.4 presents the indexes of dissimilarity by generation for educational-status groups of selected ethnic populations residing in the Toronto Census Metropolitan Area. The most interesting thing about these data is the fact that, for most of the ethnic populations, the intergenerational patterns of variation in segregation remained relatively unchanged. However, several observations need to be made. First and foremost, the classical assimilation pattern that has characterized the English, Irish, Scottish, and French remains essentially unaltered only for those components of their populations with intermediate and low educational status. At the same time, the intergenerational differences for the English, Irish, and Scottish with high status are all but eliminated. The lack of appreciable change in the generational patterns for the

TABLE 3.4
Indexes of dissimilarity for selected ethnic-origin populations 15 years and over by generation for educational-status groups; Toronto CMA, 1971

	Educational status and generation								
	Elementary			Secondary			University		
Ethnic origin	1st	2nd	3rd+	1st	2nd	3rd+	1st	2nd	3rd+
English 3rd-plus (comparison group)	–	–	–	–	–	–	–	–	–
English	23.9	20.0	20.1	14.0	13.4	4.6	31.2	31.9	30.5
Irish	28.6	26.2	22.9	19.1	16.0	10.1	36.9	38.0	34.5
Scottish	30.1	24.4	22.1	19.0	16.5	10.7	34.4	36.4	37.1
German	25.0	44.4	34.7	22.3	25.0	18.2	30.3	50.0	40.2
French	71.5	50.3	30.9	41.3	29.9	17.7	62.2	74.0	32.8
Scandinavian	52.6	–	–	32.4	38.8	47.4	56.1	70.7	–
Netherlands	46.2	–	53.8	31.4	40.7	30.0	42.7	–	68.4
Hungarian	44.4	–	–	39.7	54.7	–	51.0	–	–
Ukrainian	56.3	40.4	69.4	52.2	28.5	33.4	63.6	48.9	66.6
Yugoslav	45.7	–	–	40.6	55.6	–	49.2	–	–
Japanese	75.4	70.8	–	64.6	48.8	77.5	78.8	73.2	–
Polish	59.0	56.7	71.5	46.2	35.9	42.1	47.8	62.6	–
Russian	78.5	–	–	67.2	67.9	–	–	–	–
West Indian[a]	61.6	–	–	50.4	76.4	70.3	55.1	–	–
Greek	57.4	–	–	51.5	65.3	81.7	61.9	–	98.6
Chinese	71.9	–	–	55.8	73.2	–	52.3	–	–
Italian	63.4	43.0	66.8	54.3	33.9	41.7	55.0	63.1	–
Portuguese	75.8	–	–	53.5	–	–	77.8	–	–
Jewish	82.5	79.9	82.6	72.4	77.1	69.7	70.5	74.5	74.4

SOURCE: Indexes based on special tabulations, 1971 Census of Canada, Statistics Canada.
a Includes blacks.

remaining groups is a valid statement mainly for the intermediate-status groups because of the relatively small numbers that appear in some of the generations at both high- and low-status levels. However, it also appears to be a valid statement for the low- and high-status groups of Germans, Ukrainians, Italians, and Jews. It would appear that the importance of educational status for intergenerational variations in residential segregation is ethnic-specific. Specifically, educational status has importance for the high-status components of the British, French, and German origins. For most other ethnic populations, educational status appears to contribute very little to intergenerational variations in residential segregation.

The analysis of ethnic residential segregation in Toronto and change through successive generations has provided little support for the general validity of the classical model of urban growth and assimilation for the many ethnic populations residing in the Toronto Census Metropolitan Area. Whatever degree of socio-economic integration or assimilation that may have been achieved by individual residents has not resulted in any general diminution of residential segregation along ethnic lines. The fact that the populations of British, French, and some of the other northern and western Europeans are the only ones to show any consistent evidence of declining residential segregation through successive generations suggests the existence of barriers that operate to reduce social and physical mobility arising from either prejudice or a desire to maintain culturally distinctive ways of life, or perhaps some combination of the two.

There is no question about Toronto's diversity of ethnic populations or the existence of a considerable range in the extent to which they are residentially segregated from the more established third-plus generations of English origin who have served as the standard for comparison in this analysis. The question that remains to be answered, however, has to do with the meaning of these patterns of segregation for the individual or the ethnic community in general. The assumption underlying most of the earlier work on residential segregation was that the degree of segregation exhibited by a particular ethnic population could be taken as an indicator of the extent to which its individual members had become acculturated and assimilated into the dominant culture groups. However, given the rapid growth in population and change in urban transportation and communication systems plus the high levels of residential mobility that have occurred since the 1930s, urban sociologists have increasingly depreciated the importance of community and neighbourhood boundaries as constraints to social interaction and as significant factors influencing individual attitudes and behaviour (Webber 1970). If they are correct, the persistence of spatially identifiable ethnic communities can no longer be taken as prima facie evidence of an ethnically segregated social and economic structure; nor can ethnic residential segregation be taken as evidence of a lack of assimilation, or its disappearance be mistaken for assimilation. In either case, the persistence of relatively concentrated and residentially segregated ethnic populations in the Toronto Census Metropolitan Area could be viewed as little more than a social anachronism without either individual or social significance. The remainder of this chapter examines this problem more closely from the individual's perspective within the context of his or her own ethnic or cultural origin and the ethnic character of his or her neighbourhood of residence.

The Individual in the Urban Setting

The consequences of living in a large, ethnically diverse metropolitan centre, for the individual, cannot be thoroughly investigated through the analysis of census data alone. Many of the relevant attitudes and behaviours that might be affected by the urban experience in the particular sector of the ethnic mosaic within which one lives are not considered to lie within the proper domain of the national census. For this reason census data should be combined with the results of original field research involving more extensive personal interviews whenever appropriate research opportunities arise. Social-area analysis, combined with survey research, has been used to show how the characteristics of census-tract populations, in the aggregate, interact with individual characteristics to produce behaviour that one would not predict on the basis of the individual characteristics alone (Bell 1959). The type of data and methodological requirements for the problem to be examined here are of a similar nature in that the analysis examines the influence that neighbourhoods of varying ethnic character may have on individual behaviour (for instance, participation in ethnic-related activities as an indication of an individual's 'ethnic connectedness'). While it is recognized that other factors, such as the respondent's feelings about his or her own ethnic or cultural origin, may be more important for explaining the extent of an individual's participation in ethnic-type activities, the focus here is directed mainly to the ethnic character of an area and its possible role as a facilitator, or inhibitor, of ethnic identity and ethnic-group participation. From its earliest inception, it was clear that the Ethnic Pluralism Study would provide an excellent research opportunity to explore the significance of census measures of ethnic residential segregation with respect to the perceptions of the character of areas of residence and the ethnic-related behaviour of their residents in one of Canada's major metropolitan centres.

DATA SOURCES AND VARIABLES

It has already been noted that the Index of Dissimilarity used for the analysis of segregation was based on ethnic-origin data for census-tract areas obtained from the 1971 and 1981 censuses of Canada. Other measures of the ethnic make-up of census-tract populations, for instance, the Index of Diversity and percentage ethnic composition, utilized mother-tongue data as well, as ethnic-origin data were not collected during the 1976 census. The attitudinal and behavioural data were collected during the 1978 and 1979 field surveys of ten ethnic-origin populations in the Toronto Census Metropolitan Area. The research design and details of the sample have been more thoroughly discussed elsewhere in this volume.

The major dependent variable for this analysis, most broadly conceptualized as 'ethnic connectedness,' is measured by eight indicators of participation in various types of activities that appear to have an ethnic component or are related in some way to the ethnic or cultural origin of the respondent.[6] The major independent variables, in addition to the ethnic group's 'propensity for residential segregation' as measured by the indexes of dissimilarity and segregation, include both an objective and subjective measure of the neighbourhood's ethnic mix. While there is some evidence to indicate that individuals are perceptive of the ethnic character of those living in their general area of residence (Richmond 1972), little is known about the degree to which their perceptions correspond to more objectively defined measures of the ethnic composition of residential areas (usually census tracts), or which variable may be the more relevant one for understanding the degree of 'ethnic connectedness' that characterizes the behaviour of individuals of differing ethnic origins. For this reason, both have been included in the analysis.

The more objective measure, based on census data, is the Index of Diversity (Lieberson 1969), while the subjective measure is similar to one that was used by Reitz (1980b: 115) and Richmond (1972), and is based on the respondent's perceptive judgment as to whether the people in the general area of residence are mostly of the same ethnic origin, mostly of another ethnic origin, or mostly of mixed origins. Both of these measures differ conceptually from the major independent variable, the Index of Dissimilarity, used in the analysis of residential segregation. The Index of Dissimilarity, by itself, obviously does not indicate anything about the ethnic character of the area in which any specific individual of a given ethnic origin actually resides. It indicates, in percentage terms, the relative numbers of any specific ethnic group that would have to change residence, that is, move to different census tracts, in order to produce an overall distribution identical to that of the particular reference population being used as a comparison group, in this case the third-plus generations of the population of English origin.[7]

It is essentially a summary measure for the ethnic group as a whole showing the degree of dissimilarity (or similarity) between two residential distributions across any given set of spatially defined areas.[8] The index of segregation is a relatively simple quantitative measure of an ethnic population's propensity or tendency to residentially segregate from other populations. But, it can also be regarded as an index or measure of a characteristic of a population aggregate that summarizes the forces of attraction and repulsion contributing to the propensity of certain ethnic-groups to segregate or disperse to a greater or lesser extent than those of other origins.[9]

The three independent variables are required to answer several different but related questions concerning ethnic residential segregation. First, given the varying propensities of ethnic populations to residentially segregate, it is important to determine the extent to which the ethnic character of residential areas, as defined by the census, is actually visible to or a part of the social reality of those living in them, and how aware these individuals are of changes in an area's ethnic composition arising from rapid urban growth and changes in the origins of recent immigrant streams. Second, to what extent and under what circumstances does the perceived (or actual) ethnic character of residential areas act to facilitate or inhibit behavioural expressions of ethnic connectedness? Third, and finally, to what extent does a particular ethnic population's propensity for residential segregation, as reflected by the Index of Dissimilarity, indicate or predict the individual's degree of ethnic connectedness and the degree of acculturation or economic integration of those who are members of that ethnic population? Finding significant and logically consistent correlations in the latter case will strengthen the argument for the importance of residential propinquity in maintaining the viability of the ethnic community for individuals of various ethnic origins living in Canada's largest metropolitan centres.

PERCEPTION OF THE ETHNIC CHARACTER OF AREAS OF RESIDENCE

The Ethnic Factor in Residential Location

The persistence of ethnically and economically differentiated residential areas during periods of rapid population growth and high residential mobility suggests that the element of randomness in locational decisions is still minimal relative to ethnic and economic considerations. However, in answering questions as to why the respondents moved from their previous neighbourhood or to their present neighbourhood, over half of the reasons given were of an economic nature, while almost as many were concerned with the convenience of location. Little recognition was given to 'ethnic related' reasons. At the very most, only 10% of the reasons might have directly or indirectly involved conscious consideration of the respondent's ethnic origin or the ethnic character of the neighbourhood. Perhaps one's feelings about ethnic identity and commitment are such a natural component of 'self' that they are automatically taken into account during the decision-making process by some respondents without conscious awareness of the fact. Reasons for moving, for example, to be nearer friends or family, could be heavily influenced by one's own ethnic origin, as could decisions made on the recommendations of real-estate agents acting as 'gatekeepers' without the individual being fully cognizant of the importance of ethnic origin (Helper 1969). An accurate determination of the extent to which decisions are seen to be 'ethnic related' would appear to be problematic. In this case, the significance of ethnicity would appear to have been underestimated to a considerable extent. With so little recognition given to the ethnic factor by the respondents, its influence must operate in very subtle yet significant ways, otherwise it would be difficult to imagine how ethnic residential segregation could persist at any level for any length of time under the conditions of high residential mobility that have characterized the Toronto metropolitan area population in recent decades.

Mobility and Exposure to Ethnic Diversity

A very large part of the population mobility in the Toronto metropolitan area involves movement within or between its municipalities and from nearby communities. More precisely, over one-half, or 53%, of the population five years of age and over in the Toronto Census Metropolitan Area in 1976 had been living in a different dwelling five years earlier. About half of these had moved within the same municipality, while the remaining half had moved from some other municipality within the Toronto Census Metropolitan Area or elsewhere in the province or Canada (Statistics Canada 1978).

The mobility experience of the ten ethnic populations sampled for this study is similar to that for Toronto's population as whole. One-half of the sample reported living at their present address for five years or less, while two-thirds reported ten years or less. Only 4% had lived elsewhere in the Toronto area. Of those who had come from other places in Canada, the majority (60%) had come from small towns and cities. Just 4% had moved to their present address from outside Canada. Given the increasing ethnic diversity of the Toronto population during the post-war period, and the greater diversity of larger urban centres in comparison to smaller ones, migrants in general would be expected to encounter more ethnically diverse populations with each successive move.[10] The increasing heterogeneity of the urban mover's general neighbourhood may be seen in table 3.5, which shows the respondents' perceptions of the ethnic character of their previous neighbourhoods as well as that of their present neighbourhood of residence for the combined sample of ten ethnic populations. The decline in the proportion of respondents who have perceived themselves as living in ethnically similar, or concordant, neighbourhoods at various stages of their life cycle has been very significant, dropping from 67% for the neighbourhoods they grew up in to just 17% for their present location. The corresponding proportions of respondents experiencing more ethnically mixed neighbourhoods with successive moves were 28 and 71% respectively. The differences are even greater if the community of residence of the respondent, before coming to Canada, is taken into account.

Not only have more movers and migrants within the sample been progressively exposed to greater ethnic diversity each time they've changed residence, but a considerable number have also reported changes occurring in their present neighbourhoods since moving there. Specifically, respondents were asked, 'Since you moved to this neighbourhood, has there been any change in the ethnic or cultural backgrounds of your neighbours?' Of those reporting a noticeable change, 15% indicated that more of their neighbours were of the same ethnic background as themselves, 17% felt that there were more of some other single ethnic origin, while two-thirds of the respondents said that they thought that their neighbourhoods had become more ethnically mixed since they had been living there.

Variations in Perception by Ethnic Origin of Respondent

Table 3.5 shows that, of the combined sample of ten ethnic populations, 71% were currently living in ethnically mixed neighbourhoods and 12% in non-concordant ones in which most of the neighbours were perceived to be of some other single ethnic group. Since the ten ethnic populations selected for this study vary both in size and in terms of their propensity for residential segregation, considerable variation from the above percentages could be expected for particular ethnic groups.

TABLE 3.5
Perception of ethnic character of previous and present neighbourhoods of residence by the combined sample of ten ethnic populations;[a] Toronto, CMA, 1978–79 (percentages)

Perceived ethnic character of neighbourhood	Present neighbourhood	Previous neighbourhood	Neighbourhood grew up in	Community before coming to Canada
Ethnically concordant[b]	16.9	32.6	66.6	79.8
Ethnically non-concordant[c]	12.2	14.3	5.0	6.9
Ethnically mixed[d]	70.9	53.1	28.4	13.3
Total (%)	100.0	100.0	100.0	100.0
Number				
weighted *N*	2243	1989	1671	887
unweighted *N*	(2280)	(2012)	(1740)	(1161)

SOURCE: Ethnic Pluralism Survey, 1978–79

a The ten ethnic populations included in this study were the English, Irish, Scottish, German, Italian, Ukrainian, Portuguese, West Indian, Jewish and Chinese.

b Mostly the same ethnic origin as respondent

c Mostly another ethnic origin

d Most of mixed ethnic origins

Respondents belonging to the larger and more segregated ethnic populations in Toronto would be expected to report higher proportions living in ethnically concordant neighbourhoods than those of the less-segregated ethnic groups. This pattern is most evident for the Jews and Italians, of whom 33% perceived that their neighbourhoods were ethnically concordant, compared to just 17% for all ethnic populations combined. The smaller, but highly segregated, Portuguese group was the only other ethnic population to exceed the average for the sample as a whole (20%). The least common situation was the ethnically non-concordant neighbourhood with only 12% reporting that their neighbours were mostly of some other single ethnic group. Most of the sample respondents (71%) were living in mixed areas, with higher than average proportions reported by members of the larger and more established minority ethnic populations, for instance, the Germans and Ukrainians, as well as by most members of the smaller but rapidly growing populations, such as the Chinese, Portuguese, and West Indians.

Not only are the individuals of the various ethnic groups exposed to different patterns of ethnic diversity in their neighbourhoods (that is, concordant, non-concordant, and mixed), but the actual ethnic character of the neighbourhood also varies. Because of their size and minimal residential segregation, the population of British origins would be expected to constitute a major part of almost every census tract, except those that contain the largest segregated populations of Italian and Jewish origin. Analysis of the census data, by census tract of residence for the sample individuals, shows that for almost two-thirds of the sample, the population of British origins was, in fact, the largest ethnic population in their census tract. With respect to specific ethnic populations, it was found that the Ukrainians and Germans were more likely to live in census tracts where the British were the numerically dominant group than were those of other ethnic origins. By way of contrast, the Jews (as expected in light of their high degree of segregation) were much more likely to live in tracts where they constituted the largest single ethnic group. More specifically, 68% of the Jews lived in tracts where they were the single largest ethnic group, while 24% were in tracts where the British were numerically the largest. The remaining 8% were in Italian areas. Almost half (45%) of the Italians were living in tracts in which the Italians comprised the largest single group, with another 48% residing in tracts where the British were the largest.

Of the more recently arrived minority groups, 29% of the Portuguese were living in tracts where the Portuguese were the largest single ethnic population, while another 42% were residing in predominantly Italian tracts. The West Indians showed only a slightly greater than average propensity to locate in those tracts in which the Italians were the largest single group, while the Chinese showed only a slightly higher than average predisposition to locate in tracts where the largest single group with either British or Portuguese. The picture is exceedingly complex. Nevertheless, there is more than a hint that these patterns are a reflection of the propensities for segregation examined earlier in this chapter, as well as of perceived differences in prestige or status among the various ethnic groups.[11]

Variations in the Perception of Change

Within a growing metropolitan population characterized by ethnic diversity and differences in the sizes of ethnic populations, growth rates, and propensities for residential segregation, a large proportion of its residents can be expected to have perceived changes in the ethnic and cultural make-up of their neighbourhoods. Overall, 40% did in fact report a noticeable change; but only the respondents of English, Irish, and Scottish (the major British) origins exceeded the average proportions for the sample as a whole. Being among the larger, more dispersed and established ethnic populations in Toronto, they appear to have been even more likely to have noticed the effects of demographic change than respondents of other ethnic origins.

As might be expected, the nature of the perceived changes also varied by the ethnic origin of the respondent. The same three British origin groups (English, Irish, and Scottish), plus those of German and Ukrainian origin, were more likely to report that their neighbourhoods were becoming either more ethnically mixed or shifting towards a condition of greater non-concordance than were the respondents of other groups. By contrast, the more recent but smaller immigrant arrivals, such as the Portuguese and West Indians, and several of the larger more segregated groups (the Italians and Jewish) were more likely to perceive an increase of persons in their neighbourhoods of the same origin as themselves, that is, an increase in the direction of greater ethnic concordance.

It would appear that the perception of changes taking place in Toronto's neighbourhoods differs for individuals, depending upon their specific origin and several other factors, including recency of immigration and their group's propensity for residential segregation. Individuals of the dominant and more established ethnic populations, even though they tend to be less segregated than most, are more likely to be sensitive to the changes in the ethnic character of their established neighbourhoods. By contrast, individuals of the smaller ethnic minority groups moving to, or within, Toronto appear to be more likely to see the changes that have been occurring as a strengthening of their position as the proportion of their own ethnic-origin group increases in their areas of residence.

The patterns of ethnic segregation established on the basis of the analysis of census data by census tracts would appear to have some meaningful and consistent counterparts in the individual's perception of the ethnic character of his or her neighbourhood and of the changes that have been occurring. Having established this link, however tenuous, it is important to determine the significance of the neighbourhood's ethnic character for the individual's attitudes and ethnic behaviour, that is, the nature and degree of his ethnic 'connectedness.' This determination is important if for no other reason than to answer the long-running criticisms of segregation analysis to the effect that patterns of segregation established on the basis of relatively large and heterogeneous census tract areas are not socially meaningful at the individual level. It is also important, of course, to test the assumption that the degree of residential segregation established by a specific ethnic population is a valid indicator of the level of 'ethnic connectedness' of its individual members.

ETHNIC CHARACTER OF NEIGHBOURHOODS AND ETHNIC CONNECTEDNESS

Variations in economic achievement, combined with the vagaries of the housing market, provide ample reasons for the fact that people do not always live where they would prefer to live given complete freedom of choice. Yet, all other things being equal, if ethnicity is important to individuals, it should not be surprising to find people living in areas where there are others of similar ethnic origin. It would also seem reasonable to expect that the importance with which one regarded his or her ethnic origin would affect not only the choice of residential area, but also other aspects of ethnic connectedness, such as participation in ethnic-related activities. Undoubtedly, many other factors are involved in explaining differences in ethnic participation of one kind or another, but the major factor of concern here is the perceived ethnic character of the neighbourhood in which the individual lives, and its relation to 'ethnic connectedness.' However, since the importance of one's ethnic origin can be expected to influence one's choice of neighbourhood as well as participation in ethnic-related activities, this variable will be examined more closely.

The Importance of Respondent's Ethnic Origin and Ethnic Connectedness

There is little doubt about the importance with which most of the individuals in this study regard their ethnic origin (see table 3.6). Only one-quarter responded that their origin was 'not at all important,' while three-quarters replied that it was either 'somewhat,' 'very,' or 'extremely' important to them. For 37% of the sample, their ethnic origin was either 'very' or 'extremely' important. It is also clear from the data in table 3.6 that its importance varies significantly by ethnic origins (Cramer's $V = 0.44$). It seems to be considered least important among those of British origins and Germans, and either very or extremely important for those in the remaining groups, ranging from 53% for the Ukrainians, to a high of 70% for the Portuguese, compared to 37% for all groups combined.[12]

TABLE 3.6
Importance of ethnic origin for respondents for selected ethnic populations; Toronto CMA, 1978–79 (percentages)

Importance of ethnic origin to respondent	Ethnic origin										
	English	Irish	Scottish	German	Ukrainian	Italian	Portuguese	Jewish	West Indian	Chinese	Total
Extremely or very important	29.2	10.3	9.3	19.0	53.0	57.6	70.2	67.2	66.4	55.6	36.7
Somewhat or not at all important	70.8	89.7	90.7	81.0	47.0	42.4	29.8	32.8	33.6	44.4	63.3
Total (%)	100.0	100.0	100.0	100.0	100.0	100.0	100.0	100.0	100.0	100.0	100.0
Number											
weighted *N*	674	267	258	177	88	431	66	166	118	57	2303
unweighted *N*	(343)	(78)	(76)	(321)	(345)	(351)	(164)	(348)	(150)	(153)	(2338)

SOURCE: Ethnic Pluralism Survey, Toronto 1978–79

Not only does the sense of the importance of the respondent's ethnic origin vary significantly between ethnic groups, but so does the extent to which individuals participate in specific ethnic-related activities. Variations in the levels of participation by type of activity for the ten ethnic populations are presented in table 3.7. Participation rates, that is, the per cent participating 'sometimes to frequently,' vary from an average of just 14% for the Scottish to a high of 63% for Italians. The strength of relationships between ethnic origin and frequency of participation for each specific activity ranges from 0.30 to a maximum of 0.57. Data in tables 3.6 and 3.7 show that it is the same ethnic groups previously shown to have intermediate to high levels of residential segregation that are more likely to exhibit (1) higher proportions of individuals who regard their ethnic origin as important, and (2) higher average ethnic participation than the least segregated groups.[13]

'Perceived' Ethnic Character of Neighbourhoods and Ethnic Connectedness

In view of the preceding discussion, some relationship was expected between the perceived ethnic character of the neighbourhood and the individual's degree of participation in ethnic activities, as well as between the importance of ethnic origin and participation. As may be seen in table 3.8, the individual's perception of the ethnic make-up of the neighbourhood is only weakly related to the degree of his (or her) participation in just a few ethnic activities. Interestingly, the relationships seem worth noting only for those of English, Irish, and Scottish origins, and for just the Italians, Jews, and West Indians among Canada's non-British ethnic groups. However, the nature of the relationship where it existed, albeit weakly, was consistent with the hypothesis that ethnically concordant neighbourhoods would tend to increase the individual's likelihood of participation while neighbourhoods that were mixed or predominately of some other origin would be associated with below-average participation.[14]

Table 3.9 presents correlations for the relationships between the acknowledged importance of ethnic identity for the individual and participation in the various ethnic activities. While these relationships are still relatively moderate for all ethnic-origin groups combined, they are considerably stronger for most of the activities for those of Ukrainian origins, and somewhat stronger for the ethnic-media-type activities for those of German, Italian, Portuguese, and Jewish origins.

TABLE 3.7
Percentage 'sometimes or frequently' participating in ethnic activities for selected ethnic populations: Toronto CMA, 1978–79

Ethnic activity	Ethnic origin										
	English	Irish	Scottish	German	Ukrainian	Italian	Portuguese	Jewish	West Indian	Chinese	Total
a Dances, parties, etc.	28	12	9	20	54	61	43	46	58	28	34
b Non-ethnic dances, etc.	65	85	81	72	66	56	32	45	42	31	64
c Ethnic vacation resorts	12	1	3	4	22	13	51	27	20	9	12
d Ethnic foods on holidays	44	26	24	57	89	92	79	92	83	89	59
e Ethnic foods generally	56	30	23	79	89	97	96	91	89	96	66
f Watch/hear ethnic TV/radio	56	18	20	36	41	63	74	36	53	24	45
g Read ethnic papers, magazines	28	8	5	30	31	49	47	57	67	71	33
Total (average %)*	37	16	14	38	54	63	65	58	62	53	42
Number											
weighted *N*	677	267	258	177	89	431	66	168	116	57	2302
unweighted *N*	(343)	(78)	(76)	(321)	(354)	(351)	(164)	(348)	(150)	(153)	(2338)

SOURCE: Ethnic Pluralism Survey, Toronto, 1978–79
*Excludes item 'b.'

TABLE 3.8
Correlation coefficients (Cramer's V) for the relationship between perceived ethnic character of neighbourhood and participation in ethnic-related activities for selected ethnic populations; Toronto CMA, 1978–79

	Ethnic origin										
Ethnic-related activity	English	Irish	Scottish	German	Ukrainian	Italian	Portuguese	Jewish	West Indian	Chinese	Total
a Dances, parties, etc.	–	0.15	–	–	–	–	0.11	0.14	–	0.10	
b Non-ethnic dances, etc.	0.11	–	0.21	–	–	0.18	–	–	0.17	–	–
c Ethnic vacation resorts	–	–	0.18	–	0.12	–	–	0.13	0.16	–	0.06
d Ethnic foods on holidays	0.10	0.22	–	–	–	0.28	–	–	–	–	0.09
e Ethnic foods generally	–	0.21	0.17	–	–	–	–	–	–	–	–
f Watch/hear ethnic TV/radio	–	–	–	–	–	0.13	–	–	–	–	0.08
g Read ethnic papers, magazines	–	–	–	0.18	–	–	–	–	–	–	0.06
Total											
weighted N	665	246	248	172	88	426	64	165	109	55	2239
unweighted N	(337)	(72)	(73)	(309)	(345)	(345)	(155)	(338)	(138)	(147)	(2259)

NOTE: Correlation coefficients < 0.10 are not shown for individual ethnic-origin groups.

TABLE 3.9

Correlation coefficients (Cramer's *V*) for the relationship between the importance of respondent's origin and participation in ethnic-related activities for selected ethnic populations: Toronto CMA, 1978–79

Ethnic-related activity	Ethnic origin										
	English	Irish	Scottish	German	Ukrainian	Italian	Portuguese	Jewish	West Indian	Chinese	Total
a Dances, parties, etc.	0.12	–	0.10	–	0.40	0.19	–	0.18	–	0.11	0.26
b Non-ethnic dances, etc.	–0.14	0.14	–0.20	–	–0.17	–0.13	–0.15	–	–	–	–0.22
c Ethnic vacation resorts	–	–	–	–	0.36	0.13	0.14	0.12	–	–	0.20
d Ethnic foods on holidays	–	0.29	–	0.15	0.24	0.18	0.13	0.25	–	–	0.38
e Ethnic foods generally	–	0.15	–	0.17	0.19	–	–	0.16	–	–	0.36
f Watch/hear ethnic TV/radio	–	0.17	–	0.29	0.39	0.35	0.26	0.18	0.15	–	0.27
g Read ethnic papers, magazines	0.12	0.22	0.13	0.39	0.50	0.23	0.28	0.31	0.21	0.18	0.38
Total											
weighted *N*	674	269	258	177	88	431	64	166	116	57	2298
unweighted *N*	(341)	(78)	(76)	(319)	(359)	(351)	(159)	(344)	(147)	(152)	(2318)

NOTE: Correlation coefficients < 0.10 are not shown for individual ethnic-origin groups.

The Importance of Ethnicity and Perceived Ethnic Character of the Neighbourhood

One's ethnic origin, like the perceived ethnic character of the neighbourhood, has varying importance for ethnic participation. For groups with high proportions of individuals who regard their ethnic origin with considerable importance, such as the Chinese, Portuguese, and West Indians, the perceived ethnic character of the neighbourhood in which they live makes little difference in so far as their levels of participation are concerned. For the larger and more established groups, who on average appear to attach less importance to their ethnic origin, the perceived character of the neighbourhood may become a significant factor with respect to the individual's participation in ethnic-related activities.

Examining the relationship between the perceived character of the neighbourhood and ethnic participation, while holding constant variations in the importance of the respondent's origin, produces no dramatic effect on the correlations for the combined ethnic population. However, for the group for which ethnic origin was 'somewhat' or 'not at all important,' the correlations for six of the seven activities increased slightly, while those for the population who thought their origin to be very or extremely important decreased with respect to both the number and strength of the significant relationships. It would seem that the relationships, while weak, are not spurious correlations reflecting only the effects of the 'importance of ethnic origin' variable on ethnic participation. The significance of the perceived ethnic character of the neighbourhood for ethnic participation is not independent of the importance one attaches to one's ethnic origin. Now by treating the 'perceived ethnic character' as a control variable, further light can be shed on its significance for ethnic participation by examining the strength of the relationships between the importance of origin and participation variables within each of the types of perceived ethnic neighbourhood, that is, ethnically concordant, non-concordant, and mixed ethnic.

In table 3.10, it may be noted that living in an ethnically concordant or mixed neighbourhood appears to enhance the strength of the relationship between the importance of one's origin and ethnic participation in five of the seven ethnic-related activities. Only in the case of reading ethnic papers, etc., is the relationship between importance of origin and frequency of activity strongest in the non-concordant neighbourhoods. Living in neighbourhoods where most of the neighbours

TABLE 3.10

Measures of association (Cramer's *V*) between the importance of one's ethnic origin and frequency of participation in selected ethnic-related activities for types of 'Perceived' ethnic neighbourhoods

	Type of perceived neighbourhood			
Ethnic-related activity	All types of neighbourhoods	Ethnically concordant	Ethnically non-condordant	Ethnically mixed
a Dances, parties, etc.	0.26	0.28	–	0.29
b Non-ethnic dances, etc.	–0.22	–0.30	–0.19	–0.21
c Ethnic vacation resorts	0.20	–	–0.21	0.22
d Ethnic foods on holidays	0.38	0.38	0.33	0.39
e Ethnic foods generally	0.36	0.31	0.26	0.40
f Watch/hear ethnic TV/radio	0.27	0.29	0.24	0.29
g Read ethnic papers, magazines	0.38	0.29	0.44	0.40
Number				
range of weighted *N*s	2291–2298	375–378	269–270	1580–1582
range of unweighted *N*s	(2313–2317)	(370–371)	(265–266)	(1620–1622)

NOTE: Correlation coefficients < 0.10 are not shown.

are of the same or ethnically mixed origins seems to strengthen the relationships between the importance of one's origin and the frequency of attending ethnic dances and parties, eating ethnic foods on special occasions or on a regular basis, listening to ethnic programs on radio or watching them on television, and reading ethnic magazines, newspapers, and so on, as well as not attending ethnic dances and parties. The weaker correlations for those living in neighbourhoods where most neighbours are of some other single origin, for instance, English, may suggest the presence of generally low levels of 'importance of respondent's origins' and greater interest in socio-cultural assimilation.

The attempt to show the importance of the 'perceived' ethnic character of the neighbourhood for ethnic participation (based on the respondent's subjective judgment) has been only partially successful given the general weakness of the relationships. However, variations in this relationship for the various ethnic populations demonstrates its ethnic-specific nature. Also, examining the relationship between the importance of one's ethnic origin and ethnic participation within types of ethnic neighbourhoods permits a more precise specification of the conditions under which variations in feelings of the importance of one's ethnic origin are more likely to be reflected in participation in ethnic-group activities. Still, the magnitude of the correlations is moderate at best, as are their differences.

Ethnic Diversity of Neighbourhoods and Ethnic Connectedness

In an urban population with considerable ethnic diversity, whose ethnic populations vary significantly in their degree of residential segregation, the degree of diversity of its census-tract populations can also be expected to vary significantly. In the absence of any residential segregation, the degree of ethnic diversity would be uniform for all census tracts and equal to that for the area as a whole. However, with increasingly high levels of segregation, the degree of ethnic diversity would tend to decline in each of the residential areas, reaching zero for the limiting case of complete segregation by census tract.

The consequences of variation in area levels of ethnic diversity for the individual's ethnic participation were partially demonstrated in the previous section in which neighbourhood diversity was defined in terms of the respondent's perception of the ethnic character of the neighbourhood in relation to his or her own ethnic origin. The strength of such an index, as well as its weakness, lies in its use of the subject's own evaluation of the 'ethnic mix' of what he or she regards to be the neighbourhood of residence. The Index of Diversity provides a more objective measure of the ethnic composition of a standard area. But, while the estimate of the ethnic composition of the area would be more accurate, the census tract of resident would generally tend to encompass a larger area than what is generally regarded as one's residential neighbourhood. The use of census tracts in urban and population research has generally been criticized because of their large size and relatively heterogeneous populations. Without disavowing the possible value of smaller areas for research, this analysis examines the utility of census-tract areas and data for testing the significance of an area's ethnic composition as a contextual factor affecting the individual's participation in ethnic-related activities, that is, his/her ethnic connectedness.

An analysis of the degree of association between Lieberson's index of ethnic diversity (A'_w) for the respondent's census tract of residence and participation in eight ethnic-related activities was carried out for the ten ethnic groups individually and for the combined ethnic populations. The results are presented in table 3.11. The relationships between ethnic diversity and ethnic-related attitudes and behaviour for the combined sample are not noticeably different from those produced when using the 'perceived ethnic character' of neighbourhood as the independent variable. However, the relationships in table 3.11, as in table 3.8, are quite ethnic-specific.

Of more interest, perhaps, is the fact that the pattern of variation between ethnic diversity and participation in ethnic-related activities is generally curvilinear in nature. In most cases, participation tends to be greatest at both lowest and highest levels of diversity and least for intermediate levels. High levels of ethnic diversity in census tracts would appear to be as important for encouraging participation in ethnic-related activities as low levels that reflect greater ethnic homogeneity in areas of residence. It may be that in the absence of a significant amount of external ethnic support, some individuals may feel more compelled to assert their ethnicity in ways that they would normally feel to be unnecessary in ethnically concordant areas.

As with the previous analysis of the perceived ethnic character of neighbourhoods, combining the ten separate ethnic populations for the analysis obscures important differences between them. In this case, the very weak correlations between ethnic diversity and participation for the combined groups appear to be the result of the lack of significant correlations for any of the non-British ethnic-minority groups included

TABLE 3.11

Measures of association (Cramer's *V*) of the relationship between the ethnic diversity of the census tract of residence and selected ethnic-related attitudes and behaviours for ten ethnic-origin populations; Toronto CMA, 1978–79

Relationship between variables: index of ethnic diversity and ...	Ethnic origin										
	English	Irish	Scottish	German	Ukrainian	Italian	Portuguese	Jewish	West Indian	Chinese	Total
1 Importance of ethnic origin	0.16	0.19	0.19	–	–	–	–	–	–	–	0.08
2 Having cultural objects	0.17	–	0.31	–	–	–	–	–	–	–	0.12
3 Frequency of participation in ethnic-related activities:											
a Dances, parties, etc.	0.16	0.23	0.21	–	–	–	0.30	–	–	–	0.07
b Non-ethnic dances, etc.	–0.20	–0.35	–	–	–	–	–	–	–	–	–0.10
c Ethnic vacation resorts	–	–0.32	–	–	–	–	–	–	–	–	–
d Ethnic foods on holidays	0.12	–	0.22	–	–	–	–	–	–	–	0.09
e Ethnic foods generally	0.12	0.19	0.22	–	–	0.18	–	–	–	–	0.08
f Watch/hear ethnic TV/radio	–	–	0.20	–	–	–	–	–	–	–	0.08
g Read ethnic papers, magazines	0.20	0.37	–	–	–	–	–	0.34	0.33	–	0.10
Total											
weighted *N*	677	267	258	177	88	431	66	166	117	57	2306
unweighted *N*	(343)	(78)	(76)	(320)	(353)	(323)	(161)	(348)	(147)	(152)	(2307)

NOTE: Correlation coefficients < 0.10 are not shown for individual ethnic-origin groups.

in the sample. The English, Irish, and Scottish all showed moderately weak correlations, ranging from 0.12 to 0.37, which were, however, considerably stronger than those for all groups combined. The significance of neighbourhood ethnic diversity with respect to participation in ethnic activities is, again, clearly ethnic-specific and is limited in this case to the larger and relatively more established groups whose members generally do not regard themselves as being ethnic in the same sense that non-British immigrants tend to be regarded.

Neither the subjective perceptions of a neighbourhood's ethnic mix by the respondents, nor the more objective Index of Diversity, based on census-tract data, have provided convincing evidence of the importance of an area's ethnic composition as a factor affecting the individual's ethnic connectedness, defined in terms of participation in ethnic activities. Why there is no definitive evidence is difficult to say. Perhaps the Index of Diversity, based on census-tract areas, tends to overestimate the degree of heterogeneity of any single neighbourhood within the larger area. It is also possible that the subjective measure simply does not produce sufficient variation in the independent variable for some groups to test the hypothesis adequately. Given the high levels of participation for recent immigrant groups, there may have also been insufficient variation in the dependent variable as well.

PROPENSITIES FOR RESIDENTIAL SEGREGATION AS PREDICTORS OF ETHNIC CONNECTEDNESS

In general, the evidence suggests that those who live in an urban setting, such as Toronto's, have at least some awareness of its ethnic diversity and the nature of recent changes that is consistent with the results of residential-segregation analysis based on census data. While this awareness does not appear to make much of an independent or direct contribution to the individual's level of participation in ethnic-related activities, it may work to facilitate or inhibit such activity. It's not the ethnic character of the neighbourhood, per se, that is important for individual ethnic connectedness, but the perception of its ethnic character in conjunction with such other variables as the individual's feelings of importance about his or her ethnicity, the specific ethnic group of which she or he is a member, and the particular types of activities being considered.

Knowledge of the ethnic character of a neighbourhood by itself, based on either of the subjective or objective definitions employed here, has not been shown to be a very successful predictor of the degree of ethnic connectedness of its residents. This fact would suggest that individually perceived differences in the ethnic mix of specific neighbourhoods, arising from a group's general propensity to segregate, are a somewhat limited manifestation of a group's overall attractiveness or cohesiveness. By contrast, an index of residential segregation, as a summary measure of the residential location of all members of a particular population in relation to each other and with respect to some standard population distribution, would appear to be at least as valid and perhaps more useful as an index of the group's general cohesiveness, of which residential segregation is but one manifestation. If this were not so, the observed separation and clustering of residents in terms of their ethnic or cultural origins could only be considered the anachronistic remnants of formerly viable ethnic communities of an era when the physical limits of neighbourhoods were more effective in limiting social networks and interaction patterns.

It is the purpose of the analysis in this section to examine the assumptions underlying residential-segregation analysis and to determine the extent to which the index of segregation (dissimilarity) serves as an indicator of assimilation or acculturation for its constituent members in terms of their degree of ethnic connectedness. The general assumption underlying segregation analysis has always been that those populations showing propensities for residential segregation have done so more out of necessity than from free choice because of the general discrimination and prejudice against the more visible minority groups in the community. Residential segregation has been viewed as both an effect and a cause of other forms of differential association. The existence of near ghetto-like reception areas for arriving immigrants in the larger urban centres has reflected in part their initial disadvantaged social and economic status as well as the feelings of antipathy and prejudice towards them on the part of the established community. Once established, these ethnic enclaves have tended to set the boundaries for other forms of interaction as well. Conversely, those who managed to move away or disperse from ethnic areas opened up alternative opportunities to interact more widely with others regardless of their ethnic or cultural origins. Those who managed to move from the original areas of ethnic settlement were assumed to have done so because of their desire to assimilate and their success in overcoming their initial language, social, and economic handicaps.

A more liberal climate leading to the elimination of some discriminatory aspects of immigration legislation and regulations, beginning in

1961, combined with evidence of persisting residential segregation, seems to reflect a much greater voluntary element underlying ethnic segregation than had previously been the case. The persistence of residential segregation patterns on the part of some second and third-plus generations of non-British-origin European populations would appear to be consistent with this interpretation. Whatever the balance of voluntary and involuntary forces underlying a group's propensity for residential segregation, it is clear that their relative importance could be expected to vary from one group to another. However, the concern here is not with the determination of their relative importance, per se, but with determining how any particular balance, implicit in a group's particular propensity for segregation, reflects the individual's degree of 'ethnic connectedness.'

Reference Groups for Segregation Analysis

Data are given for two measures of segregation, the first based on an ethnic population's segregation from all other ethnic populations combined, and the second based on its segregation from the third-plus generation of the English-origin population. The first is included in the analysis because it has been the most commonly used index and provides a measure comparable to those used in other recent analyses. The second has been included because it is the more theoretically logical reference group for this particular study, and the requisite data for the separate groups of British origin became available through access to special tabulations.[15]

It is quite clear from the correlation coefficients presented in table 3.12 that both the Index of Segregation and Index of Dissimilarity are more strongly associated with the individual's ethnic behaviour than either the measure of perceived ethnic character of the neighbourhood or the measure of ethnic diversity of the respondent's tract of residence. Furthermore, it appears to make little difference which of the two indexes is used. In one respect, this is fortunate for continuing research on residential segregation in Canada's metropolitan area populations. Data required to identify the population of third and subsequent origins were last collected during the 1971 census, and their availability in future censuses is problematic. The greater loss would be the inability to examine changes in residential-segregation patterns between the first two and third-plus generations of Canadian residents. These groups are crucial for the study of the persistence of ethnocultural differences and of acculturation and assimilation processes.

TABLE 3.12
Measure of association (Cramer's V) between indexes of residential segregation for the individual's ethnic origin and generation group and ethnic-related attitudes and behaviour for the combined sample of ten ethnic populations; Toronto CMA, 1978–79

Ethnic-related attitudes and behaviour	Cramer's V	
	Index of segregation[a]	Index of dissimilarity[b]
1 Importance of ethnic origin	0.274	0.259
2 Ethnic cultural objects in the home	0.402	0.402
3 Frequency of participation in:		
a Ethnic dances, parties, etc.	0.378	0.356
b Non-ethnic dances, etc.	–0.270	–0.257
c Ethnic vacation resorts	0.274	0.258
d Ethnic foods on holidays	0.521	0.530
e Ethnic foods at other times	0.494	0.563
f Watch/hear ethnic/TV radio	0.303	0.315
g Read ethnic papers, magazines	0.356	0.361
Number		
mean of weighted *N*s[c]	2306	2306
mean of unweighted *N*s	(2338)	(2338)

SOURCE: Based on data from 1978–79 Ethnic Pluralism Survey and special tabulations from the 1971 Census of Canada, Statistics Canada.

a Compares residential distribution of an individual's ethnic and generation group with that for all other ethnic populations combined.

b Compares residential distribution of an individual's ethnic and generation group with that of the third-plus generation of the English-origin population.

c Weighted *N* for item 3c (vacation resorts) was 2299.

Indexes of Dissimilarity and Ethnic Connectedness

While there is some variation in the strength of the relationships in table 3.12, the patterns of variation are consistent with the basic hypothesis that a group's propensity for residential segregation is positively associated with greater participation in ethnic-related activities on the part of individual members, as well as with their feelings of importance about their ethnic origin. The association is moderately weak with respect to the latter and, among the eight activities included here, is weakest with respect to patronizing ethnic vacation camps or resorts and participating in non-ethnic-type activities. The link is strongest for those activities associated with the consumption of ethnic foods, either during ethnic holidays or at other times. For all items, except the non-ethnic activities, the individual is more likely to attach a greater sense of importance to his or her ethnic origin and participate more frequently in specific ethnic-related activities if her/his ethnic and generation group has a higher propensity for residential segregation than if it hasn't. To illustrate the nature of the relationship, table 3.13 presents the percentage distributions for frequency of attendance at ethnic parties and dances for the individual's ethnic and generation group categorized by high and low levels of propensities for residential segregation. A considerably higher percentage of respondents (53%) belonging to those ethnic-generation groups having high indexes of segregation attend ethnic dances and parties 'sometimes or frequently' than is the case for those individuals identified with ethnic-generation groups exhibiting low indexes (20%). As would be expected, attendance at non-ethnic dances and parties was negatively associated with a group's propensity for residential segregation (data not shown).

The question remains as to whether or not the particular items included in the analysis are the most appropriate indicators of 'ethnic connectedness.' They are representative of the types of items generally included in sociological studies of ethnic identity and ethnic-group participation. However, it would appear that they are sufficiently representative to demonstrate that the propensity for differential association, as reflected in patterns of residential segregation exhibited by the individual's ethnic-origin and generation group, is a valid indicator of the individual's ethnic connectedness.

Summary

RESIDENTIAL SEGREGATION

Results of the segregation analysis are quite similar to those of other recent studies of residential segregation in Canada's largest metropolitan centres. The rank order of the various ethnic-origin populations with respect to their degree of residential segregation appears to have remained relatively constant during the 1970s, as has their general levels of segregation. Those of British origins, that is, the English, Irish, and Scottish, and other northern and western Europeans (for instance, the Germans) exhibit the lowest degree of segregation from the rest of the population, or from the third-plus generation of English origin (used in the analysis as the general reference population in the Toronto CMA). Eastern Europeans (for instance, Ukrainians) are characterized by intermediate levels considerably lower than those exhibited by south-

TABLE 3.13
Index of residential segregation and participation in ethnic dances, parties, and other ethnic-related activities; Toronto CMA, 1978–79

Index of residential segregation	Frequently to sometimes	Very rarely or never	Total	
			%	Number
High (>30)	53.4	46.6	100.0	1377
Low (<30)	20.3	79.7	100.0	928
Total (%)	33.7	66.3	100.0	
Number				
weighted *N*	776	1529		2305
unweighted *N*	(924)	(1405)		(2329)

ern Europeans (for example, the Italians, and especially the Portuguese), who are exceeded only by those of Jewish origin. The Chinese and West Indians show levels of residential segregation about the same as other southern European-origin groups such as the Italians, but less than the Portuguese. The levels of segregation for these two more-visible minority groups may appear to be lower than they actually are in reality because of the insensitivity of the Index of Dissimiliarity (or Segregation) to the scattered pockets of residential concentrations that characterize these two particular groups.

Interestingly, the classical assimilation patterns of decreasing residential segregation in subsequent generations are observed only in the least segregated populations, that is, those of English, Irish, Scottish, and German origins. The pattern is also observed, but less pronounced, for those of Ukrainian and Italian origins, with the greatest decline occurring between the first and second generations. Intergenerational increases in segregation were observed for the Portuguese, Chinese, and West Indians, while segregation remained high for Jews of all generations. All groups exhibited a curvilinear relationship between educational status and residential segregation; but controlling for status had little effect on the intergenerational patterns previously mentioned. The notable exception was the absence of the classical intergeneration pattern for the English, Irish, and Scottish with the highest educational status. In general, however, the classical assimilation pattern of declining residential segregation appears to have relevance primarily for the British-origin groups and some of the groups of 'older' immigrant-European origins, especially the Germans, and to a lesser extent, the Ukrainians and Italians.

THE PERCEPTION OF NEIGHBOURHOOD CHANGE

The various ethnic groups did not differ significantly in their awareness of the increasing ethnic diversity of subsequent neighbourhoods of residence over time. Those with the higher propensities for residential segregation, such as Italians, Portuguese, and Jews, were also more likely to report living in ethnically concordant neighbourhoods. The existence of a preferential status or prestige hierarchy for Toronto's minority immigrant groups might be inferred from the fact that while half or more of Italians and Jews lived in areas predominantly occupied by their own origin group, the next largest proportions were in areas of British-origin dominance. Portuguese, by contrast, had relatively fewer in Portuguese-dominated areas, but the second largest proportions reported living in Italian areas.

As to perception of change in the ethnic character of residential areas, only the larger and more culturally dominant groups, that is, the English, Irish, and Scottish, had higher than average proportions reporting noticeable changes; and these same groups, plus the Germans and Ukrainians, were more likely to report their neighbourhoods as becoming more ethnically mixed or of some origin other than their own. The more recent arrivals (Portuguese and West Indians) and the more highly segregated groups (Jewish-origin) were more likely to report change in terms of increased or greater ethnic concordance.

IMPORTANCE OF ETHNIC ORIGIN AND ETHNIC CONNECTEDNESS

Of the groups included in the study, those of British and German origins had significantly lower proportions indicating that they regarded their origins as important, compared to the Ukrainians and the remaining groups who had much high proportions. There were also significant ethnic differences with respect to participation in ethnic-related activities, similar to those regarding the importance of ethnic origin. Again, those of British origin (specifically the Scottish) and the Germans were characterized by low levels of participation, while Ukrainians, Jews, and the more recent immigrants reported high participation levels. With respect to propensities for residential segregation, those whose particular ethnic-origin group exhibited intermediate to high levels of segregation were more likely to attach greater importance to their particular origin and report higher participation in ethnic-related activities.

The importance of ethnic origin was only moderately related to participation in ethnic-related activities for the combined sample. However, the relationships were consistently stronger for most of the activities for the Ukrainians, but only for ethnic-media-type activities for Germans and Italians.

PERCEPTION OF ETHNIC CHARACTER OF NEIGHBOURHOODS AND PARTICIPATION IN ETHNIC-RELATED ACTIVITIES

The relationship between the perceived character of one's neighbourhood and participation is strongest for the English, Irish, and Scottish, mainly with respect to eating ethnic foods and to dances and so on. For Germans, the relationship is strongest with respect to use of ethnic papers, magazines, and so forth; for the Italians, it is strongest around eating ethnic foods and watching ethnic television, and is negatively associated with attending non-ethnic dances. For the remaining groups, the relationships were essentially non-existent, probably because of the very high levels of participation and minimal intragroup variance.

ETHNIC DIVERSITY OF RESIDENTIAL AREAS AND ETHNIC CONNECTEDNESS

The more objective measure of an area's ethnic diversity, based on census data, exhibited a slightly curvilinear relationship to participation in ethnic-related activities, but only in the case of those of English, Irish, or Scottish origin. Diversity appears to have little or no general importance for the more recent immigrant groups or for those origins exhibiting high propensities for residential segregation, such as the Jewish.

PROPENSITY FOR RESIDENTIAL SEGREGATION AND ETHNIC CONNECTEDNESS

Propensities for residential segregation, as measured by indexes of dissimilarity based on the residential distributions of ethnic-origin and generation groups, show the strongest correlations with measures of participation in ethnic-related activities. The evidence suggests that the indexes of segregation and dissimilarity are valid indicators or measures of an ethno-generational group's degree of cultural persistence and influence on its individual members with respect to participation in ethnic-related activities. What the residential-segregation analysis suggests is that the classical assimilation model is valid only for those ethnic groups most similar to the third-plus generations of English origins (the Irish, Scottish, first- and second-generation English) and some of the northern and western European groups, such as those of German origin. The settlement and integration of other less culturally similar immigrant groups into the Canadian urban community is apparently occurring without the expected degree of residential dispersion, acculturation, and decline in participation in ethnic-related activities.

GENERAL COMMENTS

Evidence that the native-born generation tends to be less residentially segregated than the foreign-born is not new. Neither is it news that the segregation analysis has revealed significant differences in residential segregation by populations of differing ethnic and cultural origins, as well as differing status. More important, however, is the fact that the evidence of socio-cultural assimilation reflected in declining residential segregation through successive generations can be found only in a few populations of British and other western and northern European origins. Furthermore, controlling for differences in educational-attainment status does not significantly alter the intergenerational patterns even though status is shown to have a strong and persistent curvilinear relationship with residential segregation. The absence of intergenerational declines in segregation for other European and non-European populations that would be expected in the classical assimilation model would suggest that the present hierarchical patterning of Toronto's ethnic populations is very likely to persist into the future even if the volume of immigration were to decline to insignificant levels.

The field survey provided interview data from samples of ten major ethnic populations to help determine whether the observed patterns of residential segregation were merely anachronisms, or whether they still had significance as indicators of people's perceptions and attitudes or of their degree of ethnic connectedness in terms of participation in ethnic-related activities. Analysis of the interview data has shown that individuals do perceive the ethnic character of the areas in which they live in ways that are consistent with the results of the segregation analysis. The ethnic populations included in the survey differ significantly in the degree of importance with which their members tend to regard their ethnic origin, as well as in their levels of participation in ethnic-related activities.

The relationship of the ethnic character of areas of residence (either as perceived by the respondents in relation to their own ethnic origin, or as more objectively defined by the index of ethnic diversity) to the degree of ethnic connectedness was very weak for the combined sample considered as a whole. The importance with which one regards one's ethnic origin is more strongly related to participation in ethnic-related activities for all but the most recent and visible groups, but the strength of this relationship is affected somewhat by the perceived ethnic character of the neighbourhood as well as by the nature of the activity itself. Thus, it is possible that the ethnic character of the area of residence has importance as a facilitator or inhibitor of activity reflective of the individual's feelings of identification and association with his or her ethnic and cultural origin. The low correlation between the ethnic character of areas of residence (for both subjective and objective measures) and participation in various ethnic-related activities for the combined sample is due in great part to the very significant variations in this relationship for the various ethnic groups. Moderate relationships were observed for only a few activities for the English, Irish, and Scottish, and for only the Italians among the non-British immigrant groups.

Several measures of the ethnic character of areas of residence were employed in an attempt to determine which measure was most sensitive to the critical factors in residential segregation that would most likely affect the individual's behaviour. It was thought that the individual's perception of the ethnic character of the area of residence in relation to his or her own ethnic origin might be the most relevant; yet it was only weakly associated with the individual's ethnic participation for only a few of the more established groups. The more objective measure – index of ethnic diversity – detected consistently moderate relationships only for the three British-origin groups. It would appear that the generally stronger and less variant attitudes of the importance of one's origins and levels of participation simply override all other considerations as far as the more recent and visible immigrant groups are concerned. In any event, neither measure matched the simple index of an ethnic population's overall propensity for residential segregation, the Index of Dissimilarity, as a predictor of the individual's ethnic connectedness. Furthermore, the generally moderate levels of the associations between propensities for segregation and participation in ethnic-related activities would seem to be sufficient to indicate their general validity and usefulness as general measures of a group's cultural persistence, or socio-cultural assimilation.

4

Ethnic Concentrations in Labour Markets and Their Implications for Ethnic Inequality

Jeffrey G. Reitz

This chapter examines ethnic inequality in Toronto. In particular, it examines how ethnic inequality is affected by various types of ethnic concentrations in labour markets. The analysis considers ethnic concentrations in occupations, in ethnic businesses as entrepreneurs and as their employees, and in ethnic work groups and social networks within organizations. The purpose is to identify conditions under which ethnic concentrations reinforce existing inequalities, and conditions under which they may provide a basis for change.[1]

Toronto's minority ethnic groups represent different historical patterns of concentration in labour markets. Predominantly immigrant groups, such as the Portuguese, Chinese, and West Indians, often move into low-status occupations unwanted by more established groups. They have difficulty setting up independent businesses. However, even among these groups there are variations in the types of labour-market concentration. Each group has a distinctive occupational location, for example, with potentially varying effects. There are also variations in the role of small business. Among the Chinese there is a thriving 'Chinatown,' probably for several reasons. The Chinese have a longer history in Toronto, even though most Chinese in Toronto today are immigrants. As well, recent immigration from Hong Kong includes affluent businessmen who provide economic stimulus to the Chinese community, affecting other Chinese as well.

Better-established groups show still more divergent historical patterns. Italians in Toronto, as in many other North American cities, are closely identified with the construction industry. The Italian connection to construction dates from early in the century, and affected post-war Italian immigrants. Early settlers in the Jewish group became concentrated in textiles and retail trade. Later many Jewish persons moved into professional occupations. Other groups occupy somewhat less distinctive positions. Germans have worked in metal trades, and Ukrainians in railways.

Terms such as 'the ethnic economy,' 'ethnic occupations,' 'ethnic enclaves,' 'enclave-economy,' 'ethnic work settings,' 'domains,' 'job ghettos,' and so on sometimes are used to refer to specific forms of ethnic concentration in labour markets. Here we use the more encompassing term 'ethnic concentrations.' Specific forms of ethnic concentration overlap with each other. Research on one form should take account of connections to others. The term 'ethnic concentrations' has the additional advantage of being neutral about a positive or negative impact.

The theoretical approach derives from the sociology of labour markets (Kalleberg and Sørenson 1979; Granovetter 1971; Sørenson 1983; Kalleberg 1988). A central concern in recent sociological studies of labour markets is with inequities arising from the concentration of racial, ethnic, gender, and age groups in particular locations within labour markets. Labour-market concentrations may arise from discrimination or other sources. Ethnic concentrations also may overlap with the ethnic community itself. Once established, they may become social institutions that have their own effects on labour-market outcomes. This sociological approach is quite unlike classical economic theory, which sees labour markets as governed by competitive pressures likely to erode 'imperfections' such as those related to ethnic concentrations. Sociological theories suggest enduring economic effects.

The issues raised in this chapter address the broader theoretical goal of the study. This goal is to examine the impact that ethnic-community social formations have as liabilities or assets in the social incorporation of ethnic groups. Economic and occupational equality is critical to the social incorporation of minority ethnic groups, and is perhaps its most important indicator. This chapter contributes by considering ethnic concentrations in labour markets as important social formations within an ethnic community. It asks about their impact on a key indicator of social incorporation.

There is also practical and political significance in any impact of ethnic concentrations in labour markets. A practical issue faces minority-group members entering the labour market. If they enter positions associated with ethnic membership, do they face obstacles over the longer term? For those concerned with employment-equity policy there is the issue of whether to encourage minority business and economic initiatives. There are broader economic implications as well. In debates over 'free trade' and restructuring the Canadian economy, many have recognized the potential negative effects of immigrant concentration in specific industries.

Studying these issues presents problems and challenges. The first task is to identify specific ethnic inequalities in labour markets. This work involves estimating the effects of ethnic origin in human-capital regression models for income and occupational-status determination. The second problem is to identify and measure the variables representing types of ethnic concentrations likely to affect ethnic inequality. Finally, each type of ethnic concentration must be examined in relation to specific inequalities in labour markets by incorporating them in the income and status-determination models.

The chapter has six parts. The first part presents an overview of the theoretical background and empirical results from previous research, which leads to the formulation of specific research questions. The second describes ethnic inequality among eight ethnic groups in Toronto. This description, based on the survey data, is compared with previous research and with 1981 census data (from the Public Use Sample Tape). The third part develops measures for types of ethnic concentrations in labour markets. In the fourth part these measures are incorporated in the models of ethnic inequality to show relations and effects. The fifth part examines change between immigrant and Canadian-born generations among the four better-established groups. The sixth discusses the implications of the findings for specific ethnic groups and for future research.

Theoretical Issues and Previous Research

This section outlines the theoretical and methodological background to the analysis. Current theories of ethnic concentration in labour markets suggest various effects depending upon the type of concentration, and depending upon many historical circumstances. These theories have developed significantly in recent years, and so has the corresponding research. In place of earlier ad hoc speculations based on qualitative case studies, there is now emerging comparative theory which is examined in quantitative labour-force data. The design of the present study reflects a theoretical emphasis on the forms of ethnic concentration (occupations, ethnic business, and organizational niches) and on comparative ethnic histories.

DEVELOPING THEORIES OF ETHNIC LABOUR-MARKET CONCENTRATIONS

In itself, the existence of ethnic concentrations in labour markets does not imply negative effects. Ethnic concentrations often reflect the circumstances of immigration or the immediate needs of immigrants. Canadian immigration policy seeks to fit immigration to labour-market demand, often leading to specific concentrations (Reitz 1980b: 53–89). Furthermore, newly arriving immigrants themselves often seek the protection afforded by specific jobs. They may lack conventional occupational qualifications or access to the right social networks. Their particular qualifications may be better suited to the ethnic-community setting with its own businesses and occupational specialties. Ethnic-community networks can help find jobs in such settings.

If there is easy movement between ethnic labour markets and the occupational mainstream, then ethnic labour markets do not represent disadvantages. When there are no employment barriers, the normal acquisition of proper qualifications leads to abandonment of the ethnic labour market, and upward mobility. This is the classic immigrant-assimilation process.

The hypothesis of negative overall effects of ethnic concentrations in labour markets is based on the existence of institutional barriers to mobility between labour-market sectors. The hypothesis acknowledges the positive functions of ethnic concentrations in the short term, but suggests that the disadvantages arising from barriers to mobility are more important in the long term. Ethnic concentrations are *protected-but-marginal work domains.*

Qualitative case studies illustrate potential sources of barriers to mobility. Some situations create such negative implications for immigrants and minorities that they clearly outweigh any positive effect. For example, in the history of the Italian community in North American, the *padrone* system involved the exploitation of immigrants through the maintenance of dependency. Italian labour brokers manipulated Italian work groups located in majority-controlled organizations. Although Hughes and Hughes (1952) suggest that the *padrone* system has been more common in North America than most people believe, it is an extreme case.

More typically, the hypothesis of protected-but-marginal work domains suggests that ethnic concentrations generate informal barriers to mobility. Informal group processes serve to define and maintain ethnic boundaries within organizations. These boundaries then represent obstacles to mobility. Collins's (1946) study of Irish workers in a New England Yankee-owned factory is a good illustration. Irish workers dominated specific work groups and controlled the corresponding jobs, including the foreman position. The protection of the lower-level jobs, however, represented a barrier to higher-level mobility, because it reinforced Yankee control at the managerial level. Corwin's (1971) study of blacks in New York banks corroborates this theory. Rossi et al. (1974) found in Chicago that a pattern of hiring blacks benefits new black applicants, without enhancing their later prospects for upward mobility. Beattie's (1975) study of French Canadians in the Canadian federal bureaucracy showed similar patterns. In general, co-worker control of jobs applies to specific levels (see Dalton 1951; Gordon and Morton 1974).

Wiley's (1967) analysis of the 'ethnic mobility trap' emphasized another barrier to mobility caused by ethnic labour markets: the acquisition of marginal qualifications, or human capital. Wiley conceived the occupational structure, not as a simple hierarchy or ladder controlled by one group, but as a tree having many branches. The trunk represents the mainstream occupational domain. Branches correspond to ethnic work settings. The branches become 'mobility traps' because the qualifications acquired for mobility in an ethnic branch are specific to that branch, and different from those needed in the mainstream trunk. Minority-group members receive favourable treatment in the branches. Ultimately, however, they suffer because they fail to develop qualifications for mobility in the mainstream.

Competitive pressures within markets may reinforce the effects of these social barriers among occupations. Hodge and Hodge (1965) developed and tested an *occupational competition model* for the relation between occupational concentration and inequality. Their hypothesis was that when blacks or women are constrained to work in certain occupations, the lack of alternative employment drives down the wage rates for all those working in the affected occupations, including white males. Data analysis using statistical controls for job qualifications confirmed the negative income effects on white males. These effects presumably increase overall inequality, because the greatest impact is on blacks and women.

The analysis of industrial and labour-market segmentation (see Averitt 1968; D. Gordon 1972; Edwards 1979) provides yet another rationale for the negative effects of ethnic concentrations. In this theory, ethnic concentrations are *structurally disadvantaged labour-market segments.* Segmented-labour-market theory holds that certain classes of jobs are poor because they are marginal to economic production or other goals of the organization. Primary labour markets contain jobs with specialized skills and stable employment based on professional or union protection. These jobs have good wages and promotional prospects. Marginal or secondary labour markets have the opposite characteristics of low skill levels and lack of union protection. These secondary jobs have unstable employment, poor wages, and lack of career-development prospects. The theory is that discrimination against minorities and women forces them to work in the secondary segments. Secondary labour markets become ethnic enclaves, both reflecting and reinforcing ethnic inequality. They become a means for creating marginal labour, serving to reinforce divisions between levels within the labour force. The concept of labour-market segments thus links ethnic concentration to a general analysis of labour-market inequality. Wright's (1978) analysis of social-class inequality is similar, because it emphasizes structural impediments to mobility for low-status minorities.

These ideas apply also to ethnic concentrations within labour-market sectors or segments, and within specific firms and industries as well as occupations. Bonacich's (1972) discussion of 'ethnic antagonism' arising from a 'split labour market' emphasizes that segments can be based entirely on ethnicity. Any division within labour markets, including divisions at the level of the firm, may serve as an additional basis for marginality.

These various hypotheses uniformly predict an overall negative effect, but they nevertheless vary in their application. They may be most applicable to ethnic groups with the lowest status in society. In each hypothesis, low group status is a key element linking ethnic concentration to inequality. The hypotheses may also vary in their application to jobs in different locations within the occupational structure. They may apply mainly to low-status work domains within dominant-group-controlled organizations. In these situations, opportunities should be low in comparison to normally available opportunities in the mainstream.

However, positive effects of ethnic concentrations may arise when such concentrations reflect resource mobilization by group members. Dominant ethnic groups use informal and formal social relationships based on ethnic exclusivity to further their own economic interest;

minority groups may do so as well, albeit to a more limited extent. Breton (1979) has discussed the application of Weber's concept of 'social closure' both to dominant- and to minority-ethnic groups in the economic sphere. He stressed that it is the dominant groups that have greatest resources, so they benefit most from informal group relations. However, minority groups are not completely lacking in resources. Over time they may be able to mobilize those resources to the advantage of the entire group. Working within protected ethnic domains may offer advantages that in some respects outweigh disadvantages.

The prospects for such positive effects of ethnic concentrations are mentioned mainly in the discussion of *ethnic enterprise*. Minority businesses may exist in marginal industries or occupational sectors, leading to negative effects. However, minority businesses also offer the potential for structural autonomy. Hughes and Hughes (1952) described the advantages and disadvantages of small business in minority communities. Advantages include privileged access to ethnic labour markets and to ethnic consumer markets, and monopoly over certain products in larger markets. These advantages may offset any disadvantages that stem from marginality. Bonacich (1973) renewed this theme with a discussion of the 'middle-man minority.' She suggested that minority groups can gain advantages by monopolizing strategic roles linking key economic sectors. Light's (1974) analysis of ethnic enterprise would have broader implications. Success in small business for ethnic minorities may depend upon the group's capacity to mobilize its collective economic resources. This capacity, in turn, may vary with cultural characteristics (see also Light 1984, 1986). Wilson and Portes (1980) provide data suggesting that ethnic entrepreneurs can be part of the primary labour market because of the advantages of possessing specialized products and access to an ethnic work force (see also Portes 1981). Jiobu (1988) has identified some conditions for 'ethnic hegemony' in an economic sector, based on the case of California Japanese in agriculture. In general, minority business success is a function of access to capital, labour, supplies, and consumers, any of which may be structured along ethnic lines.

The advantages or disadvantages of ethnic enterprise impinge differently on employees as opposed to employer-entrepreneurs, as Sanders and Nee (1987) point out. If minority-group entrepreneurs gain from network-based access to minority labour markets, there may be exploitation and corresponding disadvantages for the minority employees. At the same time, the employees may benefit from reverse discrimination. Which effect predominates may depend upon the overall success of ethnic enterprise in the particular ethnic group.

In summary, previous theory suggests that the effects of ethnic concentrations depend upon the type of concentration, and upon diverse historical circumstances and ethnic-group characteristics. Almost any ethnic divisions in labour markets, including divisions by occupation, firm, industry, or work group, may have negative effects on the members of low-status ethnic groups. Most theorists discuss men only, but these ideas apply to women as well. Positive effects may arise in minority businesses, depending upon the conditions under which ethnic-community relationships lead to the mobilization of significant resources. Business success is complex, and the process within minority groups does not reduce to a few simple variables. Access to ethnic- and dominant-group markets for capital, labour, supplies, and products may all be important. The implications for male and female employees in minority businesses depend upon structures controlling the distribution of these resources within the group.

EMPIRICAL ASSESSMENT IN QUANTITATIVE LABOUR-MARKET RESEARCH

To study overall effects requires quantitative studies across multiethnic labour markets. Previous research has had two major limitations. One limitation is the small number of ethnic groups included in most studies, and the exclusion of women from most of them. The result is an inadequate consideration of the variety of situations in which ethnic concentrations arise. A second limitation arises from the difficulty of measuring ethnic concentration. Unfortunately, data sets most useful for measuring ethnic concentration often do not allow a proper analysis of inequality (using regression models with human-capital variables as controls).

Studies such as the one by Hodge and Hodge (1965), cited above, have provided labour-force data on occupational concentrations for U.S. blacks and women. Do negative effects arise for higher-status minorities, or for other types of ethnic concentration? To varying degrees, ethnic concentrations exist in various groups of high and low status, and they exist at various levels of the occupational structure. They also vary in the extent to which they involve ethnic autonomy in specific businesses, networks of businesses, or sectors of industries.

In Toronto, low-status groups such as the West Indians (see Pineo 1977; and also the findings reported by Breton in chapter 5 of this volume) are employed in low-status jobs as security guards and taxi drivers, but also in higher-status jobs within the health-service sector.

The Chinese, too, work in low-status service occupations, and also in technical fields and science. The Jewish work in garment trades, and also in the high-status professions of law and medicine. Occupational concentration sometimes leads to minority business, and sometimes not. The effects vary. The Italian concentration in construction includes occupational concentration, sometimes in Italian businesses and sometimes in Italian work groups in organizations managed by members of other groups. Many minority businesses do not involve occupational specialization, but do involve ethnic products or services.

Ethnic concentration has been described in quantitative studies that do not examine regression effects in human-capital models. There have been labour force-wide studies using census data (see Hutchinson 1956; Bergmann 1971; Hechter 1978), and there have been studies of concentration within specific occupations such as law (see Carlin 1966). The most comprehensive census-based study in Canada is Turritin's (1974) study of Toronto. He reported patterns of ethnic occupational concentration for hundreds of occupations, with greater concentration in low-status occupations. However, to show the actual effects of ethnic concentrations on occupational mobility for minority ethnic groups was not possible in the census data.

Model (1985a, 1985b) analysed 1910 census data on the concentration of blacks, Jewish, and Italians in 119 industries in New York City. The analysis employed regression models for occupational-status attainment, and found that the degree of industrial concentration has a negative relation to occupational success. The presence of minority group 'gatekeepers,' by contrast, had a positive effect. Although Model's regression equations contained measures of assimilation and English literacy, they excluded levels of education or other human-capital variables.

Studies of minority business have shown positive regression effects on incomes for the entrepreneurs themselves (see Aldrich 1980; Wilson and Portes 1980; Waldinger 1984; Borjas 1986; Portes and Manning 1986; Sanders and Nee 1987). However, the interpretation of income data for self-employed persons is uncertain. One problem is an inevitable selection bias arising because currently self-employed persons are relatively successful entrepreneurs. Failed entrepreneurs often return to employment. The remaining self-employed earn high incomes, but self-employment itself may lead to low incomes.

Another problem is an income-measurement bias. Income data on the self-employed are not comparable to income data on employed persons. The meaning of the term 'income' for most employed persons is the number of dollars the employer agrees to pay. It is part of a formal agreement. The meaning of income for the self-employed is different. It is a number determined in year-end accounting, based on total receipts for sales or professional fees, minus expenses. This is a complex calculation, perhaps carried out only to prepare an income tax return. Incomes reported by self-employed persons in our sample may not be comparable to income reported by employed persons. Borjas (1986: 487) noted that incomes from self-employment may include returns to physical capital as well. Reported incomes from self-employment in family businesses may include contributions by wives or other dependent family members.

In any case, regarding minority businesses, the important empirical questions concern the causes and effects of business success. What is the impact that ethnic resources have in offsetting the marginal location of ethnic businesses? How are the fruits of that success distributed among employers and employees within the ethnic group?

RESEARCH QUESTIONS AND DATA-ANALYSIS METHODS

Based on previous research and theory, this study should compare men and women in ethnic groups varying by ethnic status and occupational composition. Another requirement is to tap the following types of ethnic concentration: (a) ethnic occupations;[2] (b) minority businesses, including the self-employed entrepreneurs, and employees; and (c) ethnic work groups and other ethnic networks related to employment, including relations to supervisors, subordinates, co-workers, and customers. These variables are independent of each other; each may have direct effects or effects that are conditional. Ethnic occupations or work groups may have one set of effects for minority businesses, because they reflect access to useful group resources. They may have other effects in mainstream organizations, if they represent barriers and are seen as liabilities.

Survey data can measure all these aspects of ethnic concentration. An estimate of the extent of ethnic relationships at work is available from the 1973 Non-official Languages survey (O'Bryan, Reitz, and Kuplowska 1976). The survey asked about languages used with co-workers, among respondents in five Canadian cities (including Toronto). This criterion of language use provides only a minimum estimate, because some ethnic relationships at work do not involve the use of a minority language. Overall, about one in four workers within minority language groups said they used an ethnic language with co-workers. The highest proportions are in Italian, Greek, and Portuguese groups (one-third to one-half). Significant proportions exist for all except Dutch and Scandinavians (see Reitz 1980b).

Occupational status is the focus of some studies (for example, Model 1985a, 1985b), while income is the focus of others (for example, Wilson and Portes 1980). These may be affected in different ways by ethnic concentrations. Occupational status (or prestige) was the traditional focus of sociological studies of mobility, and is still important to the position of newly established cultural minorities. Recent sociological analyses of labour markets concern income primarily, extending work by economists. Both job rewards are important, and it is possible that mobility within an ethnic enclave may have implications for status but not income, or vice versa.

The following specific research questions are asked about each of the ethnic groups in the study, about men and women within each group, and about each type of ethnic concentration:

1 Is it necessary for minority group members to abandon ethnic concentrations if they want to achieve equality with other ethnic groups?
2 Are there actual effects of ethnic concentrations on the chances for occupational and economic mobility and equality? Are there negative effects when ethnic concentrations reflect discriminatory disadvantages and barriers? And are there positive effects in certain circumstances, when ethnic concentrations represent advantages compared to the mainstream work world? If so, which circumstances and why?

The first question is comparatively simple. It asks where, within a vertical hierarchy of rewards, one typically finds minority ethnic occupations and work-settings. To what extent does the 'ethnic enclave' consist of unattractive, poorly rewarded jobs at the bottom of the occupational hierarchy? This is a descriptive question, a question of who gets what.

This descriptive question is important because of its implications for the choices facing minority group members. If ethnic occupations are available only at certain levels of status or income, then improvement implies movement away from ethnic occupations. In effect, abandonment of an ethnic enclave is a prerequisite for ethnic equality and incorporation in society.

The second question is more complex. It asks about the advantages or disadvantages of ethnic concentrations for persons of equivalent job qualifications. To answer such questions requires comparisons of occupational status and income adjusted for the impact of varying job qualifications.

The proper method for this purpose is multiple-regression analysis. Regression procedures are conventionally used by sociologists and economists to estimate the independent contribution of individual characteristics in determining occupational status and income. In multiple-regression analysis, occupational status and income are expressed as mathematical functions of individual characteristics, including job qualifications. Coefficients of each individual characteristic measure its causal contribution to status or income determination. The estimation of successive regression equations, with different combinations of variables included, sheds light on the structure of causal sequences. Thus, ethnic origin can be added to a regression equation, with job qualifications such as education and experience included, to examine the impact of ethnic origin on status or income after taking account of the effects of job qualifications. The procedure also is used to assess the effects of ethnic concentrations within each ethnic group, after taking account of the effects of job qualifications. The analyses presented in this chapter make extensive use of multiple-regression techniques.

The analysis includes men and women in the majority group and seven ethnic minorities. (It does not include the first- and second-generation English-origin group.) The labour force includes full- and part-time employees, the self-employed, and persons laid off or looking for work (weighted $N = 1668$; $N = 1791$).

Inequalities of Occupational Status and Income among Ethnic Groups

The first step is to measure ethnic inequality. There is already a lot of research on ethnic inequality in Toronto and Canada. Data for this study parallel the results from previous studies, and also extend them in certain respects. This section begins with a review of previous research, to put the present research in context.

Porter (1965) first described for males the pattern of unequal ethnic representation in occupational groups reflecting occupational status. Using national census data, he found that Jewish and Anglo-Saxon males had the highest occupational status. The French and various north and east European groups ranked lower, while south Europeans and native Canadians had the lowest occupational status. Studies by Richmond (1967a) and Blishen (1970) confirmed Porter's findings about the relative occupational status of males in these groups.

Lack of job qualifications, mainly education, explains most of the lower occupational 'entrance statuses' for European immigrant groups in Canada. In the second and later generations, the levels of education and occupation status improve considerably. Level of education strongly influences occupational status. Research by Raynauld et al. (1969) shows that ethnic differences in status are much smaller when educational backgrounds are similar (see also Kalbach 1970; Tepperman 1975; Darroch 1979; and Reitz 1980a, 1980b).

Recent immigration has produced a rapid increase in racial minority populations, the so-called 'visible minorities.' The earlier studies gave little attention to these new minorities. The patterns observed before for European groups may not apply to racial minorities, because racial minorities appear to experience more discrimination (see MacKie 1985; Henry and Ginsberg 1985; Henry 1986; Reitz 1988a, 1988b).

Studies including racial minorities have produced varying results, however. In a 1970 Toronto survey, Goldlust and Richmond (1973) found ethnic effects on incomes among various groups of immigrant males, not just racial minorities. They showed that, given equivalent social origin, years of education, present occupational status, age, years of residence in Toronto, and years of post-secondary education, immigrant men of English and Jewish origin earned about $500–800 more than those of western European or Italian origin, $2,100–2,300 more than those of Slavic, Greek, or Portuguese origins, and $3,800 more than Asians or blacks (see Li 1978 for a reanalysis of these data).

A later study by Richmond and Verma (1978) found considerable income mobility for Canadian males of both European and Asian origin. Even in this study, however, third-generation persons of 'black and mixed racial origins' were less successful when qualifications are similar. The data did not show whether the other racial minority immigrants will experience the same income mobility as Asians. On the basis of their results, Richmond and Verma suggested that the racial minorities experience significant discrimination, and that the resulting mobility patterns vary from group to group.

Based on 1971 census data for Toronto (and certain other cities), Richmond and Kalbach (1980) also found income disadvantages for racial minority groups that did not stem from qualifications. In most ethnic groups, immigrants earn less and the Canadian-born earn more. Asian immigrants aged 35–44 earned an average of $7,733, while Canadian-born Asians of the same age earned an average of $10,447. This latter figure is only about $500 less than incomes earned by the corresponding British-origin group. There were no data on West Indian blacks. However, an 'all other' group did not experience the same income mobility. This analysis does not explicitly show the impact of education or job qualifications as explanatory variables. However, the improved position of Canadian-born Asians over foreign-born is a sign that upward income mobility is possible for Asians.

Many studies of ethnic inequality do not include women, and many studies of gender inequality do not examine ethnic groups (see Ostry 1968; Gunderson 1976; Robb 1978; Gunderson and Reid 1983). What is the position of women in each ethnic group? Very likely, ethnic and gender disadvantages to some extent combine to produce a double disadvantage for minority-group women. In the United States, there is ample evidence of disadvantage among black women, a situation of 'double jeopardy' (see Bluestone 1973; Lerner 1972; Seidman 1978).

However, ethnic inequality may not be exactly the same for men and women. Epstein (1973) showed that black-white inequality in the United States is less for women than for men in certain sectors of the labour force. Black women represent a larger proportion among all professional women than black men do among professional men. After extensively interviewing a group of black professional women, Epstein suggested two reasons for gender differences in racial inequality. First, white men may perceive less threat from black women than from black men. Second, black women may stress financial independence because of their formative experiences. Compared to white women, black women feel more responsible for their own welfare. They are less susceptible to the dream of the 'good life through marriage.' Thus, structural factors and socialization patterns may produce different patterns of ethnic inequality for women.

For Canada, Boyd (1975) suggested an opposite pattern: greater ethnic inequality among women. She compared the occupations of male and female immigrants with those of native-born Canadians. Foreign-born women have lower status compared to native-born women and to foreign-born men. There was no analysis of job qualifications in the data. However, differences in culture and socialization between native- and foreign-born groups could account for some of the inequalities (for evidence of socialization differences, see Danziger 1974 and Simmons and Turner 1976). Boyd suggests that discriminatory practices against immigrant women are particularly severe.

In sum, previous research on ethnic inequality in Canada has shown that for most European-origin ethnic groups, significant inequalities stem mainly from lack of education. Usually these inequalities end within a generation following immigration. More recent immigrants from third-world countries are less well studied. Available evidence suggests that discrimination against those groups is more significant, and may result in real inequalities among persons with similar job qualifications. Less evidence exists on minority women. We know little about the double disadvantage of ethnicity and gender.

The following data analysis replicates some findings and adds to them. It shows inequality for smaller groups such as the Chinese and the Portuguese, for women as well as men, and in relation to job qualifications. The analysis provides the background for the later analysis of the effects of ethnic concentration.

OCCUPATIONAL-STATUS INEQUALITIES AMONG ETHNIC GROUPS

Occupational status refers to the prestige of jobs as seen by the general population. High-status occupations are those that most people think of as having a high standing in the community. High status is an important job reward, and often leads as well to high incomes. The standard measure of occupational status for Canadian census occupational categories is the one developed by Blishen (see Blishen and McRoberts 1976).[3]

Ethnic inequality of occupational status in Toronto affects mainly the Italians, Portuguese, and West Indians (see table 4.1, first column). The mean occupational statuses for both men and women in these groups are significantly lower than for members of other ethnic groups included in this study. Majority Canadian males have a mean-occupational-status score of roughly 50 points, and the Germans, Ukrainians, Jewish, and Chinese follow close behind. West Indians are 8 points lower, Italians 12 points lower, and the Portuguese 18 points lower.

The mean occupational statuses of women in the sample are not very different from those of men, but the status measure is not properly sensitive to gender differences in occupations.[4] Among minority-ethnic-group women, the Germans, Ukrainians, and Jewish are within four points of the Majority Canadian women. Chinese women are 7 points lower, Italian women 10 points lower, West Indians 13 points

TABLE 4.1
Mean occupational status and income, by gender and ethnic origin

Gender	Ethnic origin	Mean occupational status[a]	Mean incomes[b]	(*WN*; *N*)[c]
Male	Majority	50.0	$18,546	(373; 109)
	German	46.2	17,450	(83; 159)
	Ukrainian	45.7	16,995	(47; 177)
	Italian	38.4	15,933	(224; 157)
	Jewish	52.0	19,984	(80; 169)
	Portuguese	32.1	14,746	(39; 99)
	Chinese	50.3	16,336	(26; 69)
	West Indian	41.5	14,522	(60; 79)
	Total	45.4	17,299	(934; 1018)
Female	Majority	52.2	10,686	(294; 86)
	German	48.2	9,802	(65; 113)
	Ukrainian	49.8	10,871	(30; 170)
	Italian	41.9	8,246	(111; 88)
	Jewish	50.3	8,663	(46; 96)
	Portuguese	33.4	7,537	(21; 49)
	Chinese	45.6	10,490	(20; 53)
	West Indian	39.1	8,699	(48; 58)
	Total	47.7	9,771	(637; 663)

a Blishen scores
b Individual gross annual income from employment. Estimates based on mid-point approximation for each income category. Highest male category ($25,000+) set at $30,000 (17.2% of weighted responses); female distribution maximum set at $15,000 (18.5% of weighted responses).
c Minimum weighted and unweighted cases. Actual cases are somewhat higher for occupational status. Total weighted *N* = 1571; unweighted *N* = 1681. Total weighted *N* in labour force = 1668; unweighted *N* = 1791. (Missing data maximum: 110 cases or 6.1%.)

lower, and the Portuguese 19 points lower. The most important difference between men and women in occupational status is among the Chinese; the relative position of the Chinese women is somewhat lower than that of Chinese men.

INCOME INEQUALITY AMONG ETHNIC GROUPS

The income figures examined in this study are individual annual incomes from employment.[5] Incomes in Toronto are only moderately related to occupational status (for men, $r = 0.445$; for women, $r = 0.470$). This finding is consistent with results reported elsewhere. Occupational status affects income, but other factors are also at work, so income must be analysed separately.

Majority Canadian men earn roughly $18,500 on the average (in 1978/79 dollars, of course; see table 4.1, second column). Jewish men earn about 8% more (close to $20,000), while the Germans, Ukrainians, Chinese, and Italians earn 5 to 15% less (between $16,000 and $17,500). The most extreme income inequalities affect the Portuguese and West Indians. Members of these groups have mean incomes near $14,500, thus earning about 23% less than members of the majority group.

These ethnic income inequalities among men to some extent are similar to the occupational-status inequalities, but there are two differences. One difference affects Italian men. Italian men have low mean occupational status (like the Portuguese and West Indians) yet earn incomes somewhat higher than expected on that basis. Italian occupational statuses are less than those of Majority Canadians by 12 points, almost one full standard deviation of 14.6. Italian incomes are lower by $2,600, much less than the standard deviation of $7,700. For Italian men, occupational-status inequality exists despite relatively little income inequality.

Chinese men, by contrast, have high occupational status but not correspondingly high incomes. Chinese occupational statuses are similar to those of Majority Canadians, but Chinese incomes average at least 10% less. For Chinese men, the main inequality is income inequality.

For women, ethnic income inequality is similar to that for men. In our estimates, the average income of women is 56.5% of that for men ($9,771 as a percentage of $17,299). German and Ukrainian women earn incomes very close to the incomes of Majority Canadian women, on the average. Italian, Portuguese, and West Indian women earn much less. The income disadvantage for these three groups of women, between $2,000 and $3,000, is less in terms of absolute dollars than the corresponding disadvantage for men, but in terms of percentages it is comparable. Thus, for example, the West Indian male incomes are $4,000 less than those of the majority group, or 22% less. The West Indian female incomes are $2,000 less than those of the majority group, which is 19% less. So in percentage terms the disadvantage of West Indian women is comparable to the disadvantage of West Indian men. Thus, for the Germans and Ukrainians on the one hand, and the Italian, Portuguese, and West Indians on the other, the female income distribution corresponds to the distribution among men.

One interesting difference between men and women in ethnic income inequality affects the Chinese. Among men the Chinese earn somewhat less than expected on the basis of occupational status; but for women this difference is not evident. The Chinese women earn incomes similar to those of Majority Canadian women. If anything, incomes for Chinese women are high in relation to occupational status.

The other difference between occupational status and income inequalities that we saw for men – the higher incomes for Italian men in relation to status – also does not appear to carry over to affect Italian women. Italian women have incomes comparable to those of Portuguese and West Indian women. Italian men have incomes somewhat higher than those of Portuguese or West Indian men.

The case of the Jewish women is also interesting. The average incomes of Jewish women are quite low. They are similar to the average incomes of Italian, Portuguese, and West Indian women. However, statistical procedures affect the computation of income averages for Jewish women. The standard deviation of incomes for Jewish women is unusually high (as it is for Jewish men). The truncation of the income distribution affects this group differently, obscuring the high-income sector of the group.

In sum, ethnic status inequalities affect mainly the Italians, Portuguese, and West Indians, for both men and women. Ethnic income inequalities affect the same groups, with some exceptions. Among men, Italians earn higher incomes than expected on the basis of status. Chinese men earn somewhat lower incomes. For women, these exceptions do not apply. Among women, the Chinese do not earn lower incomes than expected on the basis of status. Italian women do not earn higher incomes than expected on the basis of status. Ethnic status inequality is similar for men; ethnic income inequality is somewhat different.

Census Comparison

To test income data from the 1978/79 Toronto sample, it is useful to compare 1981 census data. For each ethnic group, table 4.2 presents average[6] wages and self-employment incomes for men and women aged 18 to 65 in the Toronto CMA labour force (using the Public Use Sample Tape, containing a 2% sample). There is general agreement between the two data sources, despite certain discrepancies.

For men, mean incomes in each group in the sample are within about 6% of mean incomes as measured by the census, with two exceptions:

the Jewish and Chinese. For them, the sample income means are 10.3 and 13.5% higher than the census means, respectively. The rank-order of groups in mean income level is similar for both data sources, except for the Chinese. Members of the majority group, plus Jewish, Germans, and Ukrainians, are near the top; the Italians, Portuguese, and West Indians are near the bottom.

In the sample data for men, the ethnic inequalities of income were different from the ethnic inequalities of status. Italians earned more than predicted on the basis of status; Chinese earned less. The census data show the same pattern. Chinese incomes in the census data are in fact even lower than shown by the sample data. In the sample, Chinese incomes are slightly higher than Italian incomes, and closer to those of Ukrainians. In the census, Chinese incomes are lower than Italian, closer to those of Portuguese and West Indians. Thus, the tendency for Chinese men to earn lower-than-expected incomes, noted in the survey data analysis, is if anything more extreme in the census data.

For women, the census comparison again shows significant agreement. There are certain discrepancies here as well. In the census analysis, Majority Canadian, Ukrainian, German, and Chinese women all have similar mean incomes, in agreement with the sample data. In both census and sample data, the greatest ethnic inequality affects the Portuguese, and the Italians are next-lowest in mean incomes. However, note that in the census data, the mean income for Canadian-born persons of British origin is 14.5% lower than the mean income measured for Majority Canadians in the survey data. Moreover, in the census data, the mean income for West Indian women is similar to that of the Majority Canadian women, which was not the case in the sample data. In the census, the incomes of Jewish and Italian women also appear relatively high, compared to the sample data. Thus, the census data show less ethnic inequality among women than was observed in the sample data.

In sum, the sample data and census data are consistent in many respects, though there are differences. The census shows the incomes of Chinese men to be relatively lower than shown in the sample data. The census shows the incomes of West Indian women to be relatively higher than in the sample. Incomes of Jewish women may not be well-measured in the survey data statistics. Ethnic inequality among women appears less in the census data than in the sample data.

The degree of consistency between the sample and the census supports use of the sample data for correlational analysis. Use of the data

TABLE 4.2
Comparison of sample income data with 1981 census data

Gender	Ethnic origin	Immigration status	Sample (table 4.1)	Census[a] Mean[b]	Census[a] (N)	Sample vs. census % diff.	Sample vs. census Rank order
Male	Major Can.[c]	Can.-born	18,546		–	+6.2	2-3
	British	Total	–	17,875	(8306)		
		Can.-born	–	17,463	(6331)		
	German	Total	17,450	18,694	(611)	–6.7	3-1
	Ukrainian	Total	16,995	16,727	(211)	+1.6	4-4
	Italian	Total	15,933	15,515	(1910)	+2.7	6-5
	Jewish	Total	19,984	18,117	(634)	+10.3	1-2
	Portuguese	Total	–	14,459	(529)		
		Immig.	14,746	14,632	(516)	0.8	7-6
	Chinese	Total	–	14,268	(470)		
		Immig.	16,336	14,389	(429)	+13.5	5-8
	West Indian	Total	–	14,299	(397)		
		Immig.	14,522	14,391	(377)	+0.9	8-7
	Other	Total	–	16,126	(4724)		
Female	Major Can.[c]	Can.-born	10,868		–	+17.8	2-2
	British	Total	–	9,288	(6687)		
		Can.-born	–	9,226	(5029)		
	German	Total	9,802	8,896	(477)	+10.2	4-5
	Ukrainian	Total	10,871	10,034	(254)	+8.3	1-1
	Italian	Total	8,246	8,154	(1199)	+1.1	7-7
	Jewish	Total	8,663	9,066	(475)	–4.4	6-3
	Portuguese	Total	–	7,443	(368)		
		Immig.	7,537	7,476	(349)	+0.8	8-8
	Chinese	Total	–	8,559	(432)		
		Immig.	10,490	8,634	(400)	+21.5	3-6
	West Indian	Total	–	8,846	(406)		
		Immig.	8,699	8,939	(389)	–3.0	5-4
	Others	Total	–	8,781	(3803)		

a 1981 Public use sample tape data, Toronto CMA, labour-force participants aged 18–65, 2 per cent sample.
b For census data, income distributions were capped to match sample distribution; see note b to table 4.1. Approximately the same proportions of male and female respondents were affected in census and sample data.
c For Majority Canadians, the census comparison group is Canadian-born of British origin.

to explain specific income inequalities may be uncertain in the few cases of significant sample/census discrepancies. Where there are discrepancies, these should be considered in interpreting the sample data analysis.

THE IMPACT OF JOB QUALIFICATIONS

How do ethnic differences in job qualifications, or human capital, affect ethnic differences in status and income? Which ethnic differences are not explained by job qualifications? As stated earlier, the procedure to answer these questions is multiple-regression analysis. However, several considerations affect the interpretation of such analyses.

Usually, in regression equations for status and income, effects of ethnic origin not due to job qualifications are interpreted as evidence of discrimination. This interpretation is an approximation. The amount of discrimination is both overestimated and underestimated in this approximation (see Reitz 1980b: 157–8). Discrimination is overestimated to the extent that unmeasured qualifications vary by ethnic origin. Discrimination is underestimated when job qualifications are themselves discriminatory, or when there is discriminatory access to qualifications. We know that employers sometimes rely on educational credentials as job qualifications when there is no real functional justification. This practice discriminates against immigrants lacking formal education. In addition, when discrimination reduces work experience, the effects are compounded. The regression procedures do not identify either of these discriminatory effects.

This analysis considers three job qualifications: years of formal education, years of work experience, and knowledge of English. Years of work experience is computed as the difference between current age and age of the first full-time job, minus the reported number of intervening years not working. Note that work experience to some extent also reflects on-the-job training. English proficiency also is an important job qualification (Tainer 1988). The analysis also takes account of current working hours, whether a person is currently working full-time or part-time or is unemployed.

Impact of Job Qualifications across All Ethnic Groups

The first step is to estimate regression equations for all ethnic groups combined. Table 4.3 shows zero-order correlation matrices, for men and women separately. Years of education has a negative relation to work experience, particularly for men ($r = -0.464$), but also for women

($r = -0.265$). There are two reasons. Levels of education have improved over time, so relatively inexperienced young people are better educated. Education also delays labour-force entry. The correlations also show that those with more work experience lack knowledge of English ($r = -0.353$ for men, -0.105 for women), because immigrants have more work experience. Immigrants often began working at a younger age than is typical in Canada, partly because they are less well-educated.

The regression equation for occupational-status determination (table 4.4, first column) shows that years of education has the most important effect ($\beta = 0.660$ for men, 0.544 for women). Work experience has much less impact, a sign that there is little career mobility in occupational status.

Knowledge of English and current hours have little effect on occupational status. Knowledge of English is undoubtedly an important qualification for high-status jobs, but has little impact in the regression equations, probably for at least two reasons. First, even among immigrants a practical knowledge of English is so widespread that variations are not statistically useful predictors of occupational status. Second, most immigrants lacking English also lack formal education, and for this reason move into low- or middle-status occupations. These jobs have much less stringent English-language requirements.

Two income equations have been estimated. Equation (1) includes job qualifications only. Equation (1) is reported in the second and third columns of table 4.4. Equation (2) includes occupational status as well. It is reported in the fourth and fifth columns of table 4.4. Metric regression coefficients (unstandardized *b*),[7] as well as the standardized coefficients (β), are presented.

Work experience and hours have much stronger effects on income than on occupational status, particularly among men. This can be seen in table 4.4 by comparing income equation (1) with the equation for occupational status. Progress through the career or life cycle leads to very significantly increased incomes, particularly when adjustments have been made for the lower educational level of older workers.

Education also affects income, though less than it affects status. Note that when occupational status is included in equation (2), the education effect on income is much less ($\beta = 0.111$ compared to $\beta = 0.368$ when occupational status is not included). This means that education affects income primarily because it affects occupational status, and only secondarily because it affects incomes within occupational-status groups.

TABLE 4.3
Correlation matrices for analysis of occupational status and income determination, by gender

Male (886; 963)	1	2	3	4	5	6
1. Education, years	–					
2. Work experience, years[a]	–0.464	–				
3. Current hours[b]	–0.006	0.031	–			
4. Knowledge of English[c]	0.542	–0.353	–0.004	–		
5. Occup. status	0.648	–0.206	0.122	0.401	–	
6. Income	0.264	0.125	0.214	0.169	0.445	–

Female (575; 591)	1	2	3	4	5	6
1. Education, years	–					
2. Work experience	–0.265	–				
3. Current hours	0.199	–0.064	–			
4. Knowledge of English	0.509	–0.105	0.135	–		
5. Occup. status	0.641	–0.141	0.211	0.457	–	
6. Income	0.403	0.096	0.297	0.229	0.470	–

a Work experience in years is current age, minus age at first full-time job, minus intervening years not working.
b Full-time or self-employed = 1.0; part-time = 0.5; laid off or looking for work = 0.0
c Rating by interviewer of respondents' ability to speak English: very well = 3; somewhat well = 2; not very well = 1

Occupational status in itself affects incomes, however, even after considering education and other qualifications. For men, $R^2 = 0.195$ for the effect of job qualifications and hours alone (equation 1). R^2 increases to 0.278 with occupational status in the equation (equation 2). For women, the figures are $R^2 = 0.257$, increasing to $R^2 = 0.342$. Thus, the importance of occupational status as a job reward is twofold. High status is a job reward in itself, and it increases incomes as well.

Ethnic Differences in Job Qualifications

Table 4.5 shows ethnic differences in job qualifications. The first column focuses on education. Majority Canadian men and women in the Toronto labour force both have roughly 13–14 years of education on the average. Jewish and Chinese persons average as many years of education or more. Other groups have less education. German and Ukrainians average about one year less. West Indians average just over two years less education than Majority Canadians. The least well educated

TABLE 4.4
Regression coefficients for determination of occupational status and income, by gender; with job qualifications and hours entered (1); and with occupational status also entered (2)

	Regression equation				
	Occup. status	Income			
		(1)		(2)	
	β	β	*b*	β	*b*
Male (886; 963)					
Education, years	0.660	0.368	624	0.111	189
Work experience, years	0.127	0.318	179	0.268	152
Current hours	0.122	0.206	8801	0.158	6762
Knowledge of English	0.089	0.082	1044	0.048	603
Occupational status	*[a]	*	*	0.390	200
Multiple *R*	0.672	0.442		0.528	
R^2	0.454	0.195		0.278	
Constant	–	–	–4536	–	–4822
Female (575; 591)					
Education, years	0.544	0.409	408	0.230	229
Work experience, years	0.027	0.220	75	0.211	72
Current hours	0.081	0.228	3109	0.201	2746
Knowledge of English	0.172	0.013	96	–0.043	–312
Occupational status	*	*	*	0.329	94
Multiple *R*	0.663	0.507		0.563	
R^2	0.440	0.257		0.342	
Constant	–	–	–1118	–	–262

a Star (*) indicates variables not in equation.

groups are the Italians and Portuguese. Italians average 9 to 10 years of education; Portuguese average 6 years of education.

Minority groups tend to have more work experience than Majority Canadians. Table 4.5, second column, shows that Majority Canadian men have about 15.2 years of work experience. German, Chinese, and West Indians have slightly more. Ukrainian, Italian, Jewish, and Portuguese men in Toronto have many more years of experience – between 20 and 24 years.

Ethnic differences in work experience vary for women. Majority Canadian women average 3.6 years less work experience than Majority Canadian men, mainly because of career discontinuities.[8] German,

TABLE 4.5
Occupational status and income determinants, by gender and ethnic origin

Gender	Ethnic origin	Education (years)	Work experience (years)	Current hours	Knowledge of English	(*WN*; *N*)
Male	Majority	13.7	15.2	0.96	3.00	(370; 108)
	German	12.7	19.7	0.94	2.94	(86; 162)
	Ukrainian	12.6	22.9	0.96	2.75	(47; 176)
	Italian	9.2	22.4	0.91	2.30	(231; 189)
	Jewish	14.4	20.3	0.92	2.89	(82; 175)
	Portuguese	6.0	23.4	0.93	1.73	(40; 100)
	Chinese	14.5	17.2	0.95	2.26	(27; 69)
	West Indian	11.2	17.0	0.99	3.00	(61; 80)
	Total	12.0	18.7	0.94	2.73	(943; 1029)
Female	Majority	13.6	11.6	0.89	3.00	(291; 85)
	German	12.7	14.4	0.87	2.95	(62; 109)
	Ukrainian	12.2	16.1	0.91	2.85	(30; 120)
	Italian	10.0	11.4	0.79	2.49	(113; 91)
	Jewish	14.1	11.7	0.82	2.97	(44; 93)
	Portuguese	5.9	14.5	0.90	1.80	(22; 51)
	Chinese	12.5	12.9	0.93	2.13	(21; 56)
	West Indian	11.6	14.5	0.88	3.00	(40; 47)
	Total	12.3	12.4	0.87	2.82	(624; 652)

Chinese, Portuguese, and West Indian women have somewhat greater work experience than Majority Canadians, corresponding to the pattern for men in those groups. However, unlike men, Italian, Jewish, and Chinese women do not have substantially greater work experience than Majority Canadians.

Current hours are also less for women than for men, because women more often work part-time. There are small ethnic variations. For both men and women, current hours are least for the Italian and Jewish groups. Portuguese, Chinese, and Ukrainian women have a high average. The male-female gap in hours is least in these groups.

The fourth column of table 4.5 presents ethnic variations in knowledge of English. Knowledge of English has little impact in reward allocation, and so has little relevance for later analysis. Among both men and women, the Chinese, Portuguese, and Italians have significantly less knowledge of English, corresponding to their immigrant status.

Job Qualifications and Ethnic Inequalities

The final step in the analysis of inequality is to find out which ethnic inequalities are a result of ethnic differences in qualifications, and which are not. These inequalities net of job qualifications are indicated by regression effects for ethnic origins, with job qualifications in the equations. In table 4.6 the results are presented in a slightly modified form of regression analysis known as multiple classification analysis (MCA). MCA is useful in studying population subgroups. In MCA, results show ethnic inequalities of status and income after adjustment for the overall regression effects of job qualifications. Group comparisons are facilitated because results are presented in terms of group deviations from the mean.

MCA results show that most occupational-status inequality is explained by ethnic differences in job qualifications, mainly education (see table 4.6, comparing the first two columns). For most groups, the inequalities of occupational status remaining after adjustments for job qualifications are small. The statistic 'eta' measures variation across groups. When job qualifications are considered, eta measuring group differences in status declines from 0.40 to 0.09 for men, and from 0.41 to 0.20 for women. For German and Ukrainian men, the 4- to 5-point occupational-status deficit declines to between 2 and 3 points. For Italian and Portuguese men, status deficits of 12 and 19 points, respectively decline to less than one point or less after adjustments. Among women, the Italian and Portuguese inequalities of 10 and 17 points decline to a point or less.

West Indians are an exception. For them, job qualifications do not explain low occupational status. This finding indicates that there is status discrimination against West Indians, who have high levels of education but low occupational status. For West Indian men, there is a status disadvantage of between 4 and 5 points after adjustments for qualifications. For West Indian women the status disadvantage after adjustments is 10 points.

Significant income inequalities among ethnic groups remain after adjustments for education, work experience, and hours (table 4.6, third, fourth, and fifth columns). Consider first the men. The largest inequalities affect West Indians and Chinese. Men in these two groups have mean incomes $3,500 and $2,500 lower than the majority group, respectively, after adjustments for job qualifications. This difference represents a deficit of between 14 and 19%, compared to the mean majority income of $18,546, which is not explained by qualifications.

TABLE 4.6
Mean occupational status and income, by gender and ethnic origin; unadjusted deviation from the gender mean, and adjusted for gender-specific effects of job qualifications and hours (1), and adjusted also for effects of occupational status (2) (multiple classification analysis)

		Occup. status		Income			
Gender	Ethnic origin	Unadjusted	Adjusted (1)	Unadjusted	Adjusted (1)	Adjusted (2)	(*WN*; *N*)
Male	Majority	4.63	0.99	1301	413	220	(359; 105)
	German	0.25	–1.22	–154	–662	–425	(79; 152)
	Ukrainian	–0.04	–1.75	–81	–1062	–722	(44; 138)
	Italian	–7.27	–0.39	–1286	528	604	(206; 145)
	Jewish	6.07	0.83	2765	38	–123	(76; 160)
	Portuguese	–14.26	0.50	–2891	1794	1696	(31; 91)
	Chinese	4.86	0.66	–1218	–1939	–2067	(26; 66)
	West Indian	–4.20	–3.46	–3161	–3033	–2362	(58; 76)
	Eta	0.40	0.09	0.21	0.14	0.12	(886; 963)
Female	Majority	3.89	1.13	702	239	134	(281; 82)
	German	0.04	–1.00	–10	–298	–206	(56; 100)
	Ukrainian	1.45	1.56	782	506	362	(28; 112)
	Italian	–6.27	0.09	–1254	92	83	(94; 76)
	Jewish	2.86	0.17	–746	–1053	–1069	(40; 84)
	Portuguese	–13.62	0.35	–2112	–142	–177	(17; 39)
	Chinese	–2.83	0.74	307	275	206	(20; 52)
	West Indian	–9.59	–8.79	–1061	–879	–65	(39; 96)
	Eta	0.41	0.20	0.25	0.12	0.09	(565; 591)

For West Indians, some of this inequality is related to the inequality of occupational status. However, for both Chinese and West Indians, there are significant inequalities of income even among persons with similar occupational statuses (see equation 2 in the fifth column).

All other minority groups have incomes within $1,500 of the majority group after adjustments for qualifications. In percentage terms these incomes are within about 8% of the mean majority income. The high incomes of Jewish men do not appear so high after adjustments for high qualifications. The adjustment for job qualifications has little effect on Ukrainian or German men compared to Majority Canadian men. Their mean incomes remain within $1,000 or $2,000 of the Majority Canadian incomes.

Italian and Portuguese men have fairly high mean incomes relative to their level of education and work experience. Overall, Italian men have incomes $2,500 less than Majority Canadian men. After adjustments for education and experience, net Italian incomes are near the average for Majority Canadian men. The situation of Portuguese men is similar. In fact, relative to job qualifications, there is an income advantage of Portuguese men over Majority Canadian men of about $1,400.

Among women, we also find less income inequality after adjustment for qualifications. German and Ukrainian women are mostly unaffected by adjustments for job qualifications. For women, the greatest income inequalities affect Italians, Portuguese, and West Indians. As for the men, inequalities for Italian and Portuguese women largely disappear after adjustments for the effects of low job qualifications.

West Indian women experience significant income discrimination, according to the results, though not as much as West Indian men do. The analysis for West Indian women shows an income deficit of over $1,000 compared to Majority Canadian women (about 10% less) after adjustment for qualifications. These findings should be treated with caution, however. The census comparison left doubt about the relative incomes of West Indian women.

A similar caution should be expressed about the evidence from the survey of discrimination against Jewish women. The census comparison showed higher incomes for Jewish women, compared to Majority Canadian women.

SUMMARY

The findings about ethnic inequality in Toronto are broadly consistent with the results of previous studies, and extend them in certain respects. The Germans, Ukrainians, and Jewish basically have achieved equality. Average occupational statuses and incomes in these groups are comparable to those of Majority Canadians. Italians and Portuguese have lower average occupational status and incomes mainly because they lack education. Among the men in these groups, incomes are actually somewhat higher than expected on the basis of job qualifications and occupational status.

There is evidence of discrimination against racial minorities, in this case the Chinese and West Indians. These groups experience inequality even in relation to job qualifications. Chinese and West Indians differ, however. The Chinese have high levels of education, and do not suffer serious status disadvantages in relation to job qualifications. However, Chinese men do experience income inequality both overall and in relation to job qualifications. West Indian men have lower levels of education. For West Indians, both occupational statuses and incomes are lower than expected on the basis of qualifications. West Indian and Chinese men both have significant income disadvantages, even after adjustments for qualifications or for occupational status.

Ethnic disadvantages for women are in addition to disadvantages that stem from gender. The greatest differences in patterns of ethnic disadvantage for women compared to men affect racial minorities. Chinese women do not appear to experience significant income inequality. Among Chinese women, incomes are nearly equal to those of Majority Canadians, and are not low in relation to job qualifications. Findings on the incomes of West Indian (and also Jewish) women are ambiguous, based on the census comparison.

Measurement of Ethnic Concentrations in Labour Markets

With these patterns of ethnic inequality in mind, we now consider ethnic concentrations in labour markets. This part of the chapter measures the extent of various types of ethnic concentrations in each group. The next part of the chapter examines their effects on ethnic inequality.

ETHNIC CONCENTRATION IN OCCUPATIONS

To study the effects of ethnic concentration in occupations requires a knowledge of occupational specialties for each group in Toronto. This information is available from census data, on a gender-specific basis. We use this information here to construct an index of occupational concentration. Then, the index is used to classify survey respondents. The result is a measure of the extent to which individuals and groups work in occupations in which members of their own ethnic group are over-concentrated.

An Index of Ethnic Occupational Concentration

The census data come from a special tabulation from the 1971 census for Toronto (CMA). The table includes members of the labour force between the ages of 18 and 65, and distinguishes 177 occupational categories. The table generates, for each occupation, ethnic group, and gender, a rating of the degree of concentration.

As an example, consider the occupation of tailor. In the Canadian census classification of jobs, 'tailors and dressmakers' is one category (occupation 8553). In our special tabulation, to be sure of adequate cell size,[9] this category was combined with other related categories such as furriers, milliners, hat and cap makers, and pattern makers (occupations 8550, 8551, 8555, 8557, respectively). The combined category is called 'textile products.' The degree of over-concentration of Jewish men in this larger category is measured as follows. The category contains 3,652 men (in the Toronto CMA), of which 950 are Jewish and 2,685 are not Jewish. The overall labour force contains 684,500 men, of which 29,100 are Jewish and 655,400 are not. A measure of the concentration of Jewish men in the occupation is the ratio of the odds that a Jewish male is in textile products (950:29,100) to the odds that a non-Jewish male is in textile products (2685:655,400):

$$(950/29{,}100) \div (2{,}685/655{,}400) = 7.97$$

Thus, among men in the labour force, the Jewish are about eight times more likely than others to be tailors (or work in related occupations in textiles). (Of course only a minority of Jewish men are in this occupation – 3.3% – and a minority of men in the occupation are Jewish – 26%.) Men in other ethnic groups are less concentrated in this occupation. The index value for Italians is 3.4, and for Ukrainians it is 1.0.

There are distinct index values for the ethnic occupational concentration of women. For the index, women are compared to one another. It is found, for example, that the concentration of Jewish women as tailors is 1.2; for Italians it is 6.3; for Ukrainians it is 1.1, and so on. In computing values of the index, the relative concentration of men and women is not important. For example, the fact that women are less often tailors than are men has no effect on the index.

The value of the index of ethnic occupational concentration ranges between 0 and 16.8. A value of 1.00 for a specific occupation, ethnic group, and gender indicates that members of that ethnic group are neither over-concentrated nor under-concentrated in that occupation, compared to members of other ethnic groups of the same gender. A value of more (or less) than 1.00 indicates the extent to which ethnic group members are over- (or under-)concentrated in the occupation.

Table 4.7 shows the most pronounced instances of ethnic occupational concentration for each ethnic group in the Toronto survey. In these quantitative data, we can see the most highly visible and well-known instances of occupational concentration placed alongside less well-known cases. The data also show differences between men and women in the pattern of occupational concentration in each ethnic group.

Italian men are 16.8 times more likely than others to work as masons or tilesetters, and are concentrated in other construction work. They are also 14.4 times more likely to be barbers. Italian women work in textile products (as much as 11.5 times more likely than other women), and also in metal working, factory, and other work (including in the construction industry).

Jewish men are (as was mentioned in the illustration above) 8.0 times more likely than other men to work in textile products. They are also 6.0 times more likely to be physicians, 7.9 times more likely to be lawyers, and 3.5 times more likely to be university teachers. Jewish women are three or four times more likely than other women to work in sales (particularly real estate sales). Jewish women are also concentrated as social workers (2.7 times more likely), in commercial and fine art (2.3 times more likely), and as lawyers and social scientists.

In the other established groups, there are also significant patterns of concentration, though they are less visible. German men work in tool and die making (4.2 times more likely) and other metal-working occupations, and in food preparation. German women work in electrical products and as hairdressers. Ukrainian men work in railways, baking, and hotel management. Ukrainian women work as cleaners, and in food preparation. These cases of concentration are significant enough to be known to many within the group if not always outside it.

Members of the predominantly immigrant groups are concentrated in occupations of various types. Again some are stereotypical, and others less known. Chinese men work as cooks (5.2 times more likely), and in various service occupations (3.7 times more likely; this category includes laundering but not protective services, in which Chinese are not concentrated). Other Chinese men are concentrated in medical occupations (3.2 times more likely) and science and engineering (2.7 times more likely). Chinese women have jobs that overlap with Italian women (in textiles), but that are also distinctive (electronic data processing and office-machine operators).

West Indian men are concentrated in medical and health occupations (including as physicians), as welders (3.4 times more likely), clerks, guards, and taxi drivers. West Indian women also work in the medical field as nurses, in personal services, and in data processing.

The Portuguese men, like Italians, are concentrated in construction. Even more often, however, they work as janitors (4.6 times more likely

TABLE 4.7
Occupations of ethnic concentration, by gender, 1971

Ethnic origin	Male	Index	Female	Index
Germans	Tool and die making	4.2	Electrical products	1.8
	Food processing	2.4	Hairdressers	1.7
	Metal machining	2.4	Food prep. supervisors	1.6
	Mechanical and repair	2.0	Commercial and fine art	1.6
Ukrainian	Railway transp. oper.	2.6	Cleaners	2.4
	Bakers	2.4	Food processing	2.4
	Hotel and food services	2.3	Hotel managers	2.4
	Food processing	2.1		
Italians	Masons, tilesetters	16.8	Textile products	11.5
	Barbers	14.4	Sewing	9.8
	Construction labour	12.6	Materials processing	6.6
	Plasterer	11.4	Shoe, other textiles	6.3
	Excavation, paving	6.0	Metal working	5.2
			General labour	5.1
			Construction trades	4.9
			General factory work	4.6
			Rubber, plastic process	4.5
Jewish	Medical, health occup.	10.2	Sales supervisors	4.3
	Textile products	8.0	Sales, other	3.2
	Lawyers and notaries	7.9	Real estate sales	2.8
	Physicians and surgeons	6.0	Social work	2.7
	University teachers	3.5	Sales clerks	2.5
			Commercial and fine art	2.3
			Lawyers and notaries	2.3
			Social sciences	2.2
Portuguese	Construction labour	9.2	Cleaners	10.3
	Janitors	4.6	Hotel and food services	4.7
	Welders	3.0	Textile products	4.2
	General labour	2.8	Service occupations	3.2
	Carpenters	2.6		
	Excavation, paving	2.6		
	Food processing	2.4		
	Painters, wallpaperers	2.3		
Chinese	Chefs, waiters	5.2	Sewing	3.5
	Service occupations	3.7	Data processing	3.4
	Medical, health occup.	3.2	Hotel and food services	2.2
	Science and engineering	2.7		
West Indian	Medical, health occup.	3.9	Nursing aids	7.1
	Welding	3.4	Personal serv., general	6.6
	Reception, clerk	2.4	Nurses	3.7
	Guards	2.8	Data processing	2.3
	Physicians and surgeons	2.2		
	Taxi driver	2.1		

than other men). Portuguese women work as cleaners more often than do Ukrainian women (10.3 times more likely than other women).

Variations in Ethnic-Group Occupational Concentration

To assess the extent of labour-force involvement in ethnic occupations in each ethnic group, we return to the survey data. Each respondent is assigned an index value for ethnic occupational concentration, based on occupation, ethnic origin, and gender. For example, an Italian male barber is assigned an index value of 14.4. Table 4.8, first column, shows mean log-index[10] values for men and women in each minority group, and standard deviations. It also shows the proportion with index values over 2.0.

Among men, ethnic occupational concentration is extensive for Italians, Jewish, Chinese, and Portuguese. Between 40 and 60% or more of men in these groups work in ethnic occupations. Occupational concentration is less for West Indians, and least for Germans and Ukrainians. Women tend to be less concentrated than men in ethnic occupations. Over all groups, 22.1% of women work in ethnic occupations, compared to 31.2% of men. The ethnic variations are similar, however, except for West Indian women. West Indian women work in ethnic occupations twice as often as do West Indian men.

'ETHNIC ENTERPRISE': SELF-EMPLOYED MINORITY ENTREPRENEURS AND THEIR EMPLOYEES

A second type of ethnic concentration, distinct from ethnic occupations, is ethnic enterprise. In the Toronto sample, the minority-group self-employment rate is 18.9% for men and 6.2% for women. These rates are significantly higher than the majority-group rates (11.6% for men and 3.4% for women). There is quite a bit of ethnic variation in self-employment, shown both in the census[11] and sample data in table 4.9 (first two columns). Among men, Jewish and Italians have the highest rates of self-employment. Germans, Ukrainians, and Chinese also have rates of self-employment higher than for Majority Canadians. Portuguese and West Indians have rates below that level. For women, self-employment is much less significant, but the patterns of ethnic variation are similar.

To identify employees in minority businesses, the survey asked respondents about the ethnic origin of 'the people who manage this business or company' where they work (see table 4.9, third column).[12] Minority business is a significant employer mainly for the Italians and

TABLE 4.8
Concentration in ethnic occupations, by gender and ethnic origin

		Log-index[a]		%	
		Mean	SD	high[b]	(*WN*; *N*)
Male	German	0.98	0.26	1.8	(86; 164)
	Ukrainian	1.03	0.24	5.2	(48; 179)
	Italian	1.38	0.52	39.2	(242; 166)
	Jewish	1.41	0.61	43.9	(85; 180)
	Portuguese	1.58	0.68	66.1	(40; 102)
	Chinese	1.31	0.69	46.1	(28; 73)
	West Indian	1.10	0.42	13.4	(63; 83)
	Total	1.28	0.67	31.2	(593; 947)
Female	German	1.02	0.14	0.0	(67; 118)
	Ukrainian	0.99	0.20	2.5	(31; 126)
	Italian	1.10	0.81	26.4	(129; 102)
	Jewish	1.26	0.38	24.4	(53; 109)
	Portuguese	1.60	0.94	53.5	(24; 55)
	Chinese	1.24	0.54	36.4	(19; 49)
	West Indian	1.20	0.62	28.7	(49; 58)
	Total	1.15	0.63	22.1	(372; 617)

a A log-index has been used in the correlational analysis because of the skewness in the measured index of occupational concentration; the overall mean of the non-log index is 2.01; the standard deviation is 2.58. The log-index has been calibrated to retain the value of 0 at the low extreme, and the value 1 at the neutral point representing no over- or under-representation. The exact formula is log-index = $\ln((e-1)\text{index}+1)$, where e is the base for the natural logarithms; $\ln e = 1$.

b Per cent with index-values greater than or equal to 2.00, corresponding to log-index = 1.49.

Jewish, particularly among men. Employers and employees in the Italian-managed sector comprise over 40% of the entire male Italian labour force in Toronto. They comprise nearly 20% of the female Italian labour force. Employment in the Jewish-managed sector is even more prominent within the Jewish community, and comprises over half of the male Jewish labour force, and nearly half of the female Jewish labour force.

In other groups, there are few reported employees in ethnic enterprise. This is true even for Germans, Ukrainians, and Chinese, among whom self-employment is significant. Minority businesses in these groups generate relatively little employment. Most persons in these groups work in organizations managed by members of the majority

TABLE 4.9
Self-employment, employment in minority business, and other employment, by gender and ethnic origin; sample data and census comparison

		Census[a]		Sample			
Gender	Ethnic origin	% self-employed	(*N*)	% self-employed	% employed minority business	% employed other setting	(*WN*; *N*)
Male	Majority	8.2	(6312)	11.6	–	–	(383; 112)
	German	12.6	(610)	17.9	2.2	79.9	(88; 167)
	Ukrainian	10.0	(301)	10.6	4.9	84.5	(48; 180)
	Italian	12.6	(1903)	19.2	23.4	57.4	(246; 169)
	Jewish	29.3	(631)	42.0	18.8	39.2	(87; 183)
	Portuguese	6.6	(514)	4.2	4.6	91.2	(41; 103)
	Chinese	9.6	(426)	14.1	4.1	81.8	(28; 73)
	West Indian	4.5	(377)	5.5	0.9	93.6	(63; 83)
	Total	–	–	16.1	–	–	(984; 1070)
Female	Majority	2.5	(5006)	3.4	–	–	(305; 89)
	German	6.3	(476)	6.2	3.7	90.1	(67; 118)
	Ukrainian	2.0	(252)	0.9	5.0	94.1	(31; 126)
	Italian	3.0	(1191)	5.5	12.2	82.3	(129; 102)
	Jewish	9.6	(471)	16.6	34.7	48.7	(53; 109)
	Portuguese	0.6	(348)	8.7	3.9	87.4	(25; 57)
	Chinese	4.9	(390)	3.4	0.0	96.6	(23; 59)
	West Indian	1.8	(382)	0.0	0.0	100.0	(50; 61)
	Total	1.8	–	4.9	–	–	(683; 721)

a Public use sample tape, 1981 census, as in table 4.2. Comparison groups selected as in table 4.2.

group (or in some cases members of another minority ethnic group).

Minority businesses of course tend to be small (see table 4.10). The entrepreneurs themselves often operate extremely small firms. Among self-employed minority-group members, four in five work in organizations with 25 employees or less (82.9% of men; 83.4% of women). The typical employee in a minority business also works in a small organization (though of course somewhat larger – those with more employees). About half work in organizations with 25 employees or less (44.9% of men; 64.7% of women), and most others work in organizations with 500 employees or less. By contrast, of those working in organizations controlled by the dominant group, nearly half work in organizations with over 500 employees. About one-third work in organizations with

TABLE 4.10
Per cent in each size of work organization, by status as self-employed, employed in minority business, or mainstream employment, and by gender (seven minority groups only)

Gender	Employment status	Size of organization			
		Large (500+)	Middle (26–499)	Small (25 or less)	(*WN*; *N*)
Male	Self-employed	1.7	15.3	82.9	(109; 173)
	Employed in minority business	6.5	48.6	44.9	(81; 100)
	Employed in main-stream setting[a]	49.0	34.9	16.2	(403; 674)
Female	Self-employed	13.6	3.0	83.4	(23; 44)
	Employed in minority business	4.1	31.3	64.7	(39; 69)
	Employed in main-stream setting[a]	47.5	34.5	18.0	(309; 504)

a Includes all those employed in organizations managed by members of groups other than the respondent's own ethnic group.

between 25 and 500 employees, and only one in six work in organizations with 25 or fewer employees.

ETHNIC CONCENTRATION IN WORK GROUPS AND NETWORKS

Ethnic work groups and networks within organizations are likely to have different effects in mainstream settings than in minority business. In mainstream settings they may represent barriers to advancement, while in majority settings, they may provide access to ethnic-community resources. For example, Italians in construction-related occupations may find that in organizations controlled by non-Italians, Italian work groups become isolated from other parts of the organization. By contrast, in organizations controlled by Italians, Italian work groups are the most central. The effects may be different. These different effects could be particularly important in comparing groups such as Italians with other groups in which minority business is less significant as an employer. The effects may be positive or negative, depending upon circumstances.

The interview survey asked respondents about the ethnic origins of persons they contact at work. Possible ethnic concentrations in four types of working relationships (two for the self-employed) are shown in figure 2. For employees in mainstream or minority settings, the four working relationships are those with supervisors, co-workers, subordinates, and customers or clients met on the job. For the self-employed, subordinates and customers or clients are included. Each set of persons may affect the success of the job occupant. Working in a setting in which the supervisor is from the same background may affect job success. So can working in settings in which there are opportunities to employ or supervise members of one's own ethnic group. The salesman-customer relationship may be important even though it cuts across organization boundaries.

The interviews reveal significant intra-ethnic relationships for all four types of work relationships (see table 4.11). Among minority-group men, 10.8% reported working under the supervision of someone of the same ethnic origin, 24.5% reported they had co-workers at least one-quarter of whom are of the same ethnic origin, 16.6% reported that they had subordinates at least a quarter of whom were of the same ethnic origin, and 26.4% reported that they dealt with customers or clients of whom more than 'a few' were of the same ethnic origin. For minority-group women the percentages are similar (10.6, 28.6, 4.2, and 23.6, respectively). The main gender difference is in relation to subordinates. Only 4.2% of women report that they have subordinates more than a quarter of whom are members of their own ethnic group. This difference reflects the smaller proportion of women who have supervisory roles at work.

Ethnic groups vary in the types of intra-ethnic relations that are most prominent. Italians and Portuguese most often have ethnic co-workers and supervisors, but the Portuguese have fewer ethnic subordinates or customers. This difference reflects the smaller and less well-established character of the Portuguese business community. The most distinctive feature of the Jewish networks at work is the frequency of contacting Jewish customers or clients. Over half of the Jewish work force reports doing so, among both men and women. For the Chinese and West Indians, ethnic work groups and networks are weaker, only slightly stronger than for Germans and Ukrainians. The most prominent feature is the groups of co-workers. The West Indians, and the Chinese women, tend more often to have ethnic co-workers.

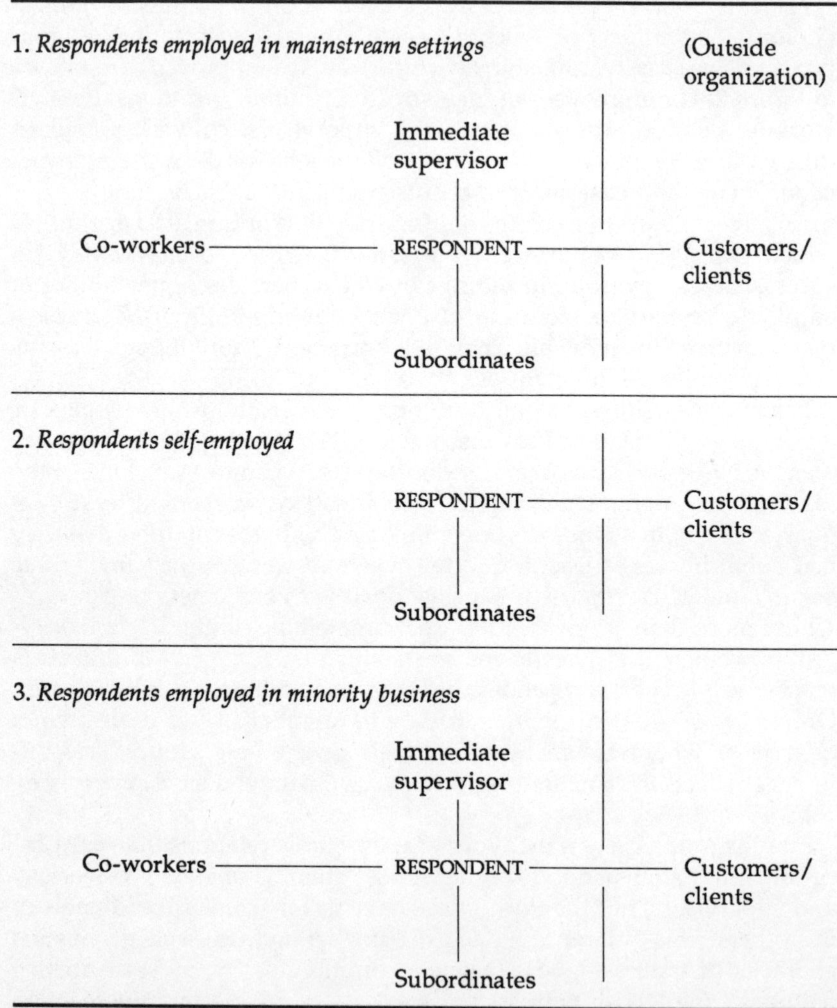

FIGURE 2 Structural diagrams representing potential ethnic work groups and networks, by employment status, measured for the Toronto Survey (survey measured ethnic composition of each position linked to respondent)

TABLE 4.11
Ethnic work groups and networks at work, by ethnic origin and gender (seven minority groups only)

Gender	Ethnic origin	Ethnic supervisor	Ethnic co-worker (25%+)	Ethnic subordinate (25%+)	Ethnic customer (more than few)	(*WN*; *N*)
Male	German	5.4	4.7	4.7	4.9	(88; 167)
	Ukrainian	5.9	11.5	6.2	7.5	(48; 180)
	Italian	18.2	38.5	28.3	38.6	(246; 169)
	Jewish	8.2	10.3	12.7	51.7	(87; 183)
	Portuguese	12.2	45.7	8.6	8.5	(41; 103)
	Chinese	1.3	10.0	15.6	9.6	(28; 73)
	West Indian	0.4	19.8	6.4	8.2	(63; 83)
	Total	10.8	24.5	16.6	26.4	(601; 958)
Female	German	7.8	3.7	2.3	8.1	(67; 118)
	Ukrainian	1.8	12.6	3.7	6.5	(31; 126)
	Italian	16.6	46.0	4.5	32.0	(129; 102)
	Jewish	11.1	28.1	9.6	50.5	(53; 109)
	Portuguese	13.1	40.1	8.2	10.8	(25; 57)
	Chinese	9.4	23.0	3.0	9.5	(23; 59)
	West Indian	3.3	24.4	0.0	17.4	(50; 61)
	Total	10.6	28.6	4.3	23.6	(378; 632)

RELATIONS AMONG TYPES OF ETHNIC CONCENTRATION

Ethnic occupations and ethnic work groups are much more prominent in minority settings (see table 4.12). In this sense, minority businesses are likely to be 'ethnic enterprises.' This fact is reflected in the data for the self-employed, and even more strongly in the data for employees in ethnic businesses. At the same time, self-employment is not always ethnic enterprise. Less than half the self-employed men (42.4%) were in ethnic specialty occupations, only one-third (36.1%) supervised persons more than a quarter of whom belong to their own ethnic group, and only half (53.2%) had more than a 'few' ethnic-group customers.

Ethnic Concentration and Ethnic Inequality

This section considers the relation between ethnic concentration and ethnic inequality. The first research question asks whether ethnic-group members must abandon ethnic concentrations to achieve equality. The

TABLE 4.12
Concentration in ethnic occupations, work groups, and networks, by status as self-employed, employed in minority business, or mainstream employment, and by gender (seven minority groups only)

Gender	Type of concentration	Measure	Employment status: Self-employed	Employed minority business	Mainstream employment[a]
Male	Ethnic occupations	log index	1.41	1.78	1.14
		% high	42.4	55.1	23.3
	Ethnic work groups and networks	% ethnic supervisor	–	37.0	8.6
		% ethnic co-worker (25%+)	–	70.2	22.0
		% ethnic subord. (25%+)	36.1	25.5	9.3
		% ethnic customer (more than few)	53.2	46.5	14.9
	(*WN*; *N*)		(109; 173)	(81; 100)	(403; 674)
Female	Ethnic occupations	log-index	1.16	1.14	1.15
		% high	10.6	21.1	23.1
	Ethnic work groups and networks	% ethnic supervisor	–	24.9	9.6
		% ethnic co-worker (25%+)	–	68.0	25.8
		% ethnic subord. (25%+)	14.8	14.5	2.3
		% ethnic customer (more than few)	49.1	65.3	16.5
	(*WN*; *N*)		(23; 44)	(39; 69)	(309; 504)

a Includes all those employed in organizations managed by members of groups other than the respondent's own ethnic group.

answers come by examining zero-order correlations (*r*). The second question asks about the impact of ethnic concentrations in actually affecting the extent of ethnic inequality. Answers to this second question come from regression analyses.

Based on the results from previous sections, some conclusions about the effects of ethnic concentrations already can be drawn. If ethnic concentrations create discriminatory barriers, they must do so in ways that vary by group. The Jewish group has achieved equality and yet is far more concentrated in labour markets than are the Germans or Ukrainians. Italians and Portuguese, as well as the Jewish, all are more concentrated in labour markets than are racial minorities. Italians and Portuguese have low occupational status, but it is the racial minorities that experience more discrimination. Among racial minorities, Chinese more often work in ethnic occupations than do West Indians, but West Indians experience more discrimination. Even further, West Indian women more often work in ethnic occupations than do West Indian men, but the men experience more discrimination. Any effects of ethnic concentrations must be highly variable to account for the very different position of each group.

Although the findings are expected to vary by group, as well as by type of ethnic concentration, the data analysis begins with the identification of effects across all minority groups combined. These overall results serve as bench-marks for the group-to-group comparisons that follow.

EFFECTS OF TYPES OF CONCENTRATION ACROSS ALL MINORITY GROUPS

Table 4.13 presents correlations and regression results for men and women across all minority groups. The table shows main effects, and separate effects for employees in mainstream settings, for entrepreneurs and for ethnic-business employees. (For women, the data are sufficient only for a separate analysis of mainstream employees.)

Correlations

Mobility to high-status occupations usually means mobility out of ethnic specializations. The correlations between ethnic occupations and occupational status are $r = -0.359$ for men and -0.524 for women. This finding supports the hypothesis that minority-group members must abandon ethnic occupations to get equality of occupational status.

The requirement to abandon ethnic occupations applies less to income equality than to status equality. For men, in fact, there is virtually no correlation at all between ethnic occupations and income, $r = 0.051$. For women, the correlation is negative, $r = -0.245$, but less strongly negative than the correlation with status.

The findings mean that ethnic occupations are a way for fairly recent immigrants who lack conventional job qualifications, particularly men, to secure a livelihood. However, to achieve social standing and prestige, most minority group members of either gender must move out of ethnic occupations.

Among men, minority entrepreneurs are often financially successful. They have average occupational status ($r = 0.091$), but earn high incomes ($r = 0.332$). Employees in such businesses, by contrast, are not as well

TABLE 4.13
Effects of ethnic concentration on occupational status and income, by gender; total, and by employment status; Pearson's *r*; regression effects with job qualifications entered (1); and with occupational status also entered (2) (seven minority groups only)

		Pearson's *r* and regression equations						
		Occup. status		Income				
					(1)		(2)	
Gender	Type of ethnic concentration	*r*	β	*r*	β	*b*	β	*b*
Male	*Total* (519; 848)							
	Eth. occup.	–0.359	–0.166	0.051	0.076	(833)	0.140	(1536)
	Self-empl.	0.091	0.000	0.332	0.209	(3873)	0.209	(3878)
	Eth. business	–0.155	–0.016	–0.024	0.053	(1106)	0.059	(1232)
	Eth. super.	–0.151	0.019	–0.063	–0.012	(–266)	–0.019	(–436)
	Eth. co-work.	–0.261	–0.036	–0.137	–0.049	(–822)	–0.035	(–590)
	Eth. subord.	0.000	–0.002	0.220	0.139	(2749)	0.140	(2769)
	Eth. customer	0.055	0.060	0.152	0.023	(369)	0.000	(–6)
	(R^2 change)		(0.027)		(0.100)		(0.113)	
	Employed in Mainstream Setting[a] (359; 613)							
	Eth. occup.	–0.412	–0.207	0.086	0.020	(220)	0.115	(1274)
	Eth. super.	0.085	0.005	0.030	0.010	(204)	0.008	(157)
	Eth. co-work.	–0.208	–0.029	–0.100	0.001	(15)	0.014	(204)
	Eth. subord.	0.075	–0.076	0.060	0.045	(945)	0.010	(207)
	Eth. customer	0.026	0.022	0.022	0.015	(258)	0.005	(88)
	(R^2 change)		(0.038)		(0.004)		(0.012)	
	Self-employed (92; 147)							
	Eth. occup.	–0.153	–0.062	0.171	0.174	(2117)	0.192	(2332)
	Eth. subord.	–0.168	–0.202	0.167	0.151	(2799)	0.208	(3863)
	Eth. customer	0.080	0.175	0.118	0.051	(915)	0.002	(29)
	(R^2 change)		(0.047)		(0.053)		(0.067)	
	Employed in Minority Business (68; 88)							
	Eth. occup.	–0.427	–0.201	0.008	0.007	(66)	0.098	(884)
	Eth. super.	–0.231	0.046	–0.015	–0.080	(–1188)	–0.010	(–1493)
	Eth. co-work.	–0.374	–0.213	–0.075	–0.077	(–1197)	0.020	(303)
	Eth. subord.	–0.008	0.078	0.334	0.339	(5770)	0.303	(5164)
	Eth. customer	0.213	0.123	–0.001	–0.080	(–1188)	0.022	(320)
	(R^2 change)		(0.078)		(0.108)		(0.109)	

TABLE 4.13 (*continued*)

		Pearson's *r* and regression equations						
		Occup. status		Income				
					(1)		(2)	
Gender	Type of ethnic concentration	*r*	β	*r*	β	*b*	β	*b*
Female	*Total* (289; 497)							
	Eth. occup.	−0.524	−0.304	−0.245	−0.110	(−661)	0.038	(228)
	Self-empl.	0.022	0.053	−0.049	−0.060	(−1181)	−0.085	(−1687)
	Eth. business	0.158	0.122	0.021	−0.021	(−262)	−0.080	(−1008)
	Eth. super.	−0.189	0.021	−0.130	0.034	(399)	0.024	(279)
	Eth. co-work.	−0.209	0.021	−0.108	0.073	(335)	0.032	(254)
	Eth. subord.	0.071	0.050	0.109	0.139	(2374)	0.115	(1955)
	Eth. customer	0.126	−0.073	−0.042	−0.139	(−1222)	−0.104	(−911)
	(R^2 change)		(0.078)		(0.040)		(0.032)	
	Employed in Mainstream Setting[a] (253; 424)							
	Eth. occup.	−0.564	−0.334	−0.266	−0.138	(−786)	0.030	(170)
	Eth. super.	−0.307	−0.033	−0.187	0.000	(−5)	0.016	(194)
	Eth. co-work.	−0.296	0.039	−0.152	0.065	(512)	0.046	(358)
	Eth. subord.	−0.023	0.000	0.004	0.038	(823)	0.038	(822)
	Eth. customer	0.011	−0.120	−0.071	−0.146	(−1431)	−0.085	(−840)
	(R^2 change)		(0.079)		(0.030)		(0.010)	

a Includes all those employed in organizations managed by members of groups other than the respondents own ethnic group.

off. Male employees have lower status (r = −0.155), and report only average incomes (r = −0.024). Female employees have somewhat higher status (r = 0.158) but also earn only average incomes (r = 0.021). Female entrepreneurs report only average status (r = 0.022) and income (r = −0.049).

The location of ethnic work groups and networks in the vertical hierarchy of status and income varies depending upon the type of intra-ethnic relationship. Respondents with ethnic co-workers and ethnic supervisors have lower status on the average, and somewhat lower incomes. These characteristics represent disadvantaged situations. Respondents with ethnic subordinates and ethnic customers, however, are average in occupational status, and have somewhat higher incomes.

The position of men in ethnic occupations and ethnic work groups varies somewhat according to the type of employment. For example, ethnic occupations are lowest in status for employed persons, in both majority settings and minority settings. Among the self-employed, those in ethnic occupations are not so low in status, and actually have higher incomes. Thus, the requirement to abandon ethnic occupations holds less for minority entrepreneurs.

Regression Effects

Regression results show that ethnic occupations have a negative effect on occupational status, even after the effect of lower job qualifications is taken into account. For men, the residual effect of ethnic occupations is β = –0.166; for women β = –0.304. These findings measure the extent of discrimination due to ethnic occupations. They show that ethnic occupations have a discriminatory effect, and consign minority-group members to a lower status than if they entered occupations based only on their qualifications. Discriminatory effects are larger for women than for men.

Income determination works differently. Regression analyses show no discriminatory effects of ethnic occupations on incomes. For men, ethnic occupations actually have a slightly positive effect on incomes (β = 0.076). Furthermore, incomes in ethnic occupations look even higher in relation to their low occupational statuses. In the final regression equations, income effects are adjusted for occupational status as well as for qualifications. These regressions show positive effects of ethnic occupations on incomes for men (β = 0.140). For women, there is a slightly negative effect of ethnic occupations on incomes (β = –0.110). This occurs mainly because of the more negative status effect for women; aside from low status there is no further effect on incomes for women (β = 0.038).

These results show that although ethnic occupations are a barrier to occupational-status attainment, they do not block income mobility. By entering ethnic occupations, immigrants with little education can protect themselves from the low incomes, though they must accept very low occupational status. In effect, ethnic occupations protect poorly educated immigrants from economic disadvantages otherwise inevitable in an occupational structure oriented towards high standards of conventional job qualifications. The price they pay is low occupational status.

For male entrepreneurs in minority businesses, the regression results agree with previous research showing positive income effects (β = 0.202). What is more interesting are the regression analyses showing how ethnic dimensions affect business success for the self-employed (available only for males). First, ethnic occupations are a plus for ethnic entrepreneurs. The occupations have no negative effects on statuses ($\beta = -0.062$), and they have a net positive effect on incomes ($\beta = 0.174$). When ethnic businesses operate in ethnic specialties, economic success is enhanced.

Another condition affecting the economic success of ethnic entrepreneurs is the employment of subordinates within the ethnic group. Ethnic subordinates make for higher incomes among minority entrepreneurs ($\beta = 0.151$). It appears that access to an ethnic labour market is helpful to minority business success. This may be one of the reasons why ethnic specialties contribute to business success – the ethnic labour supply is most ample in these specialty occupations.

Ethnic customers and clients, by contrast, have little net effect on the success of minority entrepreneurs ($\beta = 0.051$). An ethnic clientele may help businesses in certain ways, but successful businesses include those whose scope of operations cuts across ethnic boundaries.

For employees in minority businesses, ethnic occupations have discriminatory effects on occupational status, just as they do for employees in other settings. However, sometimes there are income advantages. Specifically, opportunities to supervise members of one's own ethnic group create substantial income advantages for employees in minority business ($\beta = 0.339$). Supervision has no income advantages in mainstream settings ($\beta = 0.045$). It appears that supervisory positions in ethnic businesses are recognized in the reward structures of those businesses more often than in other settings. Overall, these advantages are significant income opportunities for minority-group employees in ethnic businesses in Toronto.

For women, the status and income effects of self-employment are nil. Self-employment is an extremely marginal activity for women in most minority groups. Positive opportunities for men are not open to women. With so few cases in the data, it is not possible to examine the conditions affecting business success for minority-group women.

VARIATIONS IN EFFECTS BY ETHNIC GROUP

All these results vary by ethnic group. We can start to examine these group-to-group differences in table 4.14, which shows the impact of ethnic occupations on occupational status for men and women in each minority group. The effects of other types of ethnic concentration are not shown; only ethnic occupations have significant effects on occupational status.

TABLE 4.14
Effects of ethnic occupations on occupational status, by gender and ethnic origin; Pearson's *r* and regression effects with job qualifications entered (seven minority groups only)

Gender	Ethnic origin	Pearson's *r*	Regression β	R^2 change	(*WN*; *N*)
Male	German	0.183	0.207	0.040	(77; 149)
	Ukrainian	–0.462	–0.262	0.056	(44; 167)
	Italian	–0.656	–0.447	0.151	(203; 142)
	Jewish	0.139	0.064	0.004	(75; 157)
	Portuguese	–0.640	–0.529	0.231	(36; 91)
	Chinese	–0.224	–0.178	0.029	(26; 66)
	West Indian	–0.340	–0.223	0.046	(58; 76)
Female	German	0.196	0.249	0.057	(56; 100)
	Ukrainian	–0.511	–0.222	0.036	(28; 112)
	Italian	–0.836	–0.780	0.240	(94; 76)
	Jewish	0.062	–0.063	0.004	(40; 84)
	Portuguese	–0.847	–0.532	0.127	(16; 37)
	Chinese	–0.568	–0.246	0.043	(16; 42)
	West Indian	–0.268	–0.274	0.074	(39; 46)

Negative effects of ethnic occupations on occupational status are found in five groups: Chinese, West Indians, Portuguese, Italians, and Ukrainians. Of these, the effect is strongest for the Portuguese, a predominantly immigrant group, and for the Italians, a more well-established group. In these groups, there is a very pronounced low-status/ethnic-occupation relation for both men and women. Italians and Portuguese are distinguished by the lowest occupational status overall, and heavy concentration in occupations. For them, entering a higher-status job nearly always means moving to a non-ethnic job. There is a clear-cut link between upward status mobility and abandonment of ethnic occupations. Furthermore, most persons in the sample had done little of either. There has been little abandonment of ethnic occupations, and little status mobility.

Recall the findings reported earlier that all these groups except West Indians have occupational statuses more or less corresponding to job qualifications. Because of this fact, ethnic occupations probably are not significant for most groups in denying equal opportunity. The results here seem to arise because status determination works differently within these groups than it does in the occupational structure as a whole. A different status-determination process within the groups could explain why ethnic occupations have a negative effect on occupational status within the group, while not lowering occupational statuses in relation to other groups.

An actual discrimination effect of ethnic occupations in producing lower occupational status seems most plausible as an interpretation of the data for West Indians. This group does in fact experience job-status disadvantages in relation to education. It may be that low-status ethnic occupations lead to mobility barriers only for groups such as West Indians who have very low standing in society in relation to other ethnic groups.

For Ukrainians, education in the second generation has led to the abandonment of ethnic occupations, and upward status mobility. For Italians and Portuguese, at least, a similar process may also be under way. Formation of new middle-class ethnic occupations is a possibility, too.

For Germans and for Jewish people, there are no negative effects of ethnic occupations at all. Both groups, like Ukrainians, have achieved high status. Few Germans work in ethnic occupations, but their situation is quite different from that of Ukrainians. For Germans, abandonment of ethnic occupations has occurred despite being unrelated to occupational-status attainment. For the Jewish, abandonment of ethnic occupations also has no advantages for occupational status. However, in that case, such abandonment has not occurred. Instead, it is clear that the Jewish group has become concentrated in middle-class occupations over time.

The group-to-group income effects of four selected types of ethnic concentrations are shown in table 4.15. The overall income effects of ethnic occupations were near zero (table 4.13, above) but for the predominantly immigrant groups and racial minorities, the data in table 4.15 shows that the effects are negative. There are negative β coefficients for the income effects of ethnic occupations (with qualifications controlled) for Chinese and Portuguese men and women, and for West Indian men. Although the successfully self-employed in these groups tend to report high incomes, the effects are not great because successful self-employment is not prevalent. Where there is significant employment in minority businesses (namely among the Portuguese and Chinese men), the effect on incomes is negative.

A discrimination effect of employment in ethnic occupations and ethnic business on incomes is most plausible for West Indian and

TABLE 4.15
Effects of ethnic concentration on income, by ethnic origin and gender; Pearson's *r*; regression effects with job qualifications entered (1); and with occupational status also entered (2) (seven minority groups only)

Gender	Ethnic origin (*WN*; *N*)	Type of ethnic concentration	Pearson's *r* and regression equations				
				(1)		(2)	
			r	β	*b*	β	*b*
Male	German (77; 149)	Eth. occup.	0.112	0.040	(1064)	−0.013	(−340)
		Self-empl.	0.080	0.060	(1272)	0.052	(1114)
		Eth. bus.	−0.038	0.033	(1453)	0.026	(1229)
		Eth. subord.	0.009	−0.047	(−1790)	−0.041	(−1576)
		(R^2 change)		(0.006)		(0.003)	
	Ukrainian (44; 167)	Eth. occup.	−0.271	−0.142	(−4292)	−0.047	(−1421)
		Self-empl.	0.327	0.236	(5405)	0.240	(5505)
		Eth. bus.	−0.126	−0.196	(−7179)	−0.151	(−5525)
		Eth. subord.	−0.020	0.021	(683)	0.040	(1286)
		(R^2 change)		(0.118)		(0.084)	
	Italian (203; 142)	Eth. occup.	0.110	0.108	(884)	0.321	(2629)
		Self-empl.	0.352	0.237	(3850)	0.243	(3932)
		Eth. bus.	0.049	0.114	(1762)	0.121	(1880)
		Eth. subord.	0.404	0.254	(3726)	0.251	(3680)
		(R^2 change)		(0.194)		(0.272)	
	Jewish (75; 157)	Eth. occup.	0.195	0.047	(709)	0.021	(317)
		Self-empl.	0.342	0.193	(3583)	0.219	(4066)
		Eth. bus.	−0.180	0.005	(108)	0.027	(589)
		Eth. subord.	0.185	0.067	(1813)	0.056	(1522)
		(R^2 change)		(0.046)		(0.047)	
	Portuguese (36; 91)	Eth. occup.	−0.170	−0.146	(−1271)	−0.108	(−94)
		Self-empl.	0.520	0.589	(17807)	0.580	(17567)
		Eth. bus.	−0.171	−0.215	(−7081)	−0.211	(−6969)
		Eth. subord.	0.289	0.323	(6996)	0.310	(6721)
		(R^2 change)		(0.431)		(0.369)	
	Chinese (26; 66)	Eth. occup.	−0.152	−0.151	(−1720)	−0.033	(−372)
		Self-empl.	0.366	0.190	(4455)	0.195	(4587)
		Eth. bus.	−0.219	−0.153	(−5709)	−0.122	(−4190)
		Eth. subord.	0.143	0.053	(1106)	0.057	(1194)
		(R^2 change)		(0.088)		(0.060)	
	West Indian (58; 76)	Eth. occup.	−0.155	−0.121	(−1600)	−0.032	(−4261)
		Self-empl.	0.196	0.182	(4302)	0.138	(3273)
		Eth. subord.	−0.046	−0.013	(−276)	−0.114	(−2526)
		(R^2 change)		(0.057)		(0.036)	

TABLE 4.15 (*continued*)

Gender	Ethnic origin (*WN; N*)	Type of ethnic concentration	Pearson's *r* and regression equations				
				(1)		(2)	
			r	β	*b*	β	*b*
Female	German	Eth. occup.	0.139	0.238	(6770)	0.101	(2859)
	(56; 100)	Self-empl.	–0.141	–0.214	(–3903)	–0.136	(–2490)
		Eth. bus.	–0.054	–0.041	(–925)	–0.029	–660)
		Eth. subord.	0.110	0.113	(2622)	0.066	(1526)
		(R^2 change)		(0.092)		(0.025)	
	Ukrainian	Eth. occup.	–0.040	0.126	(2068)	0.281	(4630)
	(28; 112)	Self-empl.	–0.028	–0.062	(–1969)	0.008	(–255)
		Eth. bus.	0.004	–0.006	(–78)	0.000	(–9)
		Eth. subord.	0.001	0.080	(1274)	0.134	(2130)
		(R^2 change)		(0.025)		(0.081)	
	Italian	Eth. occup.	–0.431	–0.279	(–1196)	0.234	(1003)
	(94; 76)	Self-empl.	–0.032	0.099	(2479)	0.046	(1115)
		Eth. bus.	0.104	–0.135	(–1700)	–0.136	(–1716)
		Eth. subord.	0.170	0.118	(1693)	0.118	(1683)
		(R^2 change)		(0.056)		(0.039)	
	Jewish	Eth. occup.	0.031	–0.019	(–234)	–0.003	(–36)
	(40; 84)	Self-empl.	–0.010	–0.105	(–1443)	–0.109	(–1495)
		Eth. bus.	0.016	0.007	(68)	–0.012	(–109)
		Eth. subord.	0.167	0.143	(2162)	0.125	(1887)
		(R^2 change)		(0.025)		(0.020)	
	Portuguese	Eth. occup.	–0.532	–0.316	(–924)	–0.195	(–571)
	(16; 37)	Self-empl.	–0.102	–0.138	(–1834)	–0.107	(–1433)
		Eth. bus.	–0.024	0.092	(1786)	0.085	(1648)
		Eth. subord.	0.081	0.038	(358)	0.061	(579)
		(R^2 change)		(0.065)		(0.023)	
	Chinese	Eth. occup.	–0.510	–0.308	(–1733)	–0.155	(–872)
	(16; 42)	Self-empl.	0.000	0.000	(0)	0.000	(0)
		Eth. bus.	0.000	0.000	(0)	0.000	(0)
		Eth. subord.	0.000	0.000	(0)	0.000	(0)
		(R^2 change)		(0.068)		(0.005)	
	West Indian	Eth. occup.	–0.048	–0.035	(–170)	0.041	(210)
	(39; 42)	Self-empl.	0.000	0.000	(0)	0.000	(0)
		Eth. bus.	0.000	0.000	(0)	0.000	(0)
		Eth. subord.	0.000	0.000	(0)	0.000	(0)
		(R^2 change)		(0.001)		(0.001)	

Chinese men. These are the groups that experience the most significant income discrimination. Among West Indian women, there was evidence of income discrimination, but for them ethnic occupations have no measured effect on incomes. Thus, for West Indian women, ethnic occupations are not involved in discriminatory hiring. This is a case in which income discrimination occurs mainly within occupations, both ethnic occupations and other occupations.

Among more well-established groups, the income effects of ethnic occupations and businesses are highly variable. The most noteworthy findings concern Italian men. For them, incomes are enhanced not only by self-employment, but also by employment in Italian businesses, by employment in Italian occupations (particularly in relation to low occupational statuses), and by supervising other Italians. These variables add significantly to the explanation of income attainment for Italian men, even after adjustments for job qualifications. (They add 0.194 to R^2 before status is in the equation, and 0.272 after status is in the equation.) For Italian men of a given level of education and occupational status, working in an Italian occupation or Italian business has a fairly significant positive effect on income.

These income advantages may produce somewhat higher incomes for Italian men overall, in relation to job qualifications. Recall that Italian men have somewhat higher incomes than expected on the basis of occupational status. The difference is not large, to be sure. An additional possibility is that the lack of income discrimination against Italian men may be due at least in part to the protection afforded by the ethnic occupations. That is, to some extent higher incomes in Italian occupations may offset *lower* incomes outside the Italian occupations. There may be a degree of income discrimination against Italian men in the non-ethnic occupations.

The income-attainment process among Italians is highly gender-specific. Unlike the men, the pattern for Italian women is similar to those for both men and women in the predominantly immigrant groups. Data show negative effects of ethnic occupations and minority-business employment on the incomes of Italian women.

For the Jewish the income effects of ethnic occupations and business employment, net of job qualifications, are virtually nil.

For Ukrainians and Germans, there are a variety of effects. For Ukrainian men, there are negative income effects of minority occupations and business employment. For German men, the effects are negligible. Among women in these groups, the effects of ethnic occupations on incomes are positive.

Ethnic Concentration of Immigrants and Their Descendants

To what extent are ethnic concentrations in labour markets a phenomenon of the immigrant generation? To what extent are they abandoned by the children of immigrants and later generations? The advantages or disadvantages of ethnic concentrations are more significant if they persist across generations, or if new generations establish new patterns of concentration. This issue deserves detailed consideration, and the present section provides a preliminary view of basic trends.

Overall, ethnic concentrations in labour markets decline between generations, but this pattern varies by group as shown in table 4.16. For Ukrainians and Germans, levels of concentration are low across generations. For Italians, levels of concentration appear to decline from one generation to the next. For the Jewish, they are more likely to persist.

The low levels of ethnic labour-market concentration for Ukrainians and Germans exist even in the immigrant generation. If there is an exception to this pattern, it would be the case of self-employment among Germans. Self-employment is comparatively high for Germans, and there is a progressive decline from the immigrant generation to the second and third generations. Other measures vary little across generations.

Abandonment of Italian occupations leads to occupational-status mobility, so there is the implication of upward mobility across generations as well. No doubt increased education in the second and third generations is a factor in this trend. Note that the identification of ethnic occupations for this study is not generation-specific.[13] The Italian group has a large immigrant component, so the identification of Italian occupations may not be sensitive to new patterns of Italian concentration arising in the second or third generations. It may be significant that other patterns of Italian concentration, identified in the survey data, are significant in the second and third generations, and show little if any decline. These include self-employment, employment in Italian businesses, and relations with Italian customers. The latter are significant for the Italian women as well. In the second and third generations, Italian self-employment may still involve 'ethnic enterprise.' The immigrant occupational specialties decline, however, or change to new specialties that are not yet prominent but may become more so in the future.

Among the Jewish, ethnic concentrations are high across generations. For men, the decrease in ethnic occupations across generations is less than for Italians; for women there is an increase. For men there is an

TABLE 4.16
Per cent concentrated in ethnic occupations, self-employed, employed in minority business, and concentrated in ethnic work groups and networks at work, by gender, ethnic origin, and generation (four established minority groups only)

			Type of ethnic concentration							
Gender	Ethnic origin	Generation	Eth. occ.	Self-empl.	Min. bus.	Eth. sup.	Eth. cwk.	Eth. sub.	Eth. cust.	(*WN*; *N*)
Male	German	Immigrant	3.0	21.4	2.0	8.5	2.0	6.5	4.7	(46; 82)
		Second	0.0	16.0	0.4	0.0	5.1	4.7	5.1	(21; 37)
		Third	0.0	11.1	4.4	3.3	11.1	0.0	5.0	(19; 45)
	Ukrainian	Immigrant	9.5	2.4	6.3	7.8	10.7	7.3	12.6	(20; 89)
		Second	0.7	22.4	1.4	4.9	15.4	4.2	1.4	(16; 47)
		Third	4.1	8.3	7.2	4.1	7.2	7.2	7.2	(11; 43)
	Italian	Immigrant	46.8	18.9	25.4	21.7	43.8	30.4	40.3	(179; 103)
		Second	18.7	21.6	18.0	9.0	23.9	25.5	34.5	(53; 33)
		Third	13.5	15.1	17.2	7.1	26.3	9.1	30.3	(10; 30)
	Jewish	Immigrant	48.5	43.1	18.3	6.3	7.2	13.7	45.6	(39; 91)
		Second	41.1	40.2	15.8	9.1	10.6	10.8	58.1	(30; 55)
		Third	37.7	42.6	25.8	11.2	17.2	14.0	54.2	(16; 34)
Female	German	Immigrant	0.0	12.2	7.6	11.9	5.2	2.3	5.2	(33; 57)
		Second	0.0	0.6	0.0	0.0	0.6	0.0	7.4	(15; 24)
		Third	0.0	0.0	0.0	6.8	3.4	3.9	13.6	(19; 37)
	Ukrainian	Immigrant	6.9	0.9	1.7	1.7	14.0	0.9	3.5	(11; 54)
		Second	0.0	0.9	5.8	1.7	9.9	4.1	5.8	(14; 41)
		Third	0.0	1.0	9.3	2.1	16.5	8.2	14.4	(6; 31)
	Italian	Immigrant	34.8	5.6	11.8	21.9	54.9	4.6	24.8	(80; 47)
		Second	17.8	5.0	13.3	7.8	37.2	5.5	47.2	(40; 28)
		Third	0.0	6.6	11.0	8.8	9.9	0.0	28.6	(10; 27)
	Jewish	Immigrant	20.4	16.7	37.4	14.8	31.7	7.5	54.1	(19; 42)
		Second	21.8	16.5	24.1	10.6	21.1	13.5	47.9	(20; 37)
		Third	33.9	16.6	46.5	6.5	33.4	6.5	49.3	(14; 30)

increase in all ethnic working networks, while for women there is no decline in this respect. Ethnic occupations and work settings in the Jewish group now include professional fields associated with high job statuses and incomes, and produce no disadvantages in relation to job qualifications. These concentrations no doubt become stronger with the second and third generations.

Conclusions

This concluding section first provides an overview of the main results of this study, and then describes the results for each ethnic group separately. It also identifies directions for future research.

VARYING EFFECTS OF ETHNIC CONCENTRATIONS

The findings of this study show that ethnic concentrations do affect ethnic inequality, sometimes by restricting opportunities for upward mobility, and sometimes by creating them. The impact of ethnic concentrations in labour markets varies as a result of several factors. The impact is often negative, particularly in the predominantly immigrant groups. However, in the established groups, there are sometimes negative effects, sometimes positive effects, and sometimes no effects. Effects also vary by gender within ethnic groups. They vary according to the type of concentration, and according to whether the concern is with inequalities of occupational status or income. We can give no single answer to questions about how ethnic concentrations affect inequality. Sometimes there is a 'mobility trap,' and sometimes there is opportunity. Theory must specify the conditions and circumstances under which effects appear.

For predominantly immigrant groups in Toronto, the Chinese, Portuguese, and West Indians, ethnic concentrations in labour markets often reflect significant disadvantages. Stereotypical ethnic occupations bring low incomes, and, the data show, even lower status. Ethnic businesses have not yet helped very much. The self-employed do make relatively good money. However, successful entrepreneurship is difficult, as shown by the low rates of self-employment. The Chinese have been most successful. However, even for Chinese, the jobs created within ethnic businesses are few and poorly paid.

Ethnic occupations appear to have significant discriminatory effects in at least two instances. There is income discrimination against both West Indian and Chinese men. Men in both these groups are concentrated in a variety of low-status occupations, including service occupations. And in both cases, employment in ethnic occupations lowers incomes below what would be expected based on job qualifications. These results are consistent with a theory of discriminatory effects.

However, results across all groups show that there is no one-to-one relation between discrimination and ethnic occupations. Sometimes there is discrimination but no negative effects of ethnic occupations. West Indian women are an example. They experience income discrimination, but West Indian female occupations do not affect incomes. Their occupational concentrations are in health fields, as well as the service occupations. In other analyses, we found little evidence of discrimination, yet ethnic occupations do have negative effects. This is the case for the Portuguese and the Chinese with respect to occupational status. The negative effects of ethnic occupations within groups do not always translate into discriminatory effects across ethnic or racial groups.

Furthermore, no systematic disadvantages seem to arise from ethnic co-worker groups or ethnic supervisors within mainstream organizations for any of the ethnic groups. Previous studies identified such disadvantages in specific organizations. However, in survey data across ethnic groups, they do not appear. If ethnic work groups cause disadvantages, they must do so under more specific conditions.

Among relatively well-established ethnic groups, the Italians, Jewish, Germans, and Ukrainians, the effects of ethnic concentrations show more variation. Historically, most of these groups experienced at least some occupational concentrations in low-status positions (Reitz 1980b: 53–89), just as predominantly immigrant groups do in Toronto today. However, the passage of time brought changes of various kinds. The changes affect not only the second generation, but also later immigrants within the same groups.

Change occurs in three directions. There may be abandonment of ethnic occupations. There may be income mobility within ethnic occupations. And there may be new ethnic occupations. Some of these changes occur more often in certain groups than in others (see the comments on specific groups below). To some degree each change occurs in every group.

Upward income mobility within ethnic occupations is, according to our data, often related to establishing successful minority businesses. What factors affect the success of minority businesses? Our findings show that two conditions are important. Minority businesses are more successful for entrepreneurs within ethnic occupational specialties. They are also more successful for entrepreneurs taking advantage of ethnic labour markets. The two conditions may occur together. Ethnic occupational specialization can make available precisely the skilled labour needed in occupationally specialized businesses. By contrast, not all minority-group resources are needed for minority business success. The findings show that businesses based on consumer markets within ethnic communities do not have an advantage.

Successful ethnic businesses can generate positive employment opportunities within the group. These results for Toronto differ from those of Sanders and Nee (1987) on Cubans in Miami and Chinese in California. Sanders and Nee quite correctly distinguish 'immigrant workers' from 'immigrant bosses' in the 'enclave economy.' They also correctly argue that workers often do not share in the advantages secured by bosses. However, situations vary. In the Toronto data, the overall average income effect of employment in minority businesses across seven minority groups is nil. In predominantly immigrant groups, the impact is negative; in established groups the impact varies. In the case of Italian males, minority employees and employers both benefit from ethnic business success. Among employees, there are income benefits available because of opportunities to supervise other minority-group workers. These opportunities for supervision, which become more numerous as ethnic businesses expand, yield benefits exceeding those available outside ethnic businesses.

Upward income mobility within ethnic occupations does not improve occupational status. This fact is one reason for the general pattern, observed for predominantly immigrant groups as well, that ethnic occupations are lower in status than they are in income. Such a pattern corresponds to the priority needs of immigrants from impoverished backgrounds: economic survival takes precedence over social respectability.

A shift to new ethnic occupational specialties can lead to upward mobility in status as well as income. This change often occurs for the second, or native-born, generations, because of the requirement for high levels of education in high-status occupations.

There are a variety of avenues to upward occupational mobility for minority ethnic groups. Often attention is paid to education for the second generation, but this is only one avenue of mobility. Income mobility for immigrants themselves may be as important, perhaps more important. Greeley (1976: 25) pointed out that education often is not the first step towards upward occupational mobility for immigrant groups. 'The success of the Polish and the Italians seems to have come *first* in income, then in education, and finally in occupation.' The data show that income mobility for ethnic minorities is attained frequently in minority businesses based in resources within the ethnic community.

In a sense, upward mobility for minority ethnic groups depends in part on the capacity of the group as a whole to mobilize economic resources. This collective capacity for economic mobilization may affect the social incorporation of ethnic groups.

EFFECTS OF ETHNIC CONCENTRATIONS IN SPECIFIC ETHNIC GROUPS

The findings as summarized above apply differently to each group. The following comments elaborate the situation of particular ethnic groups.

The Germans

Germans are not extensively concentrated in labour markets, and have achieved virtual equality with the majority group. The Germans are an example that could be cited in support of the hypothesis that the abandonment of ethnic concentrations leads to equality.

However, contemporary survey data do not show whether the earliest German immigrants were concentrated in an ethnic enclave that has now been abandoned to achieve upward mobility. It seems unlikely that German concentrations in labour markets were ever as high as for Italians today, for example. Compared to other immigrant groups, Germans in Canada have always been fairly diverse occupationally. To the extent that German immigrants in the past were concentrated in low-status occupations, these have been largely abandoned. However, today German immigrants are weakly concentrated in middle-status skilled trades. If today's immigrants are comparable to German immigrants of the past, then perhaps Germans have abandoned ethnic occupations, but not as part of upward mobility.

The Ukrainians

Ukrainians, like Germans, have low ethnic concentrations in labour markets, and have attained equality. For Ukrainians, however, there may be a closer relation between the two. Earlier generations of Ukrainians were poorer, and experienced more occupational concentration, than did the Germans or more recent Ukrainian immigrants (see Reitz, 1980b: 70–1). These earlier experiences may be one reason why, now, the occupational concentration for Ukrainians is in the lower-status jobs. These instances of concentration may have been established by relatively uneducated immigrants arriving before the Second World War. If so, then a historical association between abandonment of the economic enclave and upward occupational-status mobility may apply to Ukrainians. Note that the residual ethnic occupations for Ukrainian men imply lower incomes, but the same is not true for Ukrainian women. This particular finding represents one of the variety of situations that can emerge over time.

The Italians

For Italian men, current ethnic occupations now have positive effects on incomes, despite negative effects on status. Italian men have achieved upward income mobility within low-status occupations, and as entrepreneurs and employees in ethnic businesses. Their incomes are in fact higher in these positions than in the mainstream economy. Overall, the incomes of Italian men in Toronto today are somewhat higher than would be predicted on the basis of qualifications. The question is: How has the Italian group achieved its current level of economic success within the confines of the ethnic economy?

An examination of the history of Toronto's construction industry shows one way in which an ethnic minority group can mobilize economic resources (Reitz 1980b: 75–80). The process seems to have involved several steps. In the early 1900s, many Italian immigrants were recruited to become labourers in an Anglo-Saxon-controlled construction industry. They built railways and roads. The record shows that, in this early phase, the impact of ethnic concentration on incomes undoubtedly was quite negative. The position of Italians then was at least as difficult as that of the predominantly immigrant groups today.

Slowly Italians began to develop independent businesses in the construction field. They set up small subcontracting firms with relatively little capital investment. During the Depression, the large construction firms withered. Italian construction teams, however, remained intact by building homes. As a result, they were well-placed to seize new opportunities provided by the post-war construction boom. They did so, and at the same time gave good jobs to large numbers of post-war Italian immigrants.

In short, the Italians established an organizational presence in an important industry, an industry that was partly abandoned by the dominant group, but which later enjoyed rapid expansion. It can be seen that Italians in Toronto today are by no means a newly established ethnic group, though there is a high proportion of post-war immigrants. Their position is affected by the activities of earlier immigrants arriving decades before. The earlier immigrants established an economic position, creating resources contributing to the economic incorporation of later immigrants. These resources far exceed those available to groups such as the Portuguese and the West Indians now attempting to establish themselves.

Italian women in the labour force have a drastically different experience. The findings for Italian women resemble very much the findings for Portuguese or West Indian women, showing rather negative effects of ethnic concentrations on income as well as status. This finding illustrates well the impact of gender in ethnic labour markets. It shows that the organizational factors under discussion are very much gender-specific.

The Jewish

A relation between abandonment of the economic enclave and upward mobility also has no relevance for the Jewish group. This group has achieved high statuses and incomes, and has also maintained high levels of occupational concentrations across generations. Today, ethnic occupations among the Jewish exist at many levels of occupational status and income.

Historically, the entrance statuses of Jewish immigrants were much lower. Jewish immigration to Toronto in significant numbers occurred when a key industry – the garment industry – was expanding. By establishing a foothold in this industry (including its unions), in retail trade, and through entrepreneurial skill, many Jewish immigrants seized control of significant resources. Incomes rose.

Upward mobility for the Jewish has meant, not abandonment of ethnic occupations, but finding new ones. Later generations gained professional and academic education and became influential in these fields. In addition, extremely high rates of self-employment suggest that organizational independence is still important to mobility for Jewish men and women. This self-employment may be as important as entrance into high-status occupations such as law and medicine. For Jewish men and women, ethnic occupations in themselves have no status or income effects at all, apart from the effects of successful self-employment.

The Portuguese

The current situation of Portuguese may be closer to the earlier experiences of Italians. They have a similar low entrance status and high occupational concentration. The Portuguese do not have a long history in Canada, compared to Italians, and are a much smaller group. They are concentrated in the same general type of occupations, but the income effects are quite different, possibly reflecting the relative lack of organizational control within the Portuguese community. The lack of ethnic entrepreneurship among Portuguese also may be a significant handicap in creating upward income mobility.

The Chinese

The Chinese group has relatively high levels of education. Although Chinese have been fairly successful in terms of occupational status, Chinese men experience significant income discrimination. Chinese occupations are of lower status, but do not appear to have had an impact in lowering occupational statuses. For men, there is a discriminatory income impact, however.

The weakness of Chinese entrepreneurship in providing organizational resources may be a factor in explaining these patterns. Chinese entrepreneurship is highly visible, and appears important in other settings (see Light 1974, 1986). However, in Toronto (at least at the time of this survey) such entrepreneurship was not significant for the overall economic position of the Chinese group. Self-employment was higher than for the Portuguese or West Indians, but lower than for the Italians or Jewish. Furthermore, Chinese businesses are small, judging from the small proportions of Chinese who say they work there.

The more recent influx of wealthy Chinese immigrants from Hong Kong may well have changed the situation of the Chinese group already. Among all groups, the Chinese and West Indians have experienced the most changes since the survey.

West Indians

Discrimination against West Indians is more significant than against other groups in this study, according to the survey results. Discrimination affects West Indian men and women, in both occupational status and income. The evidence from this study also shows that discrimination against West Indians occurs because of ethnic occupations.

West Indian entrepreneurship is still comparatively weak. Few West Indian men are involved in successful minority businesses, either as entrepreneurs or as employees. This factor also contributes to low incomes in the West Indian group.

Minority-Group Men and Women

Ethnic concentrations are, if anything, more strongly related to low occupational status and low incomes for women than for men. This pattern particularly applies for Italians, Portuguese, and Chinese, though not for West Indians. Low rates of self-employment for minority-group women may be related to this finding. At least for the Italians and Portuguese, the income benefits of ethnic occupations for men do not carry over to the women, though the impact on overall income levels for women in these groups is not large.

IMPLICATIONS FOR FUTURE RESEARCH

The results presented in this chapter suggest several topics for future research.

Little is yet known of the structure of opportunities within each ethnic labour-market segment. The sample sizes in this study prohibit a detailed analysis of particular ethnic labour-market segments. The findings do show that minority labour markets are not uniform. These labour-market segments vary in the extent and types of opportunities they provide. For example, the structure of opportunities for Italian men in the Italian sector is different from that available to Chinese men in the Chinese sector. Minority labour markets also vary in the specific criteria most favourable to mobility, and in the extent to which qualifications and acquired resources may be transferable to mainstream settings. Education may be more important in mainstream labour markets than in minority settings, but minority settings undoubtedly vary in this regard. The importance of access to ethnic-community resources no doubt varies, in part as a function of resource availability itself in a particular ethnic group. In some cases these resources may be useful only within minority settings, while in other cases they may provide a base for mobility in the mainstream. Further study of these issues would provide a much clearer understanding of the impact of ethnic labour markets in the social incorporation of minority groups.

To explain fully ethnic labour markets requires more knowledge of their history. In this contemporary survey, some suggested interpretations are based on historical background. Such interpretations are mostly speculative. They require further study. Historical research would show how minority businesses and occupational concentrations at one point in time affect labour-market opportunities later on, including the opportunities available to new groups of immigrants. Theories of ethnic labour markets also must incorporate this historical perspective.

The historical perspective may also inform the study of newly arrived groups. Ethnic labour-market concentrations in these new groups may affect current opportunities. They are also important if they affect the potential for expansion and development of collective opportunities in the future. For example, concentrations in particular industries may have an impact that depends upon the future prospects for that industry. These future prospects in turn can be affected by trends in industrial restructuring, technological change, and other economic trends.

Finally, the historical and structural variability of ethnic labour markets underscores the importance of comparative research. We must place findings from one city such as Toronto in the context of other similar cities in North America and elsewhere. Because of variability within this one city, there is every reason to expect variations among cities and countries as well. Comparative cross-national research is required.

In some respects, the British experience is an important comparative bench-mark (see Reitz 1988a, b). Post-war Commonwealth immigrants to Britain became concentrated in textile mills and other declining industries whose narrow profit margins and low wages sparked a white exodus. These industries experienced further sharp declines in the face of international competition. Industrial decline significantly exacerbated the negative consequences of industrial concentration for the position of these immigrants in the labour force. In comparing these experiences, it would be important to know about similarities and differences in the extent and industrial location of racial minority concentrations. Differences in the characteristics of immigrants, the viability of industries, and expected industrial trends would be part of the analysis. Most analysts of the new Canada-U.S. free trade agreement expect negative effects on the position of industries in which immigrants are concentrated today.

In the United States, the entry of Hispanic groups in Florida and California is an interesting contrast to earlier experiences in northern cities and to the findings in Toronto. These cases are receiving attention, and more contemporary and historical data on industrial location and business opportunities in these groups are needed for detailed comparisons within and between countries. The U.S. situation may differ because of the extensive industrial concentration of the indigenous black labour force. In Europe, increased labour mobility within the common market undoubtedly will also make it a major focus for research on the ethnic economy in the future.

5

The Ethnic Group as a Political Resource in Relation to Problems of Incorporation: Perceptions and Attitudes

Raymond Breton

In the course of their experience in the larger society, members of ethnic groups pursue certain values and encounter problems and opportunities. The combination of aspirations, problems, and opportunities constitutes the basis of the group's system of interests in relation to the rest of the society.[1] These can be collective phenomena because they are or could be part of the experience of a significant number of members of the group. There could be a common experience, for example, around employment aspirations, problems, and opportunities. If they are sufficiently frequent, if they have a symbolic value for the group, or if the situation of individuals depends to a significant extent on their group membership, individual problems and opportunities can become collective problems. However, groups can also face circumstances that affect them as a group, such as immigration laws, anti-discrimination programs, cultural policies, or job specifications. To a considerable degree, these are 'collective goods' (or 'bads') which, if they exist, affect all members of the community. They are largely indivisible (Olson 1965).

In order to assist their members in connection with their goals, problems, and opportunities or in order to pursue collective objectives, a more or less elaborate socio-political organization may progressively be established in the collectivity.[2] Such an organization involves ideologies, structures, and mechanisms for the pursuit of concerted action. At least three basic processes are involved: the identification of matters as being of collective interest and the articulation of related issues; the mobilization of commitment and participation, including the investment of resources; and the organization of the action itself to deal with problems identified or objectives formulated.

The components of social organization required for such processes include leadership, a decision-making apparatus, communication channels, social-control structures, and conflict-resolution and co-ordination mechanisms. In addition, the mobilization of participation and the organization of action do not depend solely on appropriate organizational structures; they also require the availability of material resources, a degree of social cohesion, an ideology, and a system of social norms. The latter give legitimacy to the social definition of aspirations, problems, and opportunities that comes to prevail in the group, to the type of action undertaken, and to the organizational system established in the community.

The results presented in this chapter deal with the latter elements, namely with some of the perceptions, ideas, and attitudes of members of ethnic groups with regard to the problems faced by their group and its members, to the type of action that could be effective in dealing with some of these problems, and to aspects of their community, its leaders, and organizations. In other words, the analysis deals with features of the public opinion that exists in various ethnic groups with regard to a number of elements deemed important for concerted action.

The views and sentiments of the ethnic publics are indeed quite relevant for the legitimacy of group action and for the mobilization of support. The definition of matters requiring collective action and resources, the course of action to be adopted, the amounts and types of resources to be used may all be affected by the views and attitudes of the relevant ethnic publics. These views and attitudes may have an impact on whether or not anything will get done or, if some action is undertaken, on its effectiveness.

Public attitudes may be manipulated. Considerable resources and effort may be invested by leaders in order to assess and shape public opinion in their community. They may attempt to control the amount or type of information transmitted. They may use a variety of strategies to mobilize public support or to neutralize the possible impact of public opinion. The constant preoccupation of those in positions of power and authority with the views and sentiments of the relevant publics attests to their importance.

This chapter limits itself to a few aspects of ethnic public opinion. The first part deals with what are perceived as problems by the members of the ethnic groups included in the study. Findings on the types of action considered more or less effective to get things done or obtain results are the object of the second part. More specifically, data on the attitudes towards the use of community organizational resources in connection with certain issues or problems are presented. The third part examines the relationship between the propensity to favour the use of ethnic organizational resources to deal with problems and the respondents' involvement in community affairs and their relationship with community leaders. The fourth and last part relates the attitudes towards ethnic organizational action to the perception of various features of the socio-political organization of the ethnic group: the decision-making structure, the efficacy of the community leadership and their relationship with societal institutions, and the factors that divide the group. It should be noted that, throughout the chapter, the data presented pertain to the *perceptions* of respondents of political matters; they do not represent a direct measurement of the socio-political phenomena. The data in the third part bear on the respondents' reports of the relation between these perceptions and their *own* experiences and relationships.

Perception of Individual and Community Problems

Generally, ethnic groups and their members can face two broad types of problems. They can, on the one hand, encounter difficulties in becoming fully incorporated in the society and, on the other, experience problems of cultural loss. This section examines the extent to which problems are perceived in these areas. As far as incorporation is concerned, the perception of problems with regard to social acceptance and discrimination will be described. This discussion will be followed by a presentation of results on the perception of problems with regard to the maintenance of traditions and customs and to the use of the group's language.

PERCEPTION OF PROBLEMS OF SOCIAL INCORPORATION

The incorporation of individuals and groups in a community and the social equality that full incorporation implies have an instrumental and an expressive dimension. They involve both matters pertaining to the position one occupies in the social structure with its associated benefits and matters related to the acceptance, respect, and status one receives from others. Thus, in attempting to improve their condition, ethnic groups and their members will seek social acceptance and will attempt to avoid discrimination. Deprivations of either type are an indication that human and civil rights are not fully enjoyed. What are the perceptions and opinions on these two components of incorporation?

Social Acceptance

Two sets of indicators are used to explore possible problems of social acceptance: one concerns interpersonal relations and the other pertains to acceptance expressed by the larger society through its immigration legislation.

Respondents were asked 'how easily the Majority Canadian group' accepts them as neighbours and as 'close relatives by marriage.' In addition, Majority Canadian respondents were asked if they would have someone from each of a number of groups as a next-door neighbour or as a close relative. The results for both sets of questions are presented in table 5.1 for each of the groups.

The upper panel (A1) of the table on acceptance as neighbours reveals considerable variations, but primarily in the *degree* of easiness with which people perceive the Majority Canadian group as accepting them. That is to say, the percentages who feel they are accepted very easily vary between 19 and 66, with the West Indians, Jews, and Chinese showing the lowest percentages and the Germans and Ukrainians the highest. If, however, we combine the 'very' and 'somewhat easily' categories, variations are considerably reduced: a strong majority in most groups feel that they would be accepted as neighbours by the Majority Canadian group. For West Indians the size of the majority is significantly smaller: 58%.

Panel A2 of the table shows the degree of acceptance of the different groups by Majority Canadians and by the minority groups combined. (Unfortunately, the distinction of degree, namely 'very' and 'somewhat easily,' is not available; the percentages refer to overall acceptance.) It can be noted that, as far as acceptance as neighbours is concerned, the expressed attitudes of the Majority Canadians are not very different from what members of the groups themselves perceive. Two discrepancies, however, are worth noting. Jewish and West Indian respondents are *less* likely to feel accepted than what the Majority Canadians declare: a 12% and 9% difference in the case of Jews and West Indians respectively. The level of acceptance as neighbours by the other ethnic minorities (combined) is about the same as by the Majority Canadian group.

The level of acceptance as close relatives is presented in panel B of table 5.1. Generally, the level of acceptance as relatives tends to be lower than as neighbours. Ever since Bogardus's work (1928), this

TABLE 5.1
Acceptance of minority groups as neighbours and as relatives (percentages)

	Chinese	German	Italian	Jewish	Portuguese	Ukrainian	West Indian
A1. Perception of acceptance as neighbours:							
Very easily	31	66	48	22	54	61	19
Somewhat easily	54	28	41	56	34	33	39
Not easily	6	3	8	16	7	2	33
Don't know	9	4	3	5	5	4	9
N – weighted	(56)	(178)	(431)	(168)	(66)	(89)	(118)
Number of interviews	(152)	(321)	(351)	(348)	(161)	(353)	(150)
A2. Acceptance as neighbours by:							
Majority Canadians[a]	83	92	85	89	84	91	67
Others[b]	85	85	83	86	84	88	68
N – weighted	(1393)	(1278)	(1058)	(1299)	(1375)	(1345)	(1334)
Number of interviews	(1861)	(1706)	(1696)	(1698)	(1844)	(1643)	(1862)
B1. Perception of acceptance as relatives:[c]							
Very easily	10	59	42	8	44	54	10
Somewhat easily	47	32	45	34	34	32	25
Not easily	23	2	7	45	7	5	43
Don't know	20	8	6	13	16	8	22
B2. Acceptance as relatives by:							
Majority Canadians[a]	65	87	84	77	68	87	49
Others[b]	52	72	70	68	66	75	39

a The weighted *N* for Majority Canadians varies between 767 and 784; the number of interviews between 224 and 229.
b 'Others' include all non-majority Canadians, except respondents for the group concerned.
c See under section A1 for the *N*'s and number of interviews.

result was to be expected. The differences in these two areas of social acceptance, however, are not the same for all groups. The greater perceived acceptance as neighbour than as relative is as follows (column A):

	A	B
Chinese	21%	11%
German	7%	4%
Italian	6%	3%
Jewish	14%	8%
Portuguese	10%	11%
Ukrainian	7%	4%
West Indian	9%	13%

It should also be noted that the difference in the percentage of those who declare not to know the attitudes of the Majority Canadian group for each type of relationship also varies among groups. This fact is shown in column B above, the positive differences meaning greater uncertainty about acceptance as relatives than as neighbours, in three of the groups in particular. A 'don't know' in this context could mean that the respondents lack the experience required to form an opinion on the matter, that they have a doubt as to whether acceptance would occur if the circumstances required it, or that they do not want to tell. The first of these possibilities is unlikely and the other two (uncertainty and willingness to tell) contain an element of hesitation that suggests a feeling of less than full acceptance.[3]

Whether the 'don't knows' are considered as negative or not, the Chinese, Jewish, and West Indian respondents are significantly less likely than the other groups to feel accepted as relatives. In addition, the Majority Canadian respondents also show less acceptance of these than of the other four groups. There is, however, a discrepancy: the Majority Canadian respondents declare a higher degree of openness than what is perceived by the members of the three minority groups concerned. The Portuguese, by contrast, perceive a level of acceptance as relatives higher than what Majority Canadian respondents show.

Finally, the ethnic minorities are somewhat less likely than Majority Canadians to accept as relatives individuals of other ethnic minorities. This finding is true for all groups, except the Portuguese. As noted earlier, this tendency of minorities to be non-accepting was not observed with regard to acceptance as neighbours.

The perception of the likelihood of discrimination if minority-group members maintain their customs and language or speak with an accent is another indicator of social (cultural) acceptance. The results presented in table 5.2 are in line with the other findings of this section on patterns of social acceptance. A substantial proportion of each group, including the Majority Canadians, feel that members of minority groups are 'more likely to encounter discrimination if they keep their customs and ability to speak their language.'[4] Among West Indians and Jews the percentages are the highest (64 and 56% respectively) as well as among the 'English – first and second generation' and among the Majority Canadians (69 and 58% respectively).

The percentage agreeing with the item about discrimination being more likely if members of minority groups 'speak with an accent than if they do not' is about as high as, and in the case of Chinese, Jews, and Ukrainians is higher than, that of those agreeing with the item about the effect of preserving one's language and customs (table 5.2). Thus, many seem to perceive the preservation of one's ethnic heritage as a disadvantage in Canadian society, especially if it is revealed through one's accent in speaking English. It should be noted that this view is held by the majority of Majority Canadians and by a strong majority of the 'English – first and second generation.'

The immigration legislation also reflects the degree to which various groups are accepted in a society. Such legislation embodies the official attitudes of a country vis-à-vis immigration generally and the immigration of particular groups. Because of this relation, the legislation will usually be a matter of some concern to members of ethnic minorities and of the majority group. The reason is that it affects their relative sizes and thus their relative importance in society and that it may have an impact on the allocation of scarce resources and social status among them. There are, of course, other reasons why people may be concerned with immigration, such as the possibility of having relatives, friends, or simply people of one's own cultural background come to Canada.

An attempt was therefore made to find out whether or not respondents see the legislation as presenting a problem for their group. Specifically, they were asked if present immigration laws make it too difficult for persons of their own origin and too easy for those of other origins to come to Canada.[5] The results appear in table 5.3 for each ethnic category.

Given the previous results, it is to be expected that West Indians and Chinese respondents will be among those who are the most likely to feel that present laws make it too difficult for people for their home country to come to Canada. This feeling is indeed what we observe,

TABLE 5.2
Discrimination is more likely if elements of cultural background are retained, by ethnic group

	Per cent agreeing that discrimination is more likely if a person:		
	keeps customs and language	speaks English with an accent	*N* (weighted)
Chinese	50	60	(57)
German	47	51	(178)
Italian	50	53	(429)
Jewish	56	73	(165)
Portuguese	47	42	(67)
Ukrainian	31	54	(89)
West Indian	64	63	(118)
Majority Canadian	58	56	(787)
English – first and second generation	69	66	(415)

although this view is even more frequent among the Portuguese. In these three groups the percentages of people who think that the laws are too restrictive (for their group) vary between 49 and 70. Other groups show significantly lower percentages (table 5.3, panel A).

Panel B of the table presents the percentages of those who feel that it is too easy for certain groups to come to Canada: in all except one of the ethnic categories, at least 45% think so (the Portuguese being the exception with only 35%).

The specific groups whose immigration is perceived as being facilitated by present laws vary considerably, depending on the ethnic origin of the respondent. Table 5.4 presents the results on this matter for three categories of respondents: Majority Canadians, English – first and second generation, and the minority groups.

The table shows that regarding Pakistanis and West Indians – two visible minorities – the percentages who find that immigration laws make it too easy to come to Canada are the highest: 53% and 41%, respectively. The percentage is the highest among all three categories of respondents. (In the cast of West Indians, the percentage is somewhat higher among first- or second-generation English respondents than among Majority Canadians and the minority groups. In the case of the Pakistanis, the percentage is somewhat lower among the members of minority groups.) It can also be noted in table 5.4 that about one in five

TABLE 5.3
Views about immigration policies and changes in relative size of groups, by ethnic group (percentages)

	Chinese	German	Italian	Jewish	Portuguese	Ukrainian	West Indian	Majority Canadian	English 1st & 2nd gen.
A. Present laws make it too difficult for group to come to Canada									
Agree	49	8	40	13	70	22	61	8	24
Disagree	34	79	47	69	20	58	28	74	64
Don't know	5	12	11	14	9	18	7	17	11
B. Present laws make it too easy for certain groups to come to Canada									
Agree	52	59	47	49	35	64	45	63	58
Disagree	19	30	37	39	31	25	34	28	29
Don't know	19	8	14	11	31	9	14	9	10
N – weighted	(57)	(178)	(431)	(168)	(67)	(88)	(118)	(787)	(415)
Number of interviews	(152)	(321)	(351)	(348)	(161)	(353)	(150)	(226)	(264)

NOTE: The 'neutral' response and the non-responses are not included; they have been included, however, for the calculation of the percentages.

TABLE 5.4
Per cent agreeing that present immigration laws make it too easy for certain groups to come to Canada

	Majority Canadians	English 1st & 2nd generation	Minority groups	Total
Too easy for:				
All groups	24	20	15	19
Pakistani	58	53	47	53
West Indians	40	49	38	41
Chinese	15	15	11	14
Italians	13	15	11	13
English	8	2	21	12
Portuguese	8	7	4	6
French	5	1	6	5
Greek	4	2	4	4
German	2	1	3	2
Jewish	1	1	3	2
Ukrainian	1	1	a	1
Other groups	16	24	30	23
N – weighted	(465)	(227)	(514)	(1206)
Number of interviews	(136)	(146)	(911)	(1193)

a Less than 1%
NOTE: This table includes only those who think that immigration laws make it too easy for certain groups to come to Canada.

(19%) think that present laws make it too easy for people of *all* origins to come to Canada, the percentage holding this view being a little higher among Majority Canadians (24%) than among the minority groups (15%). The next highest percentages are for Chinese (14%) and Italians (13%).

It should be recalled from table 5.3 that the groups most likely to find that the present laws make it *too difficult* for their group to come to Canada are the Portuguese, West Indians, Chinese, and Italians. In the case of West Indians, there is clearly a strong opposition between their own views and those of other Canadians, whether they belong to the majority or to minority groups. A similar opposition of views exists in the case of the Chinese and Italians, but it is not as pronounced. For the Portuguese, the situation is quite different: while they are very likely (70%) to find present laws too restrictive for their group, very few other Canadians (6%) find that the laws are too lax in their case.

Finally, it should be noted that among minority-group respondents, the third specific group for whom immigration laws are found to be too easy (after Pakistanis and West Indians) are the English: 21% express this view. There seems to be some concern among members of minority groups that the policy is simultaneously aimed at buttressing the numerical strength of the traditionally dominant group and at facilitating an increase in the size of less acceptable visible minorities.

A related matter concerns the size of one's group compared to that of other groups. That is to say, immigration laws may be a concern not only because of the kinds of people they directly or indirectly allow into the country, but also because of the number of people admitted.[6] Thus, members of certain groups may feel that theirs is becoming too small relative to other groups (or that other groups are becoming too large).

The views of the sample on this question are presented in table 5.5. It shows that, among members of minority groups, the view that they are 'becoming too small a group in Toronto compared to other groups' is not prevalent: a total of 5% are very concerned about the matter and another 20% are 'somewhat' and 'a little' concerned. This view is most frequently held among Jews, Ukrainians, and West Indians: between a third and 41% are at least a little concerned about this possibility in these three groups. In the other four groups the percentage is somewhat lower, varying between 18% and 28%. Three of those four groups (Portuguese, Chinese, and Italian) show fairly high percentages who feel that present immigration laws make it too difficult for their group to come to Canada, yet reveal relatively low percentages regarding a concern for the possibility of their group becoming too small. Two of these groups are already small and, as a result, getting too small may not be an issue. It may be that several members of these three groups do not see immigration in terms of building numerical strength for political purposes, but rather in terms of reunion with friends and relatives.

What is much less surprising is that among the Majority Canadians and among the first- and second-generation English the concern with the relative size of groups is significant: two-thirds are at least a little concerned 'that the non-English ethnic groups are becoming too large in Toronto compared to the English Canadian group' (table 5.5). Indeed, the census shows that for a few decades it is the population of British origin that has declined. It was seen in chapter 3 that the percentage of the population of 'British Isles' origin declined from 81.1% to 46.4%[7] between 1941 and 1981 in the Toronto metropolitan area (table 3.3).

TABLE 5.5
Concern that one's group is getting too small, by ethnic group

	Group is getting too small compared to other groups in Toronto			
	Yes %	No %	Don't know %	*N* (weighted)
Chinese	27	70	3	(57)
German	17	77	5	(177)
Italian	21	77	2	(428)
Jewish	35	62	3	(168)
Portuguese	25	72	3	(67)
Ukrainian	33	65	2	(89)
West Indian	38	55	7	(118)
Majority Canadian[a]	66	34	–	(787)
English – first and second generation	67	33	–	(415)

a The question asked to Majority Canadian and to 'English – 1st and 2nd generation' respondents referred to 'the non-English groups becoming too large' in relation to the English-Canadian group.

Discrimination

Job discrimination is among the serious problems that members of an ethnic group may face. It is an important aspect of the instrumental incorporation of persons in a society. It may be experienced by individuals or one may perceive it as a problem without having personally experienced it. Both types of questions were addressed to the respondents.

Discrimination is a phenomenon with many facets. Its complexity cannot be adequately dealt with in this context. However, this complexity is recognized in the fact that several questions were asked about the experience of discrimination or its perception. At a general level, respondents were asked if 'discrimination against members of their group as far as jobs, pay, or other working conditions are concerned' is a problem in Toronto. The percentages of those who feel that it is for their group appear in table 5.6 (panel A).

The West Indian group is the most likely to report discrimination: a majority of them (57%) think that it is either a very serious or a somewhat serious problem. The next most likely to say that discrimination is a problem are the Chinese (37%) – the other non-European group – and the Portuguese (33%). Italians and Jews follow with 20 and 15% respec-

TABLE 5.6
Perception and experience of discrimination by members of minority groups (percentages)

	Chinese	German	Italian	Jewish	Portuguese	Ukrainian	West Indian
A. Discrimination re: job, pay, and work conditions:							
A very and somewhat serious problem	37	3	20	15	33	8	57
Not too serious	42	17	37	46	26	30	23
Not a problem	17	75	41	35	33	58	14
Don't know	3	4	2	4	8	3	6
N – weighted[a]	(57)	(178)	(429)	(168)	(67)	(89)	(118)
B. Employers perceived as discriminating a lot or somewhat:							
By group itself	53	18	30	40	30	24	66
By Majority Canadians[b]	47	17	38	39	49	16	76
By minority groups[b]	37	18	32	28	37	16	61
C. Have experienced discrimination when trying to find a job	17	5	7	12	5	10	22

a The *N*'s are the same for sections A and C of the table.
b The weighted *N* for Majority Canadians is 787. For the minority groups combined, the *N* varies between 1097 and 1107.

tively. The percentages for the remaining groups are quite small (between 3 and 8%). It should be noted, however, that aside from the Majority Canadians and the 'English, first and second generation,' it is only among Germans and Ukrainians that a majority declare that job discrimination is not a problem at all (75 and 58% respectively).

These findings are consistent with the results of the analysis presented in the previous chapter on the differential allocation of job status. Indeed, it was found that for West Indians the discrepancy between actual job rewards and those expected on the basis of job qualifications was the greatest. Discrimination may well be a factor in their case and in the case of the Chinese as well. For other groups such as Jews and Italians, there may be discrimination in the majority-controlled sectors of the labour market, but it may be counterbalanced by a relative autonomy in other sectors (see chapter 4).

Respondents were also asked if various groups are treated fairly by employers or if they experience discrimination.[8] From the distribution of responses in table 5.6 (panel B), it can be noted, first, that the rank order of groups along the percentage perceiving some or a lot of discrimination by employers is about the same as the one obtained with the previous question. Another observation to be made from the table is that, with one exception, the Majority Canadian group appears to agree with each group's perception of its treatment by employers. In the case of Italians, Portuguese, and West Indians a slightly greater percentage of the Majority Canadian group perceive discrimination than of the groups themselves. In the case of the Chinese and Ukrainians, it is slightly smaller.

The Portuguese constitute an exception: a greater percentage of the Majority Canadian group (49%) than of the Portuguese themselves (30%) perceive discrimination by employers. One possible explanation could be that they are more likely than other groups to work for employers of their own ethnic origin. Thus, they would not perceive ethnic discrimination. Majority Canadians would, at the same time, respond to the question in terms of 'Majority Canadian' employers. The Portuguese, however, are unlikely to work in a business or company managed by people of their own group. Only 5% do so, in contrast to 38% among Jews and 23% among Italians – the two groups for which within-group employment is the most frequent.

Minority groups who perceive discrimination by employers and, as seen earlier, who perceive problems of social acceptance do not appear to be under the influence of a persecution complex: generally, Majority Canadians and members of other minority groups tend to agree with them. Moreover, it would seem quite doubtful that those in the majority and minority groups who declare that there are problems of discrimination and of social acceptance are all under some sort of delusion. There clearly are problems to be dealt with, especially in the case of certain minority groups. The findings presented earlier with regard to the restrictiveness of immigration laws also show that the problems perceived by members of minorities are not the result of paranoia.

Other groups not included in our sample are also perceived as being discriminated against by employers in varying degrees. The question asked included seven other groups. The percentages of Majority Canadians and of minority respondents who perceive that these groups experience some or a lot of discrimination on the part of employers appear in table 5.7. It can be observed that a sizeable majority believe that Pakistani and Canadian Indians are the object of discrimination as was the case for West Indians: 78% and 65% respectively among Majority Canadians and 64% and 48% among members of the minority groups. A much lower but still significant proportion think that employers discriminate against French and Greeks.

Another interesting finding is that in a number of cases the other minority groups are less likely to perceive discrimination on the part of employers than is the Majority Canadian group (and sometimes than is the group concerned itself). This phenomenon can be seen for Chinese, Jews, Portuguese, and West Indians in table 5.6 (part B). The differences between majority and minority Canadians in this perception vary between 10% and 15%, depending on the group they are asked about. In other words, there appears to be a greater sensitivity to the existence of employer discrimination against those four groups on the part of Majority Canadians than on the part of minority-group members.

The above questions deal with perceptions of the experience of entire groups. Information was also obtained on the respondents' own experience: they were asked if they had 'ever been discriminated against in Canada because of (their) ethnic or cultural background.' The percentages of those who say they have been subjected to job discrimination appear in table 5.6 (part C) by ethnic origin. It can be seen that the rank ordering of the groups on this question tends to be similar to the ones obtained earlier: job discrimination is more frequently reported by Chinese and West Indians, followed by Jews and Ukrainians. Very few Italians, Portuguese, Germans, Majority Canadians, and 'English – first and second generation' report any experience of job discrimination.

Although the rank order is about the same, the percentages on

TABLE 5.7
Perception of discrimination by employers vis-à-vis selected groups, by Majority Canadians and minority groups

	Per cent perceiving 'a lot of or some' discrimination	
	Majority Canadians %	Minority groups %
French	37	26
English	5	7
Irish	6	9
Scottish	5	7
Greek	33	30
Pakistani	78	64
Canadian Indian	65	48
N (weighted)	(784)	(1105)
Number of interviews	(226)	(1780)

experienced discrimination are significantly lower than those for the perception of discrimination by employers. This difference is not surprising; it only indicates that in the latter case people are referring to cases they have witnessed or have heard about in addition to their own experiences. It could also reflect the influence of the media, which, to a degree, shape popular perceptions on this as on other matters.

The experience of discrimination tends to vary by generation, but not in the same way for all groups. For three of the groups for whom generational data are available (Italian, Jewish, and Ukrainian), the experience of discrimination is reported more frequently by the second than by either the first or the third-or-more generation respondents. Among Germans, the percentage who declare they have experienced discrimination decreases significantly from the first- to later-generation respondents (table not presented).

The perception of job discrimination as a group problem, however, decreases significantly with each generation: from 29% in the first to 12% in the second and 6% in the third-or-more generation respondents. This phenomenon really applies for only two of the groups (Jews and Italians) as there are no generational differences for Germans and Ukrainians.

PROBLEMS OF CULTURAL MAINTENANCE

As a result of their minority situation, members of ethnic groups usually experience the loss of at least some elements of their culture. The loss of language, traditions, and customs may be more or less extensive. Moreover, such loss may or may not be perceived as a problem either because it is limited, because it is expected as a normal phenomenon within the Canadian context, or even because it is felt that one's cultural background should be replaced by Canadian cultural traits. The latter view may be held because it is felt as necessary to avoid discrimination or to facilitate one's acceptance by other groups, especially by Majority Canadians. Data presented in the previous section suggest that this view may well exist and may even be fairly widespread within certain minority groups.

Conversely, the maintenance of at least some cultural elements may be valued and their loss perceived as a problem. Finally, individuals may be ambivalent with regard to their cultural heritage. They may see it as a liability in the Canadian context, as indicated above; and, at the same time, they may value their culture not only in itself but also because it is an integral part of their personality.

In order to explore this matter, respondents were asked whether or not they perceive the loss of their group's traditions and customs and the decreasing use of their language as a problem and, if so, how serious a problem. The results are presented in table 5.8. First, it is only among Jews that a majority see the loss of traditions and customs as a 'very or somewhat serious' problem. About a fourth of Chinese, Italian, and Ukrainian respondents think so, as do a fifth of Germans and 15% of West Indians and Portuguese. Second, it is only among the Portuguese that the majority (55%) do not see the loss of traditions and customs as a problem at all. It is seen as a problem by a majority of the other groups, although few appear to find that it is a serious problem.

There does not seem to be much of a relationship between the perception of and the actual loss of traditions and customs. For instance, although the majority of Jews see cultural loss as a problem, it is in this group that it declines the least over generations (a decrease that varies from 1 to 7%, depending on the item considered). In the other three groups for whom generational data are available (that is, Germans, Italians, and Ukrainians), the generational decreases are much larger, except in the case of food (table 2.9). These groups, however, do not seem to be very likely to see the loss of traditions as a problem.

With few exceptions, the results are similar when the decreasing use of the group language is considered: the majority of all groups feel it is a problem, but relatively few consider it a very serious one (the question is not relevant for West Indians).[9] It is also among the Jews and the Ukrainians that it is most frequently considered a 'very or somewhat serious' problem (50 and 41% respectively).

Chapter 2 showed that the use of one's ethnic language does decrease considerably in all four groups for which generational data are available. By the third generation, 98% of Germans, 89% of Italians, 78% of Jews, and 86% of Ukrainians use their ethnic language 'rarely or never.' Yet, this situation is more likely to be seen as a serious problem by Jews and Ukrainians than by the other two groups.

A better understanding of this distribution of responses can perhaps be obtained by examining the attitudes on the desirability of forming ethnic communities. Respondents were asked if members of their group 'should try as much as possible to blend into Canadian society and not form ethnic communities.'[10] As table 5.9 shows, the majority of respondents agree with this proposition and close to one-fourth of all respondents 'strongly agree' with it. Moreover, the majority are of this opinion in all groups, except among Jews. In their case a majority (50%) disagree with the view that members of their group should blend and not form communities. It will be recalled that the Jews are also those who are the most concerned with cultural loss (traditions, customs, and language).

These two sets of data may appear contradictory: on the one hand, a majority of most groups think that the loss of traditions, customs, or language is a problem and, on the other, a majority also feel that they should blend into Canadian society. In addition, if the two questions are cross-tabulated, we observe a relationship in the expected direction: the percentage who feel that the loss of tradition and language use is a serious problem is higher (37%) among those who disagree with the view that immigrant groups should blend into Canadian society than among those who agree (24%). But this pattern does not hold for all groups. It is the reverse in the case of the Chinese. There is no difference among Italians, Ukrainians, and West Indians. In short, the expected relationship is observed only among the Germans, Jews, and Portuguese.

In order to explore this question, respondents were classified in terms of their responses to both questions. The first category are those who feel that minorities should blend into Canadian society and who do not

TABLE 5.8
Loss of traditions and customs and decreasing use of ethnic language as a group problem in Toronto, by ethnic group (percentages)

	Chinese	German	Italian	Jewish	Portuguese	Ukrainian	West Indian
A. Loss of traditions and customs							
Very or somewhat serious problem	24	19	26	51	15	26	15
Not too serious	31	32	30	24	23	28	35
Not a problem	40	44	41	23	55	43	44
Don't know	5	5	3	2	8	3	6
B. Decreasing use of group language							
Very or somewhat serious problem	24	26	30	50	22	41	–
Not too serious	30	26	23	21	32	23	24
Not a problem	42	43	46	27	44	33	76
Don't know	4	5	1	2	3	3	–
C. Either loss of traditions and customs and/or decreasing use of language a very or somewhat serious problem	33	31	38	64	25	46	15
N – weighted	(56)	(177)	(430)	(167)	(67)	(89)	(117)

TABLE 5.9
'Immigrants and members of minority groups should try to blend into Canadian society and not form ethnic communities' (percentages)

	Chinese	German	Italian	Jewish	Portuguese	Ukrainian	West Indian	Majority Canadian	English 1st & 2nd gen.
Strongly agree	10	27	16	8	39	14	20	28	27
Agree	52	45	61	34	43	43	56	47	52
Neutral	15	6	6	7	4	7	5	5	5
Disagree	19	20	16	41	12	31	17	16	14
Strongly disagree	1	3	1	9	2	5	3	3	2
Don't know	4	–	a	1	1	a	1	–	–
N – weighted	(57)	(178)	(431)	(168)	(67)	(89)	(118)	(787)	(413)

a Less than 1%

TABLE 5.10
Attitude towards ethnic community formation and perception of cultural loss[a] as a group problem (percentages)

	Chinese	German	Italian	Jewish	Portuguese	Ukrainian	West Indian
Assimilationists:							
– Favour blending into larger society							
– Do not see cultural loss as a problem	55	64	60	28	75	46	67
Pluralists – concerned:							
– Do not favour blending into larger society							
– Perceive cultural loss as a problem	4	6	5	33	3	11	4
Pluralists – satisfied:							
– Do not favour blending into larger society							
– Do not perceive cultural loss as a problem	21	17	13	20	11	27	17
Pluralists – total	25	23	18	53	14	38	21
Integrationists:							
– Favour blending into larger society							
– Perceive cultural loss as a problem	20	13	22	18	11	15	13
N – weighted	(45)	(158)	(396)	(152)	(60)	(81)	(105)
Number of interviews	(143)	(308)	(347)	(342)	(157)	(347)	(141)

a The perception of cultural loss is an index combining the item pertaining to the loss of tradition and customs and the one pertaining to the decreasing use of the group's language.

see the cultural loss as a problem.[11] These respondents do not appear to favour the maintenance of distinct ethnic identities. They could be called 'assimilationists.' The second group consists of those who feel that minorities should not blend into Canadian society: they are 'cultural pluralists.' This category consists of two subgroups depending on whether or not they are concerned with the loss of customs and traditions and with the decreasing use of the language. Finally, there is a category of respondents who favour blending into Canadian society, but nevertheless see cultural loss as a problem. They will be referred to as 'integrationists.' The distribution of respondents among these four categories (and subcategories) appears in table 5.10.

Before discussing these results, it should be emphasized that the labels used in the table were selected to facilitate the presentation of the results. They are empirical terms, so to speak. As such, they should not be given meaning beyond that of the items used to construct the categories, except hypothetically.

It can be seen that Jews show the highest percentage of 'pluralists' (53%). The next highest percentages are observed among Ukrainians (38%) and Chinese (25%). It should be noted, however, that the Jews constitute the only group of 'pluralists' concerned with cultural loss: 33% of them do not favour blending *and* perceive a problem of cultural loss. In the other groups, most pluralists do not see cultural loss as a problem.

Four groups show a pronounced 'assimilitionist' tendency: the Portuguese (75%), West Indians (67%), Germans (64%), and Italians (60%). This orientation is also quite frequent among Chinese (55%) and Ukrainians (46%). The Jews represent the only group in which it is weak: 28%.

The last segment of table 5.10 shows the percentage of 'integrationists,' that is of those who think that minorities should blend into Canadian society, yet perceive cultural loss as a problem. There is a larger percentage of 'integrationists' than of 'concerned pluralists' (except among Jews), but they are proportionately less numerous than the 'assimilationists.' This combination of responses indicates that group maintenance is not seen as being opposed to incorporation in the larger society. It may even be valued as a means towards incorporation. It could be that these respondents see their community as a locus of social integration and activity but also as a source of support and protection. Such an interpretation would lead one to expect that this last pattern of response would be more frequent among those, for instance, who perceive discrimination and social acceptance as problems than among those who do not. This is indeed what we find (table 5.11). The perception of problems of discrimination or of social acceptance is associated with cultural orientation: 'pluralists' are more likely to be found among those who perceive certain problems while 'assimilationists' are somewhat more frequently found among those who do not. It would seem, then, that a number of respondents favour ethnic-community formation for protective reasons, that is, to cope with problems of incorporation in the society.

Finally, some respondents may be ambivalent with regard to these matters. This conclusion is suggested by the fact that the respondents referred to as 'integrationists' (that is, those who favour blending while seeing cultural loss as a problem) are more frequently observed among those who 'feel that it is difficult (or a problem)' to be both an ethnic and a Canadian at the same time (28%) than among those who do not feel such a difficulty (16%).[12]

Table 5.11 presents several correlates of these cultural orientations. Not surprisingly, section A shows that 'pluralists' are more frequently found among those who feel their ethnicity is important than among those who do not; while the reverse holds for 'assimilationists.' What is perhaps less obvious, however, is that first-generation people are more likely to be 'assimilationists' than third-generation respondents while the latter are more frequently 'pluralists' than the former. The majority of all three generational groups are 'assimilationists'; but it is in the third generation that 'pluralists' are the most likely to be found. This result constitutes additional evidence for the ethnic-retention hypothesis analysed in chapter 2.

It is, however, with the concern that one's 'group is becoming too small in Toronto compared to other groups' that the orientation towards blending into Canadian society and cultural loss as a problem is the most strongly associated. Those for whom this matter is not an issue are much more likely to be 'assimilationists' (62%) than those who are somewhat or a little concerned (44%) and those who are very much concerned (31%) (table 5.11, section E).

The 'pluralists' and the 'integrationists,' by contrast, are more frequently found among those who are concerned than among those who are not concerned with relative group size. It was suggested earlier that some members of minority groups seek to retain group organization and culture for defensive or protective purposes. The relationship between attitude towards retention and the concern with relative group size suggests that a more general factor, namely political power, under-

TABLE 5.11
Attitude towards community maintenance and cultural loss as a problem, by selected variables

	'Assimilationist'	'Integrationist'	'Pluralist'	N[a]
A. Subjective importance of ethnicity				
High	50	19	31	(535/856)
Low	62	17	20	(458/757)
B. Generation				
First	59	19	22	(619/937)
Second	51	18	31	(259/369)
Third +	50	14	37	(117/314)
C. Discrimination: a group problem				
Yes	53	29	17	(214/305)
No	57	15	28	(753/1270)
D. Acceptance as neighbour or relative				
High	60	19	21	(288/446)
Medium	58	16	26	(432/661)
Low	48	21	31	(255/476)
E. Group becoming too small: a concern				
Very much	31	35	34	(55/92)
Somewhat	44	26	30	(207/381)
Not at all	62	13	25	(703/1108)

a The first number is the weighted *N*; the second refers to the number of interviews.

lies the respondents' orientation to the persistence of group organization and culture.

Finally, before concluding this section, a result presented earlier should be recalled (table 5.9): a strong percentage of the Majority Canadian group (76%) and an even stronger one among the 'English – first and second generation' (80%) agree that immigrants and members of a minority group should try to blend into Canadian society and not form ethnic communities. It seems that an 'assimilationist' orientation is prevailing in Toronto among Majority Canadians and other groups as well. As noted, respondents may have given different meanings to the item: some may not have intended to express an outright assimilationist view. However, the distribution of responses to this item is consistent with the results presented above on the distribution of views concerning the greater likelihood of discrimination if customs and language are preserved or if one speaks English with an accent (table 5.2).

The Ethnic Community as a Resource: Types of Action Favoured

There are a number of ways in which a community can be a resource for its members.[13] It can be a source of relationships for the satisfaction of one's socio-emotional needs; of assistance in dealing with matters related to job and housing; of services performed in the context of a familiar cultural context. It can be a milieu in which one finds social acceptance and is given respect and recognition, especially if such advantages are not forthcoming from the larger society; a milieu in which individuals can find support in correcting situations that harm them. As an organized social unit, it can also provide leadership and promote action to combat discrimination and pursue objectives with regard to culture maintenance and immigration policies. In short, it can be a resource in relation to individual and community needs or problems such as those discussed above.

This section examines some of the ways in which the ethnic (and the larger) community is seen as a potential resource in relation to some of the problems faced by ethnic groups. This end is achieved by focusing on the channels that respondents think would be effective in dealing with certain matters. Two problem areas have been selected: job discrimination and immigration laws and procedures. The question is what actions and, by implication, what types of resources the respondent favours in terms of getting results with regard to cases of discrimination or to changes in immigration laws and procedures.

IN RELATION TO INSTANCES OF DISCRIMINATION

There are various ways in dealing with problems encountered or of seeking certain objectives. In order to explore the views of the respondents in this area, they were asked about various courses of action in relation to a case of discrimination at work and to a desired change in immigration laws or procedures. The question dealt with the perceived effectiveness of these actions, that is, the likelihood that they would get results.[14]

In the instance of job discrimination, the possible actions presented to the respondent can be grouped under three headings:

a Individual action:
  - Complain directly to the boss or personnel manager;
  - Say nothing, but work harder than the others so as to impress the boss.

b Activation of social networks:
  - Get together with co-workers to complain to the boss;
  - Deal with the situation by contacting a friend one happens to have in the company.

c Use of organizational resources:
  - Take the case to the union or employee association, if there is one in the company;
  - Take the case to an organization of the ethnic community;
  - Take the case to a community agency like the Ontario Human Rights Commission whose purpose is to handle cases of discrimination.

The distribution of responses appears in table 5.12 for each of the ethnic groups.

Taking one's case to a 'community agency like the Ontario Human Rights Commission whose purpose is to handle cases of discrimination' is the action that, in most groups, is the most frequently seen as most likely to give results (74%). Also, with few exceptions, taking one's case to the union comes as a close second-most-favoured action (71%). Generally, then, the use of the organizational resources of the larger society appears to be the most favoured option. This is the preferred action among the Majority Canadians, among the ethnic minorities, and for the 'first- and second-generation English.'

An important observation, however, is that the organizational resources favoured appear to be those of the community-at-large, not of the ethnic community: 39% for the latter in comparison with over 70% for the other two types of organizations. Ethnic organizations are not the least favoured of all types of action, but they are thought, on the average, as significantly less efficacious than organizations of the society-at-large. They are the least favoured in two of the groups whose members are the most likely to be victims of discrimination, as we have seen earlier: only 27% of the Chinese and 19% of the West Indians think taking the case to an ethnic organization would help very much or

TABLE 5.12
Actions with regard to a case of discrimination perceived as very or somewhat helpful to change the situation (percentages)

	Chinese	German	Italian	Jewish	Portuguese	Ukrainian	West Indian	Majority Canadian	English 1st & 2nd gen.	Total
A. Individual:										
Complain directly to the boss	38	52	53	38	39	50	33	46	48	46
Work harder to impress the boss	36	47	41	35	27	39	30	45	47	42
B. Social networks:										
Get together with co-workers to complain to the boss	43	50	49	40	37	43	25	45	35	43
Deal with situation through a friend in the company	28	36	35	29	23	33	20	32	25	31
C. Organizational:										
Take case to union or employee association	57	72	69	66	52	72	59	76	71	71
Take case to an organization of the ethnic community	27	35	43	44	24	30	19	44	38	39
Take case to an agency that handles such cases	56	73	69	72	70	69	73	80	73	74
N – weighted	(56)	(178)	(429)	(168)	(67)	(89)	(118)	(787)	(413)	(2307)

somewhat to change the situation. However, the percentage for this type of action is high among Jewish respondents (44%) who are also, as seen above, among the most likely to experience problems of social rejection and discrimination.

Some of the reasons for these patterns of response will be explored later in the chapter. At this point, it is worth mentioning what much of the literature on collective action suggests, namely, the importance of organization in translating discontent, grievances, or aspirations into collective action. In social-psychological terms, this means that individuals will favour the type of action that they perceive as having the best organizational apparatus and support system for its execution. This may be the reason why societal institutions like the Human Rights Commission are the most favoured. This may also be why Jewish respondents are more likely to favour action through their own organizations than are members of other minorities: indeed, Jewish communities tend to be among the better organized for a variety of purposes, including combating anti-Semitism.

Dealing with the case of discrimination through a friend in the company is generally the least frequently selected course of action, although in some groups it is at par with or close to other actions. Among Ukrainians and Germans, for example, it is almost equally less favoured as taking the case to an ethnic organization. Among Portuguese and Italians, it is at par with working harder to impress the boss. Among Chinese respondents, however, it is favoured even more than the use of an ethnic organization.

IN RELATION TO A CHANGE IN IMMIGRATION LAWS OR PROCEDURES

A similar classification can be made of actions oriented to a change in immigration laws or procedures:

a Individual action:
- Write to a member of parliament or to government officials;
- Write letters to the editors of newspapers.

b Mobilization of social networks:
- Get as many of one's friends and neighbours as possible to write or talk to the member of parliament or to government officials;
- Organize support for or opposition to certain candidates at election time.

c Use of organizational resources:
- Work through one of the political parties to get something done;

- Work through an organization in the community to get something done.

As can be seen from table 5.13, the distribution of responses by ethnic groups does not reveal as clear a pattern as in the case of discrimination: the range of percentages favouring each type of action is not as wide and some of the different types of action are equally favoured. A reason for this distribution may be simply that the possibilities presented to the respondents can easily overlap. For example, writing to a member of parliament or to government officials can be seen as an individual action or as part of a campaign launched by an organization. Similarly, the organization of support for or opposition to a political candidate can involve one's personal networks but it can also extend to action through organizations. However, even though patterns are less pronounced, they are not absent.

First, it appears that the mobilization of social networks is perceived as the action most likely to help in bringing about a change in immigration laws or procedures (54 and 48%). The individual action items, by contrast, seem to reap the lowest percentages (31 and 35%). The use of organizational resources falls in between (44%).

It should be noted that in the case of immigration laws and procedures, community organizations are not more favoured than the political parties. Unfortunately, a difficulty with this result is that the item does not specify 'ethnic community.' Thus, some respondents may have taken it to refer to organizations of the larger community and others of the ethnic community. The impact of this ambiguity cannot be assessed.

Perception of Problems and Attitude towards the Use of Ethnic Organizational Resources

The following analysis will focus on the propensity of respondents from different ethnic groups to favour the use of community organizations. Because of space limitations, the analysis will be restricted to the case of job discrimination. It will consist of a rapid exploration of the relationship of this propensity to three phenomena: the perception of problems; the perception of certain socio-political characteristics of the community; and the linkages with the ethnic community.

What is the relationship between the propensity to favour working through community organizations and the perception and experience of discrimination problems? Table 5.14 shows that, in the sample as a whole, those who perceive job discrimination as a serious or somewhat

TABLE 5.13
Actions perceived as very or somewhat helpful to change immigration laws or procedures (percentages)

	Chinese	German	Italian	Jewish	Portuguese	Ukrainian	West Indian	Majority Canadian	English 1st & 2nd gen.	Total
A. Individual:										
Write to a member of parliament or government official	53	38	38	32	33	41	29	30	38	35
Write letters to the editors of newspapers	30	34	30	27	12	30	25	32	34	31
B. Social networks:										
Get as many friends and neighbours as possible to write to MPs or government official	36	54	53	49	40	56	32	61	54	54
Organize support for or opposition to certain election candidates	32	53	45	46	28	45	38	56	46	48
C. Organizational:										
Work through an organization in the community	28	44	45	43	27	50	30	46	45	44
Work through a political party	45	44	44	42	23	48	31	45	49	44
N – weighted	(57)	(178)	(431)	(168)	(67)	(88)	(117)	(787)	(415)	(2309)

TABLE 5.14
Per cent favouring ethnic organizational action and perception of problems, by ethnic group

	Job discrimination a group problem		Experienced discrimination	
	Yes	No	Yes	No
TOTAL	40 (224/334)[a]	39 (758/1318)	35 (300/515)	42 (708/1183)
Chinese	36 (20/44)	27 (28/84)	17 (18/45)	37 (33/87)
German	30 (6/9)	37 (154/281)	31 (40/77)	40 (126/222)
Italian	54 (83/64)	46 (294/255)	37 (103/86)	52 (280/237)
Jewish	46 (25/53)	46 (130/267)	48 (74/152)	45 (86/178)
Portuguese	34 (21/49)	20 (27/94)	20 (7/17)	27 (54/132)
Ukrainian	46 (7/31)	30 (73/289)	21 (18/84)	35 (64/244)
West Indian	24 (62/84)	12 (41/48)	28 (40/54)	17 (66/83)

a The first number is the weighted *N*; the second refers to the number of interviews.

serious problem for their group in Toronto are as likely to favour taking a case of discrimination to an ethnic organization as are those who do not so perceive: 40 and 39%, respectively.[15] However, although not pronounced, the relationship is in the expected direction in five of the seven groups. The two exceptions are the Jews, for whom there is no difference, and the Germans, for whom the small difference is in the opposite direction. (It should be noted that some of the percentages are based on a very small number of cases).

However, those who report having experienced discrimination themselves tend to be less likely than those who have not to favour the use of organizational resources to deal with a case of discrimination (42% compared to 35% for the total sample). Again, in this case, there are two exceptions: the Jews, whose views on the matter are virtually unaffected by the experience of discrimination, and the West Indians, who are a little more likely to favour the use of ethnic organizations if they have had such experiences than if they have not (28% versus 17%).

But, for most groups, there appears to be a distinction between the perception of discrimination as a community problem and its experience by individuals. A reason may be that those who perceive discrimination as a group problem are also those who are the most likely to be involved in their community and thus would be more oriented towards the use of group resources. Another reason for the difference noted may be that those who have experienced discrimination have also had the experience of attempting to use organizational channels to deal with their problem without much success. A personal failure in attempts to obtain redress may lead to disaffection with regard to particular courses of action.

Involvement with Ethnic-Community Affairs and Relationships with Leaders

The attitude towards the use of ethnic organizational resources may be associated with the extent of involvement in ethnic community affairs. It is reasonable to expect that the most active and well-connected within their community will also be the most likely to favour the use of community organizational resources. It therefore seems appropriate to examine a few dimensions of the relationship that respondents have with their ethnic community.

Two sets of measures of participation in the ethnic community will be used. First, there are items dealing with involvement in organizations and in community activities; second, there are some pertaining to the relationships of community members with community leaders.

ETHNIC-COMMUNITY ORGANIZATIONS AND ACTIVITIES

An essential component of involvement is a person's knowledge of any organizations or associations in the ethnic community. Another is actual membership in community organizations or associations and the extent to which one is active in them. A third aspect considered is the distance from the centre of community activities as perceived by the respondent. A last indicator used is the frequency at which respondents 'express their views about important community affairs either in meetings, in letters to the editor, or directly to community leaders.' After a brief examination of the extent of involvement in community affairs on the basis of these indicators, its relationship to the propensity to favour the use of community organizational resources will be considered.

Table 5.15 shows considerable variations in the degree of involvement among the ethnic groups. For most items, it is among Jewish respondents that the percentages of participation in community affairs are the highest. The level of participation is next highest among Ukrainians. These two groups show the highest percentages on three of the four items: knowing and being a member of community organizations and expressing their views on community affairs. The exception is the item pertaining to the closeness to the 'centre of activities' in the community: they occupy an intermediate position on this item. Involvement is the lowest among Germans, Chinese, and West Indians. It is slightly higher among Portuguese respondents. Italians occupy an intermediate position.

The relationship of participation with the attitude towards organizational action is limited to two items: membership in associations and the expression of views about community affairs (table 5.16). Overall, there is no relationship between participation and the propensity to favour ethnic organizational action to deal with a case of job discrimination. In the case of memberships in associations, the relationship is in the expected direction in three of the seven groups: Chinese, Portuguese, and Ukrainians. There is no relationship in the case of the Jews and the West Indians and a negative relationship for the Germans and Italians (that is, those without memberships are somewhat more likely to favour ethnic organizational action than are members).

The other item attempts to identify individuals who are likely to bring issues to the attention of community organizations. The question, indeed, refers to the expression of views about important community affairs either at meetings, in letters to the editor, or directly to community leaders. One would have expected that those who express their views would be more likely to favour ethnic organizational action than those who do not. But this expectation is not met.

For the sample as a whole, the relationship is in the expected direction, but it is weak: 43% of those who express their views compared to 38% of those who do not favour ethnic organizational action. When groups are considered individually, a relationship in the expected direction is observed only among Italians and Ukrainians.

In short, the propensity to favour ethnic channels to deal with cases of discrimination is not in any important way a function of the involvement of individuals in their ethnic community. They are almost as likely as not to favour such channels whether they are active participants or not. The Ukrainian is the only group in which a positive relationship is observed for both indicators of participation.

TABLE 5.15
Participation in ethnic-community organizations and activities (percentages)

	Chinese	German	Italian	Jewish	Portuguese	Ukrainian	West Indian
A. Know of any organizations in the community	52	46	55	94	67	70	52
B. Was or is now a member of one or more ethnic organizations	12	9	21	63	14	51	12
C. Perceived degree of closeness to centre of community activities							
Close	11	4	29	18	46	23	17
Intermediate	18	5	24	27	22	18	16
Distant	71	91	47	55	32	59	67
D. Expresses views about community affairs, at least sometimes	22	9	27	44	20	42	19
N – weighted	(56)	(177)	(430)	(167)	(67)	(89)	(117)

TABLE 5.16
Per cent favouring ethnic organizational action and participation in community affairs, by ethnic group

	Membership in ethnic associations		Expressed views about community affairs	
	Yes	No	Yes	No
TOTAL	40 (740/1164)	40 (269/536)	43 (283/511)	38 (727/1167)
Chinese	29 (44/111)	36 (6/21)	30 (13/29)	30 (37/101)
German	39 (149/273)	27 (16/26)	20 (16/31)	40 (150/256)
Italian	50 (303/267)	38 (80/56)	53 (114/91)	46 (269/229)
Jewish	46 (60/121)	47 (100/209)	46 (71/150)	47 (89/180)
Portuguese	25 (52/125)	34 (9/25)	14 (11/30)	29 (50/120)
Ukrainian	24 (39/147)	39 (43/180)	40 (36/148)	26 (47/175)
West Indian	20 (94/120)	21 (14/19)	23 (23/32)	20 (86/106)

RELATIONSHIP WITH ETHNIC LEADERS

The relationship with leaders is another aspect of incorporation in the community as a socio-political system. Are leaders known to the community members? Are there personal contacts between leaders and members? Are members informed of the activities of the leaders? And is the extent of contact with leaders related to the attitude towards the use of community organizational resources to deal with perceived problems? Before presenting the results, it should be noted that the notion of 'leader' was not defined for the respondents. They responded to the questions with their own idea of who constitutes the leadership of the community.

As with involvement in community affairs, considerable variations exist among ethnic groups in the extent of relationships with leaders, as table 5.17 shows. It is in the Jewish followed by the Ukrainian and Italian groups that leaders are the most frequently known personally by members and that there is the greatest familiarity with their acti-

TABLE 5.17
Relationship with ethnic-community leaders (percentages)

	Chinese	German	Italian	Jewish	Portuguese	Ukrainian	West Indian
A. Know leaders:							
Personally	14	5	28	48	20	37	21
Not personally	23	6	38	30	29	19	15
Not at all	63	89	34	22	51	44	64
B. Contacts with leaders:							
Frequently and occasionally	6	3	14	30	13	23	12
Seldom or never	30	7	47	42	36	30	24
Do not know leaders; and no answer	64	90	39	28	51	47	64
C. Informed about activities of leaders:							
Very much and somewhat	12	4	30	45	19	32	17
Not too well; not at all	24	7	32	28	29	21	18
Do not know leaders; and no answer	64	89	38	27	52	47	65
N – weighted	(56)	(177)	(430)	(167)	(67)	(89)	(117)

TABLE 5.18
Per cent favouring ethnic organizational action and relationship with leaders, by ethnic group

	Know community leaders	
	Yes	No
TOTAL	41 (537/869)	38 (470/828)
Chinese	27 (21/49)	32 (29/83)
German	23 (18/33)	39 (145/263)
Italian	47 (256/209)	49 (126/114)
Jewish	46 (125/261)	48 (34/69)
Portuguese	22 (30/73)	31 (31/77)
Ukrainian	38 (48/197)	24 (34/130)
West Indian	18 (38/47)	22 (71/92)

vities. Next come the Portuguese, followed by the Chinese and West Indians. Finally, among the Germans leader-member relationships are the least frequent.

As with the participation items, the relationship between knowing leaders and the attitude towards organizational action, however, is weak and inconsistent (table 5.18). In the sample as a whole, there is a positive but very small relationship (41% versus 38%). The relationship is in the expected direction only among Ukrainians. In the other groups, it is nil or negative. In short, knowing leaders does not appear to make one more likely to favour ethnic organizational action, except among Ukrainians.

Generally, there is a weak and inconsistent relationship between personal involvement in the ethnic community (as reflected in measures of participation and of relationships with leaders) and the propensity to favour the use of the community's organizational resources to deal with problems of discrimination. In spite of this fact, however, there is a certain pattern when groups are examined separately on the three items (tables 5.16 and 5.18). First, Ukrainians show a consistent positive relationship between the three community-involvement items and the propensity to favour ethnic organizational action. For them, participation affects their views on the matter. Jews and West Indians also show a consistent pattern: they show no relationship between ethnic organizational action and the three indicators of participation. Their likelihood of favouring ethnic organizational action is unaffected by the degree of involvement. There is also consistency among German respondents. In their case, there is a negative relationship on all three items. Those uninvolved are somewhat more likely to favour ethnic channels than those who are involved. Finally, there is no consistency across items among Chinese, Italian, and Portuguese respondents.

Perceived Socio-political Features of Ethnic Communities

The propensity to favour the use of ethnic organizational resources to deal with problems may be related to the perceived possibility of effective concerted action in the community. In other words, as a socio-political entity, the community may or may not be perceived as having the social and organizational characteristics required to undertake actions that would bring about results. Three sets of characteristics pertaining to the community as a socio-political entity are considered: (a) the decision-making structure; (b) the efficacy of the community leadership; and (c) the social cleavages within the community.

These variables are taken as indicators of the community's capacity for concerted action. The way decisions are made in the community, the ability of leaders to obtain results in various domains of activity, and the social cohesion of the community are among the important components of community organization for socio-political action. The present analysis deals with people's perception of these components of social organization, not with their direct measurement.

PERCEPTION OF COMMUNITY DECISION-MAKING

Three items pertaining to decision-making in the community appear in table 5.19. They deal with the perception of who makes the decisions and of the character of decision-making in the community. A first observation to be made from this table is that, as for the items presented in the previous sections, there is considerable variation among groups in the perception of how decisions are made in the community. The percentages who agree that 'the ordinary member does not have much to say about how things are run' vary between 21% (Germans)

TABLE 5.19
Perceptions of different aspects of decision making in one's ethnic community[a] (percentages)

	Chinese	German	Italian	Jewish	Portuguese	Ukrainian	West Indian	Total
A. Ordinary member does not have much to say about how things are run:								
Agree	48	21	31	31	38	27	62	34
Disagree	15	57	54	60	36	58	19	49
Don't know	24	19	10	6	18	8	16	13
B. Leaders are concerned with community problems and interests:								
Very much and somewhat	48	49	67	80	45	72	60	64
Little or not at all	33	23	25	13	41	18	19	23
Don't know	19	28	9	6	14	10	22	14
C. Effort by leaders to get community approval:								
A lot or some	32	36	50	66	43	58	42	49
Little or none	41	13	25	17	32	21	25	23
Don't know	27	51	25	17	26	21	33	29
N – weighted	(57)	(173)	(431)	(165)	(66)	(88)	(118)	(1099)

a The 'neutral' and non-responses are not included in the table, but they were included for the calculation of the percentages.

and 62% (West Indians) – a 41% difference (table 5.19, panel A). The perception that leaders are very much or somewhat concerned with community problems and interests is shared by 80% in the Jewish group and by 45% of the Portuguese – a 35% difference (panel B). Finally, 66% of Jewish respondents consider that their leaders devote a lot or some effort to get community approval in contrast with 32% of the Chinese – a 34% difference.

A second observation is that there is a certain consistency in the ranking of the groups on the three items. That is to say, the Chinese respondents tend to show a pattern of response indicating a distance between leaders and members, whether it be in terms of members not having 'a chance to say much about how things are run in the community'; of decision-makers making little or no effort 'to get approval from the members of their organizations or from the community'; and of leaders being little or not at all concerned 'with the problems and interests of the ordinary members of the community.' West Indians and Germans also tend to show a relatively low degree of integration of members and of their concerns in the decision-making process, as perceived by members.

By contrast, Jewish respondents tend to express a high degree of closeness between leaders and members in the running of community affairs. This perception holds for the three items. It is also worthwhile noting that Jewish respondents are the least likely to declare that they 'don't know' on all three items. This response suggests an awareness of the leaders and of their activities and as such could be taken as another indication of closeness between community members and leaders. Ukrainians are fairly close to the Jews in their perception of the leaders' relationship with members in the management of community affairs, as shown by their responses to the three items. Ukrainians are followed by the Italians, and then by the Portuguese.

Table 5.20 presents the percentages who favour taking the issues of cases of discrimination to a community organization among respondents with different perceptions of the community decision-making and leadership. With the first indicator, the relationship is as expected, but is not very strong: those who disagree that members do not have much to say are a little more likely to support the use of ethnic organizational resources than are those who feel they have no influence (42% versus 36% in the total sample). This result is also seen among the Chinese and Italians (but one of the percentages among Chinese respondents is quite small). There is only a weak or no relationship among

TABLE 5.20
Per cent favouring ethnic organizational action by perception of community decision making, total and by ethnic group

	Ordinary member has little to say in way community is run		Leadership concern with community problems and interests		Effort by leaders to get approval from members	
	Agree	Disagree	High	Low	A lot	Little
TOTAL	36 (352/585)	42 (502/832)	43 (651/1092)	32 (232/387)	43 (511/850)	35 (235/389)
Chinese	30 (26/65)	40 (8/25)	35 (25/66)	24 (17/46)	43 (17/39)	29 (22/62)
German	45 (36/65)	36 (93/160)	42 (83/143)	38 (39/72)	39 (60/108)	32 (23/47)
Italian	40 (125/104)	50 (213/181)	50 (260/228)	38 (95/73)	48 (204/160)	46 (98/73)
Jewish	49 (51/109)	44 (96/195)	47 (129/265)	37 (20/43)	45 (106/218)	46 (27/59)
Portuguese	36 (22/56)	25 (23/57)	31 (28/66)	26 (26/65)	31 (27/69)	26 (20/46)
Ukrainian	29 (23/97)	34 (48/185)	35 (61/241)	20 (15/59)	40 (48/189)	16 (17/69)
West Indian	20 (70/89)	22 (21/29)	24 (66/83)	14 (21/29)	27 (48/67)	12 (28/33)

Jewish, Ukrainian, and West Indian respondents, and a negative relationship among the Germans and Portuguese.

With the item pertaining to the perceived concern on the part of leaders with community problems, the relationship with the propensity to favour the use of ethnic organizational resources is somewhat stronger: 43% versus 32% in the sample as a whole. In addition, it is the first item for which the relationship is positive in all groups (although it is weak in two of them: the German and Portuguese).

Similar results obtain with the third indicator of leader-members relationships, namely the perception of the efforts of leaders to get membership approval. Those who see that they make considerable effort are somewhat more likely to favour ethnic organizational action than those who do not: 43% versus 35%. The relationship is in the expected direction in five of the seven groups. There is no relationship among Italians and Jews.

Generally, then, the perception that members' interests are incorporated in the decisions of leaders has some bearing on the propensity to favour the use of community organizational resources to deal with issues.

PERCEPTION OF THE EFFICACY OF LEADERS

Are ethnic leaders perceived as capable of bringing about results for their community? Are they perceived as sufficiently well-connected and taken seriously enough for their interventions to matter? It appears reasonable to hypothesize that the evaluation of the community leadership in these regards will be associated with the propensity to turn to community organizations to deal with instances of discrimination or to obtain desired changes in immigration legislation. Three items pertaining to the perceived efficacy of the leaders of one's ethnic community are presented in table 5.21: (A) whether or not politicians and officials are seen as taking seriously the views expressed by the leaders of ethnic communities; (B) whether or not the leaders have enough connections with important people in business and government to get important results for the community; and (C) whether the group would get more attention from politicians and officials if leaders and their organizations were more active.[16]

To repeat, the items deal with the perceptions of community members. They *do not* constitute a measure of the actual degree of efficacy of ethnic leaders. In the present context, however, they constitute the relevant kind of data. Indeed, since the concern is with the propensity

TABLE 5.21
Perceived efficacy of community leaders[a] (percentages)

	Chinese	German	Italian	Jewish	Portuguese	Ukrainian	West Indian	Total
A. Politicians do not take ethnic leaders seriously:								
Agree	42	17	28	20	37	41	54	30
Disagree	17	46	54	69	33	41	15	47
Don't know	27	33	13	9	26	15	25	19
B. Leaders do not have enough connections:								
Agree	55	15	19	7	55	29	65	26
Disagree	15	57	65	83	14	56	17	55
Don't know	22	26	14	8	28	12	18	16
C. Even if more active, leaders and organizations would not get more attention:								
Agree	35	29	23	23	40	31	37	28
Disagree	40	48	58	65	43	56	34	53
Don't know	14	20	16	8	15	11	24	16
N – weighted	(57)	(173)	(427)	(166)	(67)	(88)	(118)	(1096)

a The 'neutral' and non-responses are not included in the table, but they were included for the calculation of the percentages.

of members to favour the use of organizational resources in their community, it is their perception of the efficacy of these organizations and their leaders that needs to be considered; in fact, more so than the actual degree of efficacy.

The distribution presented in table 5.21 show as much variation among ethnic groups as we observed with the 'distance' or 'accessibility' items. There is a 54% variation among groups in the percentage who *disagree* that 'politicians do not take ethnic leaders seriously' (table 5.21, panel A). Jews are the most likely to reject this view (69%). The Italians, with 54%, are the closest to the Jews on this item. They are followed by the Germans (46%) and Ukrainians (51%). The Portuguese (33%) fall in between these relatively 'high' groups and the two that score quite low: the West Indians and Chinese with 15% and 17%, respectively.

The second item pertains to connections with the larger society (table 5.21, panel B). It is again the Jewish respondents who are the most likely to *disagree* that the leaders of their community do not have enough connections with important people in business or government to get results for the community (83%). The perception that leaders can be politically efficacious because well connected is the lowest among the Portuguese (14%), the Chinese (15%), and the West Indians (17%). There is a 69% difference between the highest and lowest group in this regard. In between are the Italians, Germans, and Ukrainians who do not differ markedly, with 65%, 57%, and 56% respectively.

Finally, the third item concerns the chances of getting more attention from politicians and officials if the leaders and organizations of the community were to be more active. The percentage who *disagree* is again the highest among Jews (65%), who are followed fairly closely by the Italians (58%) and Ukrainians (56%). The lowest percentage (34%) is observed among the West Indians (who also show the highest incidence of 'don't know') and the next lowest occurs among the Chinese. In between are the Germans and Portuguese.

The first two items dealt with the perceived political efficacy of community leaders. The third, however, pertains to the potential that leaders and organizations have not yet tapped, but could if they were more active. Thus, while Jews are the most likely to perceive their leaders as efficacious, they are also the most likely to think that they have reached the maximum of their potential efficacy. By contrast, among the Portuguese, West Indians, and Chinese, a significant percentage (40, 37, and 35% respectively) feel that the community would get more attention if leaders and organizations were more active. These three groups are the ones in which the leadership is the least likely to be perceived as being taken seriously and as well connected.

The relationship between the perception of leadership efficacy and attitude towards the use of ethnic organizational resources is presented in table 5.22. It shows that, for the sample as a whole, those who agree that politicians and officials do not take the views of ethnic leaders seriously are somewhat less likely to favour ethnic organizational action than those who disagree that such is the situation: 35% versus 43% in the sample as a whole. Similarly, those who feel that the leaders of their community are poorly connected with important people in business and government are less likely to favour organizational action: 44% versus 35%.

This pattern does not hold, however, for most group-by-group comparisons. On the first item, the relationship is positive only among Italians. In all the other groups it is negligible. The perception of the attitudes of politicians and officials appears to make little difference in the propensity to favour ethnic organizational action.

On the second item, the relationship is positive among Jews and West Indians. Among them, those who think that leaders are well connected are more likely to favour ethnic organizational action than those who agree that they do not have enough connections. Among Chinese, Germans, and Portuguese the relationship is negative (but the number of cases is sometimes small). It is nil among Italians and Ukrainians.

With the third item, dealing with an untapped potential of influence (at least to the extent of getting attention), the relationship with the propensity to favour ethnic organizational action is a little stronger: 45% of those who feel the potential of influence has been attained favour such action, compared with 32% of those who feel the opposite. In addition, the relationship is positive in five of the seven groups. The two exceptions are the Chinese (among whom the relationship is negative) and the Germans (among whom there is no relationship).

The perceived efficacy of leaders does seem to make a difference among respondents who declare a high degree of interest in national, provincial, or local issues and politics, but not among the politically uninterested (table 5.23).[17] That is to say, when political interest is low or moderate, the propensity to favour ethnic organizational action is about the same whether leaders are perceived as influential or not. But if interest is high, those who perceive efficacy in the leadership are about 14% more likely to favour such action than those who do not (13% with one indicator and 15% with the other). Similar results are

TABLE 5.22
Per cent favouring ethnic organizational action by perception of ethnic leader's efficacy, total and by ethnic group

	Politicans and officials do not take the views of leaders seriously		Leaders do not have enough connections to get results		Even if leaders were more active, group would not get more attention	
	Agree	Disagree	Agree	Disagree	Agree	Disagree
TOTAL	35 (313/532)	43 (475/789)	35 (273/485)	44 (562/921)	32 (295/519)	45 (537/876)
Chinese	27 (21/56)	24 (9/24)	33 (29/74)	26 (7/21)	37 (18/43)	28 (21/59)
German	41 (29/51)	40 (76/142)	51 (25/45)	38 (93/168)	41 (49/88)	38 (77/133)
Italian	41 (107/79)	48 (210/193)	48 (75/56)	48 (254/226)	35 (96/76)	52 (226/179)
Jewish	46 (33/69)	46 (110/226)	29 (12/27)	47 (132/273)	34 (39/84)	51 (104/210)
Portuguese	30 (24/59)	32 (19/46)	32 (35/84)	26 (10/28)	23 (25/62)	33 (27/66)
Ukrainian	33 (35/137)	30 (33/134)	30 (24/100)	34 (47/183)	28 (26/104)	36 (47/186)
West Indian	22 (63/81)	26 (17/24)	20 (73/99)	29 (19/22)	20 (43/62)	27 (35/43)

TABLE 5.23
Per cent favouring ethnic organizational action by perception of leaders' political efficacy and political interest

A. Interest in local, provincial, and federal issues

	Low	Intermediate	High
1. Politicians do not take ethnic leaders seriously:			
Agree	30	41	31
	(56/93)	(141/223)	(115/211)
Disagree	38	44	44
	(78/113)	(196/309)	(202/348)
2. Leaders do not have enough connections:			
Agree	34	39	30
	(57/98)	(117/200)	(100/184)
Disagree	37	45	45
	(88/125)	(250/383)	(225/393)
3. Even with more active leaders, group would not get more attention:			
Agree	32	31	34
	(57/105)	(129/223)	(109/191)
Disagree	37	47	45
	(86/126)	(238/368)	(213/382)

B. Closeness to the centre of ethnic community activity

	Close	Intermediate	Distant
1. Politicians do not take ethnic leaders seriously:			
Agree	30	38	34
	(78/135)	(126/203)	(107/188)
Disagree	42	48	38
	(87/144)	(213/320)	(174/303)
2. Leaders do not have enough connections to get results:			
Agree	32	35	36
	(59/114)	(127/210)	(86/155)
Disagree	45	49	37
	(114/174)	(232/349)	(215/374)
3. Even with more active leaders, group would not get more attention:			
Agree	28	33	33
	(61/119)	(114/190)	(119/210)
Disagree	45	48	40
	(110/183)	(245/371)	(181/318)

obtained with the third item dealing with the perceived untapped influence potential: there is no association between this perception and the views about ethnic organizational action when political interest is low; only when it is moderate or high.

The measure of political interest used above concerns the affairs of the larger society. The conditional effect, however, is also observed when involvement in the internal affairs of the community is taken into consideration. The indicator used in this case is the respondent's assessment of his/her closeness to the centre of community activities.[18] Perceiving the leadership as efficacious is associated with a greater likelihood of favouring ethnic organizational action among those who describe themselves as close or moderately close to the centre of community activities; not among those who say they are distant from it.

In short, the perceived efficacy of leaders appears to be associated with a positive orientation towards the use of ethnic organizational resources only among those who are politically interested or involved, whether in the affairs of their ethnic community or in the political issues of the larger society.

In addition, the perceived efficacy of leaders is generally associated with the perception that the leaders and organizations are operating at their full potential, and especially so when political interest is high.

COMMUNITY CLEAVAGES

The third feature of the ethnic community to be considered is the degree of social cohesion or, more precisely, the perceived presence of social cleavages in the group. Respondents were asked about the differences that divide their community in Toronto. The differences they were asked about are as follows: (1) between rich and poor; (2) between political groups; (3) between religious groups; and (4) between members of the group originally coming from different areas.

The percentages who think that each of these differences divides their community 'very much' or 'somewhat' are presented in table 5.24. In almost all groups, the economic differentiation is the most significant, as perceived by members of the communities. Ukrainians constitute one exception: it is the division among political groups that they mention the most frequently. Also among Jews and Ukrainians, religious division is mentioned almost as frequently as economic cleavages. Among Portuguese, all four lines of division appear to be almost equally important.

TABLE 5.24
Perception of factors that divide the community (percentages)

	Chinese	German	Italian	Jewish	Portuguese	Ukrainian	West Indian
A. Differences that divide the group very much or somewhat:							
Between rich and poor	43	39	48	64	22	31	45
Between political groups	35	23	25	29	19	46	27
Between religious groups	14	22	21	63	18	34	22
Between regional groups (in country of origin)	35	22	26	43	23	19	28
B. Number of perceived divisions in the community:							
Two or more	36	29	35	61	23	38	33
None	33	46	35	16	54	40	37
N – weighted	(56)	(177)	(430)	(167)	(67)	(89)	(117)

In order to facilitate intergroup comparisons on this dimension, it is useful to identify the lines of division mentioned as somewhat or very significant by at least one-third of the sample for each group. This analysis yields the factors shown in the table below, in order of importance, for each group.

Lines of division by order of importance

	(1)	(2)	(3)
Chinese	Economic	Regional	Political
German	Economic	–	–
Italian	Economic	–	–
Jewish	Economic	Religious	Regional
Portuguese	–	–	–
Ukrainian	Political	Religious	–
West Indian	Economic	–	–

There are intergroup differences in the number of differentiating factors as well as in their nature. Table 5.24 includes the total number of divisions perceived. For each respondent, a count was made of the factors mentioned either as very much or somewhat important. At one extreme, there are those who see all four factors as dividing the community; at the other, there are those who see no factor dividing it. The percentages in panel B of the table refer to those who mentioned two or more factors as dividing the community somewhat or very much.

This measure yields results similar to those indicated above. The Jewish group is the most frequently perceived by its members as highly divided (61%). It is followed by the Ukrainians, the Chinese, and the Italians with between 35 and 38% of the respondents seeing the group as highly divided. Next are the West Indians and Germans (33 and 29% respectively). The Portuguese, with 23%, show the smallest percentage perceiving internal divisions.

Is the perception of social cleavages related to the propensity to favour organizational action in relation to cases of discrimination? Social cohesion is frequently seen as a facilitator of community action and a divided community is less able to co-ordinate itself for effective action.[19] We would therefore expect those who perceive extensive cleavages in their community to be less inclined to favour the use of community organizational resources to deal with problems. However, the lines of social differentiation in a community may become manifest

TABLE 5.25
Per cent favouring ethnic organizational action and perception of social divisions in community, by ethnic group

	Number of perceived lines of social divisions		
	None	One	Two or more
TOTAL	35 (347/681)	40 (276/378)	43 (387/246)
Chinese	23 (14/41)	31 (17/30)	35 (19/24)
German	36 (74/149)	29 (40/62)	47 (51/41)
Italian	42 (128/119)	54 (115/74)	48 (139/50)
Jewish	53 (24/82)	42 (36/78)	46 (100/43)
Portuguese	21 (33/90)	26 (15/25)	39 (13/15)
Ukrainian	24 (32/141)	35 (19/81)	38 (32/47)
West Indian	26 (42/59)	18 (35/28)	16 (32/26)

when the community is confronted with problems or events and when, as a result, a definition of the situation must be established and a course of action identified. From this point of view, it could be argued that cleavages would tend to be more frequently perceived and organizational action more frequently favoured in the same communities since the saliency of social division is, in a way, an indicator of a politically active community. The relation between perceived cleavages and perceived organizational efficacy may, however, differ by type of cleavage. Religious or regional cleavages may reflect organizational vitality in a way that economic divisions do not. Some divisions may not prevent interaction across groupings; on the contrary, the issues that emerge may, by generating debate, increase it. Other cleavages, such as economic ones, may isolate segments of the community from each other.

Table 5.25 tends to support the latter interpretation: in the total sample, the larger the number of perceived cleavages, the more likely the support for ethnic organizational action. This result appeared among Chinese, Portuguese, and Ukrainian respondents. The relationship is in the opposite direction among Jews and West Indians, giving modest support to the first interpretation.

The relationship tends to be curvilinear among the Germans and Italians: in the case of the latter, the propensity to favour the use of community organizations is higher among those who perceive *one* cleavage of importance than among those who perceive either none or two or more. Among Germans, the propensity towards ethnic action is lower among those who perceive a single line of social division as important than among the other two categories. This curvilinear relationship may give support to both hypotheses simultaneously: the perception of cohesion is a condition for supporting group action but, at the same time, several manifest cleavages may be an indication of a politically active community. Such an interpretation, however, can only be very tentative. What the data show is that the relationship between perceived social divisions and the propensity to favour ethnic action is not unambiguously in one direction. If anything, the results tend to suggest that, to a certain extent, the perception of cleavages is an indication of political activity, not of political paralysis.

Summary and Conclusion

This chapter has attempted to describe some of the problems encountered by ethnic minorities as perceived by members of the minority groups themselves and by Majority Canadians. Generally, the rank order of the groups included in the study is similar with regard to the various instrumental and expressive aspects of social incorporation in Canadian society. The non-European-origin groups (Chinese and West Indians) and Jews are those who are the most likely to experience problems of social acceptance and job discrimination. Italians and Portuguese tend to be the next most likely to experience problems. Ukrainians and Germans are close to the Majority Canadians and the 'English – second and third generation,' who are the least likely to face discrimination or social rejection.

It is noteworthy that the perceptions of the Majority Canadian respondents tend to be the same as those of the respondents from the groups themselves. For instance, West Indians and Chinese are the most likely to report problems of social acceptance and job discrimination; it is also these groups that are the most likely to be perceived as experiencing problems by Majority Canadians and other English respondents.

With the Portuguese, the non-European-origin groups are also the most likely to perceive their groups as unequally treated by immigration laws. The Jews, however, with the Germans and Ukrainians, are the least likely to perceive difficulties in this area. This response does not mean that they are not concerned with the size of their group in Toronto relative to that of others. On the contrary, the preoccupation with group size is relatively high among Jews as well as among West Indians and Ukrainians.

The groups that are the most likely to experience problems of incorporation (social acceptance and discrimination) in Canadian society are not necessarily those that are most likely to report problems of cultural maintenance. West Indians are the most likely to declare problems of social incorporation, but are among the least likely to mention problems of cultural loss. The Portuguese show the same pattern, but at the other end of the scale: they rank higher on problems of social incorporation than of cultural loss. The situation is the reverse for Ukrainians: they rank low in the experience of social-incorporation problems, but high on the concern with cultural loss. The Germans show the same pattern (as the Ukrainians), but less pronounced: low on problems of social incorporation, but intermediate on problems of cultural loss. The Jews show the opposite pattern: intermediate on problems of social incorporation, but high on the perception of cultural loss as a problem for their group. Finally, Italians and Chinese occupy almost the same rank on both dimensions. The average rankings on these two sets of items are as given in the table below.

	Problems of social incorporation	Problems of cultural loss
Chinese	2.8	3.5
German	6.3	4.2
Italians	4.4	4.7
Jews	2.6	1.0
Portuguese	4.9	6.7
Ukrainians	5.5	2.0
West Indians	1.2	6.0

A substantial proportion of members of the different ethnic minorities do not declare that their group experiences problems of cultural loss, but also feel that minority groups should blend into Canadian society. They were referred to as 'assimilationists' in orientation. They are like the large proportion of Majority Canadians who appear to have this orientation. The proportion of 'pluralists' is significantly smaller, except in the case of Jews and Ukrainians.

For some members of minority groups, the perception of cultural loss as a problem is not necessarily associated with the desire to form distinct ethnic communities. The preliminary analysis suggested a hypothesis about the attitudes that could underlie the views of these respondents: community formation for protective or defensive purposes rather than for cultural retention as such.

The attitude with regard to different strategies to deal with instances of discrimination and to seek changes in immigration law and procedures was also described. It was found that although respondents tended to favour organizational over individual strategies, they favoured organizations of the larger society much more than those of their ethnic community.

The propensity to favour ethnic organizational resources was found to be related to the perception and experience of problems, to the degree of involvement in the ethnic community, and to the perception of certain socio-political features of that community. Table 5.26 presents the rank of the ethnic groups on the items pertaining to participation, to the relationship with leaders, and to the perception of their efficacy. It can be seen that, with a few exceptions here and there, the groups show a similar rank on most items. The Germans and Portuguese show the least consistent pattern.

It can be seen that the average rank of the groups is quite similar on the measures pertaining to the political organization of the community and with regard to the propensity to favour ethnic action on matters of discrimination and immigration laws and procedures. This similarity suggests that favouring ethnic organizational action is partly a function of the perception of the accessibility of the leadership to the community, of its concern with problems, and of the perceived possibility of making an input into the community decision-making. In addition to the internal political organization of the community, the perceived efficacy of leaders and their organizations in relation to the institutions of the larger society appears to be important.

These results, however, do not come out as clearly when the analysis is carried out at the level of individuals. Weak and inconsistent results obtain when the perception or experience of problems is related to the

TABLE 5.26

Average rank of groups on items related to discrimination, group culture, community organization, and views about ethnic organizational action

	Discrimination problems	Immigration laws too restrictive	Cultural concerns	Community participation	Openness of leaders	Efficacy of leaders	Favour ethnic action
Chinese	2.8	3	3.5	5.6	6	7	5
German	6.3	7	4.2	7	4	4	3
Italian	4.4	4	4.7	4.5	3	2	1.5
Jewish	2.6	6	1	2.2	1	1	1.5
Portuguese	4.9	1	6.7	2.7	5	6	6
Ukrainian	5.5	5	2	2.3	2	3	4
West Indian	1.2	2	6	5.2	5	5	7

NOTE: Rank 1 was assigned to the group with the highest percentage.

propensity to favour ethnic organizational action. This same pattern holds with the measures of involvement in community affairs and of relationships between leaders and members.

The propensity to favour ethnic action, however, seems to be associated with the perception of the leaders' concern for the problems of the community as well as with the possibility of making an input in the community's public policies. It is also associated with the view that leaders and organizations are operating at their full potential of political efficacy. The respondents who perceive that leaders and organizations are not as active as they could be are less likely to take cases of discrimination to an organization of their ethnic community than those who feel they are. It is not the perceived political efficacy as such that seems to matter, but the perception that leaders are prepared to use all the potential they are seen to have.

Finally, the perception of social divisions in the community is positively associated with the attitude towards ethnic action. It seems that the felt presence of divisions is an indicator of a politically active community. This correlation would, hypothetically, be the reason for the somewhat greater tendency to favour ethnic action when divisions are salient than when they are not.

Another way of summarizing the results is to present the situation of each ethnic group with regard to the various dimensions considered, which is done in the remaining paragraphs.

Chinese

The problems that the Chinese are the most likely to face in Toronto are ones of discrimination: a significant proportion declare they have experienced discrimination in the past. They are also likely to perceive employers as discriminating against members of their group, a perception with which Majority Canadians tend to agree. Close to a majority of them perceive present immigration laws as making it too difficult for their group to come to Canada. At the same time, issues of social acceptance as relatives, the loss of customs and traditions, and the decreasing use of the language are less likely to be perceived as problems: about a third of the respondents perceived these issues as problems for their group.

Relatively few of the Chinese favour the use of ethnic community organizational resources to deal with the problems faced: a little over a fourth favour the use of such channels to deal with discrimination and to obtain changes in immigration laws and procedures. Consistent with this weak inclination to use community organizational resources is a relatively low involvement in community affairs, a distant relationship with leaders, a fairly negative perception of the community decision-making structure, and a somewhat dim view of the ability of leaders to bring about change. These results suggest that the propensity to favour community action to deal with problems is not only a function of the perception of problems but also of the perception of certain features of the community organization and leadership.

Germans

Relatively few Germans perceive problems for their group in Toronto with regard to social acceptance, immigration legislation, and discrimination, although about one-third declare having experienced discrimination themselves in Canada at one time or another, mostly in areas other than work. Group problems in Toronto are more likely to be perceived with regard to the loss of tradition and customs and the decreasing use of the German language.

German respondents show a low level of involvement in ethnic-community affairs and a weak relationship with community leaders. However, they are moderately likely to favour the use of ethnic organizational resources to deal with problems of discrimination or immigration legislation and procedures. This propensity does not seem to be associated with their personal relationship with the community or with a perception of a well-functioning and responsive decision-making structure within the community, including a fairly effective leadership in relation to the élites of the larger community.

Italian

That present immigration laws make it too difficult for Italians to come to Canada is the phenomenon most frequently perceived as a problem by Italian respondents. They are less likely to either perceive or experience problems of discrimination, although such problems are mentioned by a certain proportion of them (about a fourth). Acceptance as neighbours or as relatives by Majority Canadians appears to be a negligible problem for Italians. Along with discrimination, cultural loss is a problem of intermediate magnitude for them: over one-third appear to be concerned with the loss of customs, tradition, and language among members of the community.

About 40% of Italians favour the use of community organizational resources to deal with discrimination or to obtain changes in immigration legislation. A similar percentage is involved in community affairs and has relationships with community leaders. A slightly higher percentage has positive views of the decision-making structure in the community and of the ability of their leaders to obtain results in relation to problems faced by the group.

Jews

Jewish respondents are quite likely to perceive problems in different areas, the most frequent being problems of cultural maintenance, followed closely by problems of discrimination and of acceptance as relatives. The next frequently mentioned problem is the possibility that their group is getting too small in relation to other groups in Toronto (about one-fourth).

Jews are among the most likely to favour the use of the organizational resources of their community. They are also the most likely to be involved in community affairs, to have relationships with their leaders, to perceive the community decision-making structure as responsive, and to think that their leaders can get results. Some of the other groups included in this study show an awareness of problems facing the community, but their community organization seems to fail to mobilize its members and is perceived as unable to get results. Other groups perceive few problems to be dealt with, but reveal a fairly well-organized community that presumably could launch action in the event that the group became confronted with problems of one sort or another. In the case of the Jews, however, we find a community with both sets of characteristics: it faces a number of problems and shows a willingness to use its organizational resources to deal with them, as is reflected in the high degree of involvement, and in the favourably perceived decision-making structure and leadership.

Portuguese

The only problem that Portuguese respondents perceived with any significant frequency is that present immigration laws and procedures make it too difficult for members of their group to come to Canada. No other area seems to pose significant problems for the members of this group. In fact, Majority Canadians are more likely than the Portuguese themselves to perceive problems of discrimination for Portuguese or to report difficulties in accepting them socially.

In spite of the high degree of concern with immigration laws and procedures, only about a fourth of the Portuguese respondents favour the use of community organizational action to obtain changes in them.

About the same percentage favour such action in relation to problems of job discrimination. In addition, the Portuguese are not particularly involved in the affairs of their community and in relationships with community leaders. They are among the least likely to perceive their leaders as particularly capable of obtaining results and to have a positive view of the responsiveness of the decision-making structure of their community.

Ukrainians

Few Ukrainian respondents perceive problems for their community: problems of loss of customs and tradition and of discrimination by employers are mentioned by about a fourth of the respondents. A third are concerned that the group is getting too small in relation to other groups in Toronto. Problems of social acceptance are mentioned by a very small proportion of respondents. The problem mentioned the most frequently is the decreasing use of the group's language.

Half of Ukrainian respondents favour the use of community organizational resources to obtain changes in immigration laws and procedures; a slightly lower percentage favour such channels to deal with discrimination problems. As far as community participation and perception of the community decision-making structure and leadership is concerned, it was seen that although Ukrainians do not rate as high as Jews, they (with Italians) come fairly close to them.

West Indians

In contrast with Ukrainians, West Indians perceive and experience problems in almost all areas except with regard to cultural maintenance: discrimination; restrictive immigration laws and procedures; the actual experience of discrimination; and problems of social acceptance either as neighbours or as relatives. Majority Canadians tend to share this perception of the situation of West Indians.

By contrast, the propensity to favour ethnic organizational action to deal with problems appears to be relatively low among West Indian respondents. They resemble the Chinese in this regard, although they are a little less likely than the Chinese to favour such action in relation to problems of discrimination.

Involvement in community affairs is fairly low and relationships with community leaders appear limited. However, compared with most other groups, few West Indian respondents perceive the decision-making structure of their community as responsive (as is the case among Chinese). Also, relatively few perceive their leaders as able to get results in transactions with the representatives of societal institutions (as is also the case among Chinese and Portuguese respondents). In short, the two non-European-origin groups in the study show a similar pattern of experiences and perceptions: they more frequently report experiences of discrimination by individual members and for the group as a whole; a community organizational structure that seems to be lacking in some of the internal features required for effective group action; a leadership that is perceived as being poorly connected with the institutional élites of the larger community and as relatively unable to get responses from them; and, not surprisingly given this context, a fairly low propensity to favour the use of community organizations to deal with the problems encountered.

6

Conclusion

In the preceding chapters, several findings have shown both a significant degree of incorporation in Canadian society and the continuing role of ethnicity for individuals and groups. It was seen that in many ways members of ethnic minorities are becoming part of the culture and structure of the larger society. It was also seen, however, that such a trend does not necessarily mean that ethnic identities disappear; that cultural heritages are abandoned; or that social relationships and group formation are not based on ethnicity. In addition, it was observed that although ethnicity appears to impede incorporation in the larger society, it sometimes provides the social resources that can facilitate it.

The results, however, vary considerably depending on the ethnic group and the dimension considered. These can be summarized along the major lines of variation that were, as indicated in the introduction, the focus of the analysis: variations among ethnic groups in the pattern of incorporation and in the ways in which ethnicity constitutes a basis of identity and group formation; variations in the effects (positive and negative) of retention on different aspects of incorporation; and variations across generations in the pattern of incorporation and of ethnic retention or reconstruction.

Incorporation in Canadian Society

Several more or less direct measures of incorporation were considered in the study: access to economic rewards; perceived job discrimination; perceived disadvantage if ethnic culture is retained; acceptance as neighbours and relatives; perceived acceptance by the society as reflected in immigration legislation; residential dispersion; and the sense of political efficacy, that is, of having an influence on the political institutions of the society.

The German and Ukrainian respondents showed a consistently high degree of incorporation on all these dimensions. They have equal access to economic rewards. They feel accepted socially and politically in the society. Both groups tend to be and to perceive themselves as being equal and full participants in Canadian society. As will be seen in more detail later, the two groups differ in the way they combine incorporation in the larger society and the retention of their ethnic culture and social organization – a difference suggested by the higher percentage of Germans than of Ukrainians who feel that members of ethnic minorities should blend into Canadian society, and by a residential dispersion much more similar to that of the Majority Canadian population than that exhibited by the Ukrainians.

The Jewish respondents, by contrast, do not show a consistent pattern of incorporation: they are high on the economic and political, but not on the social dimension. They have been fairly successful in becoming part of the economic structure, although a significant proportion perceive problems of job discrimination. They also show a fairly high degree of political efficacy. They are, however, the most highly segregated residentially, and the second most likely to perceive problems of acceptance as neighbours (after West Indians) and the most likely to feel not easily accepted as relatives. They are also the least likely to favour a pluralist model for Canadian society.

The Chinese and West Indians are the two groups who encounter the most problems of incorporation, whether economic, social, or political. Members of these two groups, especially the West Indians, are the least likely to have rewards in line with their qualifications. They experience problems of discrimination and social acceptance and they are the least likely to feel that they are taken seriously by the political authorities. Members of these groups show a strong tendency to favour blending into the larger society, which may be reflected in their somewhat unique patterns of residential dispersion characterized by several scattered areas of concentration.

The Italians and Portuguese occupy an intermediate position. Generally, they have rewards appropriate for their position, but a certain proportion report problems of job discrimination and social acceptance. Italians, however, are more likely than Portuguese to express a sense of political efficacy, and thus the capacity to deal with problems. Both groups are strongly in favour of blending into the larger society. Yet, the Italians show a greater tendency towards residential dispersion in later generations than is evident for those of Portuguese origin.

Ethnicity as a Basis of Identity and of Social Organization

As already indicated in the introduction and at different points in the study, incorporation in the larger society does not necessarily imply that ethnicity disappears; that it ceases to be an organizing force in the personal and social life of individuals. In the process of becoming participants in Canadian society, many individuals abandon elements of their culture; but not always all of them. Several establish ties beyond the social boundaries of their own group; but many ethnic ties are preserved. The organizations of the larger society tend to absorb the members of ethnic minorities; but elements of ethnic social organization are maintained.

There are many ways in which ethnicity can manifest itself: personal identities; knowledge and use of language; the retention of traditions and customs; participation in ethnic activities; occupational and residential concentrations; social relationships at work or elsewhere; and in socio-political organization.

For the Jewish, cultural background is the most important element in shaping their individual and collective behaviour, for all the dimensions considered: identity; economic relationships; cultural practices; and socio-political organization. Ukrainians follow fairly closely, although in their case ethnicity does not seem to have much of an impact in the economic domain. But it does have a significant role in the other areas.

The Germans, by contrast, show the lowest degree of retention in virtually all dimensions. It is not that it is absent; but it is very low compared to the other groups. In the case of the four other groups, ethnicity appears significant in some but less in other dimensions. For instance, Italians, Chinese, and Portuguese are highly concentrated in occupations. Residential segregation increases across generations for the last two (Chinese and Portuguese) as well as for the West Indians. At the same time, the three groups tend to occupy a somewhat lower position on the indicators of socio-political organization.

The Relationship of Retention with Incorporation

The above findings indicate that incorporation does not necessarily mean the loss of ethnicity. In other words, incorporation in the larger society can be associated with either high or low ethnic salience. The Jewish are quite clearly found in the first category and the Germans in the second. Ukrainians and Italians tend to be closer to the 'high' end of the continuum, while the Portuguese appear to be somewhat closer to the 'low' pole.

But there are also indications that a relatively low degree of incorporation can also be accompanied with either high or low ethnic salience. The West Indians and Chinese seem to follow the second pattern. They do not appear to lean strongly in the direction of ethnic retention or reconstruction: indeed, they show a strong aspiration to blend into Canadian society and a low degree of occupational concentration and of socio-political cohesion. Yet, they are the least incorporated of the groups considered.

The pattern followed by Italians and Portuguese is more ambiguous. Both are on the way to full incorporation in Canadian society. Whether ethnicity will continue to provide a basis of social organization for these two groups is more problematic. It seems plausible to hypothesize that, for them, incorporation will tend to be accompanied by the declining significance of the ethnic background.

Different elements of identity and culture appear to be retained as incorporation in the larger society proceeds, as happens with concrete objects such as food and artistic articles that act as symbols of the cultural background. Although less so, the same retention also occurs with social ties (friendship and marriage). Thus, these are the three items the most retained by the Germans who, it was seen, are the most incorporated. By contrast, some cultural elements seem to be less likely to be retained: language, the practice of customs, community participation, and the sense of obligation vis-à-vis the group.

In the case of residence, the best example of the classical pattern of declining segregation with subsequent generations is the population of German origin. The Ukrainians and Italians exhibit considerably higher initial levels of residential segregation that drop significantly for the second generation but remain relatively constant thereafter at intermediate levels. In the case of the other minority groups, incorporation does not seem to be associated with an increase in residential dispersion. For some groups, the visible minorities in particular, their patterns of segregation may be a partial indicator of a lack of social acceptance by the larger society.

Ethnic concentrations in labour markets have varying effects on incorporation – defined in terms of equality. Sometimes they are obstacles, but not always so. The effects actually depend on the type of concentration, the particular ethnic group, and the level of incorporation being considered. Ethnic occupations have certain discriminatory effects on Chinese and West Indians, and the Portuguese are also concentrated in very low-level occupations. However, in come of the more established groups, labour-market concentration seems to have little if any effect. The Germans, Ukrainians, and Jewish are all fairly well incorporated. Germans and Ukrainians have very low labour-market concentration. The Jewish are highly concentrated, more so than any predominantly immigrant group. Thus, a high degree of occupational incorporation is possible whether levels of ethnic concentration are high or low. Italian men represent an intermediate case. For them, extensive labour-market concentration has led to partial incorporation. Italians have established ethnic businesses enabling Italian men (but not women) to achieve income mobility while remaining, however, in low-status occupations. Later generations may be abandoning ethnic concentrations to achieve more complete incorporation. Some types of ethnic concentration, such as work groups in mainstream organizations, have little effect in any group.

Finally, the degree of socio-political organization appears to be positively related to incorporation in society, since such organization is an instrument with which to deal with the problems encountered. Two of the well-incorporated groups – Ukrainians and Jews – perceive their group as having a high degree of political cohesion, a capacity to act in a concerted way to cope with problems. The two least incorporated groups – Chinese and West Indians – are also low on most indicators of socio-political organization, as perceived by their members. The Italians and Portuguese are intermediate on both dimensions. The Germans show a different pattern: they are high on incorporation but low on socio-political cohesion.

In short, the results suggest not only that incorporation does not necessarily imply the declining salience of ethnicity, but also that ethnic identity and social organization can have an effect on the degree of incorporation in the larger society and that this impact can be either positive or negative.

In the introduction it was mentioned that the two dimensions – incorporation and ethnicity as a basis of social organization – constitute a conceptual space in which different ethnic groups can be located. The findings of the study suggest that the position of the groups included in this study is approximately as shown in the accompanying chart.

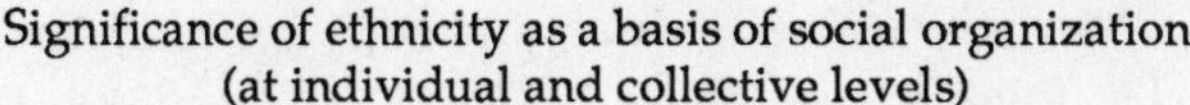

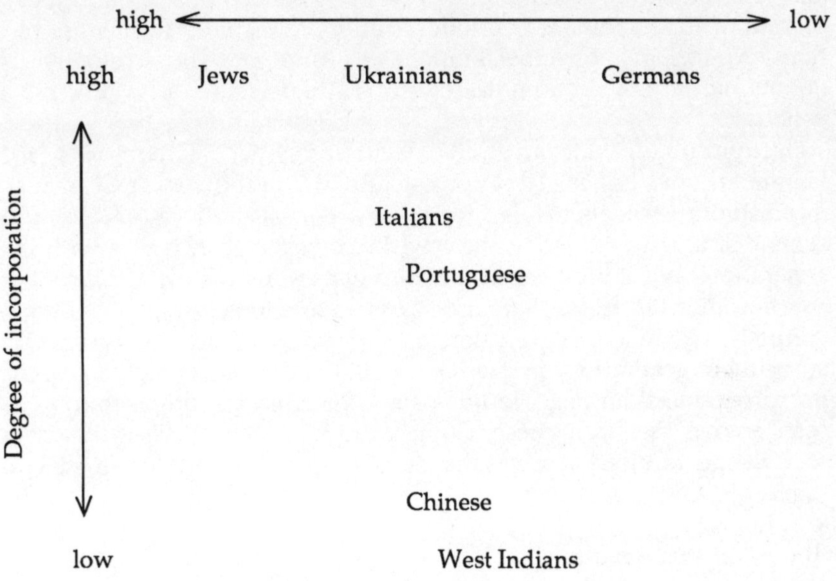

Incorporation and Retention across Generations

For Germans, Italians, Jews, and Ukrainians, generational changes were examined. The four groups do not exhibit the same pattern. It has already been observed that the Germans are the least likely to retain their culture, social ties, and elements of ethnic social organization. This pattern holds across generations as well as for the group as a whole.

The Jewish and Ukrainians were described as relatively well-incorporated 'high retainers.' Even though this description is accurate, the two groups show a different pattern across generations, although there are a few similarities. Jews are the most likely to retain the ability to read, write, and speak their language across generations. Ukrainians, by contrast, not only show a lower propensity for language retention, but the retention among them tends to be restricted to the ability to speak, not to read or write, the language. A similar pattern is revealed among Italians.

The retention of other elements (customs, artistic articles, food, social ties, and social participation) is also the highest among the Jewish. In fact, the retention increases slightly over generations, suggesting a pattern of reinforcement of ethnic identity among later Jewish generations. Among Italians and Ukrainians, cultural and social retention is not only lower than among the Jewish, it also decreases with successive generations.

Occupational concentration decreases over generations for Ukrainians and Italians (it is consistently low in the case of Germans). In addition, it seems to play for them a decreasing role for access to economic rewards. Among the Jewish, however, it increases with the generations and it involves in the third generation the establishment of concentrations in additional high-status occupations.

Finally, residential segregation, as already indicated, decreases with subsequent generations primarily among the Germans. The decrease is less pronounced among Ukrainians and Italians. The opposite trend is seen among the Portuguese, Chinese, and West Indians: it increases with the generations. Among the Jewish, it remains high for all generations.

Some General Results

In short, the study provides evidence in regard to seven propositions. *First,* it shows that, to a considerable degree, members of certain ethnic minorities become full participants in the social fabric of Canadian society: that they become incorporated in its social and institutional life.

But, *second,* it also shows that some groups or categories within groups encounter serious barriers or obstacles to their full economic and/or social incorporation. Such obstacles are most prevalent for recent immigrants. But, clearly, there is also a racial factor involved. Difficulties of incorporation are especially significant for the two non-white groups included in the sample, the Chinese and West Indians. The Jewish also experience barriers to social acceptance, even though they are well incorporated economically. Thus being non-white, a new immigrant, or Jewish continues to involve disadvantages for full and equal participation in Canadian society. In addition, it was found that a number who do not aspire to the retention of their culture and community – that is, who want to blend into Canadian society – were experiencing problems of incorporation.

Third, even if there is a significant incorporation into the larger society, a substantial degree of ethnic retention can be observed even among individuals who can, by most indicators, be considered integrated in the larger society. Thus, although their members are individually incorporated, some groups seem to retain collective goals for which they mobilize at least some degree of participation. Nevertheless, substantial loss also takes place, whether it be in terms of language, participation in activities, customs and traditions, or social ties.

A conceptual implication of these results is that the incorporation of members of ethnic minorities in a society cannot be regarded as the simple opposite of cultural retention. The definition of one is not the negative side of the other. A single concept such as integration is not sufficient since we are dealing with two distinct phenomena. They are interrelated, as we have seen, but not in such a way that if one increases the other necessarily decreases. In other words, it is not necessarily true that if members of a group are fully incorporated in Canadian society they have abandoned all elements of their ethnic identity and background. Similarly, if members of a group show a low degree of ethnic retention, it does not necessarily follow that they are highly incorporated in the social fabric of the society.

In fact, in addition to underlining the fact that ethnic retention and societal incorporation are distinct phenomena, the study shows, *fourth,* that retention can have an effect on the degree and pattern of incorporation in the larger society. That is to say, it was observed, as in other studies, that the incorporation of individuals and groups in the larger society depends on a wide range of factors. The foregoing analysis, however, emphasizes the role of ethnic retention as a factor in the incorporation of minorities in the larger society. That is to say, cultural retention and the maintenance of ethnic organizations have implications for the degree and patterns of social incorporation – implications that can be positive as well as negative. Cultural retention does not necessarily retard or impede incorporation; it may facilitate it.

The study has recognized that both retention and incorporation are multidimensional realities. Both have structural, cultural, and identificational dimensions that can manifest themselves in several domains of activities and relationships: economic, political, residential, and socio-cultural. since the study included several of these dimensions, its comparative nature has yielded a *fifth* important result: different groups do not exhibit the same pattern of retention and incorporation.

General propositions about the evolution of ethnic minorities have a very limited validity, if any. Propositions must be conditional on the situation of the groups considered. Although not the only significant one, the distinction between groups of European origin and visible minorities was found to be particularly important with regard to the rate of incorporation in society.

The *sixth* result is that the effect of retention on societal incorporation is not the same for all groups. It can be positive, negative, or nil depending on the specific internal conditions and external circumstances in which a group finds itself. Ethnic culture and organization can help in gaining access to economic resources, in gaining the attention of political authorities, and generally in coping with problems encountered.

But ethnic culture and organization can also be a liability. Again, visibility or race seems to be a particularly important differentiating factor in this connection. A comparison of the experience of the Jewish and Ukrainians, on the one hand, with that of the Chinese and West Indians, on the other, suggests that whether ethnicity is an asset or a liability depends on both internal and external factors. The behaviour of individuals and institutions in the larger society is clearly important; but so are the internal factors related to the capacity of the group to organize itself.

The *seventh* and last overall result is that incorporation and retention do not evolve in the same way across generations for all the ethnic groups considered. The results support the view that rather than being simply 'a *constant* trait that is inherited from the past, ethnicity is the result of a process that *continues to unfold*' (Yancey et al. 1976: 400; emphasis added). And because of internal and external circumstances, the process of evolution is different from one group to another. It may be that the past has a different relevance for some groups than for others; but the current situation is clearly of great significance in explaining inter-group variations in this regard.

APPENDICES

APPENDIX A

Technical Notes on the Survey Research Design

Three aspects of the survey research design are described here. First, the selection of ethnic groups for inclusion in this study is described to show the reasons why some groups were included and others not. Second, the design of the sample for the survey is described and the weighting scheme used in the presentation of data in this report is explained. Third, some information about the design of the questionnaire used in the survey, the interview procedures, and the results of interviewing is presented.

Selection of Ethnic Groups

The study required a sample that adequately represents the dominant Majority Canadian (or Anglo-Saxon) group plus a number of minority ethnic-origin groups. It was necessary to be able to make descriptive statements about these groups, and to conduct various types of multivariate analysis within groups. The sample is therefore not a random sample of the Toronto population. Instead, it includes only specific ethnic-origin groups, so that it is possible to select reasonably large sub-samples within each of the selected groups. The study also required representation by various generational groups within each ethnic-origin group, for it is concerned with experiences and behaviour not only of immigrants, but also of the children and grandchildren of immigrants, and seeks to compare these experiences with those of immigrants. Therefore, the sample should include groups with a long history of immigration.

The analysis of ethnic-identity retention required the selection of groups varying by degree of ethnic retention and ethnic social formation. The analysis of residential segregation required the selection of minority groups that vary by degree of segregation. Within each group, the sample includes persons living inside areas of ethnic residential concentration and also those living outside such areas. The analysis of the occupational position of minority-group members required a sample of men and women in the labour force varying with respect to occupational status, incomes, and ethnic concentrations in labour markets. The analysis of political collective action within ethnic groups required the selection of ethnic groups varying by degree of mobilization for collective action.

Given these constraints the sample was designed to include the Majority Canadian group plus eight minority groups. The Majority Canadian group was defined as including persons of English, Irish, or Scottish background whose families had been in Canada for three generations or more. Our analysis of census and other data indicated that in Metro Toronto four minority ethnic groups satisfy the requirements of each sub-project with respect to characteristics and variation: Italians, Germans, Jews, and Ukrainians. These groups have representation in each of three generations and vary by degree of segregation, occupational position, identity retention, and collective action. A fifth group consisting of immigrants and second-generation persons of English origin was added to permit the analysis of generational change within a dominant ethnic group. In addition, it was decided that the survey should represent the experiences of relatively newly arrived visible minorities in Toronto. Once again, however, it was felt that the selection of any one such group might be misleading. The inclusion of both West Indians and Chinese was designed to represent the variation in the occupational and social position of visible minority groups in Toronto. The Portuguese group was included to represent groups of European origin that are composed largely of immigrants. This addition permits a comparison between groups to show the effects of visible-minority status as opposed to recent-immigrant status.

Thus, in addition to the Majority Canadian group, the sample includes eight minority groups: the first- and second-generation English, Germans, Ukrainians, Italians, Jews, Portuguese, Chinese, and West Indians.

Sample Design

SAMPLE UNIVERSE

The sample is designed to represent various ethnic-origin groups within the Metropolitan Toronto area. The study area is not exactly the same as Metropolitan Toronto, however. Nor is it the same as the Toronto Census Metropolitan Area (CMA) as defined by Statistics Canada. The study area includes all of Metropolitan Toronto, plus parts of Mississauga and Richmond Hill. These suburban areas were included because they contain significant numbers of minority-ethnic-group members as a result of migrations within the Toronto area. A map showing the boundaries of the study area is shown as figure 1 (p. 22).

The sample universe was also defined to include only persons who are in the labour force and between the ages of 18 and 65. This delimitation was imposed because the sub-project on the occupational opportunity required a sample only of members of the labour force, and none of the other sub-projects required the inclusion of persons outside the labour force. For reasons relating to the sub-project on ethnic-identity retention, it was decided to include students in the sample.

NUMBERS OF INTERVIEWS

The sample was designed so that reliable descriptive statements could be made about each ethnic-origin group. To meet this objective, a desired number of interviews within each ethnic-origin and generation category was specified, as indicated in table A.1. These numbers were determined on the basis of statistical estimates and represent a compromise between statistical objectives and the realities of population distribution in the Toronto study area.

The considerable extent to which these objective were met can be seen by comparing table A.1 with table A.2, which shows the actual number of interviews completed for each ethnic-origin and generational category. In only one did the results fall below the objectives by as many as five cases: that of Ukrainian immigrants (150 interviews desired; 145 interviews completed). In many cases, the results exceeded objectives: for example, in the case of Portuguese (150 interviews desired; 164 interviews completed).

TABLE A.1
Number-of-interview objectives, by ethnic origin and generation

Ethnic origin	Immigrants	Second generation	Third generation	Total
English	150	100[a]	75[b]	325
Irish	0	0	75	75
Scottish	0	0	75	75
German	150	75	100	325
Ukrainian	150	100	100	350
Italian	150	100	100	350
Jewish	150	100	100	350
Portuguese	150	0	0	150
Chinese	150	0	0	150
West Indian	150	0	0	150
Total	1,200	475	625	2,300

a First- and second-generation English: 250
b Majority Canadian: 225

TABLE A.2
Sample results: numbers of completed interviews, by ethnic origin and generation

Ethnic origin	Immigrants	Second generation	Third generation	Total
English	156	111[a]	76[b]	343
Irish	0	0	78	78
Scottish	0	0	76	76
German	147	76	98	321
Ukrainian	145	102	107	354
Italian	149	98	104	351
Jewish	146	103	99	348
Portuguese	164	0	0	164
Chinese	153	0	0	153
West Indian	150	0	0	150
Total	1,210	490	638	2,338

a First- and second-generation English: 267
b Majority Canadian: 230

TWO-PHASE SAMPLING

A sample having the ethnic-origin and generation distribution just described could not be a simple random sample. Because of the actual sizes of the various ethnic and generational groups in the Toronto study area, a simple random sample would have produced a sample with large numbers of cases in some cells and very small numbers in others. So a procedure was needed that would over-sample in cases of small populations.

At the same time, a representative sample was needed so that reliable descriptive statements about each group in Toronto could be made. Thus, a sample was drawn in which some groups were over-sampled while others were under-sampled. In the data analysis, the over- and under-sampling is corrected by means of weighting.

The required sampling design with weighting was a two-phase sample design. Phase I involved the selection of a very large number of respondents who were then screened for eligibility on the basis of ethnic origin, generation, labour-force status, and age. From this screened sample, a sub-sample could then be selected in which the numbers of persons in each ethnic-origin and generation category could be the same as required for the main interviews in Phase II.

The Phase I screening sample was designed as follows. Census data from 1971 showed that a simple random sample of 61,250 would be needed to achieve the desired sample-size distribution by ethnic origin and generation. However, further analysis of the 1971 census data showed that by means of census tract (CT) stratification, the necessary sample could be reduced to 26,600, and by means of disproportionate selection of CT's within strata, could be reduced further to 17,100. So in the procedure adopted, seven sample strata were constructed at the CT level, an English stratum, a German stratum, a Jewish stratum, two Ukrainian strata, and two Italian strata. Within minority strata, all CT's were selected, whereas in the English stratum only 12 CT's were selected. In all, 172 CT's were selected. Within each CT, two enumeration areas (EA's) were selected, for a total of 394 EA's. Within each EA, 50 addresses were listed, for a total of 17,200 addresses. From these addresses, 17,947 households were listed for the screening interviews that covered all persons in each household.

The Phase I field screening of 17,947 households was conducted in the fall of 1977 with the following results. The completion rate was 82.9%, so a total of 14,884 households were screened. Of these, 9,881 contained eligible respondents in the sense that they fell within the target population. Finally, 17,577 individuals within the households proved to be eligible for inclusion in the sample. These individuals were distributed over ethnic-origin and generation categories as shown in table A.3. Subsequently, the first- and second-generation English, the second- and third-generation Portuguese, Chinese, and West Indians, and all Greeks were eliminated from the sample. So the respondents who completed the Phase I screening are 15,305 in number.

The Phase II sample was designed as follows. Within each of the ethnic-origin and generation cells, respondents were sub-sampled to meet the desired numbers of interviews. In only one case, third-generation Italians, did the number of eligible respondents fall below the target: only 76 respondents were identified. In that case, a supplementary sample of 28 was created by a snowball procedure. Since this snowball sample is not a probability sample, no weights could be calculated, and these respondents were not included in the weighted data analysis. In effect, all members of the snowball sample are assigned a weight of zero.

The Phase II was actually designed in two parts. The English, Irish, Scottish, Germans, Ukrainians, Italians, and Jews were sampled first, for interviewing in the spring of 1978. For this sample, 2,802 respondents were selected. Of these 148 had moved, and 76 turned out to be ineligible. Of the base sample of 2,578, 1,840 interviews were completed, for a response rate of 71.3%.

The second part of the Phase II sample included the Portuguese, Chinese, and West Indians, who were selected for interviewing in the spring and summer of 1979. For this sample, 930 respondents were selected. Of these, 184 had moved and 18 turned out to be ineligible. The larger percentage of respondents having moved (19.8% compared to 5.3% for the interviews conducted a year earlier) reflects the greater elapsed time since the screening. Of the base sample of 728, 470 interviews were completed, for a response rate of 64.6%. Note that in these three additional groups, the sample tends to under-represent individuals likely to be geographically mobile.

The distribution of completed interviews by ethnic origin and generation was presented above, as table A.2.

Sample weights are calculated to compensate for disproportionate sampling by ethnic origin, generation, and sample strata. For the Germans, Italians, Jewish, and Ukrainians, weights were calculated separately for respondents in each generational group according to whether they lived in the sample stratum (or strata) for the group in

TABLE A.3
Target population: number of screening interviews, by ethnic origin and generation (Phase I)

Ethnic origin	Immigrants	Second generation	Third generation	Total
English	925	1,210 [a]	2,164	4,299
Irish	340	432	1,118	1,890
Scottish	494	535	1,036	2,065
German	519	151	247	917
Ukrainian	448	454	176	1,078
Italian	3,121	647	104	3,872
Jewish	305	409	171	885
Portuguese	1,062	19	4	1,085
Greek	333	34	5	372
Chinese	329	38	1	368
West Indian	709	30	7	746
Total	8,585	3,959	5,033	17,577

a First- and second-generation English: 2135
b Majority Canadian: 4418

TABLE A.4
Sample results: weighted N's, by ethnic origin and generation (Phase II)

Ethnic origin	Immigrants	Second generation	Third generation	Total
English	232	182 [a]	263 [b]	677
Irish	0	0	267	267
Scottish	0	0	258	258
German	88	46	44	178
Ukrainian	32	37	20	89
Italian	269	137	25	431
Jewish	64	64	40	168
Portuguese	67	0	0	67
Chinese	57	0	0	57
West Indian	118	0	0	118
Total	929	965	917	2,310

a First- and second-generation English: 415 (varies from sum of numbers in table because of rounding)
b Majority Canadian: 787 (varies from sum of numbers in table because of rounding)

question, or some other stratum. For the Chinese, Portuguese, and West Indians, there were no distinctive strata, and respondents were mainly distributed across the various German, Italian, Jewish, and Ukrainian strata. So weights for these groups were assigned to compensate for disproportionate sampling across the minority strata. Majority Canadian respondents, and the first- and second-generation English, were found both in the English stratum and in the various minority strata. No weights were used for these groups. Analysis of results shows few significant differences in characteristics among these respondents according to the particular stratum of residence. The weighted-sample *N*'s by ethnic origin and generation are shown in table A.4. Note that the *N* is 2,310, which is smaller than the number of interviews (2,338) because of the exclusion of 28 third-generation Italians selected by the snowball technique.

Because the sample is weighted, standard statistical procedures for testing the reliability of findings are not applicable. An efficient procedure for such testing is not available. Procedures known as 'random sub-sample replication' have been described by Bernard M. Finifter (1972) in an article in *Sociological Methodology*. These procedures, however, are quite complex and are not used in the data analysis presented in this volume.

Questionnaire Design and Interviews

The questionnaire used in the main (Phase II) interviews was designed in such a way as to incorporate the research requirements of each of the four sub-projects, and so as to average approximately one and one-half hours in length. There was considerable overlap among the various sub-projects in variables of importance to the research. For this reason, there was also overlap in the questionnaire items required for the study. The questionnaire consisted of a set of common questionnaire items and four sets of items needed for the purposes of each of the four sub-projects. The development of items for each of the sub-projects was undertaken through the use of preliminary interviewing carried out by the four researchers independently.

IDENTIFICATION OF RESPONDENT ETHNICITY

The ethnic origin of the respondents to the survey was determined using a question identical to that used in the Canadian census. The question is 'To what ethnic or cultural group did you or your ancestors (on the male side) belong on coming to North America?' This question has the advantage that the respondent is able to place himself or herself in an appropriate category. For example, although the category 'Jewish' often is not considered to be an ethnic category, but rather a religious category, respondents to the survey were not classified as Jewish unless they themselves reported that they belonged to this group.

The use of the census question has the distinct disadvantage that it refers only to the male side of the family and not to the female side. It would be desirable of course to interview respondents about whatever ethnic origin they consider to be most relevant or most meaningful to them. However, this could not be done in the present case because the sample was designed using Canadian census data, and sample representativeness could not be guaranteed unless the respondents were treated as though they were members of the ethnic-origin group defined in the same way as in the Canadian census.

The use of the census question represents a potential liability for this research. However, it appears not to be a very serious liability. The questionnaire asked respondents about their ethnic or cultural ancestry on the female side, and also asked the respondent to indicate the relative importance of the two ethnic origins. The results of this questioning are shown in table A.5. In minority ethnic groups, the vast majority of respondents reported that the ethnic origin on the female side was the same as on the male side. For example, in the case of male-side Chinese, Italians, Jews, Portuguese, and West Indians, over 90% of the sample reported the ethnic origin on the female side to be the same as that on the male side. Among male-side Ukrainians, the figure is 84.3%, and among male-side Germans, the figure was 62.0%. Moreover, in most cases where the female ethnic origin was different from the male, most respondents reported that the ethnic origin on the male side was more important to them than the ethnic origin on the female side. For male-side Ukrainians, among the 15.7% who said that the female-side ethnic origin was different, about half (7.6%) said the male (Ukrainian) side was more important, and less than a third (4.0%) said the female (non-Ukrainian) side was more important. For male-side Germans, among the 38.0% who said the female-side ethnic origin was different, the designation of the male side as more important occurred in 12.7% of the cases, and the designation of the female (non-German) side as more important occurred in about 10.4% of the cases. So in this instance we can conclude that interviewing the respondents about their German origin results in potential distortions in only 10.4% of the cases. Among the various minority groups interviewed for the survey,

TABLE A.5
Percentage having each type of ethnic origin on the female side, by ethnic origin on the male side

	Female ethnic origin					
		Different				
Male ethnic origin	Same as male	Male more important	Male & female equal	Female more important	No answer	(*WN*; *N*)
English	69.6	15.3	4.8	6.8	3.4	(677; 343)
Irish	30.8	25.6	12.8	20.5	10.3	(267; 78)
Scottish	26.5	42.4	10.6	13.9	6.6	(258; 76)
Chinese	96.0	1.5	0.5	0.7	1.3	(57; 153)
German	62.0	12.7	7.6	10.4	7.3	(178; 321)
Italian	94.6	2.9	0.6	0.9	1.0	(431; 323)
Jewish	96.7	1.7	1.0	0.6	0.0	(168; 348)
Portuguese	99.6	0.0	0.0	0.0	0.4	(67; 164)
Ukrainian	84.3	7.6	2.5	4.0	1.6	(89; 354)
West Indian	99.2	0.0	0.0	0.8	0.0	(118; 150)
Total	70.0	14.2	4.9	7.1	3.8	(2,310; 2,310)

the German case is the most problematic. The Ukrainian case is less problematic, and in all the other cases only less than 1% of the respondents reported that their ethnic origin on the female side was not the same as that on the male side and was also more important than the latter.

In the dominant ethnic groups, the situation is somewhat different. For the English group, which includes significant numbers of immigrants and persons of the second generation, the male-side designation is nearly as appropriate as it is for most minority groups, easily as appropriate as for the Germans. For the Majority Canadian respondents, male- and female-side ethnic origin varies considerably. However, in many of these cases, the female-side origin is in the British categories and is, at any rate, less often the most important.

THE PRE-TEST

Prior to the Phase II interviewing, the questionnaire draft was extensively pre-tested in the field, in each of the ethnic groups included in the study. The pre-test resulted in some questions being dropped and others being significantly modified. In the interviews, several of the questions made reference to the respondents' perceptions of the Anglo-Saxon, or dominant majority, ethnic group in Toronto. The interviews showed that there is no standard terminology for describing this group that prevails in all of the ethnic-origin groups in Toronto. Many respondents did not understand the term 'Anglo-Saxon' and while some respondents preferred to describe this dominant group as 'Canadian,' this is not a satisfactory term for all respondents. To deal with this problem, a standard definition of what we called the 'Majority Canadian group' was used for the interviewing. This standard definition was available to be read to the respondents in cases of confusion. It read as follows: 'The Majority Canadian group consists of Canadians of English or French background, or whose families have been in Canada for several generations.' It can be seen that this definition itself is somewhat ambiguous, for it provides for the possibility that persons in Canada for several generations will be considered as part of the Majority Canadian group even if their ethnic origin is not English or French. This is not the same definition as we have used in our research to describe the Majority Canadian group, since there we only include persons of English, Irish, or Scottish origin whose families have been in Canada at least three generations as part of the 'Majority Canadian group.'

TRANSLATIONS

In only two groups, the Portuguese and Chinese, were problems of language encountered in the interviewing significant enough that translation of the interview schedule seemed necessary. In these cases translation of the questionnaire was provided by professional translators. Multilingual interviewers were used as well, and were in fact employed wherever possible throughout the interviewing in all groups. In the case of the Chinese, there are so many different dialects and styles of speaking that even a standard translation has its liabilities. In the field, Chinese interviewers were given latitude in adapting questions as appropriate in the specific interview situation.

FIELD EXPERIENCE

In selecting interviewers for use in the study, care was taken to ensure that wherever possible interviewers would be of the same ethnic origin as the interviewees. In the case of West Indians, this approach was not possible because of the difficulty of recruiting West Indian interviewers. In this case, at least 40% of the interviews were conducted by West Indian interviewers. It is possible to compare the results obtained as they vary by ethnic origin of the interviewer, but this analysis has not yet been conducted. It is worth noting that in the case of the Chinese and West Indian respondents, the interviewers classified the racial origin of the respondent. For the Chinese, virtually all respondents were classified as being Asian in racial origin. In the case of West Indians, 91.9% were classified as being black, 5.8% as being 'white,' and 2.3% as being Asian. The presence of white and Asian West Indians in the sample was not intended, and should be taken into account in interpreting the results of the survey.

APPENDIX B

The Interview Schedule

Survey Research Centre
Institute for Behavioural Research
York University

January 1979

Project #227

Ethnic Pluralism in an Urban Setting: Determinants and Consequences

---

IMPORTANT NOTE TO INTERVIEWERS: The term 'MAJORITY CANADIAN GROUP' is used in this interview. If unclear, the following definition is provided: 'The *Majority Canadian group* consists of Canadians of English or French background, or whose families have been in Canada for several generations.'

START TIME: ________

SECTION A: ETHNIC BACKGROUND AND DESIGNATION OF (GROUP)

1 a. [*INTERVIEWER, CODE RACE*: White (1); Black (2); Other (3)]

b. [*INTERVIEWER, CODE SEX*: Male (1); Female (2)]

2 a. To what ethnic or cultural group did you or your ancestor (on the *male* side) belong on coming to this continent? Chinese (01); English (02); French (03); German (04); Greek (05); Hungarian (06); Irish (07); Italian (08); Jewish (09); Netherlands (10); Polish (11); Portuguese (12); Scottish (13); Ukrainian (14); West Indian (15); Other [*SPECIFY*] (16)

[*INTERVIEWER: USE MALE ETHNICITY AS (GROUP).*]

b. To what ethnic or cultural group did you or your ancestor (on the *female* side) belong on coming to this continent? Chinese (01); English (02); French (03); German (04); Greek (05); Hungarian (06); Irish (07); Italian (08); Jewish (09); Netherlands (10); Polish (11); Portuguese (12); Scottish (13); Ukrainian (14); West Indian (15); Other [*SPECIFY*] (16)

[*INTERVIEWER: IF FEMALE ETHNICITY SAME AS MALE ETHNICITY, GO TO Q. 4.*]

3 Which of these two different ethnic or cultural backgrounds (Q. 2a and 2b) do you think is *relatively more important to you*? Chinese (01); English (02); French (03); German (04); Greek (05); Hungarian (06); Irish (07); Italian (08); Jewish (09); Netherlands (10); Polish (11); Portuguese (12); Scottish (13); Ukrainian (14); West Indian (15); Other [*SPECIFY*] (16)

4 [*INTERVIEWER*] In several parts of this interview I will ask questions about your background on the *male* side, (*group*).

How important is your ethnic or cultural background to you? Extremely important (1); Very important (2); Somewhat important (3); Not at all important (4); Don't know (8)

5 a. Are you married, single, or something else at present? Single (1); Married (2); Widowed (3); Separated (4); Divorced (5); Common law (6) [*IF (1), GO TO Q. 6*]

b. What is (or was) the ethnic or cultural background of your spouse? Chinese (01); English (02); French (03); German (04); Greek (05); Hungarian (06); Irish (07); Italian (08); Jewish (09); Netherlands (10); Polish (11); Portuguese (12); Scottish (13); Ukrainian (14); West Indian (15); Other [*SPECIFY*] (16)

6 What is your age? __

7 Now I would like to ask where your parents and grandparents were born. Choose from: Canada (01); Elsewhere [*SPECIFY*]; Don't know (98)

a. Father __
b. Father's father __
c. Father's mother __
d. Mother __
e. Mother's father __
f. Mother's mother __

8 In what country were *you* born? Canada (01); Elsewhere [*SPECIFY*]

SECTION B: LANGUAGE

9 [*ASK EVERYONE.*] What language did you first learn in childhood and are still able to understand? English (01); Italian (02); German (03); Yiddish or Hebrew (04); Ukrainian (05); Chinese (06); Portuguese (07); Greek (08); Other [*SPECIFY*]; INAP (99)

[*IF RESPONDENT CLEARLY SPEAKS ENGLISH WELL, CHECK __ AND GO TO Q. 11; IF RESPONDENT DOES NOT SPEAK ENGLISH WELL, GO TO Q. 10.*]

10 How well would you say you speak and understand spoken English yourself? Very well (1); Fairly well (2); Not very well (3); INAP (9)

a. Speak English. __
b. Understand English. __

11 How well do you read and write English? Very well (1); Fairly well (2); Not very well (3); INAP (9)

a. Read English. __
b. Write English. __

INTERVIEWER NOTE:

12 How well would you say the respondent can speak English? Very well (1); Somewhat well (2); Not very well (3); INAP (9)

13 Does the respondent have any kind of non-British accent? If so, how much of an accent does he/she have? No identifiable accent (1); Slight accent (2); Definite accent (3); Heavy accent (respondent is difficult to understand at times) (4); INAP (9)

14 [*IF BRITISH OR WEST INDIAN GO TO Q. 17; IF MOTHER TONGUE (SEE Q. 9) IS (GROUP), SKIP TO Q. 14d.*]

a. Do you know any (*language*) at all? Yes (1); No (2); Don't know (8); INAP (9)
[*IF (2) OR (8), GO TO Q. 17.*]

b. How well do you understand (*language*) when you hear others speak it? Very well (1); Fairly well (2); Not very well (3); Not at all well (4); INAP (9)

c. How well do you speak (*language*) yourself? Very well (1); Fairly well (2); Not very well (3); Not at all well (4); INAP (9)

d. How well do you read (*language*)? Very well (1); Fairly well (2); Not very well (3); Not at all well (4); INAP (9)

e. How well can you write (*language*)? Very well (1); Fairly well (2); Not very well (3); Not at all well (4); INAP (9)

15 [*ASK ONLY IF RESPONDENT SPEAKS (Language).*] How often do you speak in (*language*)? Every day (1); Often, but not daily (2); Occasionally (3); Rarely (4); Never (5); INAP (9)
[*IF (5), GO TO Q. 17.*]
[*HAND R. CARD 1.*]

16 Which language do you use when speaking to the following persons? Almost always English (1); mostly English (2); Frequently either language (3); Mostly (*language*) (4); Almost always (*language*) (5); INAP (9)

a. Parents ___

b. Brothers or sisters ___

c. Best friends ___

d. Family doctor ___

e. Priest, minister, or rabbi ___

f. People at work [*Students code INAP*] ___

g. Spouse [*if applicable*] ___

h. In-laws [*if applicable*] ___

SECTION C: GROWING UP

17 [*IF BORN IN CANADA (SEE Q. 8), GO TO Q. 19; OTHERS ASK THE FOLLOWING.*] At what age did you move to Canada? Age ___

18 [*IF MOVED TO CANADA AT AGE 18 OR OLDER, GO TO Q. 27; OTHERS ASK THE FOLLOWING.*] In what country did you spend *most* of your time growing up? Canada (1); Elsewhere [*SPECIFY*] (2); INAP (9)
[*IF (2), GO TO Q. 27.*]

19 [*IF BRITISH (ENGLISH, IRISH, OR SCOTTISH) OR WEST INDIAN GO TO Q. 21.*]

What languages did your parents tend to use in speaking to you? English only (1); Ethnic language only (2); Ethnic language and English (3); INAP (9)

20 And what language did you usually use in speaking to them? English only (1); Ethnic language only (2); Ethnic language and English (3); INAP (9)

21 [*HAND R. CARD 2.*]
While you were growing up, was your *parents' ethnic* or cultural background very important *to them*, somewhat important, not very important, or not at all important? Very important (1); Somewhat important (2); Not very important (3); Not at all important (4); Don't know (8); INAP (9)

22 And yourself, while you were growing up, was *your ethnic* or cultural background very important *to you*, somewhat imporant, not very important, or not at all important? Very important (1); Somewhat important (2); Not very important (3); Not at all important (4); Don't know (8); INAP (9)

23 Think of the three closest friends you had when you were a teenager. How many were from the same ethnic or cultural background as yourself? None (1); One (2); Two (3); Three (4); Don't know (8); INAP (9)

24 a. When you were growing up, did you ever date anyone who was not (*group*)? Yes __; No (2)
[*IF (2), GO TO Q. 25.*]

b. Did your parents ever disapprove, or not want you to date this person because of his/her ethnic or cultural background? Yes __; No (2)
[*IF (2), GO TO Q. 25.*]

c. How serious was the problem with your parents over this? Not very serious (1); Sometimes serious (4); Often very serious (5); Don't know (8); INAP (9)

25 [*IF BRITISH, GO TO Q. 31; IF WEST INDIAN, ASK Q. 25a, c, and d.*]
Did you ever have problems with your parents over things like the following? Yes (1); No (2); INAP (9)

a. Friendships with persons of some other ethnic or cultural background __
b. Use of (*group*) language __
c. Attendance at (*group*) affairs __
d. Attendance at church services __

26 a. When you were growing up, did you go to a (*group*) school or classes in Canada that were attended only by students of (*group*) background? Yes (1); No (2); INAP (9)
[*IF (2), GO TO Q. 31.*]

b. For how long did you attend this school? __ years
[*GO TO Q. 31.*]

27 When you arrived in Canada did you expect to return home eventually? Yes (1); No (2); INAP (9)

28 Were the first two or three friends you made in Canada mostly (*group*), or mostly from other groups, or what? Mostly (*group*) (1); Mostly other groups (2); Mixed (3); INAP (9)

29 [*IF R. IS WEST INDIAN GO TO Q. 30; IF BRITISH, GO TO Q. 31.*]
How well could you speak English when you arrived in Canada? Very well (1); Fairly well (2); Not very well (3); Not at all (4); INAP (9)

30 How well could you read and write English when you arrived in Canada? Very well (1); Fairly well (2); Not very well (3); Not at all (4); INAP (9)

SECTION D: MIGRATION AND RESIDENCE

31 [*ASK EVERYONE.*] How would you describe the people who live in this neighbourhood? Is their ethnic or cultural background mostly the same as your own (1); another (2); mixed (3)? Don't know (8)

32 a. Since you moved to this neighbourhood, has there been any change in the ethnic or cultural backgrounds of your neighbours? Yes (1); No (2); Don't know (8)
[*IF (2) OR (8), GO TO Q. 32c.*]

b. In what way have they changed? Are they now more the same as yourself (1); another (2); mixed (3)? Don't know (8)

c. Since you have been living here, has there been a change in the ethnic or cultural backgrounds of the students attending the schools that serve your neighbourhood: Yes (1); No (2); Don't know (8)

33 Are the religious backgrounds of people in this neighbourhood mostly the same as your own (1); another (2); mixed (3)? Don't know (8)

34 a. Approximately how many adult relatives do you have in the Metro Toronto area? (Include those in your household; include spouse's relatives.) Number ___

b. Of these relatives, how many *know each other* on a first name basis? All or almost all (1); More than half (2); About half (3); Less than half (4); Few or none (5); Don't know (8); INAP (9)

c. Are most of them (*group*), from the majority Canadian group, another group, or mixed? Same as self (1); Majority Canadian group (2); Another group (3); Mixed (4); Don't know (8); INAP (9)

35 Of your neighbours, how many would you say you know

a. *well* (have dinner, social evenings, vacation together)? Most of them (1); Few (2); None (3)

b. *casually* (occasional coffee or conversation on a first name basis)? Most of them (1); Few (2); None (3); INAP (9)

c. *by sight only*? Most of them (1); Few (2); None (3); INAP (9)
[*IF (3) IN Q. 35b AND c, GO TO Q. 36.*]

d. How many of your neighbours do you know well, or at least casually? [*COUNT A COUPLE AS TWO.*]

e. Of these neighbours you know well or casually, how many *know each other* on a first name basis? All or almost all (1); More than half (2);

About half (3); Less than half (4); Few or none (5); Don't know (8); INAP (9)

f. Are most of them (*group*) from the Majority Canadian group, another group, or mixed? Same as self (1); Majority Canadian group (2); Another group (3); Mixed (4); Don't know (8); INAP (9)

36 How many years have you lived in this neighbourhood? Less than two years (1); Two to five years (2); Six to ten years (3); More than ten, but not always (4); Always (5)
[*IF (5), GO TO Q. 46.*]

37 Why did you (or your family) move to *this* neighbourhood? [*CIRCLE ALL MENTIONED.*] Had the right kind of housing (size, price, etc.) (01); Good access to public transportation (02); Close to place of work (03); Close to schools and shops (04); It was a nicer neighbourhood (cleaner, safer, etc.) (05); Encouraged by family or friends (06); Encouraged or directed here by a real estate agent (07); Others of the same ethnic background live here (08); Because the people weren't from one ethnic background (09); Other [*SPECIFY*]; Don't know (98)

38 Where did you live before you moved here? Elsewhere in Metro Toronto (1); Elsewhere in Ontario (2); Elsewhere in Canada (3); Outside Canada (4)
[*IF (1), GO TO Q. 40; IF (4), GO TO Q. 43.*]

39 a. How would you describe where you lived before coming to Toronto? Farm or rural (1); Village (2); Small town or city (3); Big city or its suburb (4); Don't know (8); INAP (9)

b. How many years did you live there? Less than two years (1); Two to five years (2); Six to ten years (3); More than ten years (4); INAP (9)

40 In the previous place (or neighbourhood) you lived in, *before* moving here, were the ethnic or cultural backgrounds of the people living there at that time mostly the same as your own (1); another (2); mixed (3)? Don't know (8); INAP (9)

41 Were the religious backgrounds of the people living there at that time mostly the same as yourself (1); another (2); mixed (3)? Don't know (8); INAP (9)

42 When you moved out of your previous neighbourhood, what was the most important reason for leaving? [*CIRCLE ALL MENTIONED.*] Inadequate housing (too small, too costly, etc.) (01); Didn't like the neighbourhood or neighbours (02); Wanted to buy my own house (03); Change in marital status (got married, divorced, etc.) (04); Too far from work, change of jobs, etc. (05); Too far from family or friends (06); House we lived in no longer available (lease up, etc.) (07); Ethnic or racial character of neighbourhood changing (08); Wanted to get away from family or relatives (09); Other [*SPECIFY*]; Don't know (80); INAP (99)

43 [*IF BORN IN CANADA, GO TO Q. 44a.*]

In the last place (community) you lived in before coming to Canada, were the ethnic or cultural backgrounds of the people living in your neighbourhood mostly the same as your own (1); another (2); mixed (3)? Don't know (8); INAP (9)

44 a. Was your previous place of residence (before moving to your present address) the place where you spent most of your years growing up, that is where you lived most of the time before you became 18 years of age? Yes (1); No (2)
[*IF (1), GO TO Q. 46.*]

b. How would you describe the place where you spent most of your years before you became 18 years of age? [*NOTE: If respondent mentions two or more places where equal time was spent, ask for the one in which he lived first.*] Farm or rural area (1); Village (2); Small town or city (3); Medium size or big city (4); Don't know (8); INAP (9)

45 In the neighbourhood where you spent most of your years growing up, were the ethnic or cultural backgrounds of the people mostly the same as your own (1); another (2); a mixture (3)? Don't know (8); INAP (9)

SECTION E: ATTITUDES ON ISSUES

46 [*ASK EVERYONE.*] Now I would like to get your opinions on a number of issues. [*HAND R. CARD 3.*]

How do you think women are now treated by employers in Toronto? Do they receive fair treatment (1); experience some discrimination (2); experience a lot of discrimination (3); have an advantage (7)? Don't know (8)

47 I'd like to ask the same question about various ethnic groups. Are they now being treated fairly by employers, or do they experience some discrimination or a lot of discrimination? Treated fairly (1); Some discrimination (2); A lot of discrimination (3); They have an advantage (7); Don't know (8)

a. Ukrainians ___
b. French ___
c. Germans ___
d. Jews ___
e. English ___
f. Irish ___
g. Scottish ___
h. Italians ___
i. Greeks ___
j. Chinese ___

k. West Indians ___

l. Portuguese ___

m. Pakistanis ___

n. Canadian Indians ___

48 [*INTERVIEWER: SUBSTITUTE [ ] FOR ENGLISH R'S ONLY.*] What do you think is the main reason that some (*group*) [immigrants or members of a minority group] in Toronto take jobs where they work alongside other (*group*)? Avoid discrimination (1); Cannot speak English, need language group (2); Find better opportunity (3); Prefer to work with own kind (4); Want to contribute to own group (5); Have special training or ability for that type of work (6); Only job they can get (7); Other [*SPECIFY*] (8); Don't know (9)

49 a. [*INFO ONLY*] Chinese (1); German (2); Greek (3); Italian (4); Jew (5); Portuguese (6); Ukrainian (7); West Indian black (8); Woman (9)

b. What do you think should be done when a group of workers in a company isn't willing to work alongside a qualified (*group*)? [*SEE CIRCLED GROUP ABOVE.*] Should the employer move him (her) to another job to keep the peace, or should he make the workers learn to accept that person even if there is some trouble? Move (*group*) to another job (1); Make workers learn to accept (2); Other [*SPECIFY*] (3); Don't know (8)

[*HAND R. CARD* 4]

I would like to know whether you agree or disagree with the following statements (Q. 50 to Q. 54). [*Interviewer: Substitute [ ] for English R's only.*]

50 (*Group*) [Immigrants or members of a minority group] should try as much as possible to blend into Canadian society and not form ethnic communities. Strongly agree (1); Agree (2); Neutral (3); Disagree (4); Strongly disagree (5); Don't know (8)

51 (*Group*) [Immigrants or members of a minority group] are more likely to be discriminated against if they speak with an accent than if they do not. Strongly agree (1); Agree (2); Neutral (3); Disagree (4); Strongly disagree (5); Don't know (8)

52 (*Group*) [Immigrants or members of a minority group] are more likely to encounter discrimination if they keep their customs and ability to speak their language. Strongly agree (1); Agree (2); Neutral (3); Disagree (4); Strongly disagree (5); Don't know (8)

53 The French-Canadians are demanding more than they have a right to. Strongly agree (1); Agree (2); Neutral (3); Disagree (4); Strongly disagree (5); Don't know (8)

54 Native Indians and Eskimos are demanding more than they have a right to. Strongly agree (1); Agree (2); Neutral (3); Disagree (4); Strongly disagree (5); Don't know (8)

55 [*HAND R. CARD 5.*]

How would you rate the social standing or prestige of the following groups in Canada? Excellent (1); Very good (2); Good (3); Fair (4); Poor (5); Don't know (8)

a. Ukrainians ___
b. French ___
c. Germans ___
d. Jews ___
e. English ___
f. Irish ___
g. Scottish ___
h. Italian ___
i. Greeks ___
j. Chinese ___
k. West Indians ___
l. Portuguese ___
m. Pakistanis ___
n. Canadian Indians ___

56 If you were completely free to decide yourself would you have a ______ as a next door neighbour or would you prefer not to? [*Repeat Q. for all groups, but OMIT R'S OWN GROUP.*] Yes (1); Prefer not to (2); Not sure, depends (7); Don't know (8)

a. Ukrainian ___
b. French ___
c. German ___
d. Jew ___
e. English ___
f. Irish ___
g. Scottish ___
h. Italian ___
i. Greek ___
j. Chinese ___
k. West Indian ___
l. Portuguese ___
m. Pakistani ___
n. Canadian Indian ___

57 If you were free to decide, would you have a ______ as a close relative or would you prefer not to? [*OMIT R'S OWN GROUP.*] Yes (1); Prefer not to (2); Not sure, depends (7); Don't know (8)

a. Ukrainian __
b. French __
c. German __
d. Jew __
e. English __
f. Irish __
g. Scottish __
h. Italian __
i. Greek __
j. Chinese __
k. West Indian __
l. Portuguese __
m. Pakistani __
n. Canadian Indian __

58 [*IF BRITISH, GO TO Q. 60.*]
How easily does the majority Canadian group accept (*group*)
a. as neighbours? Very easily (1); Somewhat easily (2); Not easily at all (3); Don't know (8); INAP (9)
b. as close relative by marriage? Very easily (1); Somewhat easily (2); Not easily at all (3); Don't know (8); INAP (9)

59 Compared to other (*group*) in Toronto, how would you say you get along and are accepted by the majority Canadian gorup? Much better (1); A bit better (2); About the same (3); A bit worse (4); Much worse? (5); Don't know (8); INAP (9)

60 a. Have you ever been discriminated against in Canada because of your ethnic or cultural background? Yes (1); No (2)
[*IF (2), GO TO Q. 61.*]
b. What was the situation? [*DO NOT READ OUT – CODE ALL RESPONSES MENTIONED.*] When I was trying to get a job (1); Socially, by people of other ethnic groups who did not want to associate with me (2); When I was trying to rent an apartment, or buy or rent a house (3); By not being accepted to a school I wanted to go to (4); Other [*SPECIFY*]; INAP (9)

61 [*HAND R. CARD 6.*]
Suppose a member of an ethnic group has trouble getting a good job in a company because he is discriminated against. How much do you think the following actions he could take would help to change the situation? Very much (1); Somewhat (2); A little (3); Not at all (4); Don't know (8)
a. Complain directly to the boss or personal manager __
b. Get together with his co-workers to complain to the boss __

c. Deal with the situation by contacting a friend one happens to have in the company ___
d. Say nothing, but work harder than the others so as to impress the boss ___
e. Take his case to the union or employee association, if there is one in the company ___
f. Take his case to an organization in his ethnic community ___
g. Take his case to a community agency like the Ontario Human Rights Commission whose purpose is to handle cases of discrimination ___

62 [*HAND R. CARD 6.*]

Suppose someone wanted to change Canadian immigration laws or procedures. How much do you think the following actions would help? Very much (1); Somewhat (2); A little (3); Not at all (4); Don't know (8)

a. Write to a member of parliament or to government officials ___
b. Work through one of the political parties to get something done ___
c. Write letters to the editors of newspapers ___
d. Work through an organization in the community to get something done ___
e. Get as many of one's friends and neighbours as possible to write or talk to the member of parliament or to government officials ___
f. Organize support for or opposition to certain candidates at election ___

63 [*HAND R. CARD 4.*]

Do you strongly agree, agree, disagree, or strongly disagree with the following statements on immigration? Strongly agree (1); Agree (2); Neutral (3); Disagree (4); Strongly disagree (5); Don't know (8)

a. Present immigration laws make it *too difficult* for (*group*) to come to Canada. ___
b. Present immigration laws make it *too easy* for certain ethnic groups to come to Canada.
[*IF (3), (4), (5), OR (8), GO TO Q. 63d.*]
c. Which ones? [*CIRCLE ALL RESPONSES MENTIONED.*] Canadian Indian (01); Chinese (02); English (03); French (04); German (05); Greek (06); Irish (07); Italian (08); Jewish (09); Pakistani (10); Portuguese (11); Scottish (12); Ukrainian (13); West Indian (14); All ethnic groups (15); Other [*SPECIFY*] (16); Don't know (98)
d. The government does not do enough to help (*group*) immigrants find jobs after they have been admitted to Canada. ___

64 Suppose the leaders of ethnic communities tried to change immigration laws or procedures; how much effect do you think it would have on government policies? A lot (1); Some (2); A little (3); None at all (4); Don't know (8)

65 [*HAND R. CARD 7*]

I would like to have your opinion on some problems that are faced by some ethnic groups in Toronto today. Could you tell me if the following are very serious (1), somewhat serious (2), not too serious (3), or not a problem at all (4) for (*group*) in Toronto? Don't know (8); INAP (9)

a. Discrimination against (*group*) as far as jobs, pay, or other working conditions are concerned __
b. Unemployment among (*group*) in Toronto __
c. The difficulty for (*group*) in finding good housing at a reasonable cost __
   [*IF BRITISH, GO TO Q. 67.*]
d. The loss of (*group*) traditions and customs in Toronto __
e. [*IF WEST INDIAN, GO TO Q. 66.*]
   The decreasing use of (*group*) language among (*group*) in Toronto __

66 Are you concerned that (*group*) are becoming too small a group in Toronto compared to other groups? Very much (1); Somewhat (2); A little (3); Not at all (4); Don't know (8); INAP (9)

67 [*NON-BRITISH GO TO Q. 68; ASK BRITISH Q. 67.*]

How concerned are you that the Non-English ethnic groups are becoming too large in Toronto compared to the English Canadian group? Very much (1); Somewhat (2); A little (3); Not at all (4); INAP (9)

[*GO TO Q. 74a*]

68 [*HAND R. CARD 6*]

Using this card would you tell me how much you think the following differences divide the (*group*) community in Toronto? Very much (1); Somewhat (2); A little (3); Not at all (4); Don't know (8); INAP (9)

a. Differences between rich and poor __
b. Differences between political groups __
c. Differences between religious groups __
d. Differences between (*group*) originally coming from different areas __

69 [*HAND R. CARD 4*]

Do you strongly agree, agree, disagree, or strongly disagree with the following statements about the (*group*) community? Strongly agree (1); Agree (2); Neutral (3); Disagree (4); Strongly disagree (5); Don't know (8); INAP (9)

a. In general, politicians and officials *do not* take seriously the views expressed by the (*group*) community leaders. __
b. The ordinary member of the (*group*) community does not have a chance to say much about how things are run in the community. __

c. Even if the leaders and organizations of the (*group*) community in Toronto were more active, we would not get more attention from politicians and government officials. __

d. Leaders of the (*group*) community do not have enough connections with important people in business and government to get important results for the community. __

70 [*HAND R. CARD 8*]

a. Would you look at this card and rate the two best ways to become a leader in the (*group*) community. [*CIRCLE THE APPROPRIATE RESPONSES.*] Education (01); Money or wealth (02); Personality (03); Length of time in Canada (04); Establishing good relations with people who are already leaders (05); Being successful in organizing an activity in the community (06); Political orientation (07); Being a member of the clergy (08); Don't know (98)

b. Of these two ways which is (a) best? (b) second best? __

71 How concerned do you think the leaders of the (*group*) community in Toronto are with the problems and interests of the ordinary members of the community? Very much (1); Somewhat (2); A little (3); Not at all (4); Don't know (8); INAP (9)

72 In general, do the important decisions in the (*group*) community in Toronto tend to be made by the same small group of people or does the group change each time a new problem comes up? Same small group (1); Group changes (2); Other response (3); Don't know (8); INAP (9)

73 How much effort is made by decision-makers in the (*group*) community to get approval from the members of their organizations or from the community? A lot (1); Some (2); A little (3); None at all (4); Don't know (8); INAP (9)

SECTION F: ETHNIC CULTURAL RETENTION

74 [*ASK EVERYONE.*]

a. How close are the ties which you maintain with other (*group*) in Canada? Very close (1); Moderately close (2); Not very close (3); Not at all close (4)

b. Do you feel that you are closer to (*group*) in Canada now than you once were, less close, or staying about the same? Closer (1); Less close (2); Staying about the same (3); Don't know (8)

c. Do you feel that it is difficult (or is a problem) to be both a (*group*) and a Canadian at the same time? Yes (1); No (2); Depends (3); Don't know (8)

75 How do you usually think of yourself, as a (*group*), or a (*group*)-Canadian, or a Canadian, or what? (*Group*) (1); (*Group*)-Canadian (2); Canadian (2); Canadian of (*group*) origin (4); Some other group (5); Don't know (8)

76 a. I would like you to think about your three closest friends who are not relatives. Of these three friends how many are (*group*)? None (1); One (2); Two (3); Three (4); Don't know (8)
[*IF (4), GO TO Q. 76c*]

b. What is the ethnic or cultural background of your friends who are not (*group*)? Choose from Chinese (01); English (02); French (03); German (04); Greek (05); Hungarian (06); Irish (07); Italian (08); Jewish (09); Netherlands (10); Polish (11); Portuguese (12); Scottish (13); Ukrainian (14); West Indian (15); Other [*SPECIFY*] (16)

c. How many friends have you seen socially (for lunch, dinner, social gatherings) in the past month? __
[*IF NONE, GO TO Q. 77.*]

d. Of these friends, how many did you meet in your neighbourhood? __

e. How many at work? __

f. How many did you meet in church or in a club or other social organization? __

77 [*HAND R. CARD 9*]

How often do you do the following? Frequently (1); Fairly often (2); Sometimes (3); Very rarely (4); Never (5)

a. Attend (*group*) dances, parties, or informal social affairs __

b. Attend Canadian (*non-group*) dances, parties, or informal social affairs __

c. Go to (*group*) vacation resorts, summer camps, etc. __

d. Eat any food that is associated with (*group*) [English, but not typically Canadian] holidays or special events __

e. Eat any (*group*) [English, but not typically Canadian] food at other times __

f. Listen to (*group*) radio broadcasts or watch (*group*) television programs [that are English, but not Canadian] __

g. Read any (*group*) newspapers, magazines, or other periodicals [that are English but not Canadian] __

78 [*ASK EVERYONE.*]

a. Do you practise any religious or non-religious (*group*) customs (such as on Christmas, Hannukah, Easter) [that have an *English* origin and are not typically Canadian]? Yes (1); No (2)
[*IF (2), GO TO Q. 79a*]

b. Which ones? [*RECORD BELOW UNDER OBSERVANCES*]

c. *How often* do you practise these customs: every time the occasion comes, often, sometimes, or only rarely?

Observances	Every time	Often	Some-times	Rarely	INAP
1. ______________	1	2	3	4	9
2. ______________	1	2	3	4	9
3. ______________	1	2	3	4	9
4. ______________	1	2	3	4	9

79 a. Are there (*group*) religious or non-religious customs [of English origin] that you used to practise but no longer do? Yes (1); No (2) [*IF (2), GO TO Q. 80a*]

b. Which ones?
1. ______________________________
2. ______________________________
3. ______________________________
4. ______________________________

c. Why did you stop practising them? [*CIRCLE ALL MENTIONED.*] Married non-(*group*) (1); Too much time, trouble (2); In Canada, should follow Canadian customs (3); Don't believe in religion anymore (4); Friends stopped, no one to do it with (5); Other (6); Don't know (8); INAP (9)

80 a. Do you have (*group*) artistic articles, religious objects, or traditional clothing, such as statues, pictures, embroidery, dresses, shirts [that are of English origin, but are not typically Canadian], in your home? Yes (1); No (2)

b. Are there any historical events concerning the (*group*) which you feel the Canadian public should know more about and pay attention to? [*CIRCLE ALL MENTIONED.*] No (1); Yes ___. Which ones? Political events (2); Sports events (3); Religious events (4); Cultural events (5); Economic events (6); Other [*SPECIFY*] (7); Don't know (9)

c. Can you name two or more well-known (*group*) whom you most admire? No (01); Yes ___. What is there occupation? ___ Politician or statesmen (02); Businessmen (03); Artists or musicians (04); Poets or writers (05); Scholars or scientists (06); Religious leaders (07); Athletes (08); Other [*SPECIFY*] (09)
[*IF (01), GO TO Q. 81.*]

81 What is your present religion?

No preference (01)

IF PROTESTANT SPECIFY: Anglican (02); Lutheran (03); Presbyterian (04); Baptist (05); Salvation Army (06); United Church (07); Other Protestant (08)

IF JEWISH SPECIFY: Orthodox (09); Reform (10); Conservative (11)

Roman Catholic (12); Ukrainian Catholic (13); Ukrainian Orthodox (14); Greek Orthodox (15); Other [*SPECIFY*] (16)
[*IF (01), GO TO Q. 83a.*]

82 a. How strong would you say your own religious beliefs are today? Very strong (1); Somewhat strong (2); Somewhat weak (3); Very weak (4); Refusal (7); Don't know (8); INAP (9)

b. How often do you personally attend services at a church (or a synagogue or temple or other place of worship)? More than once a week (1); Once a week (2); One to three times a month (3); Three to eleven times a year (4); Only one to three times a year (5); Never (6); INAP (9)

c. [*IF JEWISH, GO TO Q. 83a; OTHERS ASK THE FOLLOWING.*] What proportion of the members of the church you attend are from the same ethnic group as yourself? All or almost all (1); More than half (2); About half (3); Less than half (4); Few or none (5); Don't know (8); INAP (9)

83 a. When you were growing up, what was your mother's religion? __
[*USE CODES BELOW.*]

b. When you were growing up, what was your father's religion? __
[*USE CODES BELOW.*]

No religious preference (01)

IF PROTESTANT SPECIFY: Anglican (02); Lutheran (03); Presbyterian (04); Baptist (05); Salvation Army (06); United Church (07); Other Protestant (08)

IF JEWISH SPECIFY: Orthodox (09); Reform (10); Conservative (11)

Roman Catholic (12); Ukrainian Catholic (13); Ukrainian Orthodox (14); Greek Orthodox (15); Other [*SPECIFY*] (16); Don't know (98)
[*IF (01), GO TO Q. 85.*]

84 a. When you were growing up how strong was your mother's religion? __
[*USE CODES BELOW.*]

b. What about your father's? __
[*USE CODES BELOW.*]

c. And yourself *at that time*? __
[*USE CODES BELOW.*]

Very strong (1); Somewhat strong (2); Somewhat weak (3); Very weak (4); Don't know (8); INAP (9)

85 How many children do you have? None (00); Number __
[*IF (00), GO TO Q. 92.*]

86 [*IF BRITISH, GO TO Q. 92; OTHERS ASK THE FOLLOWING.*] Are any of your children six years or older? Yes (1); No (2); INAP (9)
[*IF (2), GO TO Q. 91.*]

87 a. Have your children ever attended a school *or courses run for* (*group*) in Canada? Yes (1); No (2); INAP (9)
[*IF (2), GO TO Q. 90.*]

b. How many of your children? Number ___; INAP (99)
NOTE: IF MORE THAN ONE: I would like to ask you a few questions about the one who attended for the longest period of time.

88 a. Is this child now going to this school? Yes (1); No (2); INAP (9)
[*IF (2), GO TO Q. 89.*]

b. What are the main reasons you are sending your child to the (*group*) school? [*CIRCLE ALL MENTIONED.*] So child can be a good (*group*) (1); So child can understand (*language*) (2); So child remembers who his parents were (3); So child can return to (*country*) and be able to talk to people there (4); So child can help other (*group*) if need be (5); Other [*SPECIFY*] (6); INAP (9)
[*GO TO Q. 91.*]

89 Why did your child stop going to that school? [*CIRCLE ALL MENTIONED.*] Wasn't learning (1); Teachers were old-fashioned (2); Child didn't want to go anymore (3); Took too much time (4); Transportation problems (5); Completed program (6); Other [*SPECIFY*] (7); INAP (9)
[*GO TO Q. 91.*]

90 a. Have you ever considered sending your children to such a school? No (1); Yes (2); INAP (9)
[*IF (1), GO TO c.*]

b. What made you decide against sending them? [*CIRCLE ALL MENTIONED.*] Transportation problems (1); Child unwilling (2); School of little use (3); No school available (4); Teachers not qualified (5); Other [*SPECIFY*] (6); Don't know (8); INAP (9)
[*GO TO Q. 91.*]

c. Is there any special reason why you have not? [*CIRCLE ALL MENTIONED.*] Child can learn at home (1); Learning (*language*) will not help child get ahead (2); No (*group*) schools nearby (3); Takes too much time, work (4); Other [*SPECIFY*] (5); No, don't know (8); INAP (9)

91 [*IF R. IS WEST INDIAN, GO TO Q. 92; IF R. KNOWS NO (LANGUAGE), GO TO Q. 92; OTHERS ASK THE FOLLOWING.*]

a. Which language does (do) your child (children) use when speaking to you? Almost always English (1); Mostly English (2); Either language equally (3); Mostly (*language*) (4); Almost always (*language*) (5); INAP (9)

SECTION G: COMMUNITY PARTICIPATION

92 [*HAND R. CARD 10.*]

Do you, or did you ever, belong to any organizations in Canada similar to the ones on this list? Yes (1); No (2)
[*IF (2), GO TO Q. 94.*]

93 a. Which ones? [*Check after (a) below.*]

b. Do you or did you ever attend meetings regularly and play an active role in the organizations? [*Check after (b) for each type of organization R belongs to.*]

c. Are or were any of the organizations (*group*) [English rather than Canadian] organizations? [*Check after (c).*]

d. Do you still belong? [*Check after (d).*]

(a) Belong or belonged; (b) Active; (c) Ethnic; (d) Still belong

CHURCH related groups, such as church committee, church choir: (a) __; (b) __; (c) __; (d) __

JOB related associations, such as business or professional association, labour union: (a) __; (b) __; (c) __; (d) __

RECREATIONAL groups, such as bowling league, hobby clubs, sports group, garden club: (a) __; (b) __; (c) __; (d) __

FRATERNAL-SERVICE organizations such as Kiwanis Club, Knights of Columbus, hospital auxiliary, school association: (a) __; (b) __; (c) __; (d) __

POLITICAL groups, such as political party, citizen action groups, ratepayers associations: (a) __; (b) __; (c) __; (d) __

COMMUNITY organizations FOR YOUTH, such as YMCA/YWCA, Scouts: (a) __; (b) __; (c) __; (d) __

CULTURAL groups, such as literary groups, film clubs, art and study groups: (a) __; (b) __; (c) __; (d) __

94 How interested are you in local issues or events (which *do not* relate specifically to [*group*] such as new by-laws or local politics? Very (1); Somewhat (2); Slightly (3); Not at all (4); Don't know (8)

95 How about provincial or national affairs? Very interested (1); Somewhat interested (2); Slightly interested (3); Not at all interested (4); Refused (5); Don't know (8)

96 a. Do you know of any Toronto politicians, officials, or community leaders who are not (*group*)? Yes (1); No (2)
[*IF (2), GO TO Q. 97.*]

b. Do you know any of them personally? Yes (1); No (2); INAP (9)
[*IF (2), GO TO Q. 97.*]

c. How often would you say you are in contact with one or more of them? Frequently (1); Occasionally (2); Seldom (3); Never (4); Don't know (8); INAP (9)

97 [*IF BRITISH, GO TO Q. 101; OTHERS ASK THE FOLLOWING.*]

a. Do you know of any leaders in the (*group*) community in Toronto? Yes (1); No (2); INAP (9)
[*IF (2), GO TO Q. 98.*]

b. Do you know any of them personally? Yes (1); No (2); INAP (9)

c. How often would you say you are in contact with one or more of them? Frequently (1); Occasionally (2); Seldom (3); Never (4); Don't know (8); INAP (9)

d. In general, how informed would you say you are about their activities? Very well (1); Somewhat (2); Not too well (3); Not at all informed (4); Don't know (8); INAP (9)

98 Do you know of any organizations or associations in the (*group*) community in Toronto? Yes (1); No (2); INAP (9)

99 How often do you express your views about important (*group*) community affairs either in meetings, in letters to the editor, or directly to community leaders? Frequently (1); Occasionally (2); Seldom (3); Never (4); INAP (9)

100 [*HAND R. CARD 11.*]

Suppose the circle on this card represented the activities that go on in the (*group*) community in Toronto. How far from or how close to the centre of these activities would you be? Code response ___; Don't know (8); INAP (9)

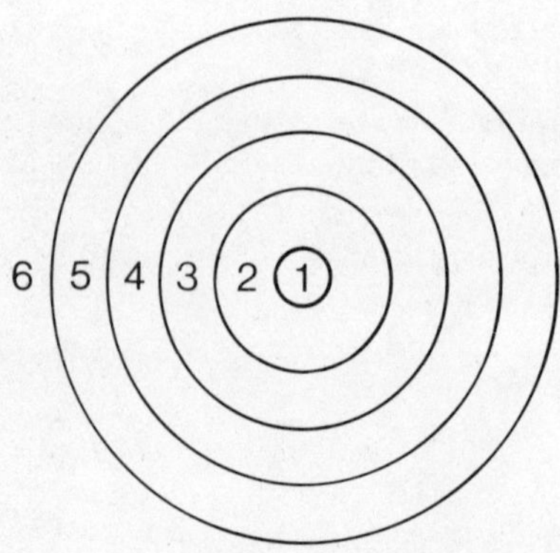

SECTION H: SELF-IMAGES AND FEELINGS

101 [*HAND R. CARD 12.*]

Please look at each of the characteristics on this card and tell me which number describes most closely *your* own view of *yourself.*

a. warm & friendly	1	2	3	4	5	cold & reserved
b. competitive	1	2	3	4	5	uncompetitive
c. strict	1	2	3	4	5	liberal
d. independent	1	2	3	4	5	conformist
e. ambitious	1	2	3	4	5	not ambitious
f. cautious	1	2	3	4	5	adventurous
g. artistic	1	2	3	4	5	practical
h. rule-abiding	1	2	3	4	5	flexible
i. hard-working	1	2	3	4	5	lazy
j. noisy	1	2	3	4	5	quiet
k. religious	1	2	3	4	5	non-religious
l. proud	1	2	3	4	5	humble

102 Looking again at the card, which number describes most closely your impression of what (*group*) are like as a group?

a. warm & friendly	1	2	3	4	5	cold & reserved
b. competitive	1	2	3	4	5	uncompetitive
c. strict	1	2	3	4	5	liberal
d. independent	1	2	3	4	5	conformist
e. ambitious	1	2	3	4	5	not ambitious
f. cautious	1	2	3	4	5	adventurous
g. artistic	1	2	3	4	5	practical
h. rule-abiding	1	2	3	4	5	flexible
i. hard-working	1	2	3	4	5	lazy
j. noisy	1	2	3	4	5	quiet
k. religious	1	2	3	4	5	non-religious
l. proud	1	2	3	4	5	humble

103 [*HAND R. CARD 4.*]

Now I would like you to think about the (*group*) in Canada and some situations that might be to *their* advantage. How strongly do you agree or disagree with each of these statements? Strongly agree (1); Agree (2); Neutral (3); Disagree (4); Strongly disagree (5); Don't know (8); INAP (9)

a. When a (*group*) person is choosing a career he should think whether such an occupation will help (*group*) as a group. ___

b. When a (*group*) is an employer he should try to place persons of (*group*) background into better jobs. ___

c. People of (*group*) origin really shouldn't go out of their way to help other (*group*) to get jobs. ___

d. (*Group*) should encourage their children to marry (*group*). ___

e. (*Group*) should support special needs and causes of the group. ___
[*IF BRITISH, GO TO Q. 104.*]

f. It is important for (*group*) children to learn to speak (*group*). ___

104 [*ASK EVERYONE; HAND R. CARD 4.*]

The following questions are similar to those I just asked. This time, however, think only about *your own* advantage. How strongly do you agree or disagree with each of these statements? Strongly agree (1); Agree (2); Neutral (3); Disagree (4); Strongly disagree (5); Don't know (8); INAP (9)

a. It is important for me to have a job that will benefit the (*group*) as well as myself. ___

b. If I were hiring people I should try to get (*group*) people into good positions. ___

c. It is not important to me to help people of (*group*) background get jobs. ___

d. It is important that my children should marry other (*group*) (or would be, if I had children)___

e. I personally feel that I should support the special causes and needs of the (*group*). ___

[*IF BRITISH, GO TO Q. 106; IF WEST INDIAN, GO TO Q. 105; OTHERS CONTINUE.*]

f. It is important (or would be) that my children learn to speak the (*group*) language. ___

g. It is impossible to think of (*group*) traditions and customs in a language other than (*language*).

105 What part of the (*group*) way of life is most important if the (*group*) group is to survive in Canada? (*Group*) holiday celebrations (01); Friendships among (*group*) (02); (*Group*) food (03); Keeping religious practices (04); Active organizations and leadership (05); (*Group*) language (06); Marriage with other (*group*) (07); Other [*SPECIFY*] (08); Don't know (98); INAP (99)

106 [*ASK EVERYONE; HAND R. CARD 4.*]

Do you strongly agree, agree, disagree, or strongly disagree with these points of view about life? Strongly agree (1); Agree (2); Neutral (3); Disagree (4); Strongly disagree (5); Don't know (8)

a. It is hardly fair to bring a child into the world the way things look now. ___

b. Most people don't really care what happens to the next fellow. ___

c. These days I get a feeling that I'm just not part of things. ___

d. In spite of what some people say, the lot of the average man is getting worse, not better. ___

e. There is not much that I can do about most of the important problems that we face today. —

f. In order to get ahead in the world today you are almost forced to do some things which are not right. —

g. I don't really enjoy most of the work that I do, but I feel that I must do it in order to have other things that I need and want. —

107 Here are three very different statements about life in general, and I would like to know which you think is best.

1 Some people believe it best to give most attention to what is happening now in the present

2 Other people think that the ways of the past were the best, and as changes come, things get worse.

3 Still other people believe that change in the future will bring improvements.

a. Which of these ways of looking at life do *you* think is best? Number 1 (1); Number 2 (2); Number 3 (3); Don't know (8)

b. Which of the three do you think most other (*group*) would think is best? Number 1 (1); Number 2 (2); Number 3 (3); Don't know (8)

108 [*HAND R. CARD 13.*]

If you had to choose among the following things, which would seem (a) best to you? — (b) second best? — Don't know (8)

1 Maintaining order in the country

2 Giving the people more say in important political decisions

3 Fighting rising prices

4 Protecting freedom of speech

109 [*HAND R. CARD 4.*]

Tell me whether you agree or disagree with these statements about work. Strongly agree (1); Agree (2); Neutral (3); Disagree (4); Strongly disagree (5); Don't know (8)

a. In a company, the person who really gets ahead is one who spends a lot of time making friends with the boss, even if his/her work is not the best. —

b. Education is not as important to getting ahead as a lot of people think it is. —

c. Realistically, success depends more on family contacts and connections than it does on anything an individual can do for himself. —

d. A person who goes to university generally has a better life, even if he doesn't make more money. —

e. If I inherited or won so much money that I didn't have to work, I'd still work at the same thing I am doing now. —

f. I enjoy my spare-time activities much more than my work. —

g. It is extremely important to me to have a higher income. __
h. Getting money and material things out of life is very important to me. __

SECTION I: EDUCATION AND OCCUPATION

110 And now I'd like to ask you some questions about your education and work experience.
a. How many years of full-time schooling have you completed? __
b. Of these years, how many did you spend in Canadian schools? __
c. Of these years, how many were spent in schools where English was the main language of instruction? __

111 a. Did you ever attend a community college, trade school, business or commercial school, or some other special vocational school of this kind? Yes __; No (1)
[*IF 'NO,' GO TO Q. 112.*]
b. Did you graduate and get a diploma or certificate from the school? Yes (2); No (3); INAP (9)
[*IF (3), GO TO Q. 112.*]
c. What occupation were you trained to do? ______________________
d. [*IF BRITISH, GO TO Q. 112a; OTHERS ASK THE FOLLOWING.*]
Was this school an English-language school? Yes (1); No (2); INAP (9)

112 [*IF RESPONDENT ATTENDED 10 YEARS OF SCHOOL OR LESS (SEE Q. 110a), CHECK HERE __ AND GO TO Q. 113a; IF MORE THAN 10 YEARS, ASK THE FOLLOWING.*]
a. Did you ever attend a university? Yes __; No (1)
[*IF 'NO,' GO TO Q. 113a.*]
b. Did you graduate and get a degree or diploma from a university? Yes (2); No (3); INAP (9)
[*IF (3), GO TO Q. 113a.*]
c. What was your field of specialization? ______________________
d. [*IF BRITISH, GO TO Q. 113a; OTHERS ASK THE FOLLOWING.*]
Was this college or university an English-language school? Yes (1); No (2); INAP (9)

113 a. [*ASK EVERYONE.*] Are you working at the present time; are you self-employed, unemployed, a student, or what?
Self-employed (01); Employed full-time (02); Employed part-time (03)
[*GO TO Q. 114a.*]
Looking for work (04); Laid-off temporarily (05); Retired or permanently disabled (06); Housewife (07)
[*GO TO Q. 113b.*]

If student, what kind of school? Secondary (08); Technical, vocational, Community college (09); University (10); No job yet (11) [*GO TO Q. 156.*]

b. When were you working last? In last 6 months (1); Between six months and one year (2); More than one year ago (3); INAP (9)

[*INTERVIEWER: THE FOLLOWING QUESTIONS (114–134) RELATE TO R.'S MOST RECENT EMPLOYMENT.*]

114 a. What kind of work do you do? [*PROBE FOR EXACT JOB DESCRIPTION.*]

____

b. In what kind of organization, business, or industry is that?

____

115 In the company where you work, how many employees are there altogether? Include the entire company or organization under the same ownership or control, not just your own office or branch. [*DO NOT INCLUDE SEPARATE, LOCALLY OWNED FRANCHISES.*] 1–10 (1); 11–25 (2); 26–100 (3); 101–250 (4); 251–500 (5); Over 500 (6); Don't know (8)

116 Comparing your present job situation with that of other persons in Toronto, would you say it is: much better (1); somewhat better (2); about the same (3); somewhat worse (4); much worse (5)? Don't know (8); INAP (9)

117 Comparing your present job situation with that of other persons having the same education and experience that you have, would you say it is: much better (1); somewhat better (2); the same (3); somewhat worse (4); much worse (5)? Don't know (8); INAP (9)

118 Comparing your own job with your father's job when he was your age, would you say you are doing: much better (1); somewhat better (2); about the same (3); somewhat worse (4); much worse (5)? Don't know (8); INAP (9)

119 [*IF BRITISH, GO TO Q. 120; ASK OTHERS THE FOLLOWING.*]

Comparing your job situation with other (*group*) in Toronto, would you say it is: much better (1); somewhat better (2); about the same (3); somewhat worse (4); much worse (5)? Don't know (8); INAP (9)

120 [*IF R. SELF-EMPLOYED, GO TO Q. 129a; ASK OTHERS THE FOLLOWING.*]

I'd like to ask you how you found your present job. Did you find it by looking in the newspapers, or by going to an employment agency, Canada Manpower, a union, or through someone you knew who could help? Newspaper (1); Employment agency (private) (2); Canada Manpower (3); Union (4); Applied directly to employer (5); Was approached by employer (6); Someone I knew who could help (7); INAP (9) [*IF (7), GO TO Q. 122.*]

121 Was there anyone you knew who helped you in any way to get the job? Yes (1); No (2); INAP (9)
[*IF (2), GO TO Q. 127.*]

122 Was this person a member of your family, another relative, a friend, a neighbour, someone known through a previous job, or someone else? Family (1); Other relative (2); Friend (not a neighbour) (3); Neighbour (4); Someone known through a previous job (5); Other [*SPECIFY*] (6); INAP (9)
[*IF (1), GO TO Q. 124a.*]

123 At that time, would you say this person was a close friend (relative), not very close, or not at all close? Close (1); Not very close (2); Not at all close (3); INAP (9)

124 a. How did this person happen to know about the job? Was working or had worked in the same place (1); Was in same line of work (2); Learned about it through friends (3); Other (4); Don't know (8); INAP (9)
[*IF (2), (3), (4), OR (8), GO TO Q. 125.*]

b. Was the position of this person in the company higher than yours, about the same, or lower? Higher (1); Same (2); Lower (3); Don't know (8); INAP (9)

125 Did this person help you by just telling you about the job, or did he/she introduce you to the employer, put in a good word, or help in some other way? [*CODE ALL RESPONSES MENTIONED.*] Just told me about the job (1); Introduced me to the employer (2); Put in a good word (3); Was the person doing the hiring (4); Other [*SPECIFY*] (5); INAP (9)

126 a. Was this person also (*group*)? Yes (17); No
[*IF 'YES,' GO TO Q. 127.*]

b. Do you know his/her ethnic origin? Yes: Chinese (01); English (02); French (03); German (04); Greek (05); Hungarian (06); Irish (07); Italian (08); Jewish (09); Netherlands (10); Polish (11); Portuguese (12); Scottish (13); Ukrainian (14); West Indian (15); Other [*SPECIFY*] (16). No: Don't know (98)

127 [*IF BRITISH, GO TO Q. 132a.*]
Are the people who manage this business or company also (*group*), or are they from the majority Canadian group or something else? Same as self (1); Majority Canadian group (2); Other group (3); More than one group (4); No particular group (5); Don't know (8); INAP (9)

128 a. Is there someone who is your supervisor, other than the employer himself? Yes (1); No (2); INAP (9)
[*IF (2), GO TO Q. 129a.*]

b. Is your supervisor also (*group*), from the majority Canadian group, or from some other ethnic group? Same as self (1); Majority Canadian group (2); Some other group (3); Don't know (8); INAP (9)

129 a. How many other persons where you work are working directly under the same supervisor (or foreman, immediate superior) as yourself in the same department? __

[*IF SELF-EMPLOYED ASK THE FOLLOWING.*] How many other persons do roughly the same work as yourself? None (00); Don't know (98); Number of persons __

[*IF (00) OR (98), GO TO Q. 130a.*]

Of those who do roughly the same work, how many are:

b. (*group*)? Number __; Don't know (98); INAP (99)

c. from the majority Canadian group? Number __; Don't know (98); INAP (99)

d. men? Number __; Don't know (98); INAP (99)

130 a. Are there any persons working under your supervision? Yes (1); No (2); INAP (9)

[*IF (2), GO TO Q. 131a.*]

b. How many are there? Number __; INAP (99)

c. (*group*)? Number __; Don't know (98); INAP (99)

d. from the majority Canadian group? Numbers __; Don't know (98); INAP (99)

131 a. In this job, how often do you come into contact with customers, clients, or others outside the company? Every day (1); Regularly but not every day (2); Only occasionally (3); Rarely or never (4); Don't know (8); INAP (9)

[*IF (4) OR (8), GO TO Q. 132*a.]

b. Of these persons, what proportion are (*group*)? All or almost all (1); More than half (2); About half (3); Less than half (4); Few or none (5); Don't know (8); INAP (9)

c. What proportion are from the majority Canadian group? All or almost all (1); More than half (2); About half (3); Less than half (4); Few or none (5); Don't know (8); INAP (9)

132 a. Think of all the people you work with or come into contact with on your job. How often do you spend time with any of them outside of work? Regularly (1); Occasionally (2); Rarely or never (3); INAP (9)

[*IF (3), GO TO Q. 133a.*]

b. [*IF BRITISH, GO TO Q. 133a; OTHERS ASK THE FOLLOWING.*]

Are the ethnic backgrounds of these people (*group*), from the majority Canadian group, or from some other gorup? Mostly same as self (1); Mostly from the majority Canadian group (2); Mostly other groups (3); No particular group (4); Don't know (8); INAP (9)

133 a. Is there a union for persons who have your job? Yes (1); No (2); Don't know (8); INAP (9)

[*IF (2), GO TO Q. 134.*]

b. Did you join the union? Yes (1); No (2); Don't know (8); INAP (9)

c. [*IF BRITISH, GO TO Q. 134.*]

Are members of the union local mostly also (*group*), mostly Canadian, or mostly some other group? Mostly same as self (1); Mostly Canadians (2); Mostly other groups (3); No particular group (4); Don't know (8); INAP (9)

134 [*HAND R. CARD 14.*]

In your present job, what is your annual income (before taxes)? A, Less than $1,000 (01); B, $1,000–$1,999 (02); C, $2,000–$2,999 (03); D, $3,000–$3,999 (04); E, $4,000–$4,999 (05); F, $5,000–$5,999 (06); G, $6,000–$6,999 (07); H, $7,000–$7,999 (08); I, $8,000–$8,999 (09); J, $9,000–$9,999 (10); K, $10,000–$11,999 (11); L, $12,000–$13,999 (12); M, $14,000–$15,999 (13); N, $16,000–$19,999 (14); O, $20,000–$24,999 (15); P, $25,000 or more (16); Refusal (97); Don't know (98); INAP (99)

135 Now I would like to ask about your occupation *10 years ago*, at this time in 1969.

a. Were you working at that time, were you self-employed, unemployed, or something else? Self-employed (1); Employed full-time (2); Employed part-time (3); Looking for work (4); Laid off temporarily (5); Unemployed and not looking for work (6); Housewife (7); Full-time student (8); Part-time student (9)
[*IF (3)–(9), GO TO Q. 135c.*]

b. Were you working in Canada? Yes (1); No (2) INAP (9)
[*IF (1), GO TO Q. 136a.*]

c. When did you first work *full-time* in *Canada*? One year ago or less (1978) (01); Two years ago (1977) (02); Three years ago (1976) (03); Four years ago (1975) (04); Five years ago (1974) (05); Six years ago (1973) (06); Seven years ago (1972) (07); Eight years ago (1971) (08); Nine years ago (1970) (09); Never (10); More than 10 years ago (11); INAP (99)
[*IF (10), GO TO Q. 156; IF (11), GO TO Q. 147.*]

d. Were you self-employed? Yes (1); No (2); INAP (9)

[*INTERVIEWER: PLEASE NOTE THAT THE FOLLOWING QUESTIONS (Q. 136–146) STILL REFER TO R's FIRST FULL-TIME EMPLOYMENT IN CANADA IN THE* LAST TEN YEARS.]

136 a. What kind of work did you do then? [*PROBE FOR EXACT JOB DESCRIPTION.*] ______________________________

— [*INTERVIEWER: CHECK IF* EXACTLY *SAME* KIND OF WORK *AS TODAY.* (*See Q. 114*)]

b. In what kind of organization, business, or industry was that?

____

137 In the company where you worked, how many employees were there at the time? (Include the entire company or organization under the same

ownership or control, not just your own office or branch. Do not include separate locally owned franchies.) 1–10 (1); 11–25 (2); 26–100 (3); 101–250 (4); 251–500 (5); Over 500 (6); Don't know (8)

[IF R. SELF-EMPLOYED (SEE Q. 135a OR 135d), CHECK HERE ___ AND GO TO Q. 141a.]

138 Is the same employer you have now? Yes (1); No, different employer (2); INAP (9)
[IF (1), GO TO Q. 140a.]
[IF BRITISH, GO TO Q. 144a; FOR OTHERS GO TO Q. 139.]

139 Were the people who managed this business or company where you worked ten (nine, ...) years ago also (*group*), or were they from the majority Canadian group or some other group? Same as self (1); Majority Canadian group (2); Other group (3); More than one group (4); No particular group (5); Don't know (8); INAP (9)

140 a. In that job, was there someone who was your supervisor, other than the employer himself? Yes ___. Yes, same supervisor as today (1); No (2)
[IF (1) OR (2), GO TO Q. 141a.]

b. Was your supervisor also (*group*) or from the majority Canadian group or some other group? Same as self (1); Majority Canadian group (2); Other group (3); More than one group (4); No particular group (5); Don't know (8); INAP (9)

141 a. How many other persons where you worked ten (nine ...) years ago were working directly under the same supervisor (or foreman, immediate supervisor) as yourself? *IF R. IS SELF-EMPLOYED ASK*: How many other persons do roughly the same work as yourself: None (00); Exactly same co-workers as today (97); Don't know (98); Number of persons ___
[IF (00), (97), OR (98), GO TO Q. 142a.]

Of those who do roughly the same work, how many were:

b. (*group*)? Number ___; Don't know (98)

c. from the majority Canadian group? Number ___; Don't know (98)

d. men? Number ___; Don't know (98)

142 a. Were there any persons working under your supervision? Yes (1); Yes, same persons as today (2); No (3)
[IF (2) OR (3), GO TO Q. 143.]

b. How many were there? ___

143 a. In this job, did you come into contact with customers, clients, or others outside the company? Yes ___; Exactly same persons as today (1); No (2)
[IF (1) OR (2), GO TO Q. 144.]

b. How often did you come into contact with such persons? Every day (1); Regularly but not every day (2); Only occasionally (3); Don't know (8); INAP (9)

c. Of these persons, what proportion were also (*group*)? All or almost all (1); More than half (2); About half (3); Less than half (4); Few or none (5); Don't know (8); INAP (9)

d. What proportion were from the majority Canadian group? All or almost all (1); More than half (2); About half (3); Less than half (4); Few or none (5); Don't know (8); INAP (9)

144 a. Of all these people you worked with or came into contact with on your job, how often did you spend time with any of them outside of work? Regularly (1); Occasionally (2); Rarely or never (3)
[*IF (3), GO TO Q. 145a.*]

b. [*IF BRITISH, GO TO Q. 145a.*]
Were the ethnic backgrounds of these people you spent time with mostly (*group*), from the majority Canadian group, or from some other group? Mostly same as self (1); Mostly from the majority Canadian group (2); Mostly other groups (3); No particular group (4); Don't know (8); INAP (9)

145 a. Was there a union for persons who had your job? Yes (1); No (2); Don't know (8)
[*IF (2), GO TO Q. 146.*]

b. Did you join the union? Yes (1); No (2); INAP (9)
[*IF BRITISH, GO TO Q. 146.*]

c. Were the members of the union local also mostly (*group*), mostly from the majority Canadian group, or from some other group? Mostly same as self (1); Mostly from the majority Canadian group (2); Other group (3); Mixture (4); Don't know (8); INAP (9)

146 [*HAND R. CARD 14.*] [*INTERVIEWER: Q. 146 refers to the same job as in the previous questions.*]
Using this card, would you tell me, in that job ten (nine ...) years ago, what was your annual income (before taxes)? A, Less than $1,000 (01); B, $1,000–$1,999 (02); C, $2,000–$2,999 (03); D, $3,000– $3,999 (04); E, $4,000–$4,999 (05); F, $5,000–$5,999 (06); G, $6,000–$6,999 (07); H, $7,000–$7,999 (08); I, $8,000–$8,999 (09); J, $9,000–$9,999 (10); K, $10,000–$11,999 (11); L, $12,000–$13,999 (12); M, $14,000–$15,999 (13); N, $16,000–$19,999 (14); O, $20,000–$24,999 (15); P, $25,000 or more (16); Refusal (97); Don't know (98); INAP (99)

147 Finally, I would like to ask about *your first regular full-time job*, I mean, your first job after leaving school to enter the work force.

a. What kind of work did you do? [*Probe for exact job description.*]

___

b. In what kind of organization, business, or industry was that?

---

148 At what age did you start this job? __

149 a. Since you started this first job, have you *always* worked, or were there times of *more than a year* when you were not working? Always worked (1); Times not working for a year or more (2)
[*IF (1), GO TO Q. 150.*]

b. If you added together the time when you were *not working*, about how many years would that be? __ years; Don't know (98)

150 When you had this first job were you living in Canada? Yes (1); No (2)
[*IF (1), GO TO Q. 153.*]

151 a. What kind of work did you do *just after coming to Canada*?

---

b. In what kind of organization, business, or industry was that?

---

152 How many years ago did you take this first job after coming to Canada? Ten years or less (1); More than ten years (2); Don't know (8)
[*IF (1), GO TO Q. 154a.*]

153 [*IF BRITISH, GO TO Q. 155a.*]

Were the people you worked with primarily (*group*), primarily another group, or something else? Primarily (*group*) (1); Primarily other group (2); Mixed (3); Don't know (8); INAP (9)

154 a. In looking for any of the jobs you have had in Canada did you want to work mainly with other (*group*), or with the majority Canadian group, or wasn't this ever a consideration? Yes, I wanted to work with (*group*) (1); Yes, I wanted to work with the majority Canadian group (2); No, it wasn't a consideration (3); INAP (9)
[*IF (3), GO TO Q. 155a.*]

b. What was the main reason? Was it a question of how much opportunity you would have (1) or the kind of people you liked to be with (2)? Other (3); INAP (9)

155 a. How many people that you have met through your present and past jobs do you keep in touch with? __

b. Of these, how many *know each other* on a first name basis? All or almost all (1); More than half (2); About half (3); Less than half (4); Few or none (5); Don't know (8); INAP (9)

c. Are these people you met through work mostly (*group*), mostly from the majority Canadian group, or from some other group? Same as self (1); Majority Canadian group (2); Other group (3); Mixed (4); Don't know (8); INAP (9)

156 Now a few questions about your family.

a. What was the highest educational level completed by your father? __
b. What was the highest education level completed by your mother? __
USE THESE CODES: Never attended school (01); 1–4 years elementary (02); 5–8 years elementary (03); Some high school (no diploma) (04); High school graduate (05); Post-secondary technical or vocational (non-university) (06); Some university (no degree) (07); Postgraduate degree (08); University degree (09); Don't know (98)

157 a. What kind of work did your father do most of the time when you were growing up (that is, up to age 18)? [*PROBE FOR JOB DESCRIPTION*.]

______

b. In what kind or organization, business, or industry was that?

______

158 [*IF R. BRITISH, OR IF R. GREW UP* OUTSIDE CANADA, *GO TO Q. 159; FOR OTHERS ASK THE FOLLOWING*.]

Were the people your father worked with primarily (*group*), primarily from another group, or some other group? Primarily (*group*) (1); Primarily other group (2); Mixed (3); Works alone (4); Don't know (8); INAP (9)

159 [*IF NOT MARRIED OR NOT LIVING WITH SPOUSE, GO TO Q. 165*.]

a. For how many years did your spouse go to school? Years __; INAP (99) [*IF 11 YEARS OR LESS, GO TO Q. 160*.]

b. Did he (she) ever attend a university? Yes (1); No (2); Don't know (8); INAP (9)
[*IF (2) OR (8), GO TO Q. 160*.]

c. Did he (she) earn a degree? Yes (1); No (2); Don't know (8); INAP (9)

160 Is your spouse working at the present time; does he (she) have his (her) own business, is he (she) unemployed, or what? Self-employed (1); Employed full-time (2); Employed part-time (3); Laid off temporarily (4); Out of a job (5); Retired or permanently disabled (6); Full-time student (7); Housewife (8); INAP (9)
[*IF (7) OR (8), GO TO Q. 164*.]

161 a. What kind of work does (did) he (she) do?

______

b. What kind of business or industry is that?

______

162 Do the persons where your spouse works tend to be of the same ethnic origin as your spouse? Yes (1); No (2); Mixed (3); Works alone (3); Don't know (8); INAP (no spouse) (9)

163 [*HAND R. CARD 14*.]

What is your spouse's current income, before taxes? A, Less than $1,000 (01); B, $1,000–$1,999 (02); C, $2,000–$2,999 (03); D, $3,000– $3,999 (04); E, $4,000–$4,999 (05); F, $5,000–$5,999 (06); G, $6,000–$6,999 (07); H, $7,000–

$7,999 (08); I, $8,000–$8,999 (09); J, $9,000–$9,999 (10); K, $10,000–$11,999 (11); L, $12,000–$13,999 (12); M, $14,000–$15,999 (13); N, $16,000–$19,999 (14); O, $20,000–$24,999 (15); P, $25,000 or more (16); Refusal (97); Don't know (98); INAP (99)

164 What was your spouse's father's main occupation *at the time you were married*? ______

[*INTERVIEWER: PLEASE REFER TO Q. 2a AND 2b. IF RESPONSES ARE THE SAME, CHECK HERE* __ *AND TERMINATE THE INTERVIEW. IF RESPONSES ARE NOT THE SAME, RECORD FEMALE ETHNICITY HERE* ______ *AND CONTINUE.*]

You mentioned that your ancestry on your mother's side was (*female ethnicity*) and I'd like to ask you a few questions about that.

165 How close are the ties which you maintain with other (*female ethnicity*) in Canada? Very close (1); Moderately close (2); Not very close (3); Not at all close (4); Don't know (8); INAP (9)

166 How do you usually think of yourself, as a (*female ethnicity*), or a (*female ethnicity–Canadian*), or a (*male ethnicity*), or a (*male ethnicity–Canadian*), or a Canadian, or what? Female ethnicity (1); Female ethnicity–Canadian (2); Male ethnicity (3); Male ethnicity–Canadian (4); Canadian (5); Other [*SPECIFY*] (6); Don't know (8); INAP (9)

167 [*HAND R. CARD 11.*]

Suppose the circle on this card represented the activities that go on in the (*group*) community in Toronto. How far or how close from the centre of these activities are you? Code response __; Don't know (8); INAP (9)

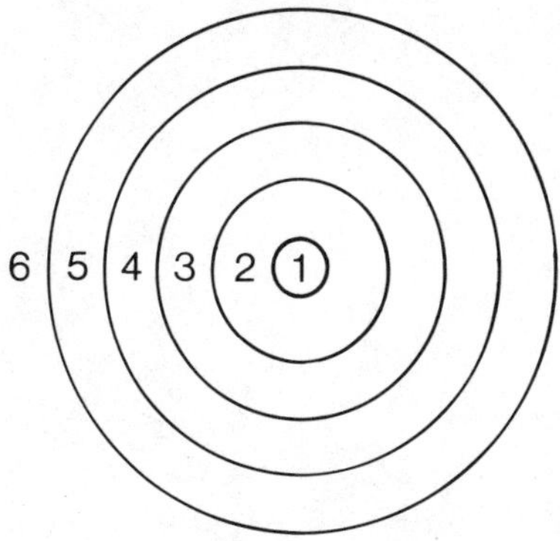

THANK YOU VERY MUCH FOR YOUR CO-OPERATION!

FINISH TIME: ______

Notes

CHAPTER 1

1 Changes in the wording of the ethnic-origin question in the 1981 Census of Canada, and instructions encouraging respondents to 'specify as many (origins) as applicable,' preclude any direct comparison of 1981 census data with earlier censuses. Of the total, 46.7% indicated they were of British origin only, while another 5.6% indicated some multiple combination of origins including British. An estimate of the proportion of the population of British origin in 1981, based on a definition comparable to the one used in the 1971 census, would undoubtedly lie somewhere between 46.7 and 52.3%.

2 The source of the data in these maps showing the distributions of ethnic-origin populations in the Toronto CMA is Statistics Canada, 1981 Census of Canada. The maps were drawn by Madeline Richard of the Population Research Laboratory, Erindale College, University of Toronto. Note that the study area for the survey is not the same as the Toronto CMA, as defined by Statistics Canada, but includes all of Metropolitan Toronto plus parts of Richmond Hill and Mississauga.

3 The data analyses reported in this book are based on an assignment of weights that is somewhat different from that used in earlier working papers distributed through the University of Toronto Centre for Urban and Community Studies (see Breton, Isajiw, Kalbach, and Reitz 1981). The weights used here have been refined to improve the accuracy of our results. In most cases, however, results do not vary widely from those reported earlier.

CHAPTER 3

1 As measured by Lieberson's Index of Diversity (A'_w), based on thirteen ethnic categories, the index increased from 0.36 in 1941 to 0.70 in 1971. For a discussion of the adjusted index see Lieberson (1969: 850–62). The index varies between 0, for complete homogeneity, and 1 for maximum diversity. The formula for A_w and the adjusted index, A'_w, is shown below, where P_i represents the proportion of the ith ethnic population and N is the number of ethnic categories, that is $N = 13$ in this case:

$$A'_w = \frac{A_w}{1 - 1/N} \text{ where } A_w = 1 - \sum_{i=1}^{N} (P_i)^2.$$

2 Analysis by Balakrishnan (1976: 481–97) of the 1951 and 1961 censuses provided some evidence of decline during the interim period, but a similar analysis of changes in the 1961–71 decade did not show any continuation of a downward trend. He could only conclude that 'ethnic pluralism' in Canada as revealed by ethnic residential segregation is not only persistent, but high for certain groups (Balakrishnan 1976: 25).

3 Simple percentage-distribution maps cannot directly show the extent to which a population may be 'over' or 'under'-represented in a particular area. The index of relative concentration, employed for the maps presented in chapter 1, does permit a direct interpretation. For example, an index of 110 means that the population is over-represented by 10 per cent, while an index of 80 indicates an under-representation of 20 per cent. An index of 100 indicates that its percentage of the area's (census tract) population is identical to its percentage of the total metropolitan area population and neither over- or under-represented in the particular tract or area.

4 While the index of dissimilarity used for the analysis of segregation of the 1971 census data is the same as that employed for the earlier historical period presented in table 1, the indexes used for the major analysis reported in this chapter are based on a slightly different reference group. Rather than using the total English-origin population as the population for comparison, access to special tabulations of the data by census tract for 1971 permitted the use of a theoretically more relevant population for assessing the nature of residential segregation in Toronto, the third-plus generations of English origin. One additional difference should be noted with respect to the actual calculation of indexes of dissimilarity. Rather than using the total population, the analysis was limited to the population 15 years of age and over. This limitation was necessary because the educational attainment variable, when used as a control for socio-economic status, makes sense only when applied to a population old enough to be

included in the labour-force population and for which most would have completed their formal education.

5 The 1971 census is the only Census of Canada during the post-war period that collected data on the birthplace of parents, permitting the identification of the second and third-plus generations of Canadians.

6 The eight indicators include attendance at ethnic dances, parties, or informal social affairs; attending non-ethnic affairs; patronizing ethnic vacation resorts, summer camps, and so on; eating foods associated with ethnic holidays or special events; eating ethnic foods generally as part of one's regular diet; listening to ethnic radio broadcasts or watching ethnic television programs; reading ethnic newspapers, magazines, or other periodicals; and displaying ethnic or cultural objects in the home.

7 There is a minor difference in the definition of the basic reference group used in the segregation analysis relative to the 'Majority Canadian' group used in the other chapters. The segregation analysis, based on census data, was completed much earlier than the analyses for the other sub-projects based on the sample survey data collected in 1978–9. For the segregation analysis, the third-plus generation of the population of English origin was chosen as the basic standard or reference group because of the generally high prestige and status they have enjoyed as a group in Toronto since its original settlement. There were considerable status differences between the English, Irish, and Scottish in Toronto's early days, and it was thought important to maintain the distinction between these groups so that their present residential patterns could be compared and assessed with respect to the possible validity that a combined 'British origin' group might have as an alternative reference group in segregation studies. The special interests reflected in the analyses presented in the other chapters required the use of a somewhat different reference group for the ethnic-minority groups included in the study at a time when many of the early status distinctions between the various components of the combined British-origins group have ceased to exist. The 'Majority Canadian' group used elsewhere differs only in that it includes the third-plus generations of Irish and Scottish origins in addition to those of English origin.

8 An index of 100 would indicate a condition of total segregation, that is, that the individuals of one ethnic origin were located only in those areas in which individuals of the other ethnic origin did not reside. Provided that the numbers of census tracts exceeded the number of ethnic-origin groups, it would be theoretically possible, but highly unlikely, to have an urban community in which all of the ethnic groups were totally segregated from one another.

9 These forces would include such factors as the strength of an individual's feelings of ethnic identity and commitment, feelings of prejudice experienced or expected in the community, degree of facility with the English language, desire or convenient access to ethnic markets, or existence of

relatives and friends of one's own ethnic group.

10 Those least likely to encounter more ethnically diverse populations in their day-to-day routines would be the non-movers remaining in the smaller communities outside the reach of the larger metropolitan centres.

11 Residential segregation, that is, the Index of Dissimilarity, is weakly correlated (Cramer's $V = 0.22$) with the perceived ethnic character of the neighbourhood and moderately related ($V = 0.47$) to the prestige ratings of ethnic groups, as judged by those in the sample of English origin who reported that they had not attained more than an elementary education. Correlations between residential segregation and prestige ratings were somewhat less for those of English origin with higher educational status.

12 Part of these differences can be attributed, of course, to variations in the generational composition of each of the ten ethnic populations. The correlation (Cramer's V) between generation and importance of respondent's origin is 0.39. Fifty-seven per cent of the first generation considered their origins to be either very or extremely important compared to 40 and 15% for the second and third-plus generations respectively.

13 The rank-order correlation between the group's Index of Segregation and average ethnic participation is +0.71, based on the ten ethnic groups presented in tables 3.6 and 3.7.

14 Reitz (1980) reported that the respondent's perception of the ethnic character of the neighbourhood was the least successful of six measures in predicting ethnic-community attachment. While the variable was employed somewhat differently in this analysis, the correlations with similar types of ethnic-participation variables were essentially the same, that is, between 0.10 and 0.20.

15 During the interview of the field survey, respondents were asked to make certain comparative-type judgments involving themselves, as well as other groups, with respect to the 'Majority Canadian' group. This group included the third-plus generations of English-, Irish-, and Scottish-origin populations. As the indexes of segregation, based on census tabulations, had been calculated for individual ethnic populations by generation, the third-plus generation of the English-origin population seemed to be the most appropriate and comparable group to use as the standard for comparison in the segregation analysis.

CHAPTER 4

1 This chapter is a revision, consolidation, and extension of two papers (Reitz, Calzavara, and Dasko 1981; and Reitz 1982) previously made available in the 'Ethnic Pluralism' research paper series of the University of Toronto Centre for Urban and Community Studies. The collaboration of Liviana Calzavara and Donna Dasko in the early stages of this research is gratefully acknowledged. The author also wishes to express special thanks to Raymond Breton, Mark Granovetter, Ron Gillis, John Hagan, Ivan

Light, and Suzanne Model for comments and suggestions that have contributed to this research.

2 The term 'ethnic occupations' is used here as shorthand for 'ethnic concentrations in occupations.' Use of the term 'ethnic occupations' does not in any way imply the existence of occupations which are the official domain of any ethnic group. Rather, it is always meant to imply 'ethnic concentrations in occupations,' a purely statistical concept.

3 Blishen and McRoberts (1976) describe a scale for 1971 occupational categories used in this study. The scale estimates occupational prestige for 480 occupational titles listed in the census manual. For each occupation, data on average educational and income levels are used to estimate occupational prestige, using the known relationships of education and income to occupational prestige for 85 occupational titles rated in previous survey research by Pineo and Porter (1967).

4 Job status as measured here may be a poor indicator of gender inequality (cf. Guppy and Siltanen 1977). First of all, job statuses vary more among men than among women. Men more often have very high-status jobs *and* very low-status jobs. The standard deviation in job status is 14.58 for men, compared to only 12.76 for women. But, more important, the overall equality between men and women may be an artefact of the Blishen-scale measurement procedure. In the construction of the Blishen scale, only the occupations of the male labour force were used. Thus, the occupational prestige of the female labour force is measured using criteria derived from an analysis of the male labour force. The mean job status for women is very much affected by their mean level of education, since the latter determines the ratings given to occupations where they predominate. If women tend to remain in school on the average nearly as long as men, then the mean educational level of the occupations in which they are concentrated will parallel that of men, whatever the actual 'status' of the occupations.

5 Actual disposable incomes available to individuals may be somewhat different. This is because some individuals have non-employment incomes, and some share incomes with other household members who are employed. The latter possibility may affect ethnic inequalities because of ethnic differences in the sharing of household or family incomes. However, the interest in this study is specifically in income distribution occurring within labour markets and the occupational structure. Therefore, individual income from employment is the appropriate variable for analysis.

6 To make the census data as closely comparable to the sample data as possible, upper limits to incomes were set for men and women in the census data in a way that corresponds to the upper limits set for men and women in the sample survey data. See table 4.1, note b, and table 4.2, note b.

7 The unstandardized coefficients can be interpreted as the numbers of dollars of additional income that can be attributed to each additional unit of the independent variable.

8 Women also start to enter the labour force later, but the effect of this fact on current experience is offset by the higher average age of women currently in the labour force.

9 Since the census is a complete enumeration, one would not expect cell size to present statistical problems. However, Statistics Canada special tabulations all present cell frequencies rounded to the nearest number ending in 0 or 5 (a device to protect the confidentiality of individuals enumerated). This means that cell frequencies are only approximate, and if the absolute number in particular cells becomes small, the accuracy of estimates is endangered. To hold errors to a minimum, the tabulation was designed so that the smallest expected cell size (based on the null hypothesis that persons of a particular ethnic origin are neither over-concentrated nor under-concentrated in any occupation relative to others of the same gender) is 50.

10 See table 4.8, note a.

11 The census data on self-employment come from the variable 'class of worker.' The question on self-employment in the survey was very direct, and appears to have identified a larger proportion of the labour force. The group-to-group differences are similar in the census and survey data.

12 The place of work was defined as 'the entire company or organization under the same ownership or control, not just your own office or branch.' Locally owned franchises were considered as separate organizations.

13 It was not practical for Statistics Canada to produce a table showing occupation by ethnicity by sex by generation. We therefore do not know in which occupations the various generations are concentrated. The fact that, overall, Italian males are highly concentrated in construction occupations does not indicate that this pattern is true for males of each generation. Each generation may be concentrated in a unique set of occupations.

CHAPTER 5

1 For a discussion of ethnic interests in relation to ethnic structure and behaviour, see for example Siegel 1970, Cohen 1974b (especially the papers by Cohen himself, Deshen, Hannerz, and Charlsley), Zielyk 1975, and Breton 1978.

2 The literature on the organizational requirements for collective action is extensive. See, for instance, Dahrendorf 1959, Pinard 1968, Clark 1975, Tilly 1975, and Brym 1978.

3 The question on acceptance as neighbours or relatives included a number of groups in addition to those in the sample. The results that refer to overall acceptance (without distinctions as to the degree of acceptance) are

as follows. The figures are the percentages of Majority Canadians and of all other groups combined who would accept the groups listed as neighbours and as close relatives.

	Would have as neighbour			Would have as close relative		
	Majority Canadians	English 1st & 2nd	Minority groups	Majority Canadians	English 1st & 2nd	Minority groups
French	90	90	87	87	87	73
English	92	–	92	93	–	77
Irish	97	92	91	94	91	75
Scottish	94	93	91	95	93	75
Greek	84	84	87	78	78	68
Pakistani	59	55	63	43	39	37
Canadian Indian	82	75	80	73	64	50

It should be noted that the extent of social acceptance is lower for the Pakistani than for any other group considered in the study, except among the minority-group respondents, who rate Pakistani with West Indians as relatives.

4 For members of minority groups, the questions pertained to their own group; for respondents of British ancestry, the questions referred to 'immigrants or members of a minority group.'

5 The statements read to respondents were as follows: 'Present immigration laws make it too difficult for (group) to come to Canada' and 'Present immigration laws make it too easy for certain groups to come to Canada.' The five response options ranged from 'strongly agree' to 'strongly disagree.'

6 The relative size of groups does not depend only on immigration. It also depends on factors such as differential fertility, mortality, and assimilation or acculturation.

7 The 1981 census allowed a respondent to mention multiple origins. The percentage given here refers to those listed as 'British only.'

8 The question was asked as follows: 'I'd like to ask the same question about various ethnic groups. Are they now being treated fairly by employers, or do they experience some discrimination or a lot of discrimination? How about ... (each group named separately)?' The response options were: 'treated fairly,' 'some discrimination,' 'a lot of discrimination,' 'they have an advantage,' and 'don't know.'

9 West Indians may perceive the variety of English they speak as different from the variety of English spoken in Canada, but this matter has not been explored in this study. The question is therefore not applicable in their case.

10 The respondents of British ancestry were asked about 'immigrants or members of a minority group.'

11 Cultural loss is seen as a problem when either the loss of customs and traditions or the decreasing use of the group's language or both are perceived as very or somewhat serious problems faced by the group.

12 The question is the following: 'Do you feel that it is difficult (or a problem) to be both a (group) and a Canadian at the same time?' The response options are: 'yes,' 'no,' 'depends,' 'don't know.'

13 As will become apparent from the discussion that follows, the notion of resource is used here in its very general sense.

14 The two questions are the following: 'Suppose a member of an ethnic group has trouble getting a good job in a company because he is discriminated against. How much do you think the following actions he could take could help to change the situation: very much, somewhat, a little, or not at all?' (The list of actions appears in table 5.12.) 'Suppose someone wanted to change Canadian immigration laws or procedures. How much do you think the following actions would help? Very much, somewhat, a little, not at all.' (The list of actions appears in table 5.13.)

15 The same results are observed with the question about employer discrimination against members of one's group.

16 Respondents were asked if they agreed or disagreed with the following statements: 'In general, politicians and officials do not take seriously the views expressed by the (group) community leaders.' 'Leaders of the (group) community do not have enough connections with important people in business and government to get important results for the community.' 'Even if the leaders and organizations of the (group) community in Toronto were more active, we would not get more attention from politicians and government officials.'

17 The index of political interest is based on the following two questions: 'How interested are you in local issues or events [which *do not* relate specifically to (group)] such as new bylaws or local politics?' 'How about provincial or national affairs? Are you ...' The response options were: 'very,' 'somewhat,' 'slightly,' 'not at all.'

18 The question asked is the following: 'Suppose the circle on this card represented the activities that go on in the (group) community in Toronto. How far or how close from the centre of these activities are you?' Closeness or distance could vary between 1 and 6.

19 On this question see, for example, Warner 1945, Spiro 1955 and Hannerz 1974.

References

Aboud, Frances E. 1981. 'Ethnic self-identity.' In R.C. Gardner and R. Kalin, eds, *A Canadian Social Psychology of Ethnic Relations*. Toronto: Methuen Publications

Abramson, Harold J. 1973. *Ethnic Diversity in Catholic America*. New York: Wiley

– 1975. 'The religioethnic factor and the American experience: Another look at the three-generations hypothesis.' *Ethnicity* 2: 163–77

Alba, Richard D. 1976. 'Social assimilation among American Catholic national-origin groups.' *American Sociological Review* 41: 1030–46

– 1985a. 'The twilight of ethnicity among Americans of European ancestry: The case of Italians.' *Ethnic and Racial Studies* 8 (1): 134–58

– 1985b. *Italian Americans: Into the Twilight of Ethnicity*. Englewood Cliffs, NJ: Prentice-Hall

– 1985c. *Ethnicity and Race in the U.S.A.* Boston: Routledge & Kegan Paul

Alba, Richard D., and Mitchell B. Chamlin. 1983. 'A prelimary examination of ethnic identification among whites.' *American Sociological Review* 48: 240–7

Aldrich, Howard. 1980. 'Asian shopkeepers as a middleman minority: A study of small business in Wandsworth.' In Alan Evans and David Eversley, eds, *The Inner City: Employment and Industry*, 389–407. London: Heinemann

Averitt, R.T. 1968. *The Dual Economy*. New York: Norton and Co.

Aversa, Alfred, Jr. 1978. 'Italian neo-ethnicity: The search for self-identity.' *The Journal of Ethnic Studies* 6 (2): 49–56

Baar, Ellen. 1983. 'Patterns of selective accentuation among Niagara Mennonites.' *Canadian Ethnic Studies* 15 (2): 77–91

Balakrishnan, T.R. 1976. 'Ethnic residential segregation in the metropolitan areas of Canada.' *Canadian Journal of Sociology* 1 (4): 481–98

– 1982. 'Changing patterns of ethnic residential segregation in the metropolitan areas of Canada.' *Canadian Review of Sociology and Anthropology* 19 (1): 92–110

Beattie, Christopher. 1975. *Minority Men in a Majority Setting*. Toronto: McClelland and Stewart

Bell, Daniel. 1975. 'Ethnicity and social change.' In Nathan Glazer and Daniel P. Moynihan, eds, *Ethnicity: Theory and Experience*. Cambridge, MA: Harvard University Press

Bell, W. 1959. 'Social areas: Typology of urban neighborhoods.' In M.B. Sussman, ed., *Community Structure and Analysis*. New York: T.Y. Crowell Co.

Bergman, B. 1971. 'The effect on white incomes of discrimination in employment.' *Journal of Political Economy* 79: 294–313

Berry, J.W., R. Kalin, and D.M. Taylor. 1977. *Multiculturalism and Ethnic Attitudes in Canada*. Ottawa: Minister of Supply and Services

Blishen, Bernard R. 1970. 'Social class and opportunity in Canada,' *Canadian Review of Sociology and Anthropology* 7: 110–27

Blishen, Bernard R. and Hugh A. McRoberts. 1976. 'A revised socioeconomic index for occupations in Canada.' *Canadian Review of Sociology and Anthropology* 13 (1): 71–9

Bluestone, B. 1973. *Low Wages and the Working Poor*. Ann Arbor: University of Michigan

Bogardus, E.S. 1928. *Immigration and Race Attitudes*. Boston: Heath

Bonacich, E. 1972. 'A theory of ethnic antagonism: The split labor market.' *American Sociological Review* 37: 547–59

– 1973. 'A theory of middle-man minorities.' *American Sociological Review* 38: 583–94

Borhek, J.T. 1970. 'Ethnic group cohesion.' *American Journal of Sociology* 76: 33–46

Borjas, George J. 1986. 'The self-employment experience of immigrants.' *The Journal of Human Resources* 21 (4): 485–506

Boyd, Monica. 1975. 'The status of immigrant women in Canada.' *Canadian Review of Sociology and Anthropology* 12: 406–16

Breton, Raymond. 1978. 'Stratification and conflict between ethnolinguistic communities with different social structures.' *Canadian Review of Sociology and Anthropology* 15: 148–57

– 1979. 'Ethnic stratification viewed from three theoretical perspectives.' In J.E. Curtis and W.G. Scott, eds, *Social Stratification: Canada* 271–293. Toronto: Prentice-Hall

Breton, Raymond, Wsevolod W. Isajiw, Warren Kalbach, and Jeffrey G. Reitz. 1981. 'Ethnic pluralism in a urban setting: Conceptual and technical overview of a research project.' Research paper no. 121, University of Toronto Centre for Urban and Community Studies

Brym, Robert J. 1978. 'Regional social structure and agrarian radicalism in Canada: Alberta, Saskatchewan, and New Brunswick,' *Canadian Review of Sociology and Anthropology* 15: 339–51

Burgess, E.W. 1925. 'The growth of the city: An introduction to a research project.' In R.E. Park, E.W. Burgess, and R.E. McKenzie, eds, *The City*, 47–62. Chicago: University of Chicago Press

Burnet, J.R. 1972. *Ethnic Groups in Upper Canada*. Toronto: Ontario Historical Society

Canada, Department of Manpower and Immigration. 1974a. *Canadian Immigration and Population Study*, vol. I, *Immigration Policy Perspectives*. Ottawa: Information Canada

– 1974b. *Canadian Immigration and Population Study*, vol. II, *The Immigration Programmer*. Ottawa: Information Canada

Carlin, J. 1966. *Lawyer's Ethics*. New York: Russell Sage Foundation

Chrisman, Noel J. 1981. 'Ethnic persistence in an urban setting.' *Ethnicity* 8: 256–92

Clark, Samuel. 1975. 'The political mobilization of Irish farmers.' *Canadian Review of Sociology and Anthropology* 12: 483–99

Cohen, Abner. 1974a. 'Introduction: The lessons of ethnicity.' In Abner Cohen, ed., *Urban Ethnicity*. London: Tavistock Publications

– 1974b. *Urban Ethnicity*. London: Tavistock Publications

Collins, O. 1946. 'Ethnic behavior in industry: Sponsorship and rejection in a New England factory.' *American Journal of Sociology* 51: 293–8

Connor, John W. 1977. *Tradition and Change in Three Generations of Japanese Americans*. New Brunswick, NJ: Transaction Books

Corwin, R.D. 1971. *Racial Minorities in Banking: New Workers in the Banking Industry*. New Haven, CT: College and University Press

Crispino, James A. 1980. *The Assimilation of Ethnic Groups: The Italian Case*. Staten Island, NY: Center for Migration Studies

Dahlie, Jorgen, and Tissa Fernando, eds. 1982. *Ethnicity, Power and Politics in Canada*. Toronto: Methuen

Dahrendorf, Ralf. 1959. *Class and Class Conflict in Industrial Society*. Stanford, CA: Stanford University Press

Dalton, M. 1951. 'Informal factors in career achievement.' *American Journal of Sociology* 56: 407–15

Danziger, K. 1974. 'The acculturation of Italian immigrant girls in Canada.' In C. Beattie and S. Crysdale, eds, *Sociology Canada Readings*. Toronto: Butterworths and Co.

Darroch, Gordon A. 1979. 'Another look at ethnicity, stratification, and social mobility in Canada.' *Canadian Journal of Sociology* 4: 1–25

Darroch, Gordon A., and Wilfred G. Marston. 1969. 'Ethnic differentiation: Ecological aspects of a multidimensional concept.' *International Migration Review* 4 (Fall): 71–95

– 1971. 'The social class bias of ethnic residential segregation: The Canadian case.' *American Journal of Sociology* 77 (November): 491–510

– 1984. 'Patterns of urban ethnicity: Toward a revised ecological model.' In Noel Iverson, ed., *Urbanism and Urbanization: Views, Aspects and Dimensions*. Leiden: E.J. Brill

Dashefsky, Arnold. 1970. 'Interaction and identity: The Jewish case.' Paper presented at 65th annual meeting, American Sociological Association

– 1972. 'And the search goes on: The meaning of religio-ethnic identity and identification.' *Sociological Analysis* 33 (4): 239–45

– 1975. 'Theoretical frameworks in the study of ethnic groups: Toward a social psychology of ethnicity.' *Ethnicity* 2: 10–18

Dashefsky, Arnold, and Harold M. Shapiro. 1974. *Ethnic Identification among American Jews: Socialization and Social Structure*. Lexington, MA: Lexington Books

Deshen, Shlomo. 1974. 'Political ethnicity and cultural ethnicity in Israel during the 1960s.' In Abner Cohen, ed., *Urban Ethnicity*. London: Tavistock Publications

Deutschmann, Linda Bell. 1979. 'Decline of the WASP?: Dominant group identity in a multi-ethnic society.' Unpublished PhD thesis, University of Toronto

Doucette, Lori, and John Edwards. 1987. 'Ethnic salience, identity and symbolic ethnicity.' *Canadian Ethnic Studies* 19 (1): 52–62

Driedger, Leo. 1975. 'In search of cultural identity factors: A comparison of ethnic students.' *Canadian Review of Sociology and Anthropology* 12: 150–62

– 1977. 'Toward a perspective on Canadian pluralism: Ethnic identity in Winnipeg.' *Canadian Journal of Sociology* 2: 77–96

– 1978. 'Ethnic boundaries: A comparison of two urban neighborhoods.' *Sociology and Social Research* 62: 193–211

– 1980. 'Jewish identity: The maintenance of urban religions and ethnic boundaries.' *Ethnic and Racial Studies* 3 (1): 67–88

Driedger, Leo, and Glenn Church. 1974. 'Residential segregation and institutional completeness: A comparison of ethnic minorities.' *Canadian Review of Sociology and Anthropology* 11: 30–52

Edwards, John, and Lori Doucette. 1987. 'Ethnic salience, identity and symbolic ethnicity.' *Canadian Ethnic Studies* 19 (1): 52–62

Edwards, Richard. 1979. *Contested Terrain*. New York: Basic Books

Epstein, Arnold Leonard. 1978. *Ethos and Identity: Three Studies in Ethnicity*. London: Tavistock Publications

Epstein, C.F. 1973. 'Positive effects of the multiple negative.' *American Journal of Sociology* 78: 912–35

Farber, Bernard, Leonard Gordon, and Albert J. Mayer. 1979. 'Intermarriage and Jewish identity: The implications for pluralism and assimilation in American society.' *Ethnic and Racial Studies* 2 (2): 222–30

Finifter, Bernard M. 1972. 'The generation of confidence: Evaluating research findings by random subsample replication.' In H. Costner, ed., *Sociological Methodology 1972*, 112–75. San Francisco: Jossey Bass Inc., Publishers
Fischer, Claude S. 1975. 'Toward a subcultural theory of urbanism.' *American Journal of Sociology* 80: 1319–41
Fishman, Joshua A., Vladimir C. Nahirny, John E. Hofman, and Robert G. Hayden. 1966. *Language Loyalty in the United States: The Maintenance and Perpetuation of Non-English Mother Tongues by American Ethnic and Religious Groups*. The Hague: Mouton and Co.
Frideres, J.S., and S. Goldenberg. 1977. 'Hyphenated Canadians: Comparative analysis of ethnic, regional and national identification of Western Canadian university students.' *Journal of Ethnic Studies* 5 (2): 91–100
Gans, Herbert. 1956. 'American Jewry: Present and future.' *Commentary* 22, nos. 5 and 6
– 1962. *The Urban Villagers*. New York: The Free Press
– 1979. 'Symbolic ethnicity: The future of ethnic groups and cultures.' *Racial and Ethnic Studies* 2: 1–20
Geismar, Ludwig. 1954. 'A scale for the measurement of ethnic identification.' *Jewish Social Studies* 16: 33–60
Glaser, Daniel. 1958. 'Dynamics of ethnic identification.' *American Sociological Review* 23: 31–40
Glazer, Nathan, and Daniel P. Moynihan. 1963. *Beyond the Melting Pot*. Cambridge, MA: MIT Press
Goering, John. 1971. 'The emergence of ethnic interest: A case of serendipity.' *Social Forces* 49: 379–84
– 1972. 'Changing perceptions and evaluations of physical characteristics among Blacks, 1950–1970.' *Phylon* 33: 231–41
Goldlust, J., and A. Richmond. 1973. 'A multi-variate analysis of the economic adaptation of immigrants in Toronto.' York University Institute for Behavioural Research, Downsview, ON
Gordon, David. 1972. *Theories of Poverty and Underdevelopment: Orthodox, Radical, and Dual Labor Market Perspectives*. Lexington, MA: Lexington
Gordon, M.N., and T.E. Morton. 1974. 'A low mobility model of wage discrimination – with special reference to sex differentials.' *Journal of Economic Theory* 7: 241–53
Gordon, Milton. 1964. *Assimilation in American Life: The Role of Race, Religion and National Origins*. New York: Oxford University Press
Granovetter, Mark. 1981. 'Toward a sociological theory of income differences.' In Ivar Berg, ed., *Sociological Perspectives on Labour Markets*, 11–47. New York: Academic Press
– 1985. 'Economic action and social structure: The problem of embeddedness.' *American Journal of Sociology* 91: 481–510
Greeley, Andrew M. 1972. 'The transmission of cultural heritage: The case of

the Irish and the Italians.' Paper presented to the American Academy of Arts and Sciences, Conference on Ethnic Problems in the Contemporary World, Boston

– 1974. *Ethnicity in the United States: A Preliminary Reconnaissance*. New York: John Wiley and Sons

– 1976. 'The ethnic miracle.' *The Public Interest* 45 (Fall): 20–36

Greeley, Andrew M., and William C. McCready. 1974. 'Does ethnicity matter?' *Ethnicity* 1: 91–108

Guest, A.M., and J.A. Weed. 1976. 'Ethnic residential segregation: Patterns of change.' *American Journal of Sociology* 81: 1088–1111

Gunderson, Morley. 1976. 'Work patterns.' In G. Cook, ed., *Opportunity for Choice*. Ottawa: Statistics Canada and C.D. Howe Research Institute

Gunderson, Morley, and Frank Reid. 1983. *Sex Discrimination in the Canadian Labour Market: Theories, Data, and Evidence*. Ottawa: Women's Bureau, Labour Canada

Guppy, L.N., and J.L. Siltanen. 1977. 'A comparison of the allocation of male and female occupational prestige.' *Canadian Review of Sociology and Anthropology* 14: 320–30

Hannerz, Ulf. 1974. 'Ethnicity and opportunity in urban America.' In Abner Cohen, ed., *Urban Ethnicity*, 37–76. London: Tavistock Publications

Hansen, Marcus Lee. 1962. 'The third generation in America.' *Commentary* 14: 496

Hasakawa, Fumiko. 1973. 'Social interaction and ethnic identification among third generation Japanese.' Unpublished doctoral dissertation, University of California, Los Angeles

Hauser, Stuart. 1972. 'The black and white identity development: Aspects and perspectives.' *Journal of Youth and Adolescence* 1: 113–30

Hechter, M. 1978. 'Group formation and the cultural division of labor.' *American Journal of Sociology* 84 (2): 293–318

Helper, R. 1969. *Racial Policies and Practices of Real Estate Brokers*. Minneapolis: University of Minnesota Press

Henry, Frances. 1986. 'Race relations research in Canada today: A "state of the art" review.' Canadian Human Rights Commission Colloquium on Racial Discrimination, 25 September

Henry, Frances, and Effie Ginzberg. 1985. *Who Gets the Work? A Test of Racial Discrimination in Employment*. Toronto: The Urban Alliance on Race Relations and the Social Planning Council of Metropolitan Toronto

Herberg, Will. 1955. *Protestant-Catholic-Jew*. New York: Doubleday and Co.

Hodge, R., and P. Hodge. 1965. 'Occupational assimilation as a competitive process.' *American Journal of Sociology* 71: 249–64

Hughes, Everett C., and Helen MacGill Hughes. 1952. *Where Peoples Meet: Racial and Ethnic Frontiers*. Glencoe, IL: The Free Press

Hurh, Won Moo. 1980. 'Towards a Korean-American ethnicity: Some theoretical models.' *Ethnic and Racial Studies* 3 (4): 444–64

Hutchinson, E. 1956. *Immigrants and Their Children, 1850–1950*. New York: Wiley

Isaacs, Harold R. 1975. 'Basic group identity: The idols of the tribe.' In Nathan Glazer and Daniel P. Moynihan, eds, *Ethnicity: Theory and Experience*. Cambridge, MA: Harvard University Press

Isajiw, Wsevolod W. 1974. 'Definitions of Ethnicity.' *Ethnicity* 1 (2): 111–24

– 1975. 'The process of maintenance of ethnic identity: The Canadian context.' In P. Migus, ed., *Sounds Canadian: Languages and Cultures in Multi-Ethnic Society*, 129–38. Toronto: Peter Martin Associates.

– 1977. 'Olga in Wonderland: Ethnicity in technological society.' *Canadian Ethnic Studies* 9 (1): 77–85

Isajiw, Wsevolod W., and Tomoko Makabe. 1982. 'Socialization as a factor in ethnic identity retention.' University of Toronto Centre for Urban and Community Studies, Research paper no. 134

Jiobu, Robert M. 1988. 'Ethnic hegemony and the Japanese in California.' *American Sociological Review* 53: 353–67

Kalbach, Warren E. 1970. *The Impact of Immigration on Canada's Population*. Ottawa: Dominion Bureau of Statistics, Queen's Printer

– 1980. 'Historical and generational perspectives of ethnic and residential segregation in Toronto, Canada: 1851–1971.' University of Toronto Centre for Urban and Community Studies, Research paper no. 118

Kalbach, Warren E., and W.W. McVey. 1971. *Demographic Bases of Canadian Society*. Toronto: McGraw-Hill

– 1979. *Demographic Bases of Canadian Society*. 2d ed. Toronto: McGraw-Hill Ryerson

Kalleberg, Arne L. 1988. 'Comparative perspectives on work structures and inequality.' *Annual Review of Sociology* 14: 203–25

Kalleberg, Arne L., and Aage B. Sørenson. 1979. 'The sociology of labour markets.' *Annual Review of Sociology* 5: 351–79

Kallen, Evelyn. 1977. *Spanning the Generations: A Study in Jewish Identity*. Toronto: Longman Canada

Kantrowitz, N. 1969. 'Ethnic and racial segregation in the New York metropolis, 1960.' *American Journal of Sociology* 74: 685–95

Kienetz, Alvin. 1986. 'Ethnic identity in Northern Canada.' *Journal of Ethnic Studies* 14 (1): 129–34

Kralt, J. 1976. *The Urban and Rural Composition of Canada's Population*. 1971 census profile study. Ottawa: Information Canada

Kramer, J., and S. Leventman. 1961. *Children of the Gilded Ghetto: Conflict Resolutions of Three Generations of American Jews*. New Haven, CT: Yale University Press

Lazarewitz, Bernard, and L. Rowitz. 1964. 'The three-generations hypothesis.' *American Journal of Sociology* 69: 529–38

Lenski, Gerhard. 1961. *The Religious Factor: A Sociological Study of Religious Impact upon Politics, Economics and Family Life*. New York: Doubleday and Co.

Lerner, G. 1972. *Black Women in White America*. New York: Pantheon Books

Lewin, Kurt. 1948. *Resolving Social Conflicts: Selected Papers on Group Dynamics*. New York: Harper and Row, Publishers

Li, Peter S. 1978. 'The stratification of ethnic immigrants: The case of Toronto.' *Canadian Review of Sociology and Anthropology* 15: 31–40

Lieberson, Stanley. 1961. 'The impact of residential segregation on ethnic assimilation.' *Social Forces* 40: 52–7

– 1963. *Ethnic Patterns in American Cities*. New York: The Free Press

– 1969. 'Measuring population diversity.' *American Sociological Review* 34 (December): 850–62

– 1980. *A Piece of the Pie: Black and White Immigrants since 1880*. Berkeley: University of California Press

– 1985. 'Unhyphenated whites in the United States.' *Ethnic and Racial Studies* 8 (1): 159–80

Light, Ivan. 1974. *Ethnic Enterprise in America*. Berkeley: University of California Press

– 1984. 'Immigrant and ethnic enterprise in North America.' *Ethnic and Racial Studies* 7 (2): 195–216

– 1986. 'Ethnicity and business enterprise.' In Mark Stolarik and Murray Friedman, eds, *Making It in America*, 13–32. London and Toronto: Associated University Presses

Lyman, Stanford, and W.A. Douglas. 1973. 'Ethnicity: Strategies of collective and individual impression management.' *Social Research* 40: 344–65

MacKie, Marlene. 1985. 'Stereotypes, prejudice and discrimination.' In R.M. Bienvenue and S.E. Goldstein, eds, *Ethnicity and Ethnic Relations in Canada*, 219–39. Toronto: Butterworths

MacKie, Marlene, and Merline Brinkerhoff. 1984. 'Measuring ethnic salience.' *Canadian Ethnic Studies* 16 (1): 114–31

Makabe, Tomoko. 1976. 'Ethnic group identity: Canadian born Japanese in Metropolitan Toronto.' Doctoral dissertation, University of Toronto

– 1978. 'Ethnic identity and social mobility: The case of the second generation of Japanese in Metropolitan Toronto.' *Canadian Ethnic Studies* 10 (1): 106–23

– 1979. 'Ethnic identity scale and social mobility: The case of Nisei in Toronto.' *Canadian Review of Sociology and Anthropology* 16 (2): 136–46

Masuda, Minoru, G.H. Matsumoto, and G.M. Meredith. 1970. 'Ethnic identity in three generations of Japanese Americans.' *Journal of Social Psychology* 81: 199–207

Mayhew, Leon. 1968. 'Ascription in modern societies.' *Sociological Inquiry* 38: 112–16

McCready, William C. 1974. 'The persistence of ethnic variation in American families.' In A.M. Greeley, ed., *Ethnicity in the United States: A Preliminary Reconnaissance*, 156–76. New York: John Wiley

– ed. 1983. *Culture, Ethnicity and Identity: Current Issues in Research*. New York: Academic Press

Model, Suzanne. 1985a. 'A comparative perspective on the ethnic enclave: Blacks, Italians, and Jews in New York City.' *International Migration Review* 19 (1): 64–81

– 1985b. 'The effects of ethnicity in the work place on Blacks, Italians, and Jews in 1910 New York.' Center for Studies of Social Change, New School for Social Research, New York, Working paper no. 7

Montero, Darrel. 1981. 'The Japanese Americans: Changing patterns of assimilation over three generations.' *American Sociological Review* 46: 829–39

Morse, Stan, and K.J. Gergen. 1970. 'Social comparison, self-consistency and concept of self.' *Journal of Personality and Social Psychology* 16: 148–56

Mulvany, C.P. 1884. *Toronto: Past and Present*. Toronto: W.E. Craiger Publisher

Murdie, R.A. 1969. *Factorial Ecology of Metropolitan Toronto, 1951–1961*. Chicago: University of Chicago Press

Nelsen, Hart M., and H.D. Allen. 1974. 'Ethnicity, Americanization and religious attendance.' *American Journal of Sociology* 79: 906–21

Nicks, Trudy. 1985. 'Mary Anne's dilemma: The ethnohistory of an ambivalent identity.' *Canadian Ethnic Studies* 17 (2): 103–14

Novak, Michael. 1971. *The Rise of the Unmeltable Ethnics: Politics and Culture in the Seventies*. New York: Macmillan Publishing Co.

O'Bryan, K.G., J.G. Reitz, and O. Kuplowska. 1975. *Non-Official Languages: A Study in Canadian Multiculturalism*. Ottawa: Supply and Services Canada

Olson, Mancur. 1965. *The Logic of Collective Action*. Cambridge, MA: Harvard University Press

Ostry, S. 1968. *The Female Worker in Canada*. Ottawa: Dominion Bureau of Statistics

Patel, Bharat N. 1978. Sample design report for the study 'Ethnic pluralism in an urban setting.' York University Survey Research Centre, Downsview, ON

Pinard, Maurice. 1968. 'Mass society and political movements: A new formulation.' *American Journal of Sociology* 73: 682–90

Pineo, Peter. 1977. 'The social standing of ethnic and racial groupings.' *Canadian Review of Sociology and Anthropology* 14 (May): 147–57

Pineo, Peter C., and John Porter. 1967. 'Occupational prestige in Canada.' *Canadian Review of Sociology and Anthropology* 4: 24–40

Polite, Craig K. 1974. 'Ethnic group identification and differentiation.' *Journal of Social Psychology* 92: 149–50

Porter, John. 1965. *The Vertical Mosaic: An Analysis of Social Class and Power in Canada*. Toronto: University of Toronto Press

– 1972. 'Dilemmas and contradictions of a multi-ethnic society.' Royal Society of Canada, *Proceedings and Transactions*, 4th ser., 10: 193–205

– 1975. 'Ethnic pluralism in Canadian perspective.' In Nathan Glazer and Daniel P. Moynihan, eds, *Ethnicity: Theory and Experience*. Cambridge, MA: Harvard University Press

Portes, Alejandro. 1981. 'Modes of incorporation and theories of labour immigration.' In Mary Kritz, Charles Keely, and Silvano Tomasi, eds,

Global Trends in Migration, 279–97. New York: Center for Migration Studies
Portes Alejandro, and Robert D. Manning. 1986. 'The immigrant enclave: Theory and empirical examples.' In Susan Olzak and Joane Nagel, eds, *Competitive Ethnic Relations*, 47–68. New York: Academic Press
Raynauld, A., G. Marion, and R. Beland. 1969. 'La repartition des revenus selon les groups ethniques au Canada.' Quoted in the Royal Commission on Bilingualism and Biculturalism, *The Work World* (book III). Ottawa: Queen's Printer
Reitz, Jeffrey G. 1980a. 'Immigrants, their descendants, and the cohesion of Canada.' In Raymond Breton, Jeffrey G. Reitz, and Victor Valentine, *Cultural Boundaries and the Cohesion of Canada*, 329–417. Montreal: Institute for Research on Public Policy
– 1980b. *The Survival of Ethnic Groups*. Toronto: McGraw-Hill Ryerson
– 1982. 'Ethnic group control of jobs.' University of Toronto Centre for Urban and Community Studies, Research paper no. 133
– 1988a. 'The institutional structure of immigration as a determinant of inter-racial competition: A comparison of Britain and Canada.' *International Migration Review* 22 (1): 117–46
– 1988b. 'Less racial discrimination in Canada, or simply less racial conflict?: Implications of comparisons with Britain.' *Canadian Public Policy* 14 (4): 424–41
Reitz, Jeffrey G., Liviana Calzavara, and Donna Dasko. 1981. 'Ethnic inequality and segregation in jobs.' University of Toronto Centre for Urban and Community Studies, Research paper no. 123
Richmond, Anthony H. 1964. 'Social mobility of immigrants in Canada.' *Population Studies* 18: 53–69
– 1967a. *Post-War Immigrants in Canada*. Toronto: University of Toronto Press
– 1967b. *Immigrant and Ethnic Groups in Metropolitan Toronto*. York University Institute for Behavioural Research, Ethnic Research Programme, Downsview, ON
– 1972. *Ethnic Residential Segregation in Metropolitan Toronto*. York University Institute for Behavioural Research, Downsview, ON
Richmond, Anthony H., and J. Goldlust. 1974. 'Multivariate analysis of immigrant adaptation.' York University Institute for Behavioural Research, Ethnic Research Programme, Downsview, ON
Richmond, Anthony H., and Warren E. Kalbach. 1980. *Factors in the Adjustment of Immigrants and Their Descendants*. 1971 census monograph. Ottawa: Minister of Supply and Services
Richmond, Anthony H., and R.P. Verma. 1978. 'Income inequality in Canada: Ethnic and generational aspects.' *Canadian Studies in Population* 5: 25–36
Ringer, Benjamin B. 1967. *The Edge of Friendliness: A Study of Jewish-Gentile Relations*. New York: Basic Books
Robb, R.E. 1978. 'Earnings differentials between males and females in Ontario, 1971. *Ontario Journal of Economics* 11 (2): 350–9

Rossi, P., R. Berk, and B. Edison. 1974. *The Roots of Urban Discontent*. New York: Wiley

Sandberg, Neil C. 1974. *Ethnic Identity and Assimilation: The Polish-American Community*. New York: Praeger

– 1986. *Jewish Life in Los Angeles: A Window to Tomorrow*. Landham, MD: University Press of America

Sanders, Jimy, and Victor Nee. 1987. 'Limits of ethnic solidarity in the enclave economy.' *American Sociological Review* 52: 745–73

Seidman, A., ed. 1978. *Working Women: A Study of Women in Paid Jobs*. Boulder, CO: Westview Press

Sharot, Stephen. 1973. 'The three generations thesis and the American Jews.' *The British Journal of Sociology* 24: 151–64

Siegel, B.J. 1970. 'Defensive structuring and environmental stress.' *American Journal of Sociology* 76: 11–32

Simirenko, Alex. 1964. *Pilgrims, Colonists, and Frontiersmen: An Ethnic Community in Transition*. New York: The Free Press of Glencoe

Simmons, A.B., and J.E. Turner. 1976. 'The socialization of sex roles and fertility ideals: A study of two generations in Toronto.' *Journal of Comparative Family Studies* 7: 255–71

Sklare, Marshall, and J. Greenblum. 1967. *Jewish Identity on the Suburban Frontier: A Study of Group Survival in the Open Society*. New York: Basic Books

Sørenson, A. 1983. 'Sociological research on the labour market: Conceptual and methodological issues.' *Work and Occupations* 10 (2): 261–87

Spiro, Melford E. 1955. 'The acculturation of American ethnic groups.' *American Anthropologist* 57: 1240–52

Statistics Canada. 1978. *1976 Census of Canada*. Census tracts. Population and housing characteristics, Toronto (Bulletin 6.27). Ottawa: Minister of Supply and Services

Tainer, Evelina M. 1988. 'English language proficiency and the determination of earnings among foreign-born men.' *The Journal of Human Resources* 32 (1): 108–22

Taylor, Ronald L. 1979. 'Black ethnicity and the persistence of ethnogenesis.' *American Journal of Sociology* 84: 1401–23

Tepperman, Lorne. 1975. *Social Mobility in Canada*. Toronto: McGraw-Hill Ryerson

Thomas, William I., and Florian Znaniecki. 1927. *The Polish Peasant in Europe and America*. New York: Alfred Knopf

Tilly, Charles. 1975. *The Rebellious Century, 1830–1930*. Cambridge, MA: Harvard University Press

Toch, Hans H., A.I. Rabin, and D.M. Wilkins. 1962. 'Factors entering into ethnic identification: An experimental study.' *Sociometry* 25: 297–312

Tricarico, Donald. 1984. 'The "new" Italian-American ethnicity.' *The Journal of Ethnic Studies* 12 (3): 75–93

Turner, Victor W. 1969. *The Ritual Process: Structure and Anti-Structure.* Chicago: Aldine Publishing Co.

Turritin, Anthony H. 1974. 'Ethnicity and occupational stratification in Metropolitan Toronto, 1961.' Unpublished manuscript

Uyeki, Eugene. 1960. 'Correlates of ethnic identification.' *American Journal of Sociology* 65: 468–74

Waldinger, Roger. 1984. 'Immigrant enterprise and the New York garment industry.' *Social Problems* 32 (October): 60–71

Warner, William L., and Leo Srole. 1945. *The Social Systems of American Ethnic Groups*. New Haven, CT: Yale University Press

Webber, M.M. 1970. 'Order in diversity: Community without propinquity.' In R. Gutman and D. Popenoe, eds, *Neighborhood, City and Metropolis*, 791–811. Toronto: Random House of Canada

Whiteside, Mary Jane. 1971. 'Evaluation of a successful rival: An experimental investigation of jealousy.' Unpublished PhD dissertation, University of Texas, Austin

Wiley, Norbert. 1967. 'The ethnic mobility trap and stratification theory.' *Social Problems* 15: 147–59

Wilson, K.L., and A. Portes. 1980. 'Immigrant enclaves: An analysis of the labor market experiences of Cubans in Miami.' *American Journal of Sociology* 86 (2): 295–319

Wong-Rieger, Durhane. 1981. 'Self identity and adaptation to social change: Self conceptions among Cree Indians in a French Canadian town.' *Canadian Ethnic Studies* 8 (3): 127–42

Wright, Erik O. 1978. 'The class structure of advanced capitalist societies.' In his *Class, Crisis and the State*. London: NLB

Yancey, William B., Eugene P. Ericksen, and Richard N. Juliani. 1976. 'Emergent ethnicity: A review and reformulation.' *American Sociological Review* 41: 391–403

Zenner, Walter P. 1985. 'Jewishness in America: Ascription and choice.' *Ethnic and Racial Studies* 8 (1): 117–33

Zielyk, Ihor V. 1975. 'Two types of ethnic communities.' In P. Migus, ed., *Sounds Canadian: Languages and Cultures in Multi-Ethnic Society*, 147–57. Toronto: Peter Martin Associates

Name Index

Subject Index